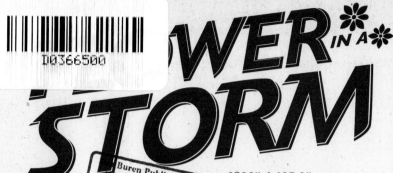

OWER IN A STORM

STORY & ART BY
Shigeyoshi Takagi

What are you two doing?
Time for class!

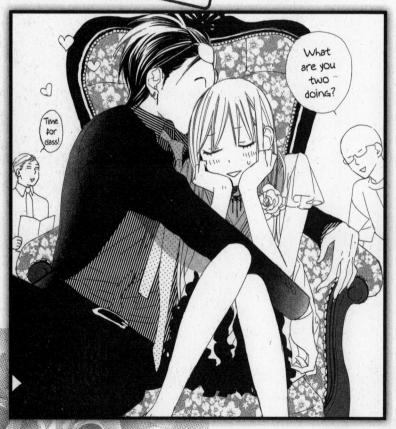

VOLUME ONE

CONTENTS

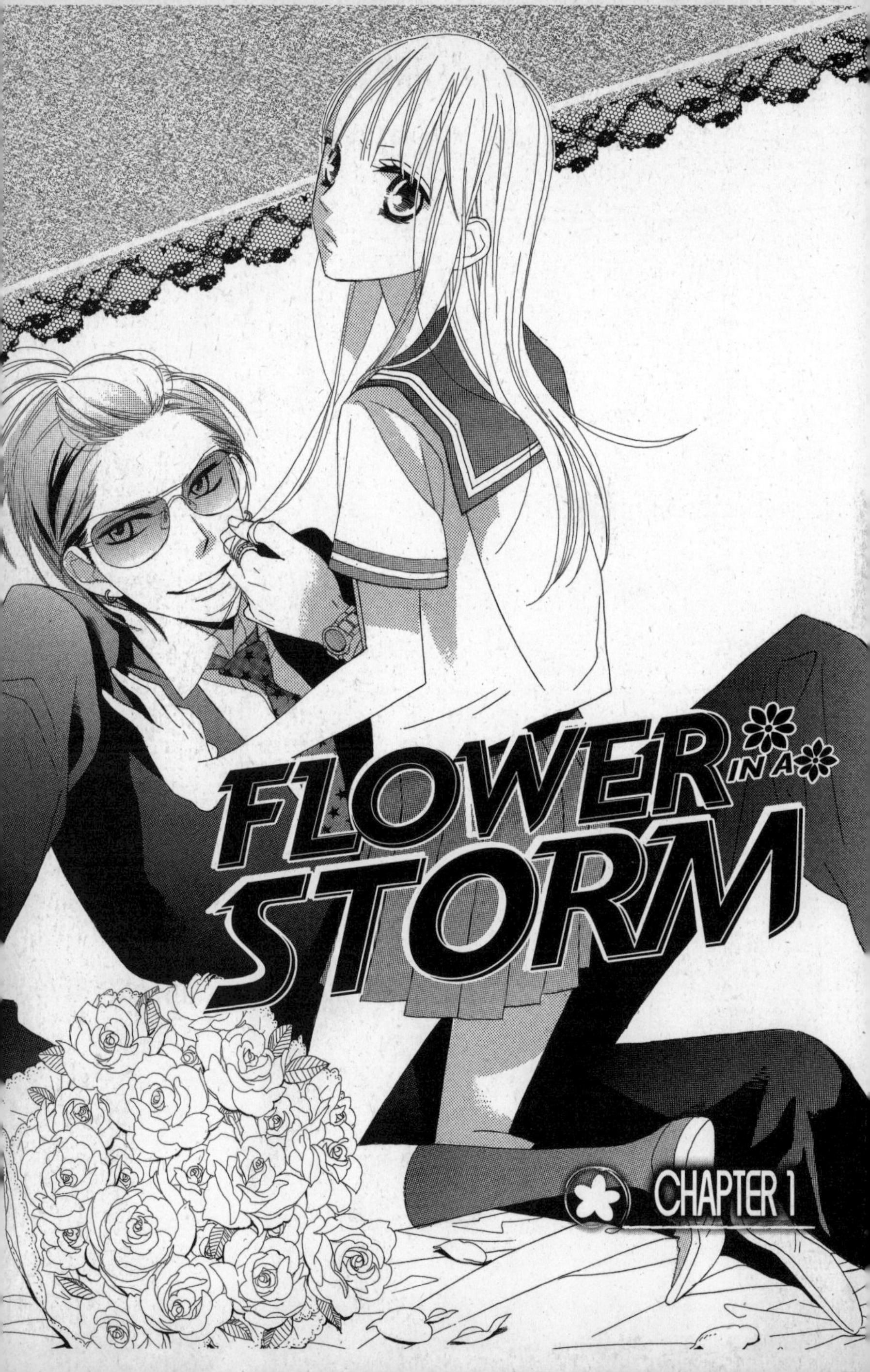
FLOWER IN A STORM
CHAPTER 1

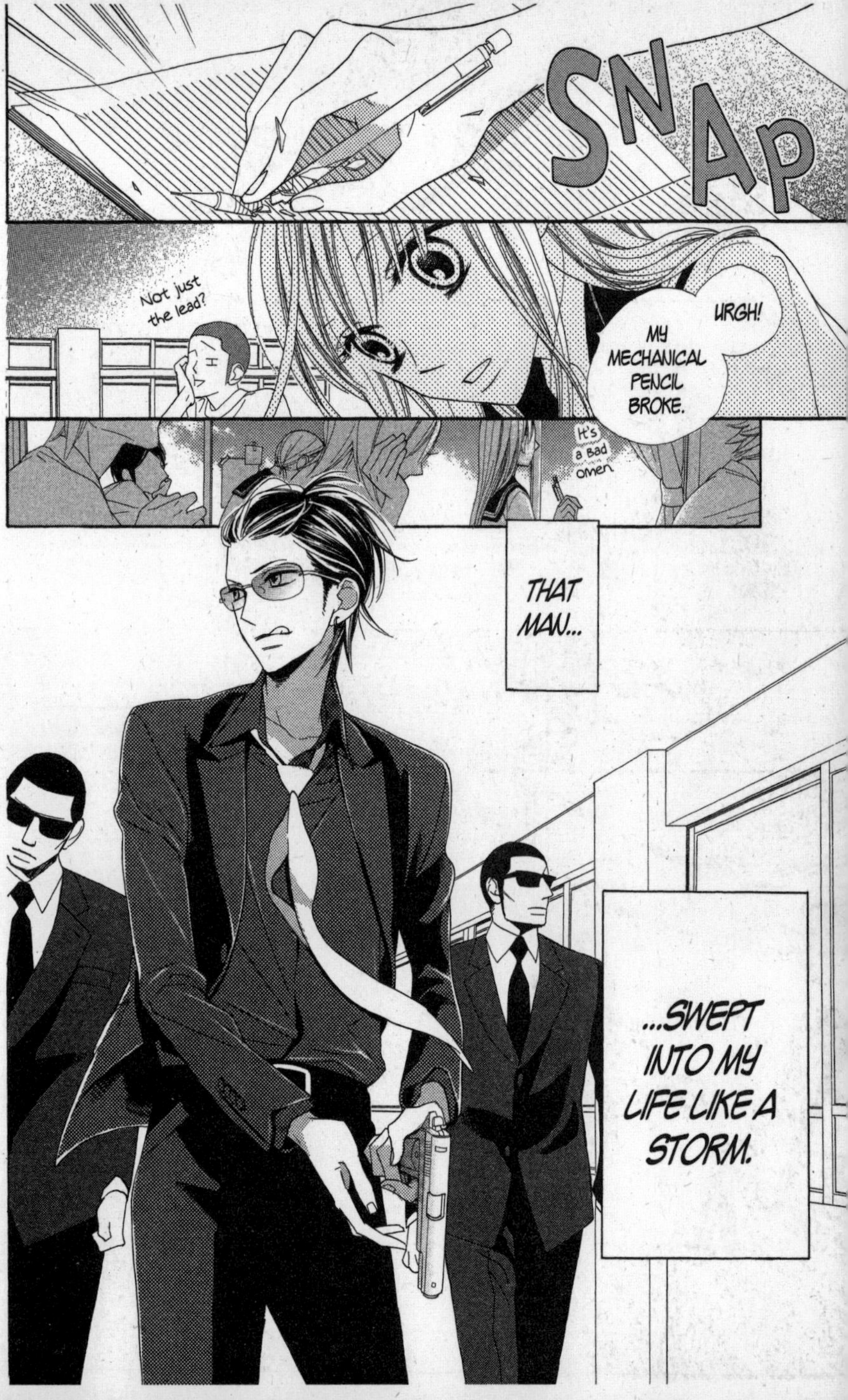
SNAP
URGH! MY MECHANICAL PENCIL BROKE.
Not just the lead?
It's a bad omen.
THAT MAN...
...SWEPT INTO MY LIFE LIKE A STORM.

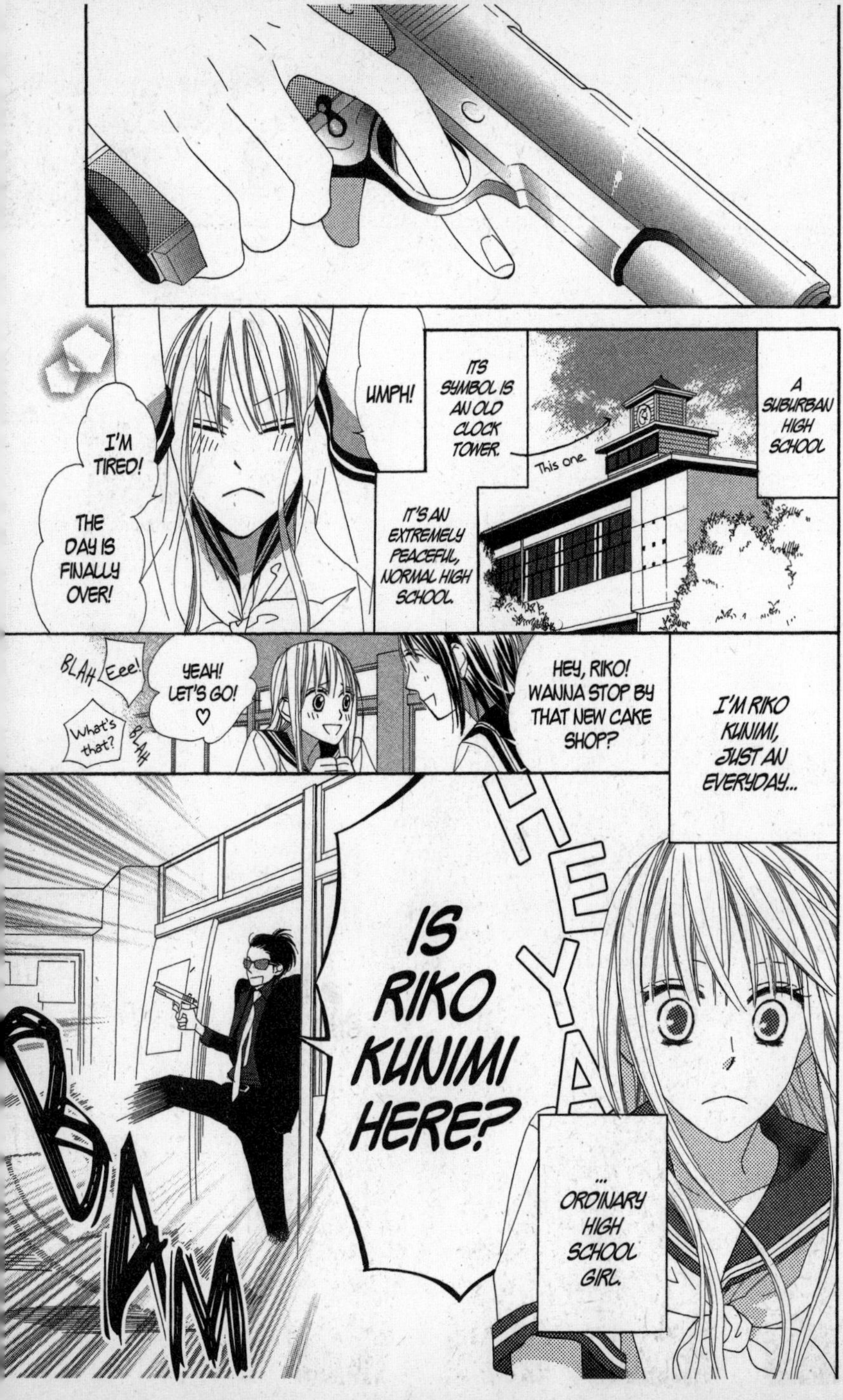
A SUBURBAN HIGH SCHOOL
ITS SYMBOL IS AN OLD CLOCK TOWER.
This one.
IT'S AN EXTREMELY PEACEFUL, NORMAL HIGH SCHOOL.
UMPH!
I'M TIRED!
THE DAY IS FINALLY OVER!
I'M RIKO KUNIMI, JUST AN EVERYDAY...
HEY, RIKO! WANNA STOP BY THAT NEW CAKE SHOP?
YEAH! LET'S GO! ♡
Eee!
What's that?
BLAH BLAH
... ORDINARY HIGH SCHOOL GIRL.
HEYA
IS RIKO KUNIMI HERE?
BAM

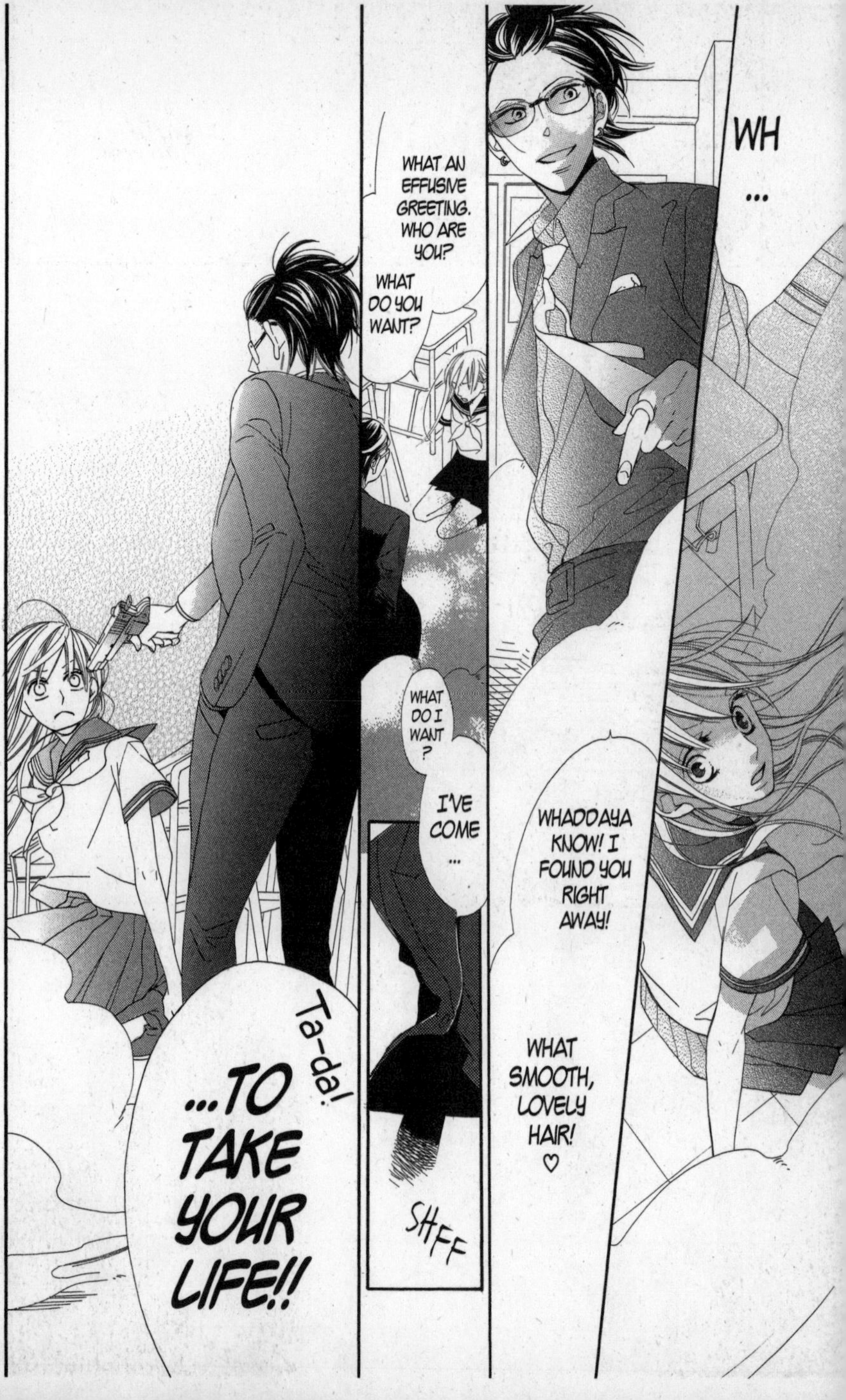
WH ...
WHADDAYA KNOW! I FOUND YOU RIGHT AWAY!
WHAT SMOOTH, LOVELY HAIR! ♡
WHAT AN EFFUSIVE GREETING. WHO ARE YOU?
WHAT DO YOU WANT?
WHAT DO I WANT?
I'VE COME ...
SHFF
Ta-da!
...TO TAKE YOUR LIFE!!

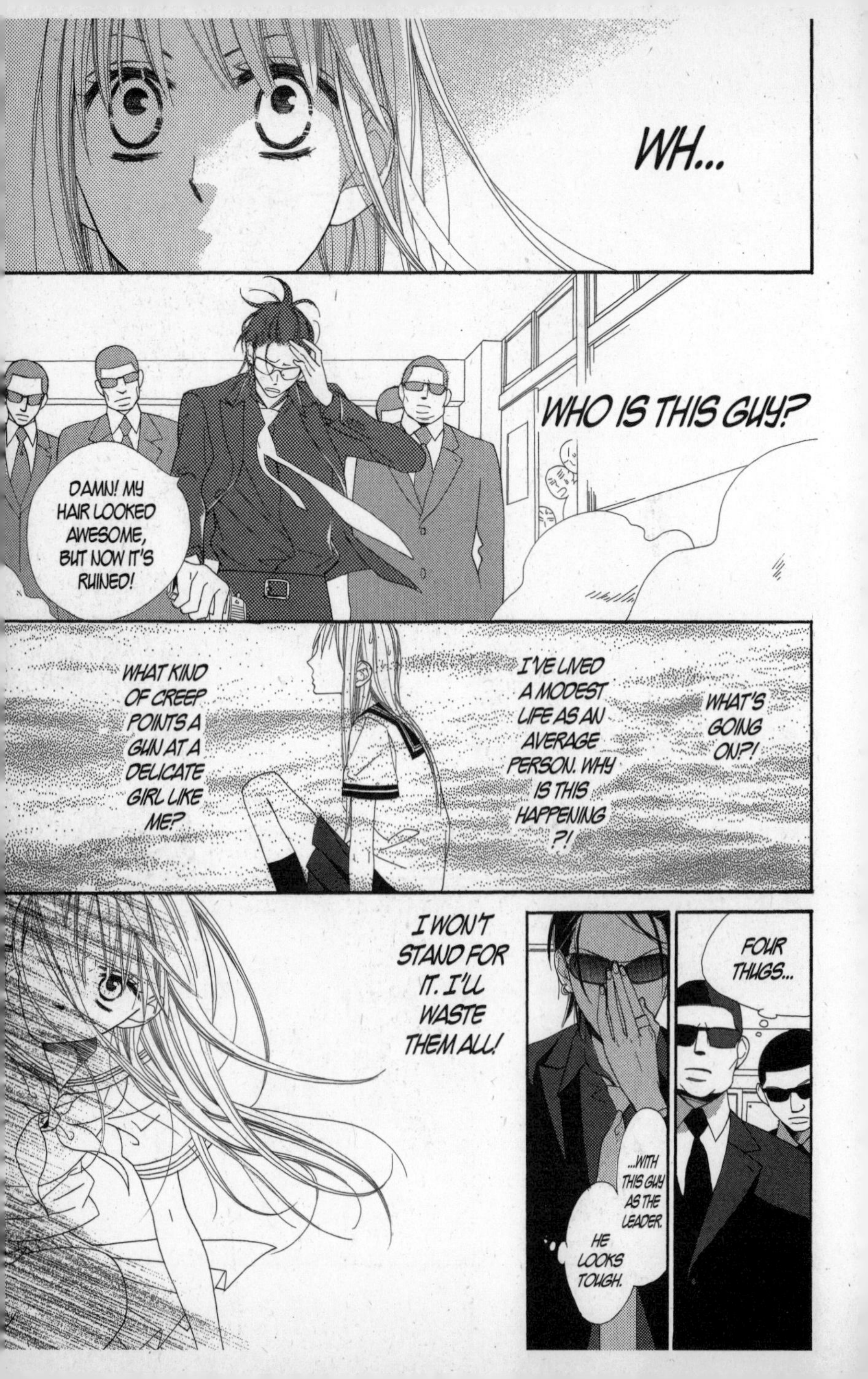
WH...
WHO IS THIS GUY?
DAMN! MY HAIR LOOKED AWESOME, BUT NOW IT'S RUINED!
WHAT'S GOING ON?!
I'VE LIVED A MODEST LIFE AS AN AVERAGE PERSON. WHY IS THIS HAPPENING?!
WHAT KIND OF CREEP POINTS A GUN AT A DELICATE GIRL LIKE ME?
FOUR THUGS...
...WITH THIS GUY AS THE LEADER.
HE LOOKS TOUGH.
I WON'T STAND FOR IT. I'LL WASTE THEM ALL!

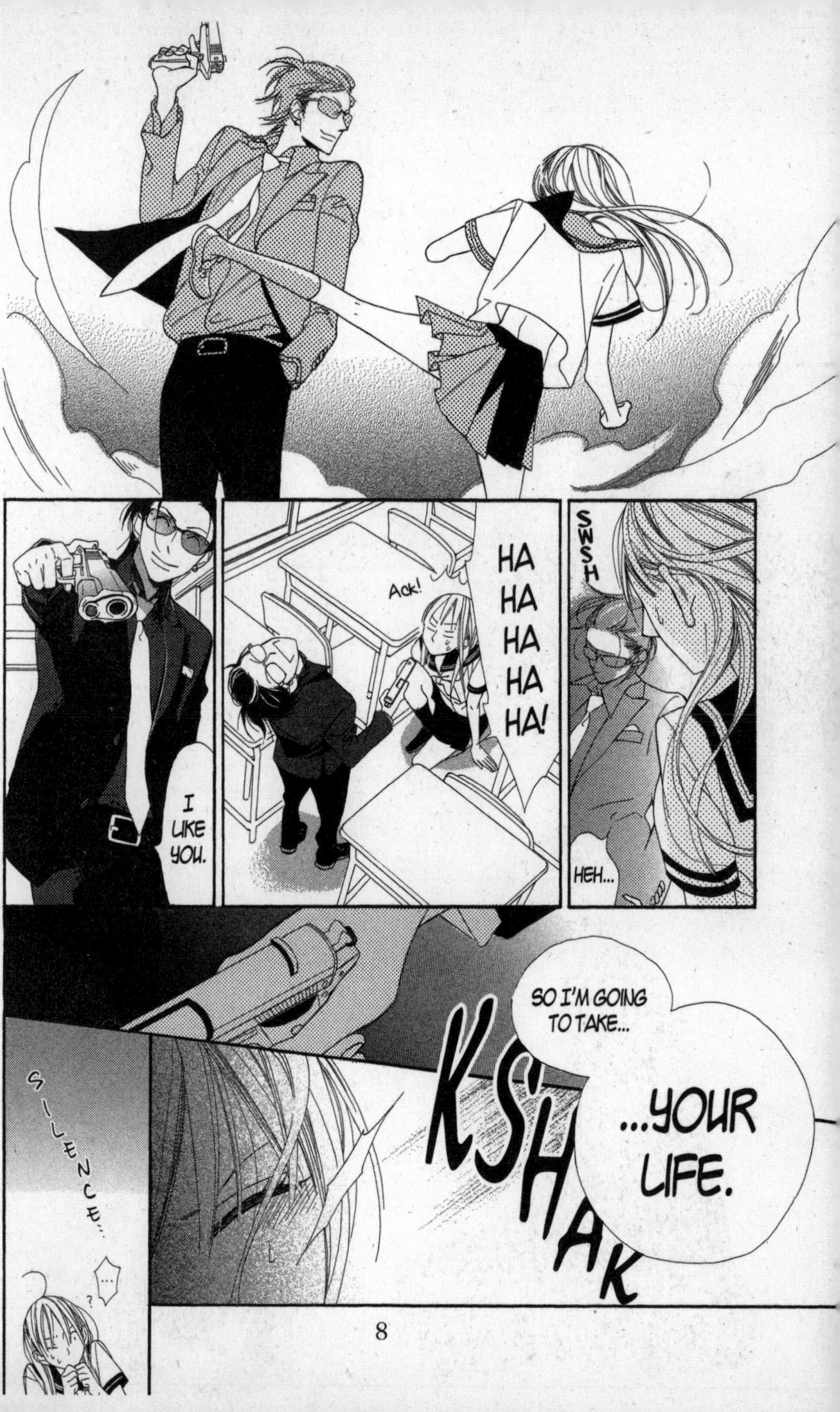
SWSH
HEH...
HA HA HA HA HA!
Ack!
I LIKE YOU.
SO I'M GOING TO TAKE...
KSHAK
...YOUR LIFE.
SILENCE...
...
?

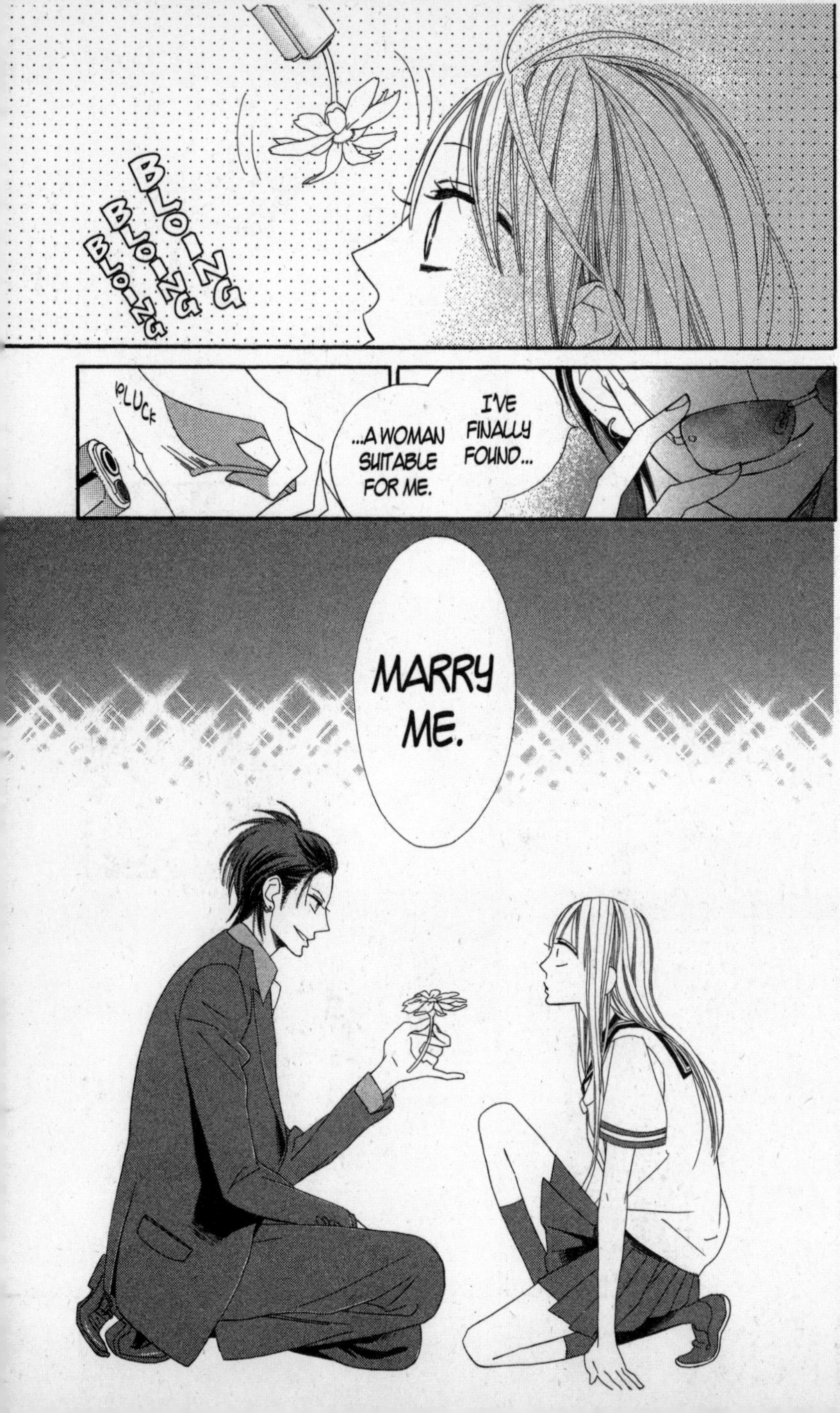
BLOING BLOING BLOING
I'VE FINALLY FOUND...
...A WOMAN SUITABLE FOR ME.
PLUCK
MARRY ME.

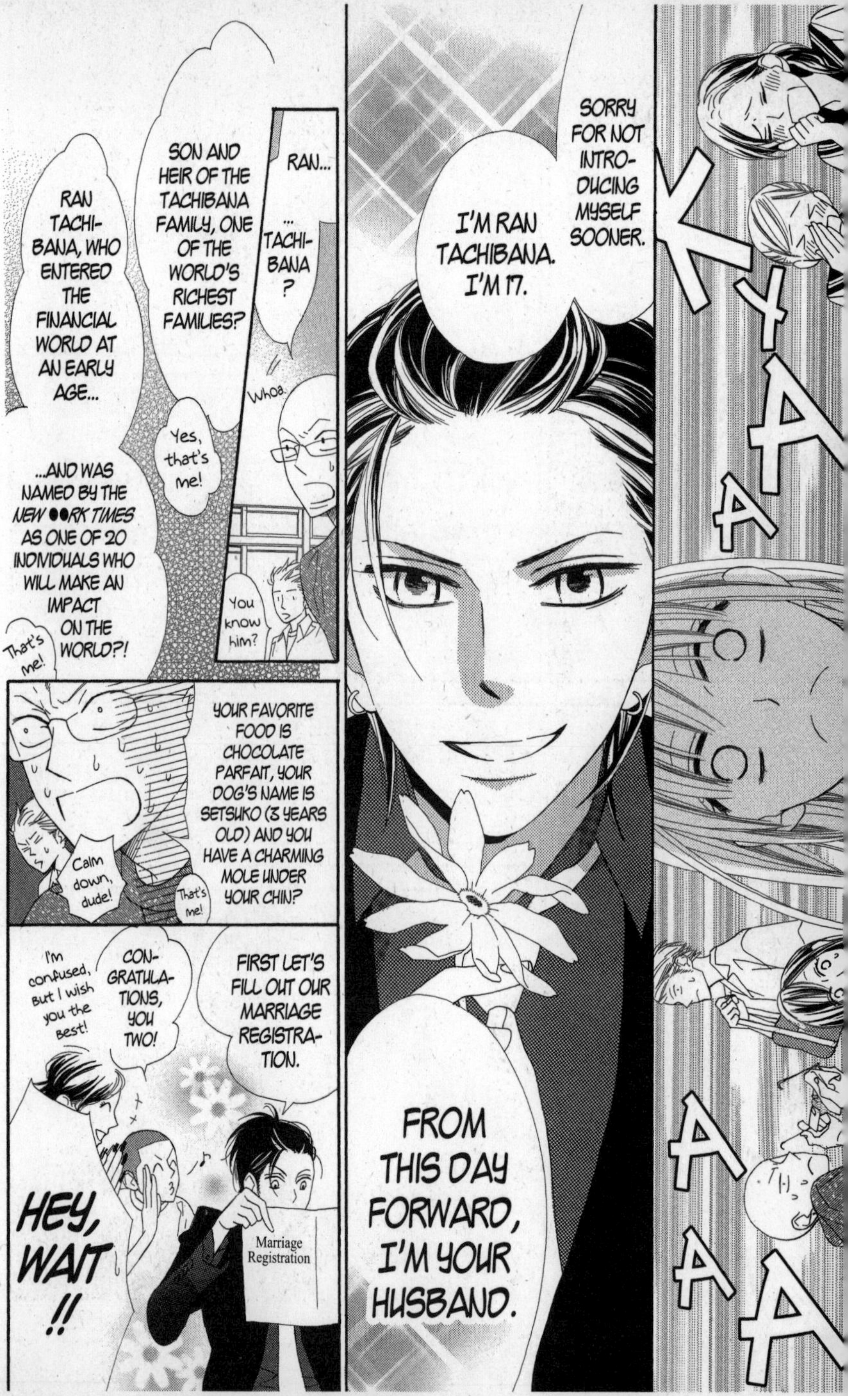
KYAAA
AAAA
SORRY FOR NOT INTRO-DUCING MYSELF SOONER.
I'M RAN TACHIBANA. I'M 17.
FROM THIS DAY FORWARD, I'M YOUR HUSBAND.
RAN...
...TACHI-BANA?
Whoa.
SON AND HEIR OF THE TACHIBANA FAMILY, ONE OF THE WORLD'S RICHEST FAMILIES?
Yes, that's me!
RAN TACHI-BANA, WHO ENTERED THE FINANCIAL WORLD AT AN EARLY AGE...
...AND WAS NAMED BY THE *NEW ●●RK TIMES* AS ONE OF 20 INDIVIDUALS WHO WILL MAKE AN IMPACT ON THE WORLD?!
You know him?
That's me!
YOUR FAVORITE FOOD IS CHOCOLATE PARFAIT, YOUR DOG'S NAME IS SETSUKO (3 YEARS OLD) AND YOU HAVE A CHARMING MOLE UNDER YOUR CHIN?
That's me!
Calm down, dude!
FIRST LET'S FILL OUT OUR MARRIAGE REGISTRA-TION.
CON-GRATULA-TIONS, YOU TWO!
I'm confused, but I wish you the best!
Marriage Registration
HEY, WAIT!!

IT DOESN'T MATTER WHAT YOU WANT.

Tch!

IF I SAY YOU'RE MY WIFE, YOU'RE MY WIFE.

RRIP
RRIP

JUST LIKE THAT?! I WON'T DO IT!

MARRY YOU? IS THIS A JOKE?

COME BACK AFTER YOU'VE LEARNED SOME COMMON SENSE!

WHAT KIND OF REASONING IS THAT?

WHOOSH

!

IF YOU DON'T, I'LL FORCE YOU TO.

I'd rather not though...

RIKO

TOMORROW ... I LEAVE FOR ENGLAND.

STOP RESISTING AND COME WITH ME.

11

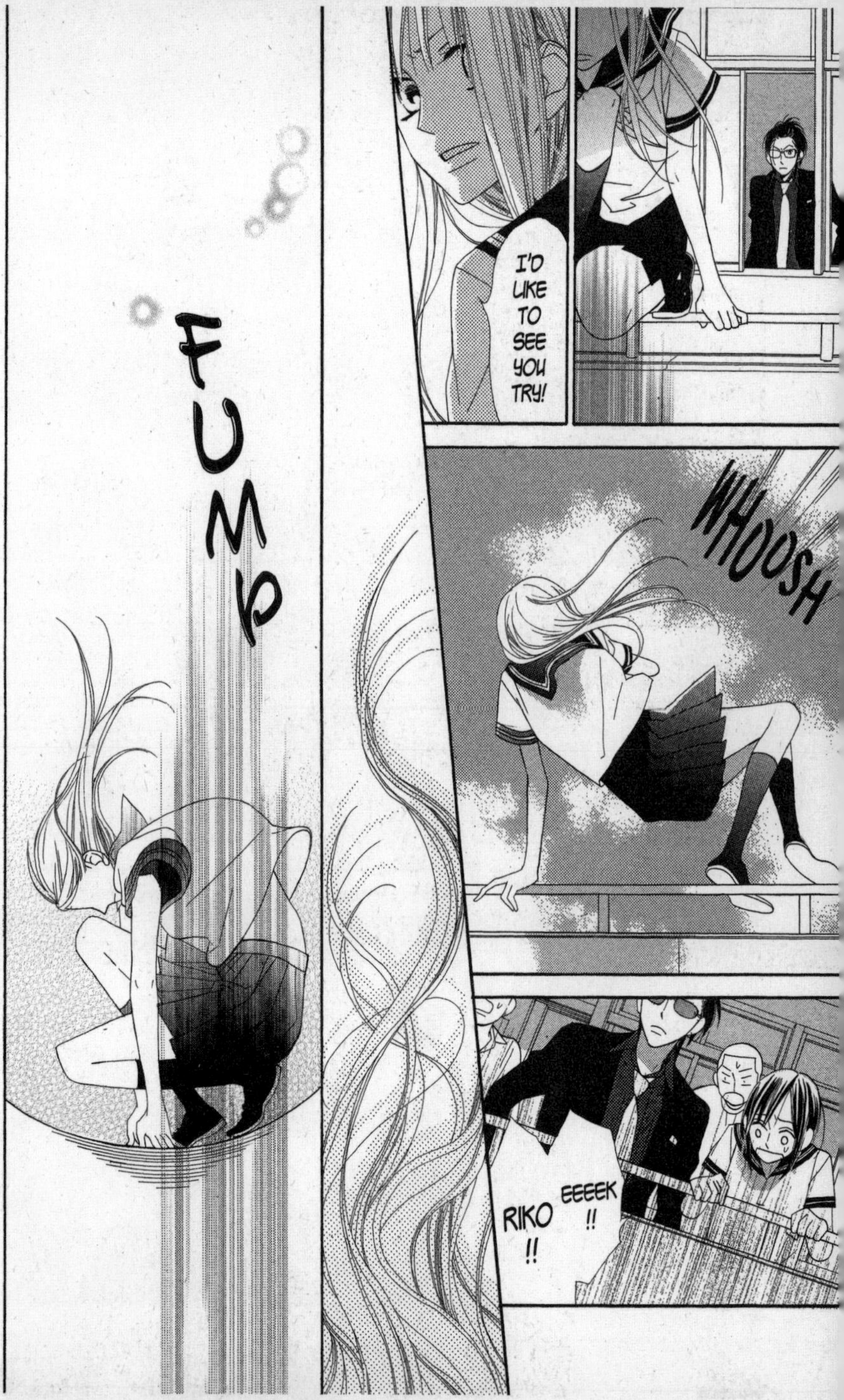
I'D LIKE TO SEE YOU TRY!
WHOOSH
EEEEK !!
RIKO !!
FUMP

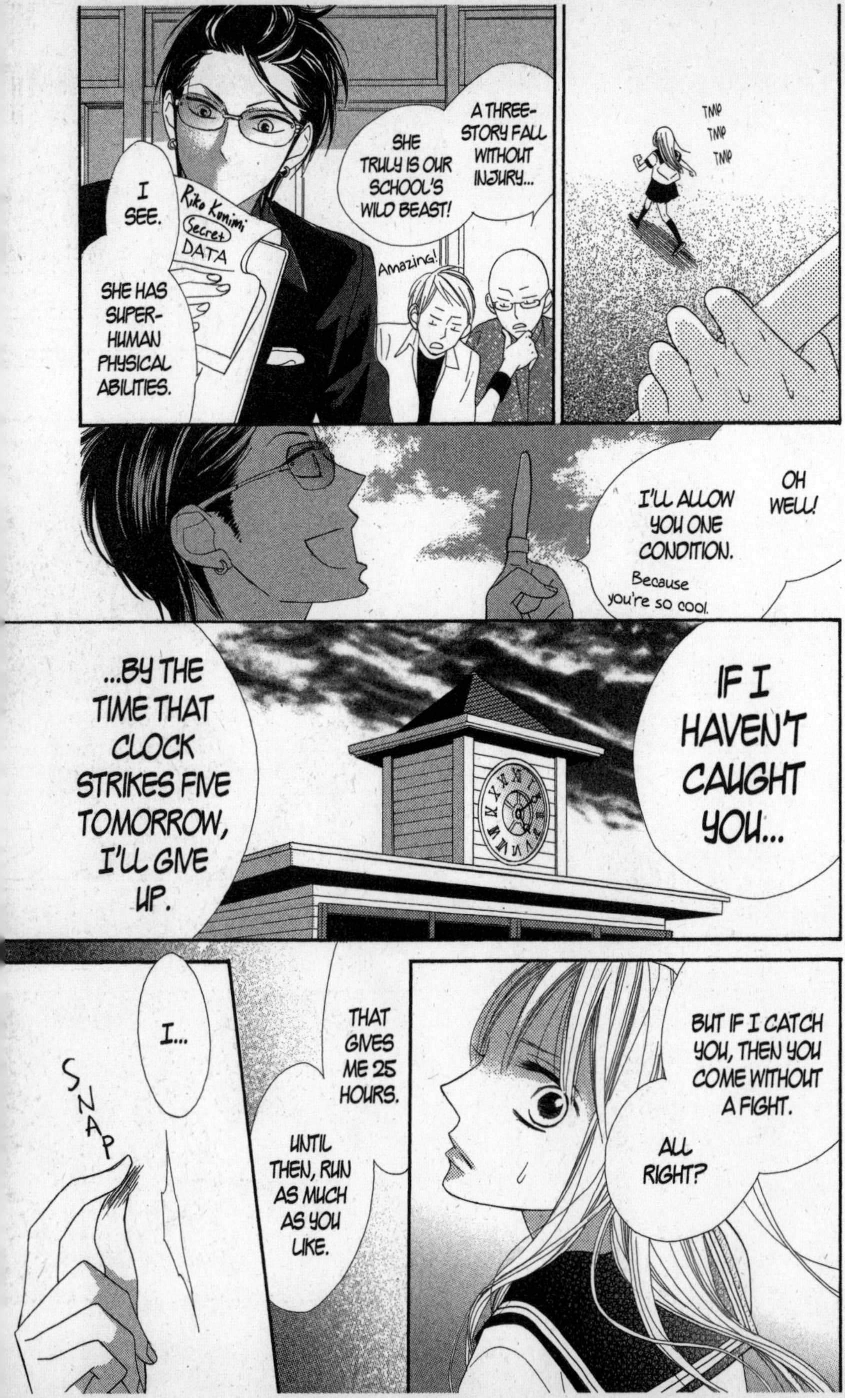
TMP
TMP
TMP
A THREE-STORY FALL WITHOUT INJURY...
SHE TRULY IS OUR SCHOOL'S WILD BEAST!
Amazing!
I SEE.
Riko Kunimi Secret DATA
SHE HAS SUPER-HUMAN PHYSICAL ABILITIES.
OH WELL!
I'LL ALLOW YOU ONE CONDITION.
Because you're so cool.
IF I HAVEN'T CAUGHT YOU...
...BY THE TIME THAT CLOCK STRIKES FIVE TOMORROW, I'LL GIVE UP.
BUT IF I CATCH YOU, THEN YOU COME WITHOUT A FIGHT.
ALL RIGHT?
THAT GIVES ME 25 HOURS.
UNTIL THEN, RUN AS MUCH AS YOU LIKE.
I...
SNAP

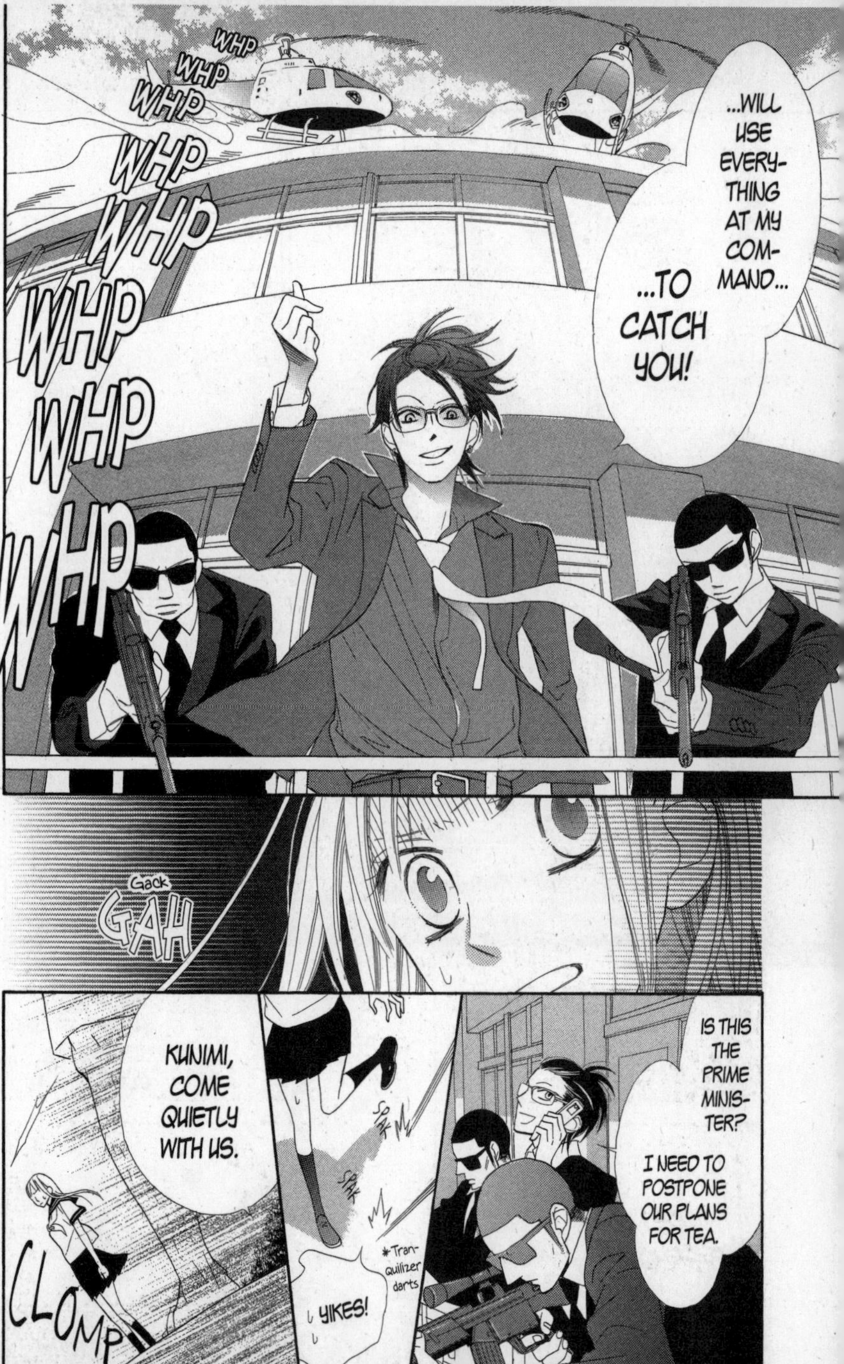
...WILL USE EVERY-THING AT MY COM-MAND...
...TO CATCH YOU!
WHP WHP WHP WHP WHP WHP WHP WHP
Gack GAH
IS THIS THE PRIME MINIS-TER?
I NEED TO POSTPONE OUR PLANS FOR TEA.
*Tran-quilizer darts
YIKES!
KUNIMI, COME QUIETLY WITH US.
CLOMP

WHAT ARE YOU GUYS DOING?

Sorry! Martial arts are expensive!

WH...

The sports dudes were persuaded by money.

I CALLED IN SOME FAVORS.

Just in case.

DADUM

YOU SHALL NOT PASS!!

WHY WON'T THEY JUST LEAVE ME ALONE?

SHEESH...

WHY CAN'T I HAVE A NORMAL LIFE?

...FOR A FUN CAKE-AND CHAT-FEST!

I WAS GOING TO GET TOGETHER WITH A FRIEND...

...JUST AN EVERYDAY...

GRRRP

I'M...

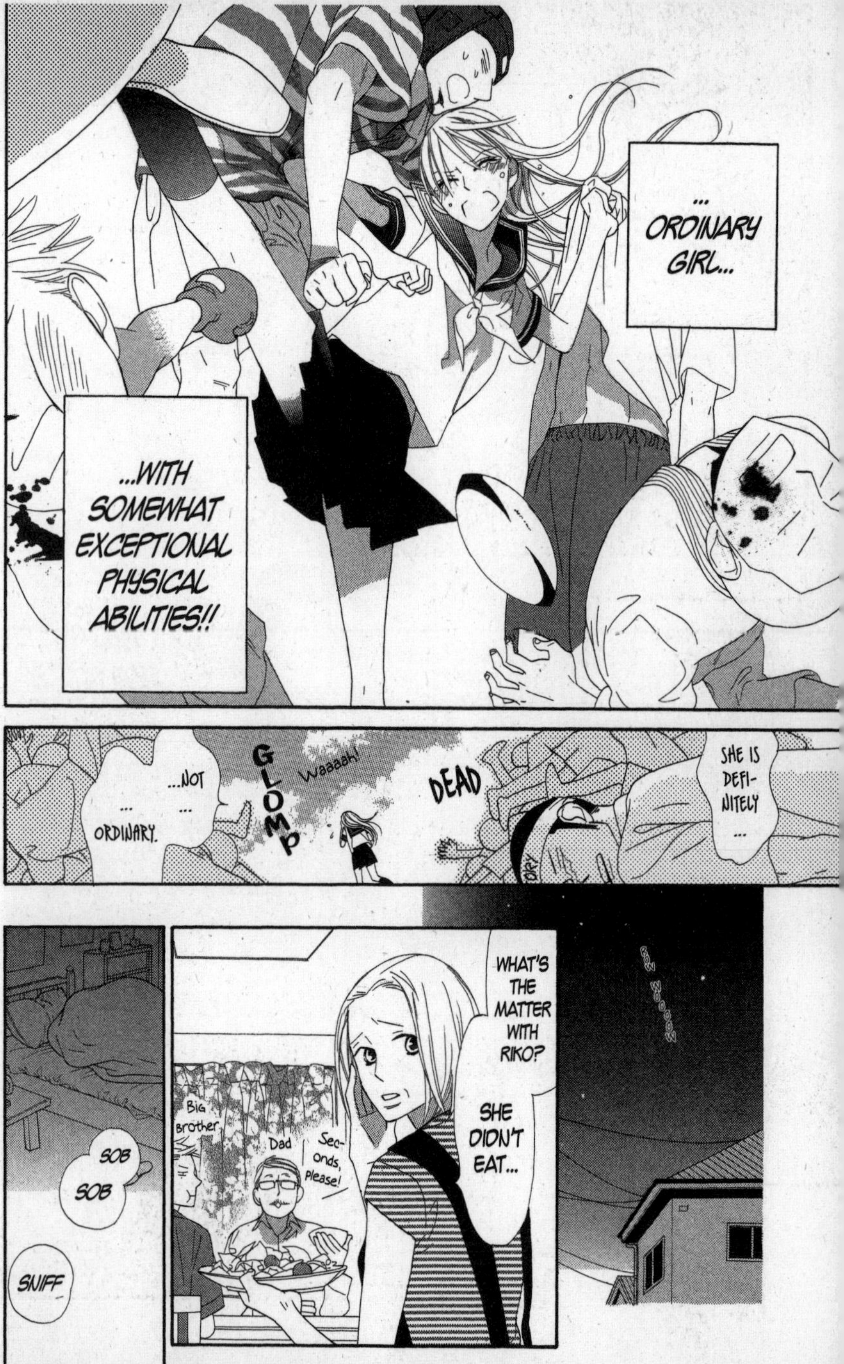
...ORDINARY GIRL...
...WITH SOMEWHAT EXCEPTIONAL PHYSICAL ABILITIES!!
SHE IS DEFINITELY ...
DEAD
Waaaah!
GLOMP
...NOT ... ... ORDINARY.
BOW WOOOOW
WHAT'S THE MATTER WITH RIKO?
SHE DIDN'T EAT...
Seconds, please!
Dad
Big brother
SOB SOB
SNIFF

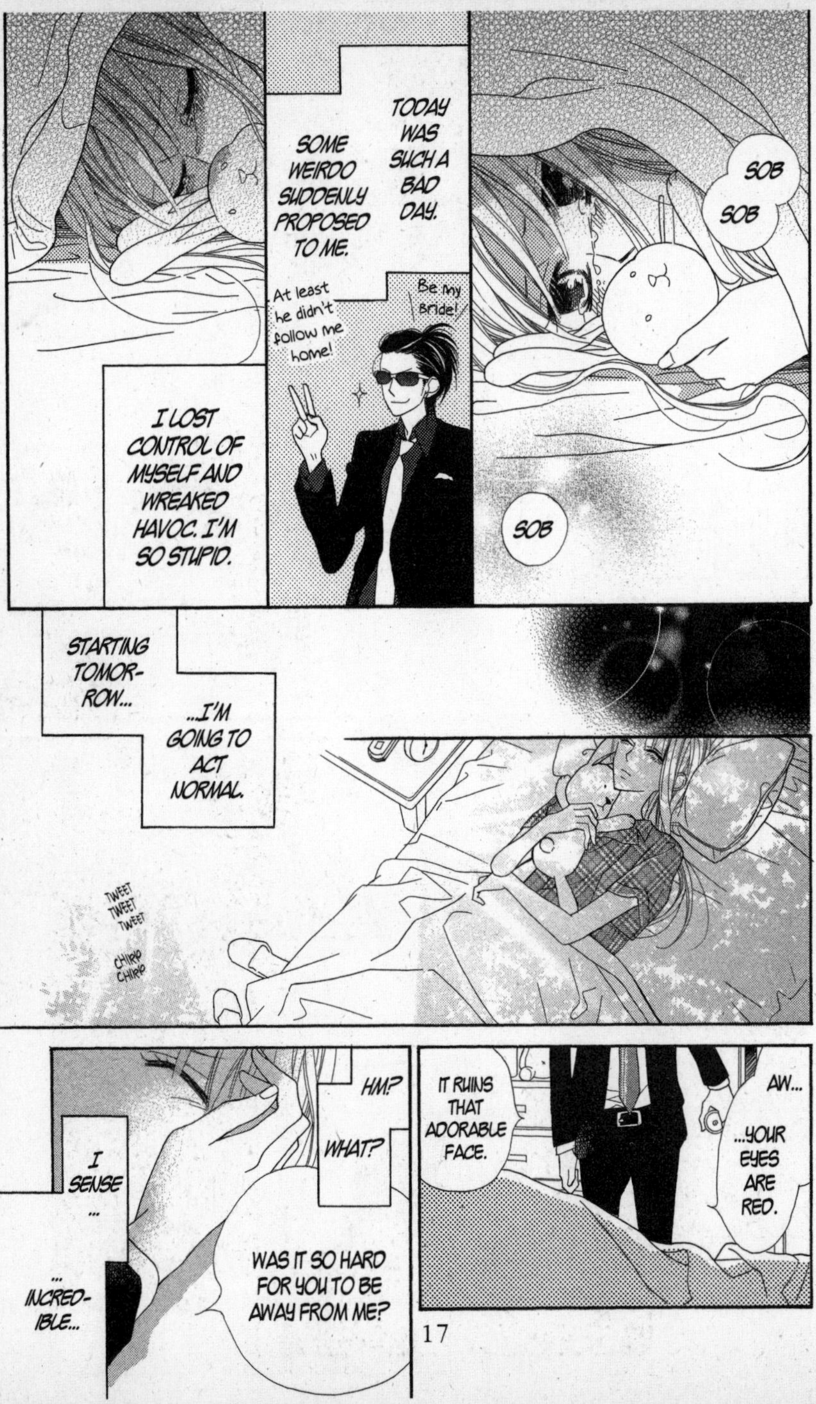
SOB
SOB
SOB
TODAY WAS SUCH A BAD DAY.
SOME WEIRDO SUDDENLY PROPOSED TO ME.
Be my Bride!
At least he didn't follow me home!
I LOST CONTROL OF MYSELF AND WREAKED HAVOC. I'M SO STUPID.
STARTING TOMOR-ROW...
...I'M GOING TO ACT NORMAL.
TWEET TWEET TWEET
CHIRP CHIRP
AW...
...YOUR EYES ARE RED.
IT RUINS THAT ADORABLE FACE.
HM?
WHAT?
WAS IT SO HARD FOR YOU TO BE AWAY FROM ME?
I SENSE...
...INCREDI-BLE...

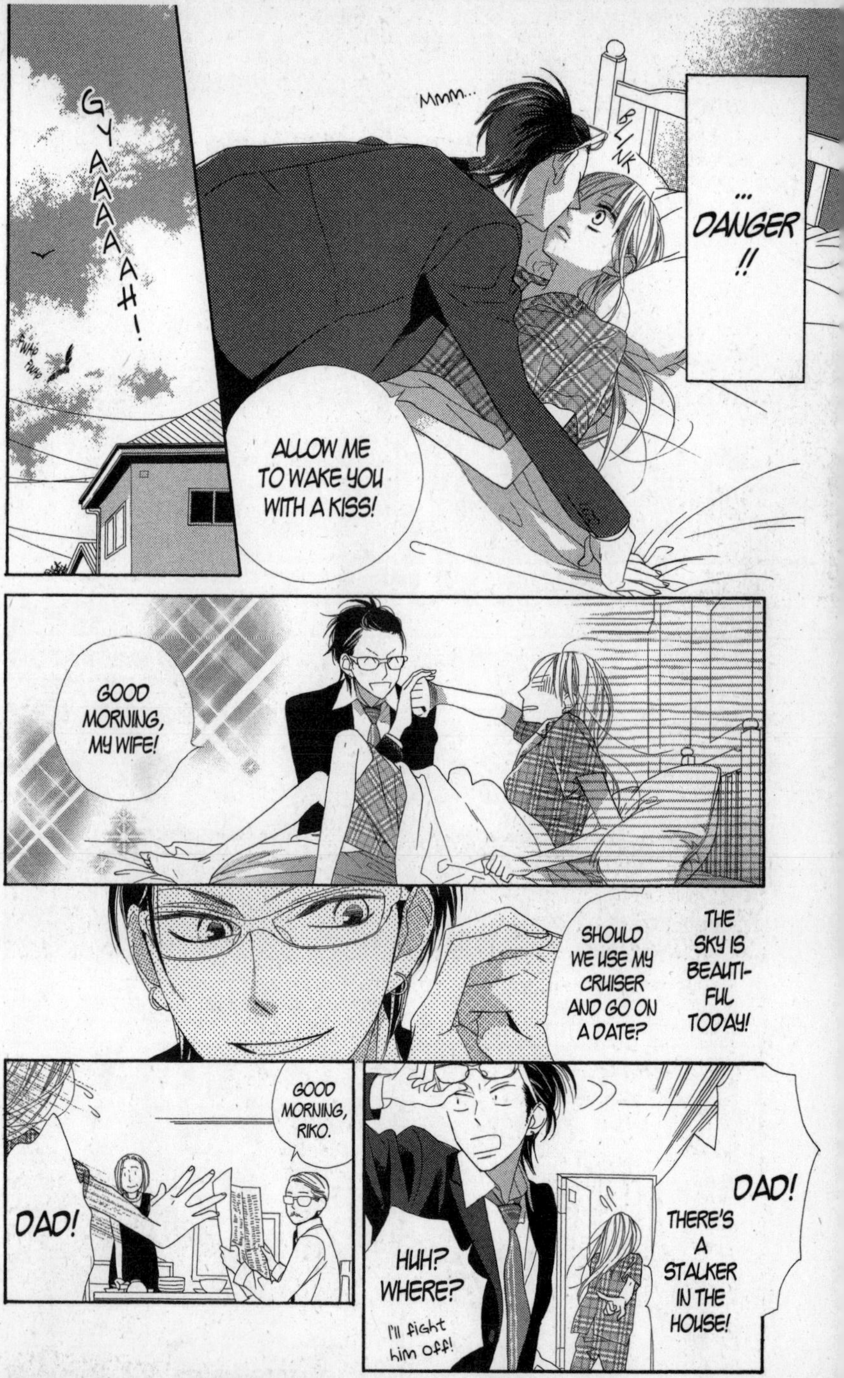
...DANGER!!
MMM...
BLINK
ALLOW ME TO WAKE YOU WITH A KISS!
GYAAAAAH!
FWAP FWAP
GOOD MORNING, MY WIFE!
THE SKY IS BEAUTIFUL TODAY!
SHOULD WE USE MY CRUISER AND GO ON A DATE?
DAD!
THERE'S A STALKER IN THE HOUSE!
HUH? WHERE?
I'll fight him off!
GOOD MORNING, RIKO.
DAD!

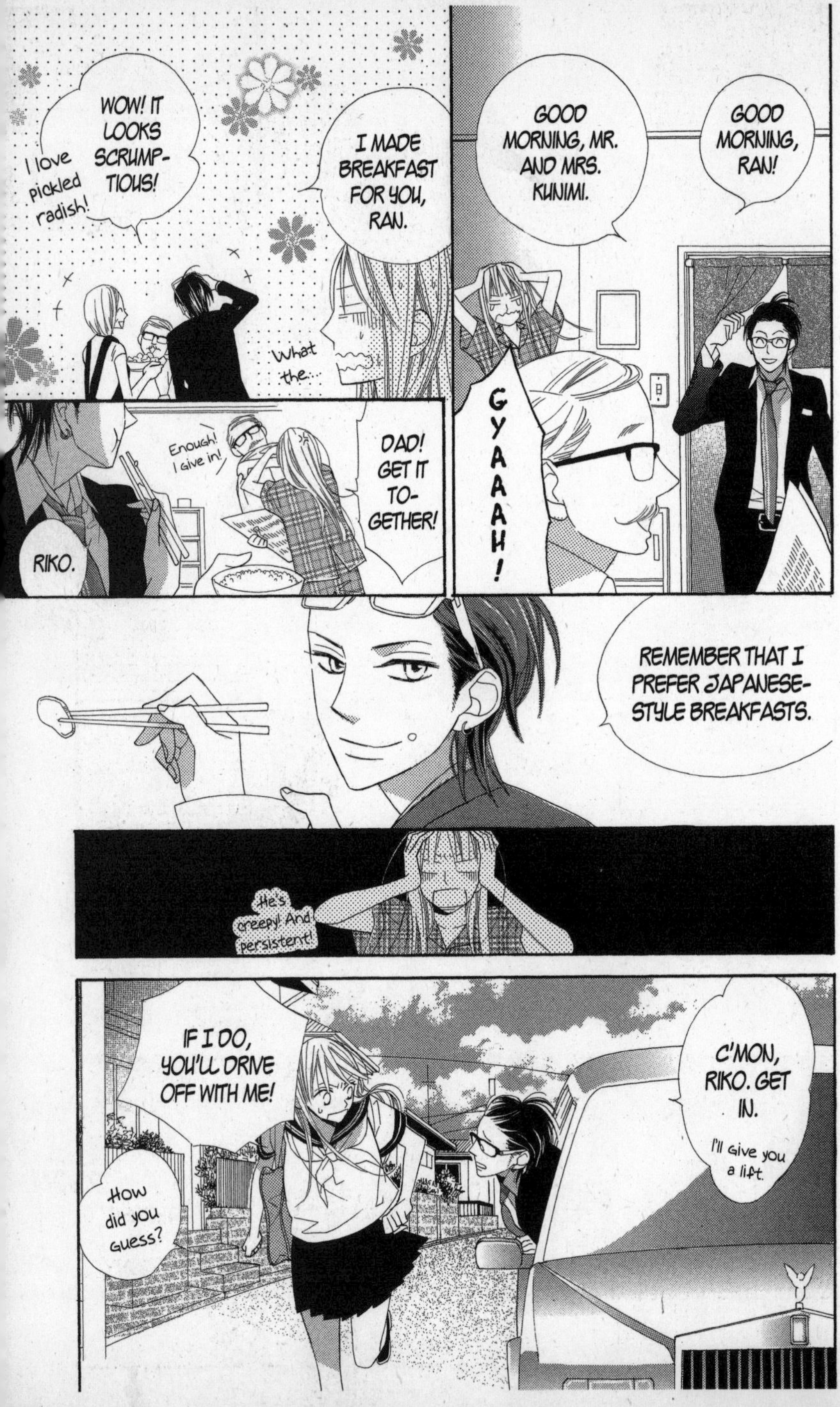
GOOD MORNING, RAN!
GOOD MORNING, MR. AND MRS. KUNIMI.
GYAAAAH!
I MADE BREAKFAST FOR YOU, RAN.
WOW! IT LOOKS SCRUMP-TIOUS!
I love pickled radish!
What the...
DAD! GET IT TO-GETHER!
Enough! I give in!
RIKO.
REMEMBER THAT I PREFER JAPANESE-STYLE BREAKFASTS.
He's creepy! And persistent!
C'MON, RIKO. GET IN.
I'll give you a lift.
IF I DO, YOU'LL DRIVE OFF WITH ME!
How did you guess?

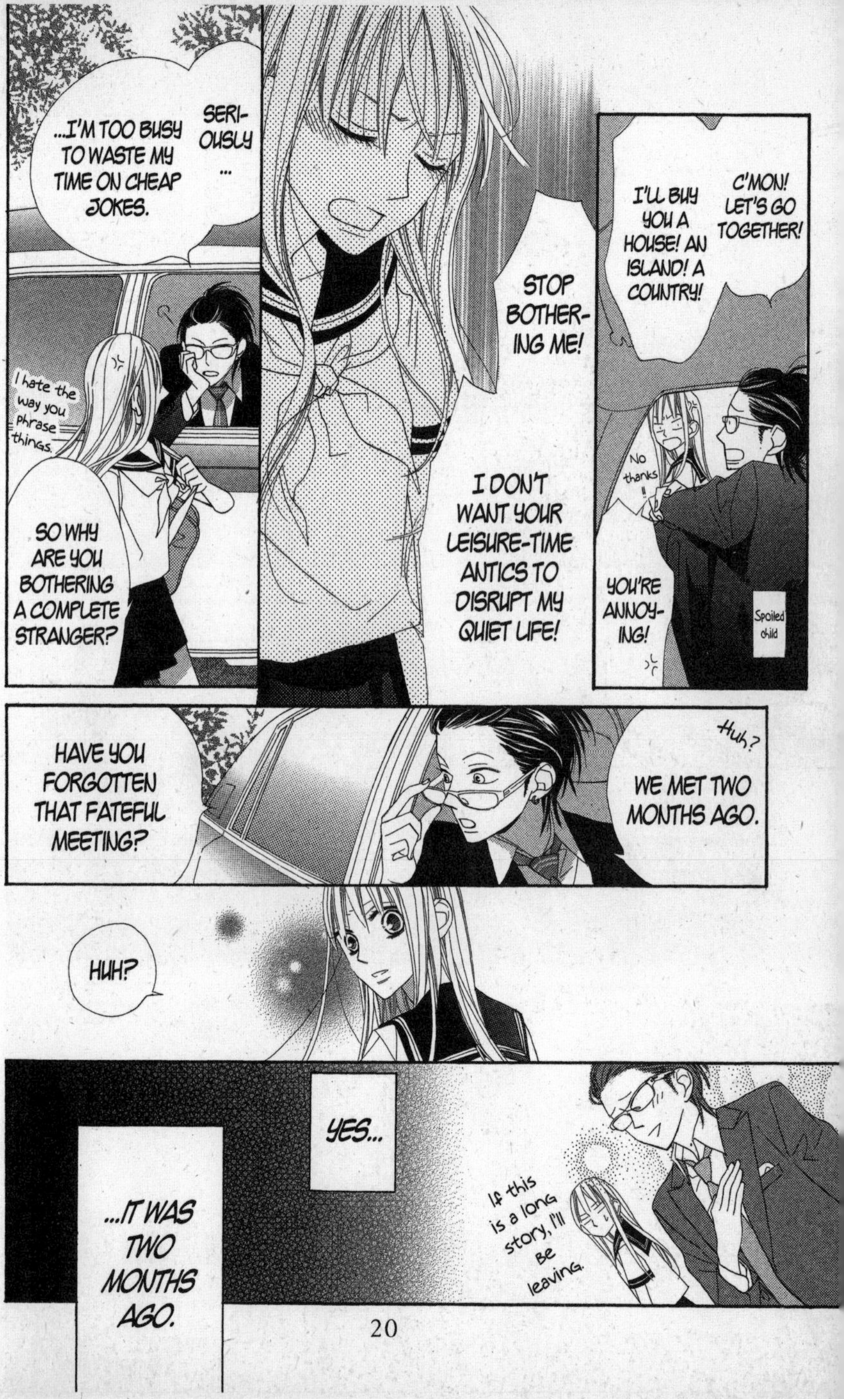
C'MON! LET'S GO TOGETHER!
I'LL BUY YOU A HOUSE! AN ISLAND! A COUNTRY!
No thanks!!
YOU'RE ANNOY-ING!
Spoiled child
STOP BOTHER-ING ME!
I DON'T WANT YOUR LEISURE-TIME ANTICS TO DISRUPT MY QUIET LIFE!
SERI-OUSLY...
...I'M TOO BUSY TO WASTE MY TIME ON CHEAP JOKES.
I hate the way you phrase things.
SO WHY ARE YOU BOTHERING A COMPLETE STRANGER?
Huh?
WE MET TWO MONTHS AGO.
HAVE YOU FORGOTTEN THAT FATEFUL MEETING?
HUH?
YES...
If this is a long story, I'll be leaving.
...IT WAS TWO MONTHS AGO.

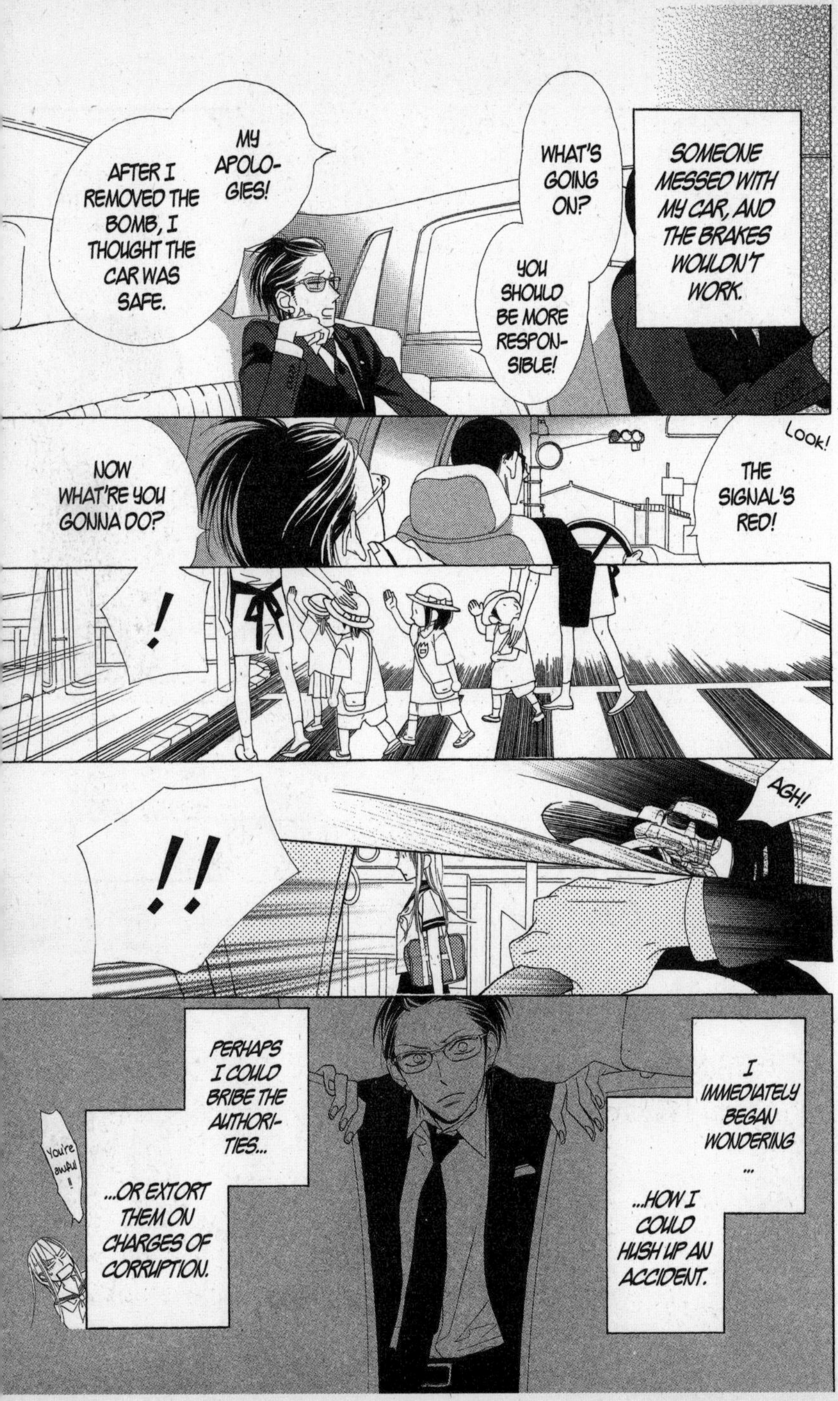
SOMEONE MESSED WITH MY CAR, AND THE BRAKES WOULDN'T WORK.
WHAT'S GOING ON?
YOU SHOULD BE MORE RESPONSIBLE!
MY APOLOGIES!
AFTER I REMOVED THE BOMB, I THOUGHT THE CAR WAS SAFE.
Look!
THE SIGNAL'S RED!
NOW WHAT'RE YOU GONNA DO?
!
AGH!
!!
I IMMEDIATELY BEGAN WONDERING ...
...HOW I COULD HUSH UP AN ACCIDENT.
PERHAPS I COULD BRIBE THE AUTHORITIES...
...OR EXTORT THEM ON CHARGES OF CORRUPTION.
You're awful!!

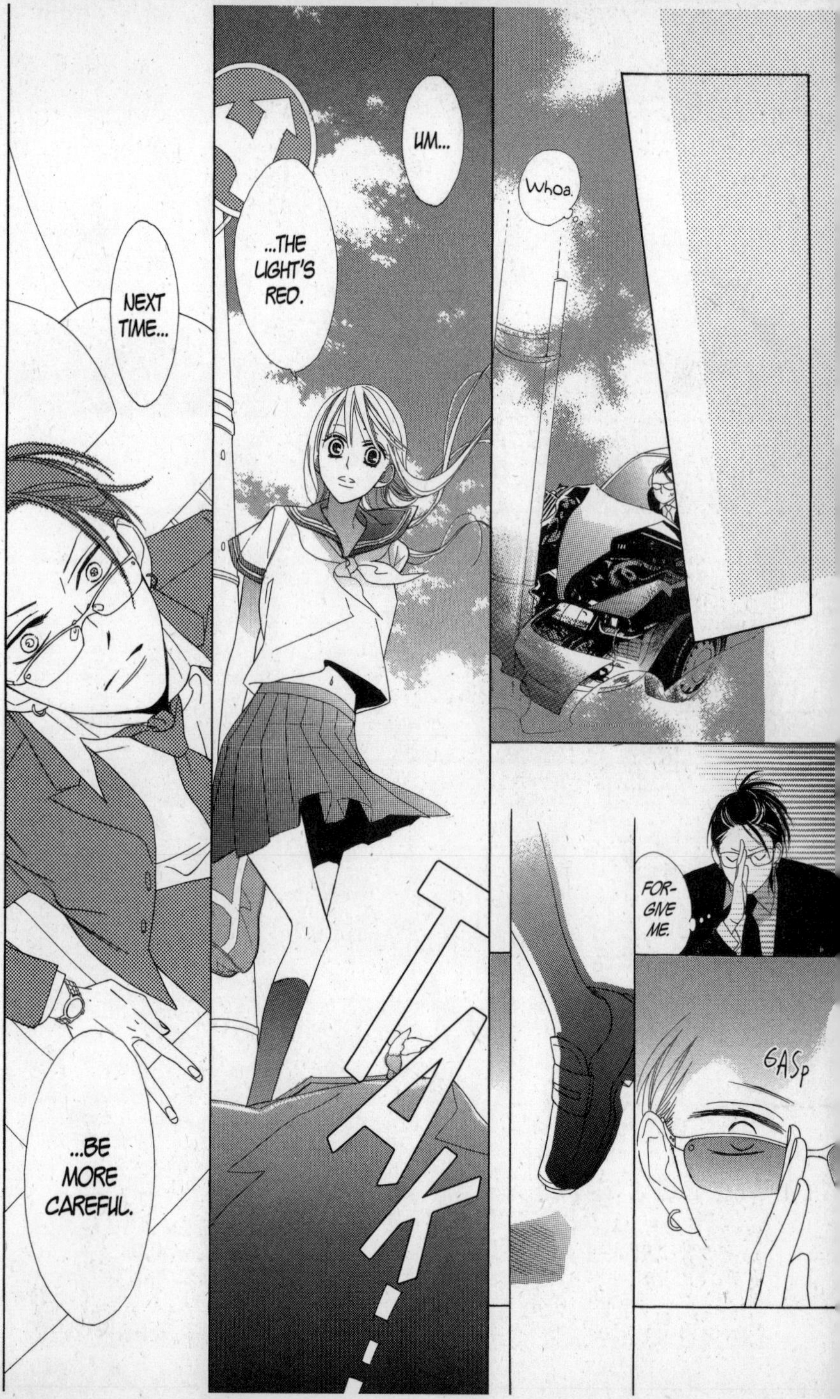
Whoa.
FOR-GIVE ME.
GASP
UM...
...THE LIGHT'S RED.
TAK
NEXT TIME...
...BE MORE CAREFUL.

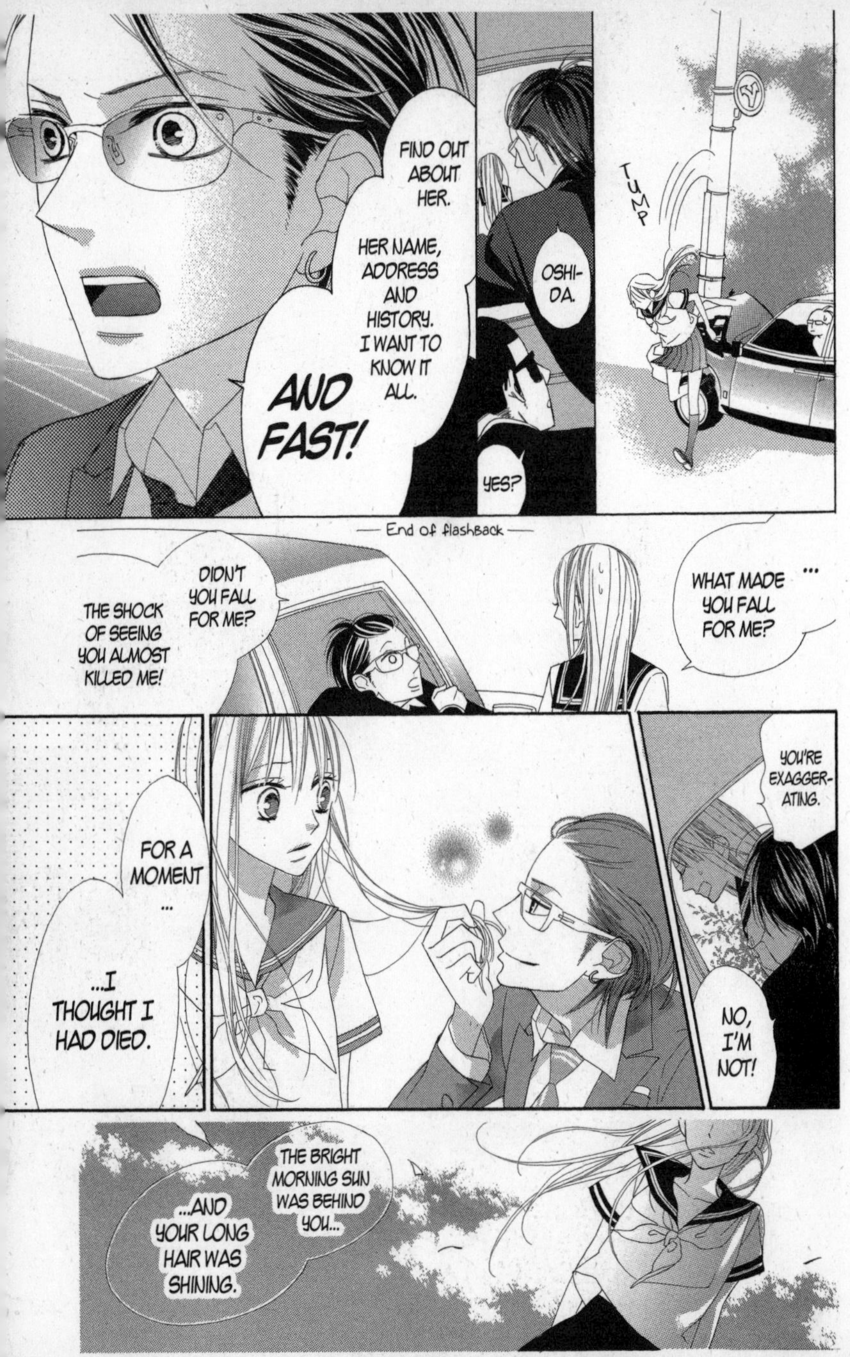
TUMP
OSHI-DA.
YES?
FIND OUT ABOUT HER.
HER NAME, ADDRESS AND HISTORY. I WANT TO KNOW IT ALL.
AND FAST!
— End of flashback —
WHAT MADE YOU FALL FOR ME? ...
DIDN'T YOU FALL FOR ME?
THE SHOCK OF SEEING YOU ALMOST KILLED ME!
YOU'RE EXAGGER-ATING.
NO, I'M NOT!
FOR A MOMENT ...
...I THOUGHT I HAD DIED.
THE BRIGHT MORNING SUN WAS BEHIND YOU...
...AND YOUR LONG HAIR WAS SHINING.

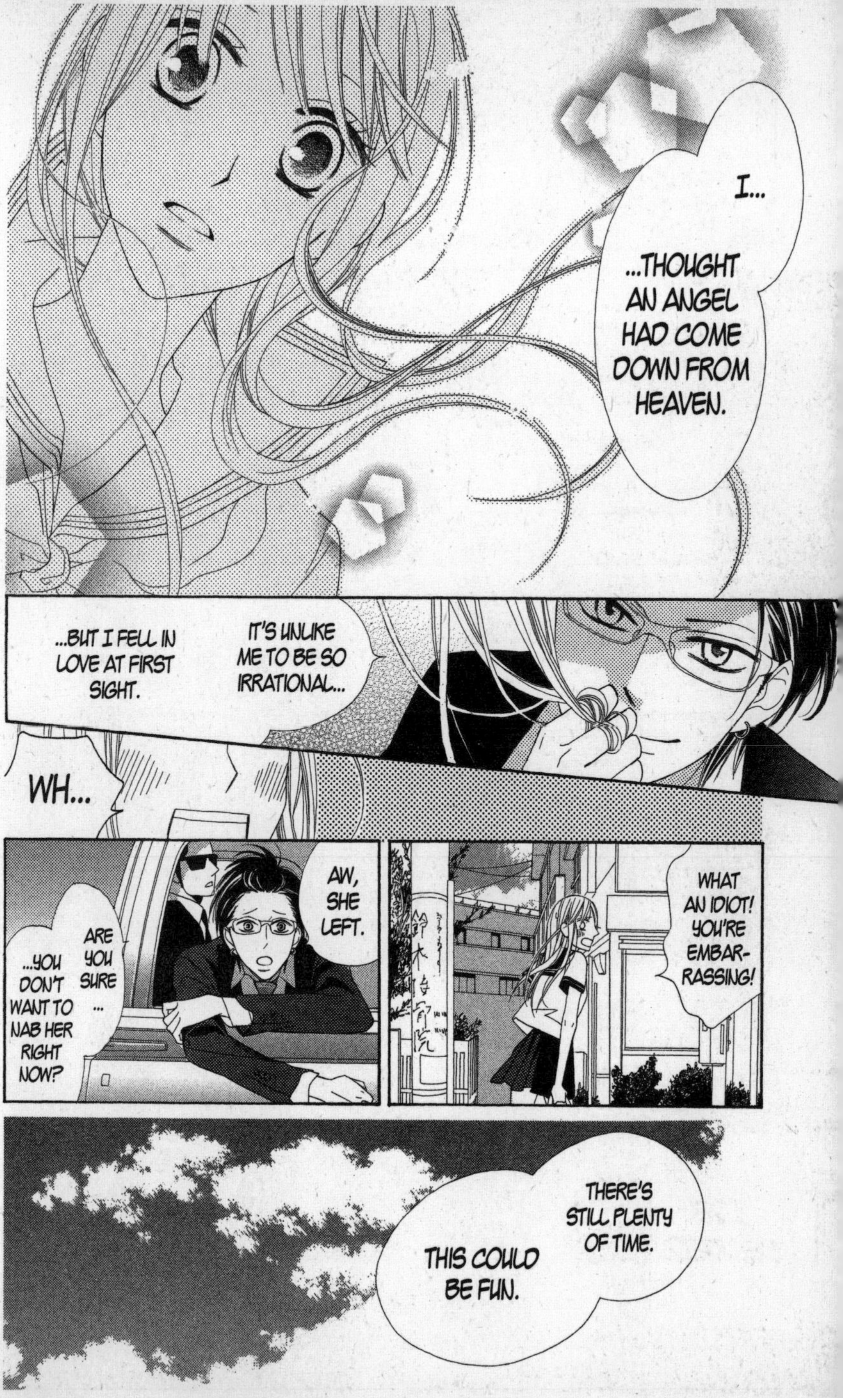
I...
...THOUGHT AN ANGEL HAD COME DOWN FROM HEAVEN.
IT'S UNLIKE ME TO BE SO IRRATIONAL...
...BUT I FELL IN LOVE AT FIRST SIGHT.
WH...
WHAT AN IDIOT! YOU'RE EMBARRASSING!
AW, SHE LEFT.
ARE YOU SURE...
...YOU DON'T WANT TO NAB HER RIGHT NOW?
THERE'S STILL PLENTY OF TIME.
THIS COULD BE FUN.

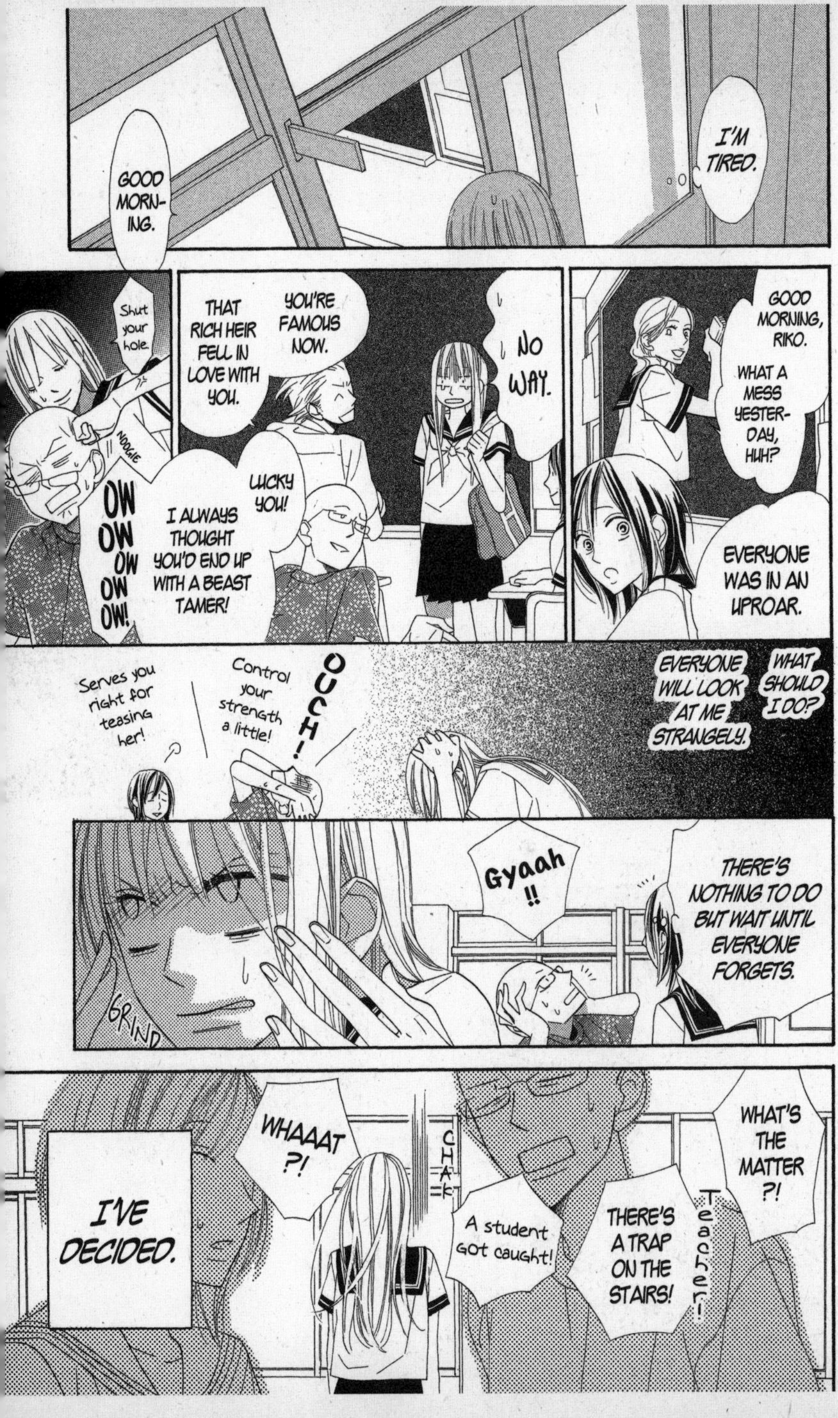
I'M TIRED.
GOOD MORNING.
GOOD MORNING, RIKO.
WHAT A MESS YESTERDAY, HUH?
EVERYONE WAS IN AN UPROAR.
NO WAY.
YOU'RE FAMOUS NOW.
THAT RICH HEIR FELL IN LOVE WITH YOU.
LUCKY YOU!
I ALWAYS THOUGHT YOU'D END UP WITH A BEAST TAMER!
Shut your hole.
NOOGIE
OW OW OW OW OW!
WHAT SHOULD I DO?
EVERYONE WILL LOOK AT ME STRANGELY.
OUCH!
Control your strength a little!
Serves you right for teasing her!
THERE'S NOTHING TO DO BUT WAIT UNTIL EVERYONE FORGETS.
Gyaah !!
GRIND
WHAT'S THE MATTER ?!
Teacher!
THERE'S A TRAP ON THE STAIRS!
A student got caught!
CHAK
WHAAAT ?!
I'VE DECIDED.

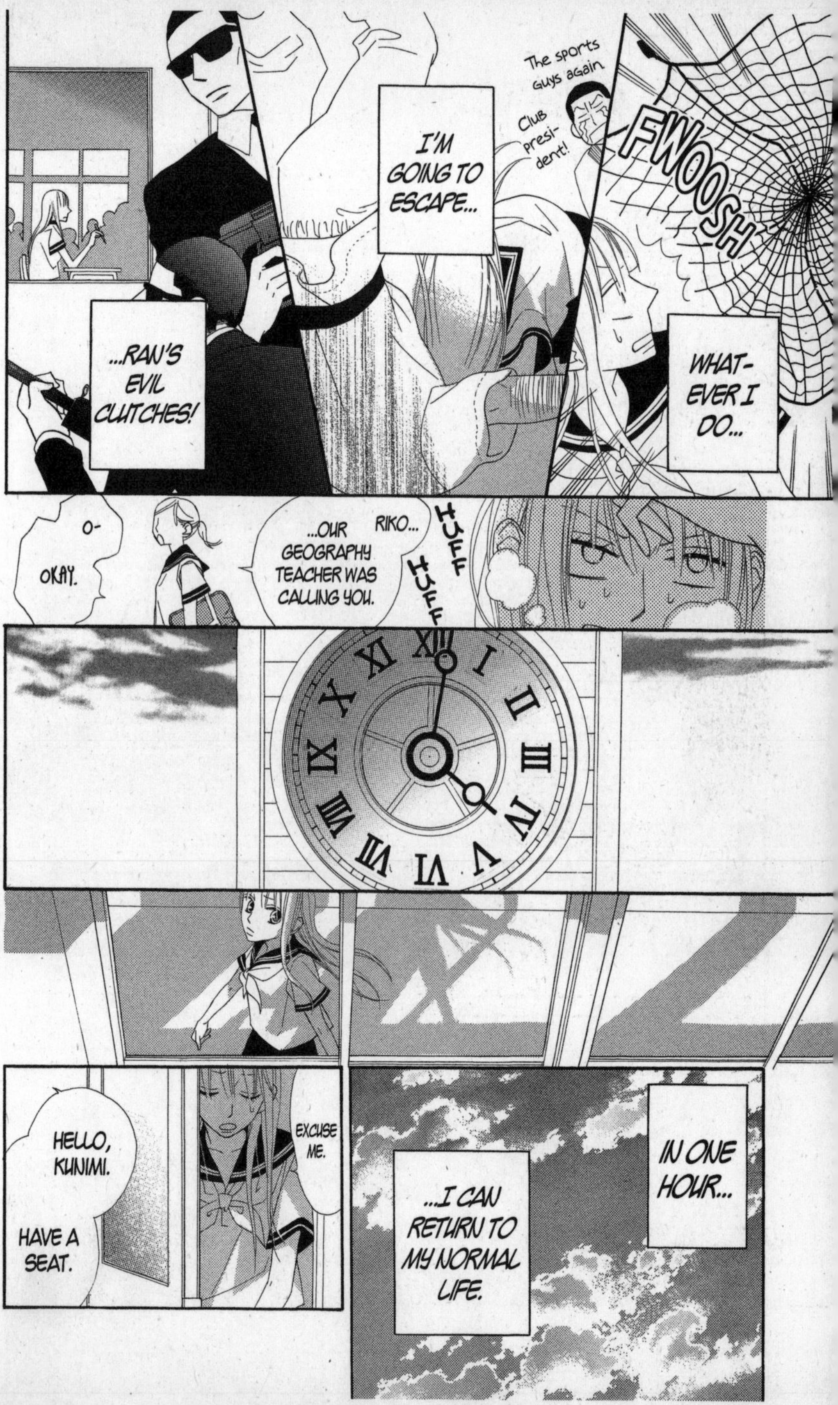
The sports Guys again.
Club president!
FWOOSH
WHAT-EVER I DO...
I'M GOING TO ESCAPE...
...RAN'S EVIL CLUTCHES!
HUFF HUFF
RIKO...
...OUR GEOGRAPHY TEACHER WAS CALLING YOU.
O- OKAY.
IN ONE HOUR...
...I CAN RETURN TO MY NORMAL LIFE.
EXCUSE ME.
HELLO, KUNIMI.
HAVE A SEAT.

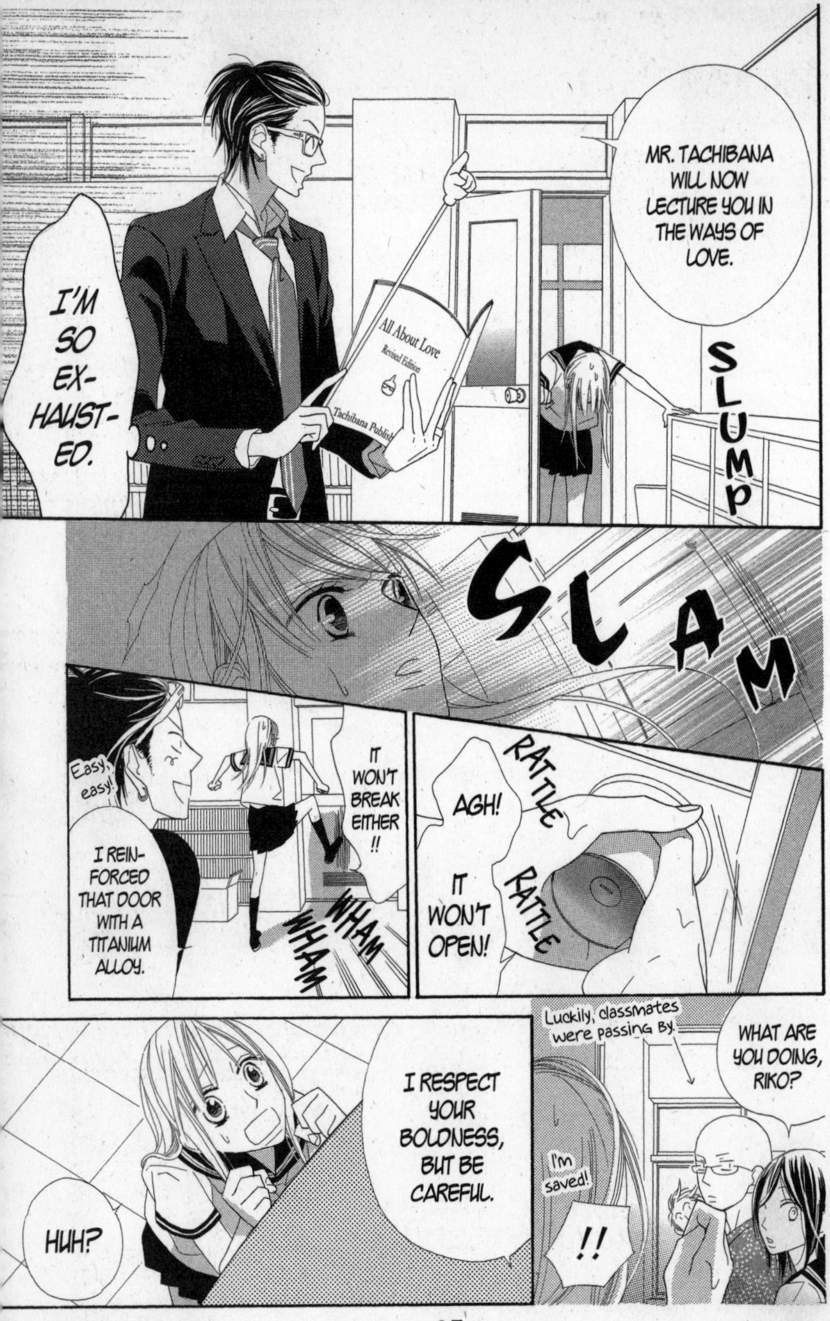
MR. TACHIBANA WILL NOW LECTURE YOU IN THE WAYS OF LOVE.
SLUMP
All About Love
Revised Edition
Tachibana Publish
I'M SO EX-HAUSTED.
SLAM
RATTLE
AGH!
RATTLE
IT WON'T OPEN!
IT WON'T BREAK EITHER!!
WHAM WHAM
Easy, easy!
I REINFORCED THAT DOOR WITH A TITANIUM ALLOY.
Luckily, classmates were passing By.
WHAT ARE YOU DOING, RIKO?
I'm saved!
!!
I RESPECT YOUR BOLDNESS, BUT BE CAREFUL.
HUH?

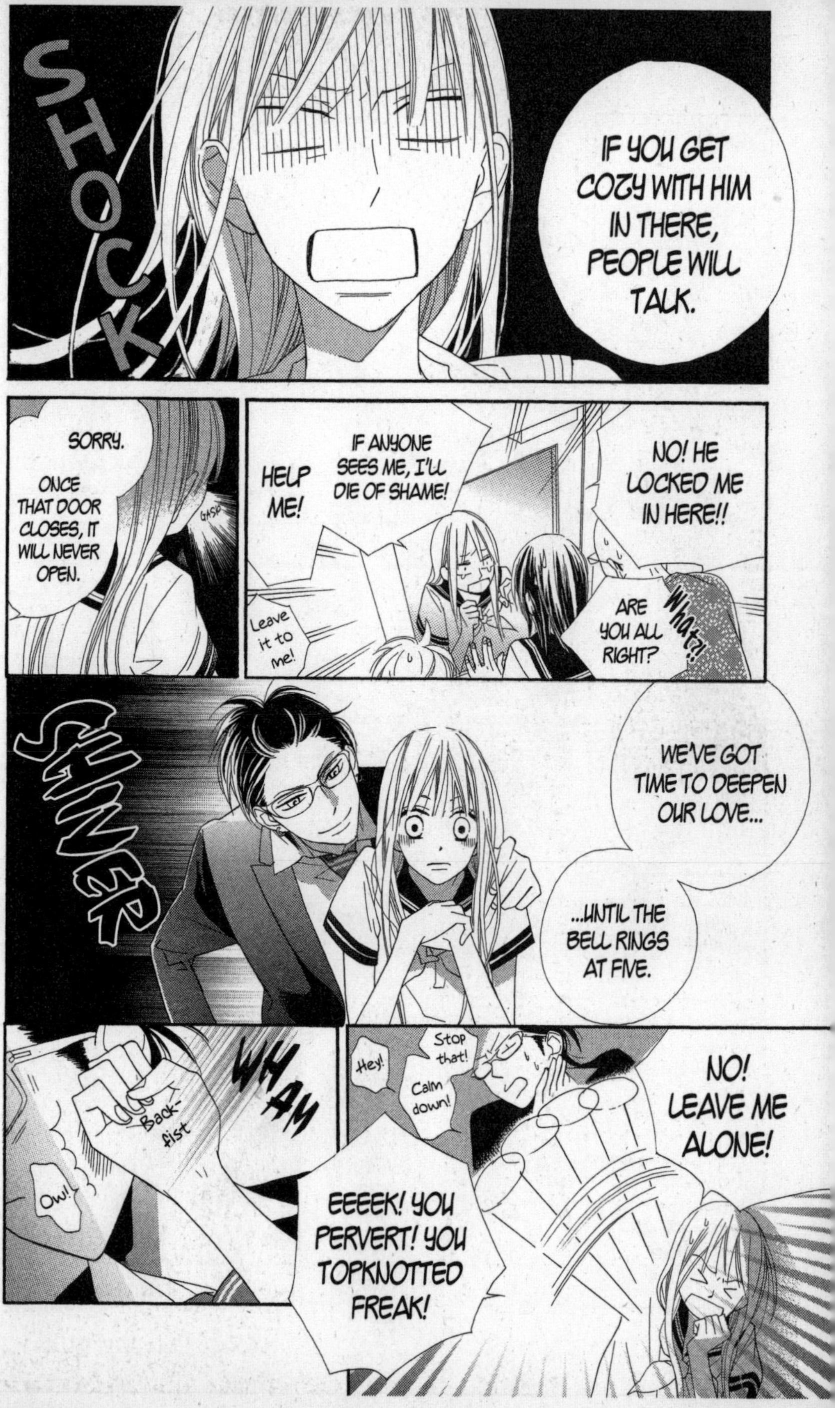
IF YOU GET COZY WITH HIM IN THERE, PEOPLE WILL TALK.
SHOCK
NO! HE LOCKED ME IN HERE!!
What?!
ARE YOU ALL RIGHT?
IF ANYONE SEES ME, I'LL DIE OF SHAME!
HELP ME!
Leave it to me!
SORRY.
ONCE THAT DOOR CLOSES, IT WILL NEVER OPEN.
WE'VE GOT TIME TO DEEPEN OUR LOVE...
...UNTIL THE BELL RINGS AT FIVE.
SHIVER
NO! LEAVE ME ALONE!
Stop that!
Hey!
Calm down!
EEEEK! YOU PERVERT! YOU TOPKNOTTED FREAK!
WHAM
Back-fist
Ow!

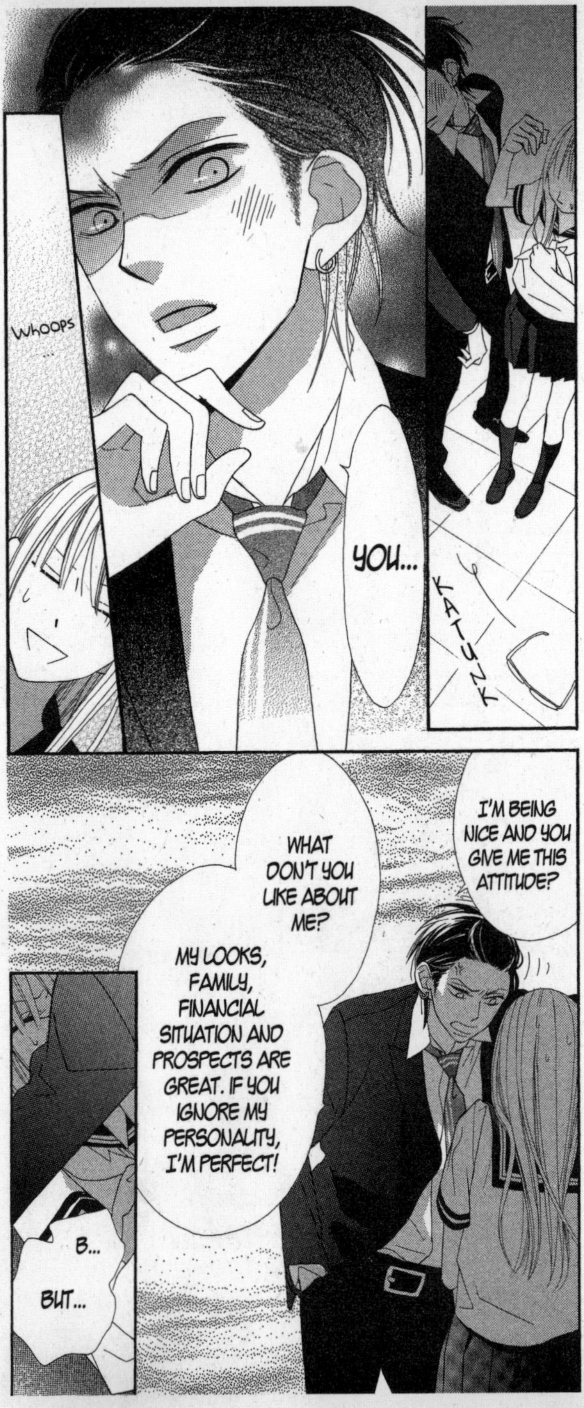
KATUNK
YOU...
Whoops...
I'M BEING NICE AND YOU GIVE ME THIS ATTITUDE?
WHAT DON'T YOU LIKE ABOUT ME?
MY LOOKS, FAMILY, FINANCIAL SITUATION AND PROSPECTS ARE GREAT. IF YOU IGNORE MY PERSONALITY, I'M PERFECT!
B...
BUT...

• Character Profile Part 1 •

Riko Kunimi

Age 17, 5' 1-1/2"

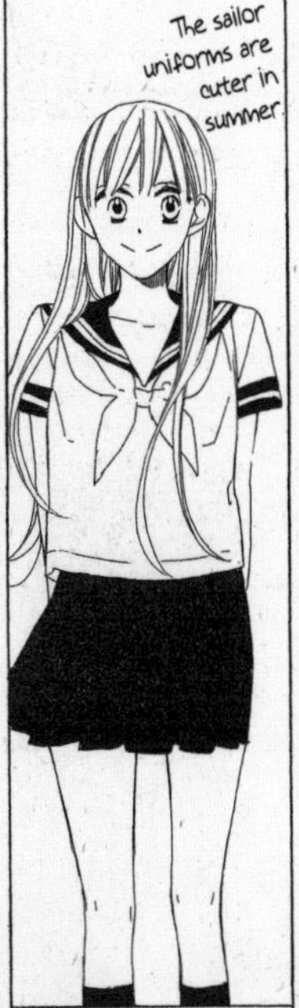
The sailor uniforms are cuter in summer.

I think Riko is the most normal girl I have ever drawn in any of my manga. I tried to make her look cute, but drawing her hair was difficult. Isn't it strange that even when she's flying through the air or jumping you can never see her panties?

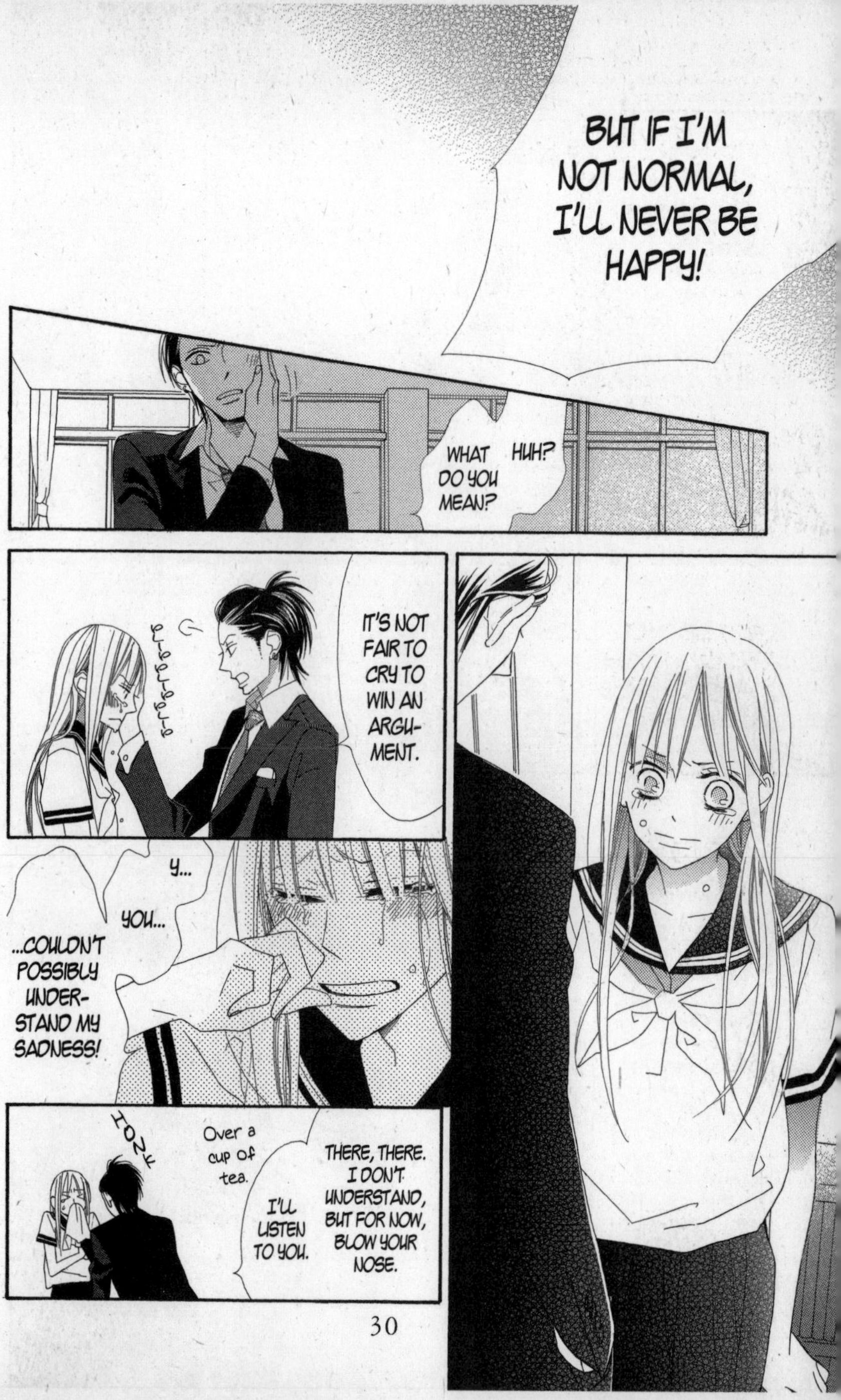
BUT IF I'M NOT NORMAL, I'LL NEVER BE HAPPY!
HUH?
WHAT DO YOU MEAN?
IT'S NOT FAIR TO CRY TO WIN AN ARGU-MENT.
Y...
YOU...
...COULDN'T POSSIBLY UNDER-STAND MY SADNESS!
THERE, THERE. I DON'T UNDERSTAND, BUT FOR NOW, BLOW YOUR NOSE.
I'LL LISTEN TO YOU.
Over a cup of tea.
HONK

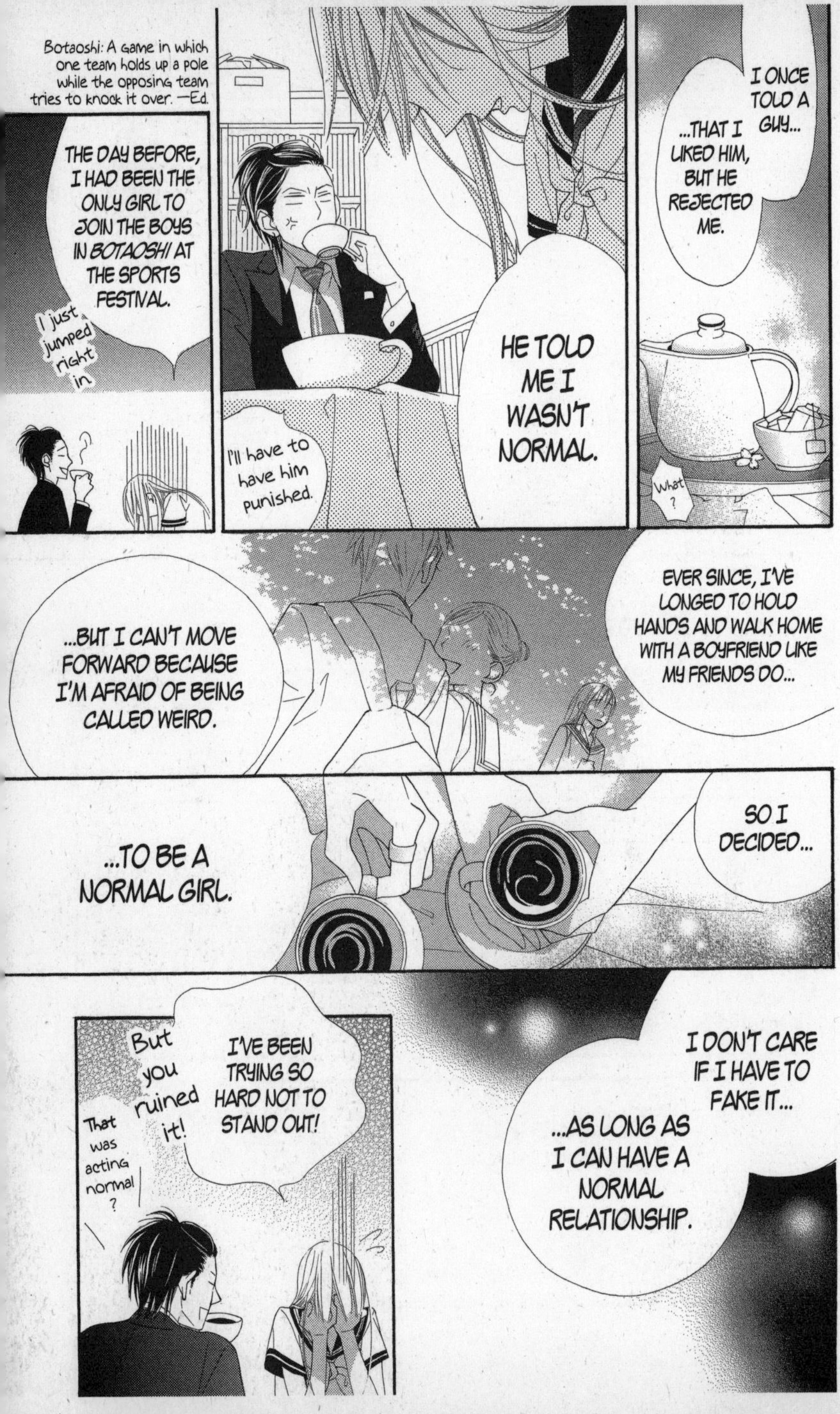
I ONCE TOLD A GUY...
...THAT I LIKED HIM, BUT HE REJECTED ME.
What?
HE TOLD ME I WASN'T NORMAL.
I'll have to have him punished.
Botaoshi: A game in which one team holds up a pole while the opposing team tries to knock it over. —Ed.
THE DAY BEFORE, I HAD BEEN THE ONLY GIRL TO JOIN THE BOYS IN *BOTAOSHI* AT THE SPORTS FESTIVAL.
I just jumped right in.
EVER SINCE, I'VE LONGED TO HOLD HANDS AND WALK HOME WITH A BOYFRIEND LIKE MY FRIENDS DO...
...BUT I CAN'T MOVE FORWARD BECAUSE I'M AFRAID OF BEING CALLED WEIRD.
SO I DECIDED...
...TO BE A NORMAL GIRL.
I DON'T CARE IF I HAVE TO FAKE IT...
...AS LONG AS I CAN HAVE A NORMAL RELATIONSHIP.
I'VE BEEN TRYING SO HARD NOT TO STAND OUT!
But you ruined it!
That was acting normal?

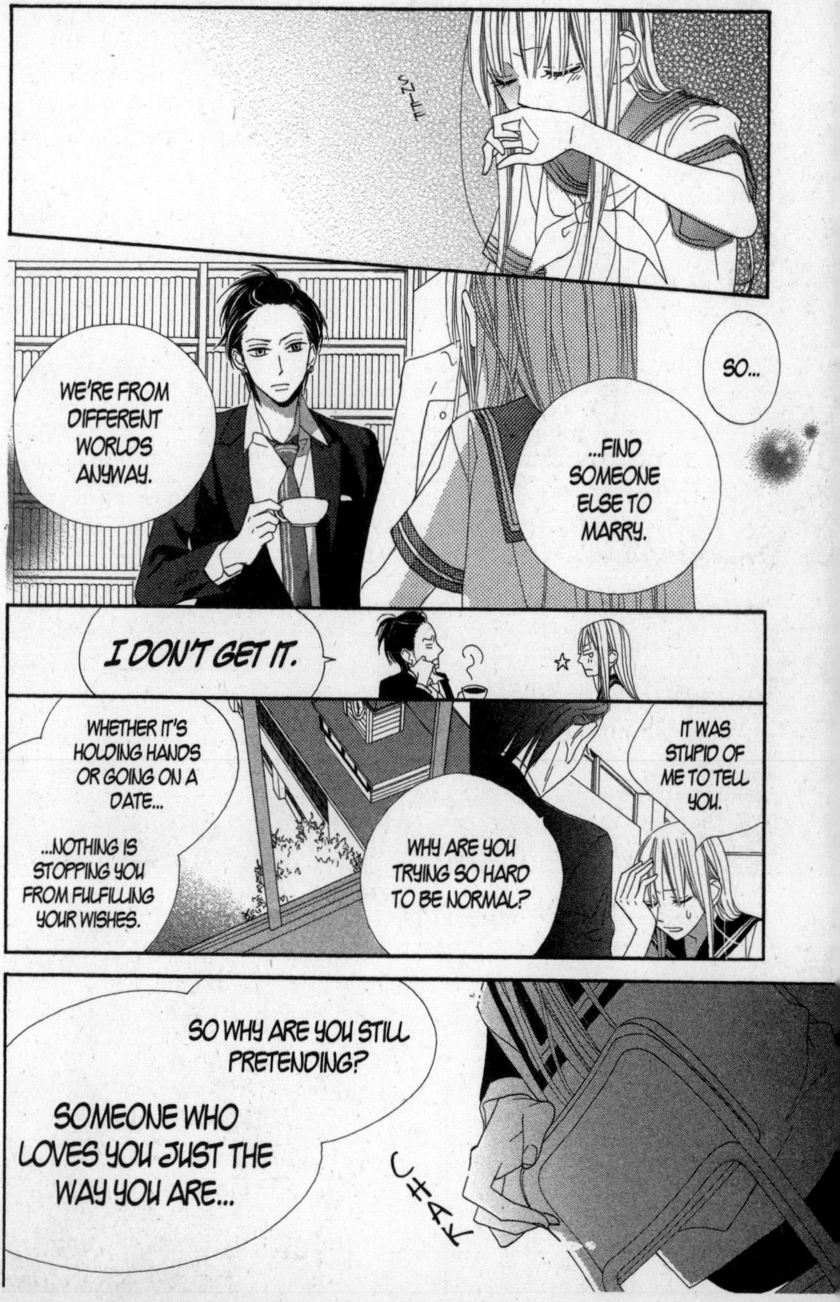
SNIFF
SO...
...FIND SOMEONE ELSE TO MARRY.
WE'RE FROM DIFFERENT WORLDS ANYWAY.
I DON'T GET IT.
IT WAS STUPID OF ME TO TELL YOU.
WHY ARE YOU TRYING SO HARD TO BE NORMAL?
WHETHER IT'S HOLDING HANDS OR GOING ON A DATE...
...NOTHING IS STOPPING YOU FROM FULFILLING YOUR WISHES.
CHAK
SO WHY ARE YOU STILL PRETENDING?
SOMEONE WHO LOVES YOU JUST THE WAY YOU ARE...

...IS RIGHT...

...HERE.

HOW CAN HE...

...SO EASILY SAY WHAT I'VE ALWAYS WANTED TO HEAR?

RIKO!

HOW? It's a titanium alloy.

HEH!

SORRY FOR THE WAIT!

WE CAN HELP YOU NOW!

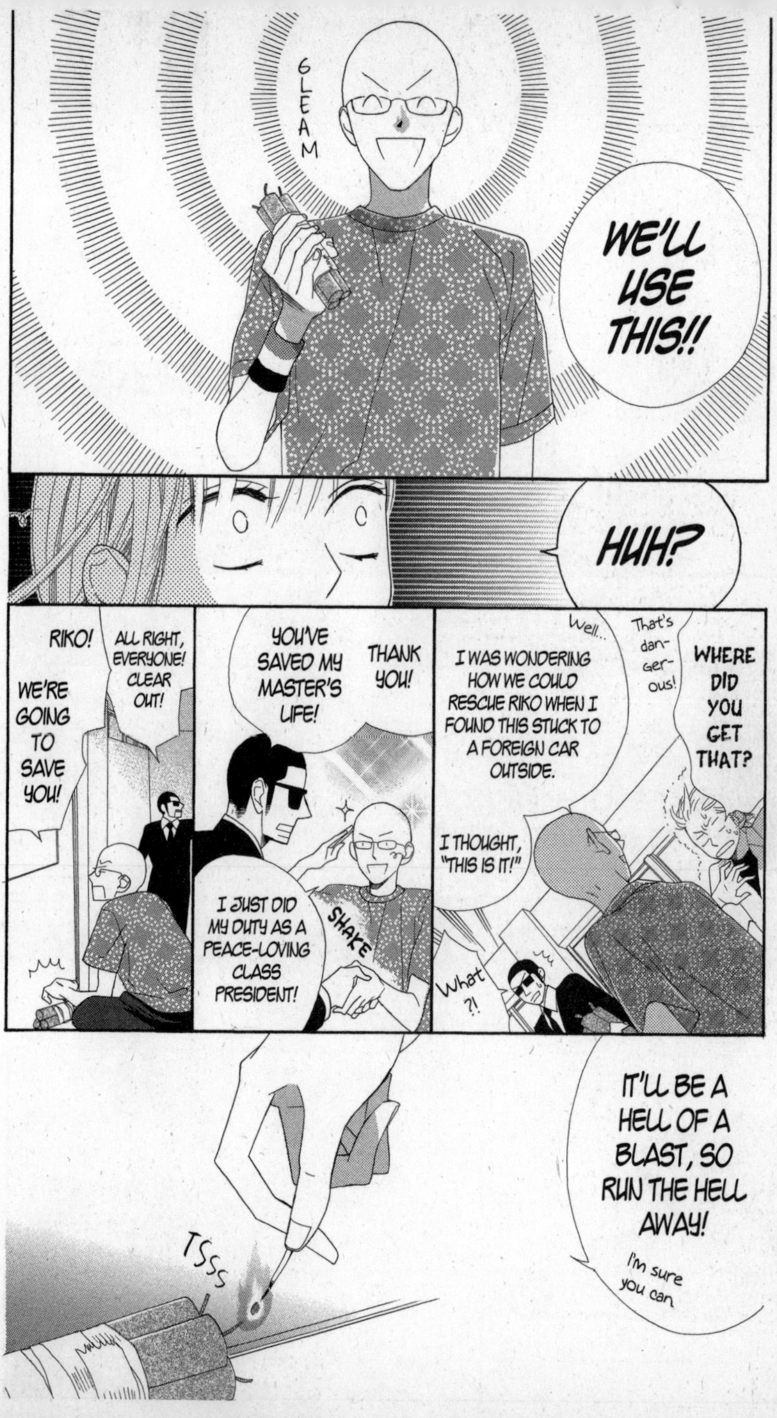
GLEAM
WE'LL USE THIS!!
HUH?
WHERE DID YOU GET THAT?
That's dan-ger-ous!
Well...
I WAS WONDERING HOW WE COULD RESCUE RIKO WHEN I FOUND THIS STUCK TO A FOREIGN CAR OUTSIDE.
I THOUGHT, "THIS IS IT!"
What?!
THANK YOU!
YOU'VE SAVED MY MASTER'S LIFE!
I JUST DID MY DUTY AS A PEACE-LOVING CLASS PRESIDENT!
SHAKE
ALL RIGHT, EVERYONE! CLEAR OUT!
RIKO!
WE'RE GOING TO SAVE YOU!
IT'LL BE A HELL OF A BLAST, SO RUN THE HELL AWAY!
I'm sure you can.
TSSS

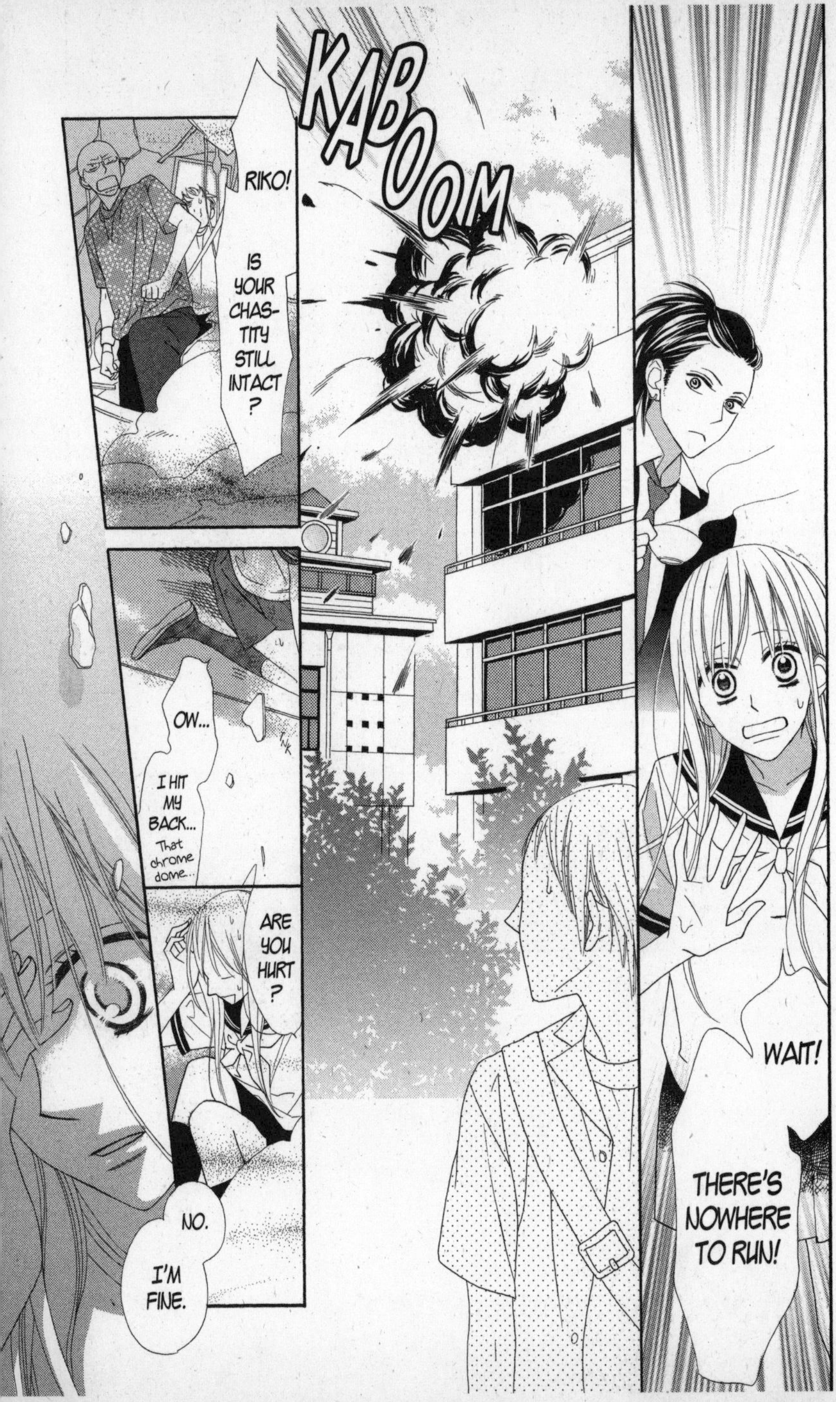
WAIT!
THERE'S NOWHERE TO RUN!
KABOOM
RIKO!
IS YOUR CHASTITY STILL INTACT ?
OW...
I HIT MY BACK...
That chrome dome...
ARE YOU HURT ?
NO.
I'M FINE.

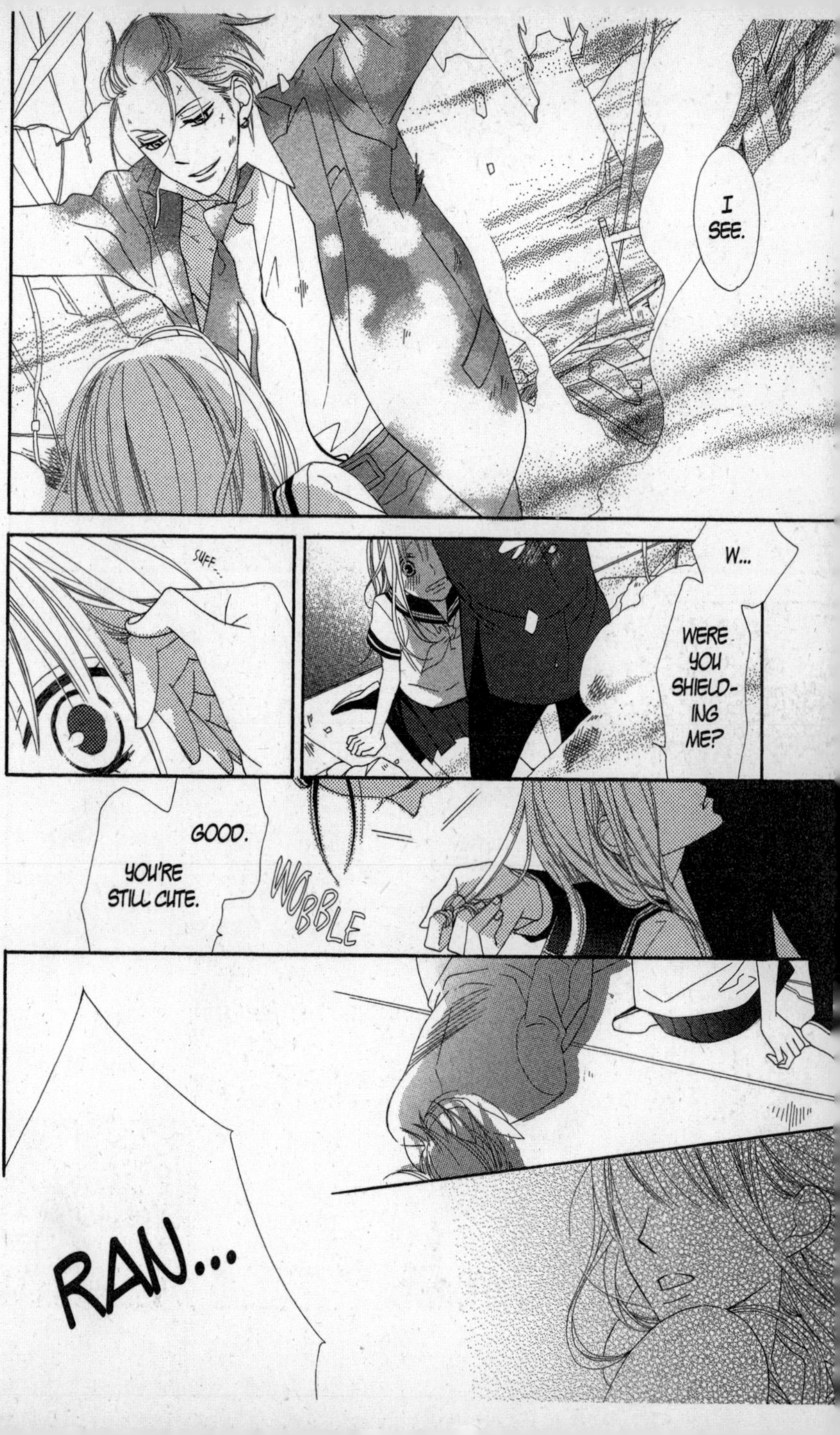
I SEE.
W...
WERE YOU SHIELDING ME?
SNIFF...
GOOD.
YOU'RE STILL CUTE.
WOBBLE
RAN...

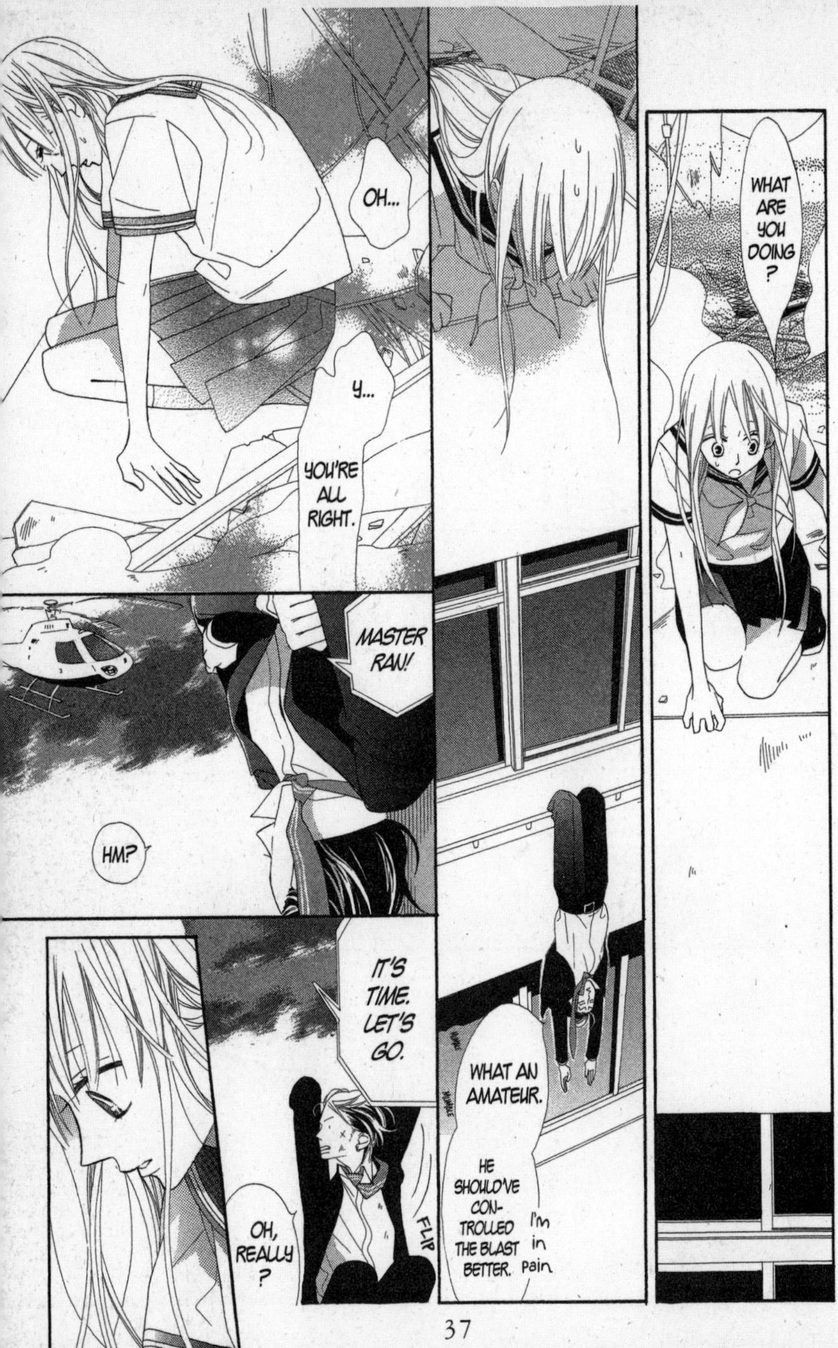
WHAT ARE YOU DOING ?
OH...
Y...
YOU'RE ALL RIGHT.
WHAT AN AMATEUR.
HE SHOULD'VE CON-TROLLED THE BLAST BETTER.
I'm in pain
MUMBLE
MASTER RAN!
HM?
IT'S TIME. LET'S GO.
OH, REALLY ?
FLIP

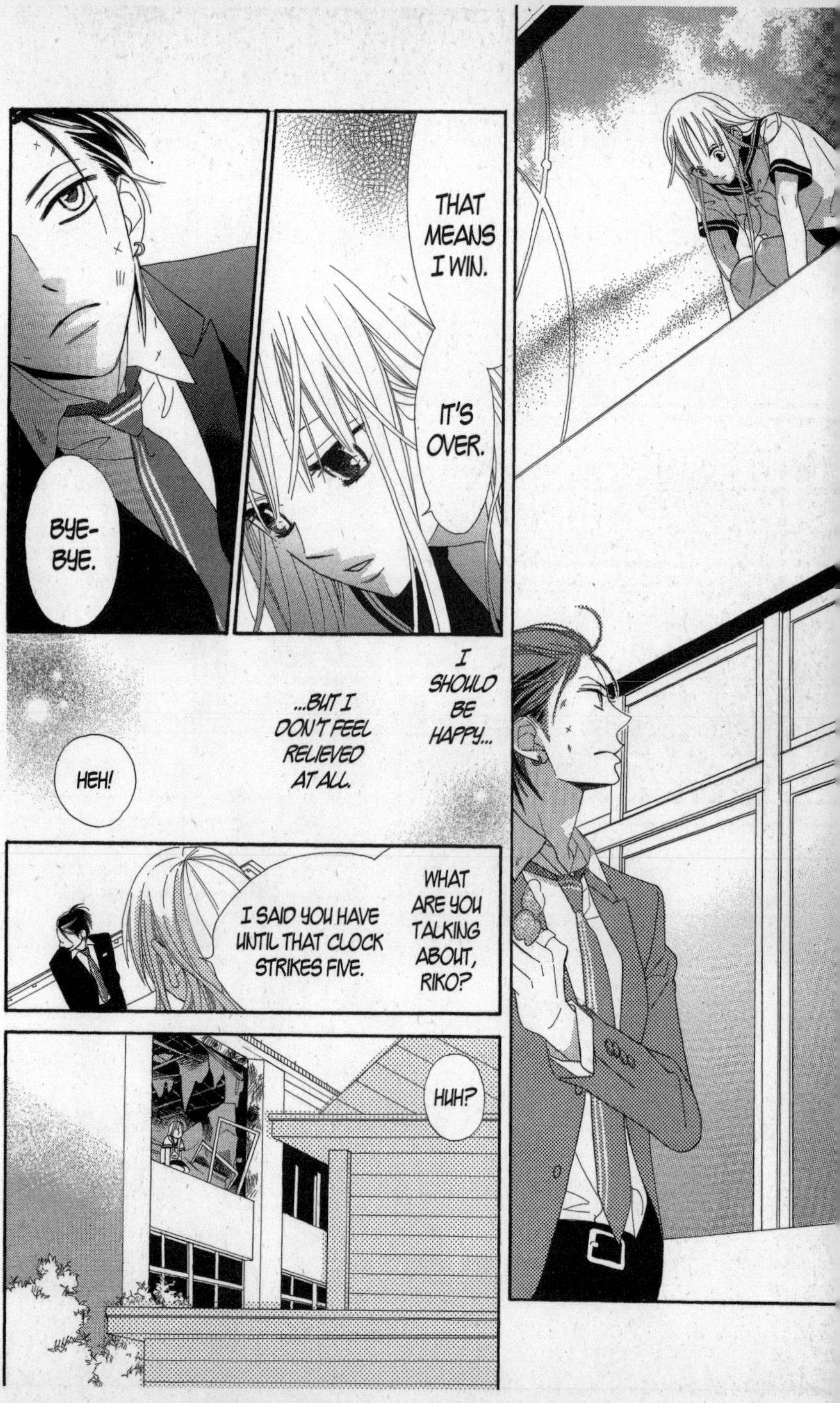
THAT MEANS I WIN.
IT'S OVER.
BYE-BYE.
I SHOULD BE HAPPY...
...BUT I DON'T FEEL RELIEVED AT ALL.
HEH!
WHAT ARE YOU TALKING ABOUT, RIKO?
I SAID YOU HAVE UNTIL THAT CLOCK STRIKES FIVE.
HUH?

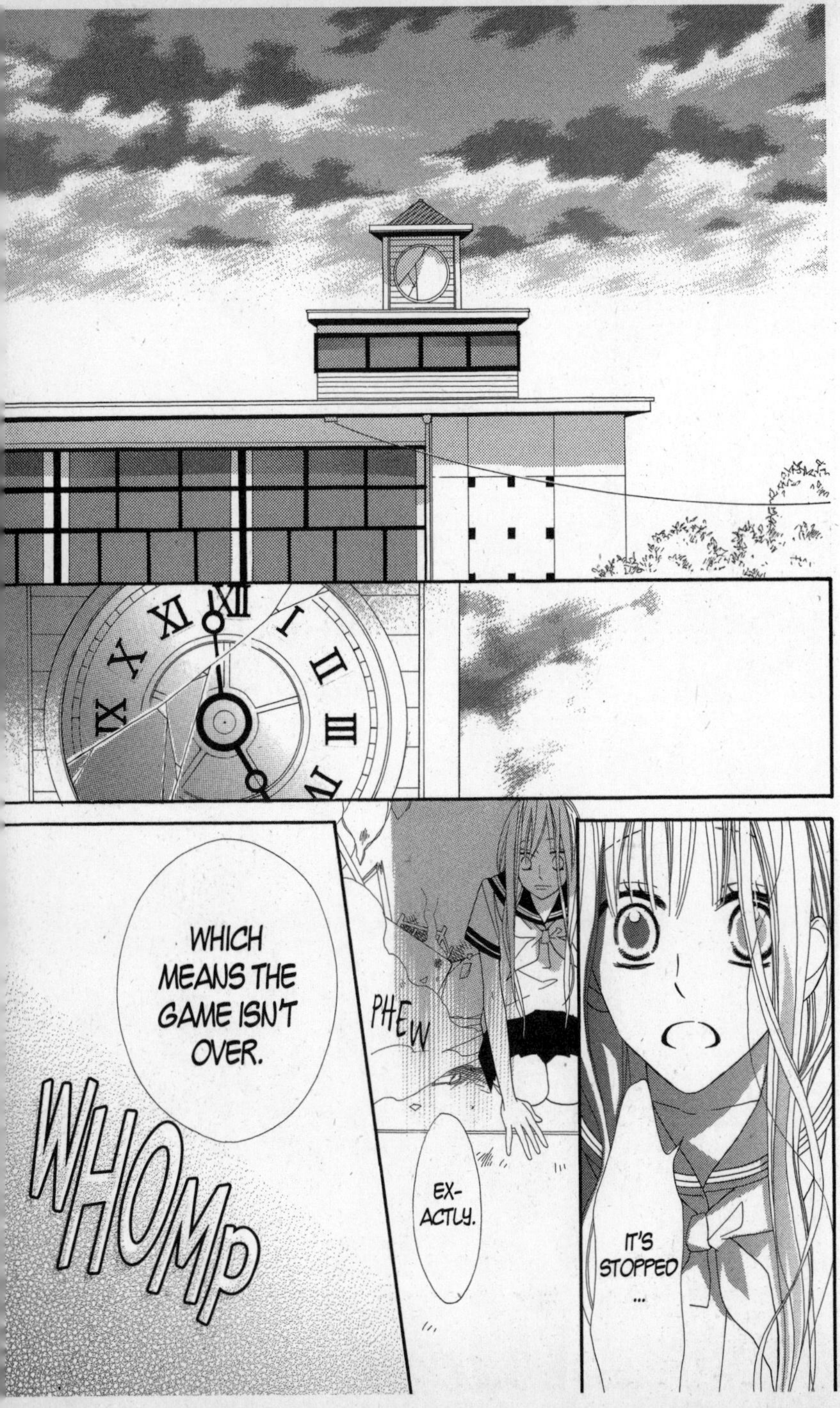
IT'S STOPPED ...
PHEW
EX-ACTLY.
WHICH MEANS THE GAME ISN'T OVER.
WHOMP

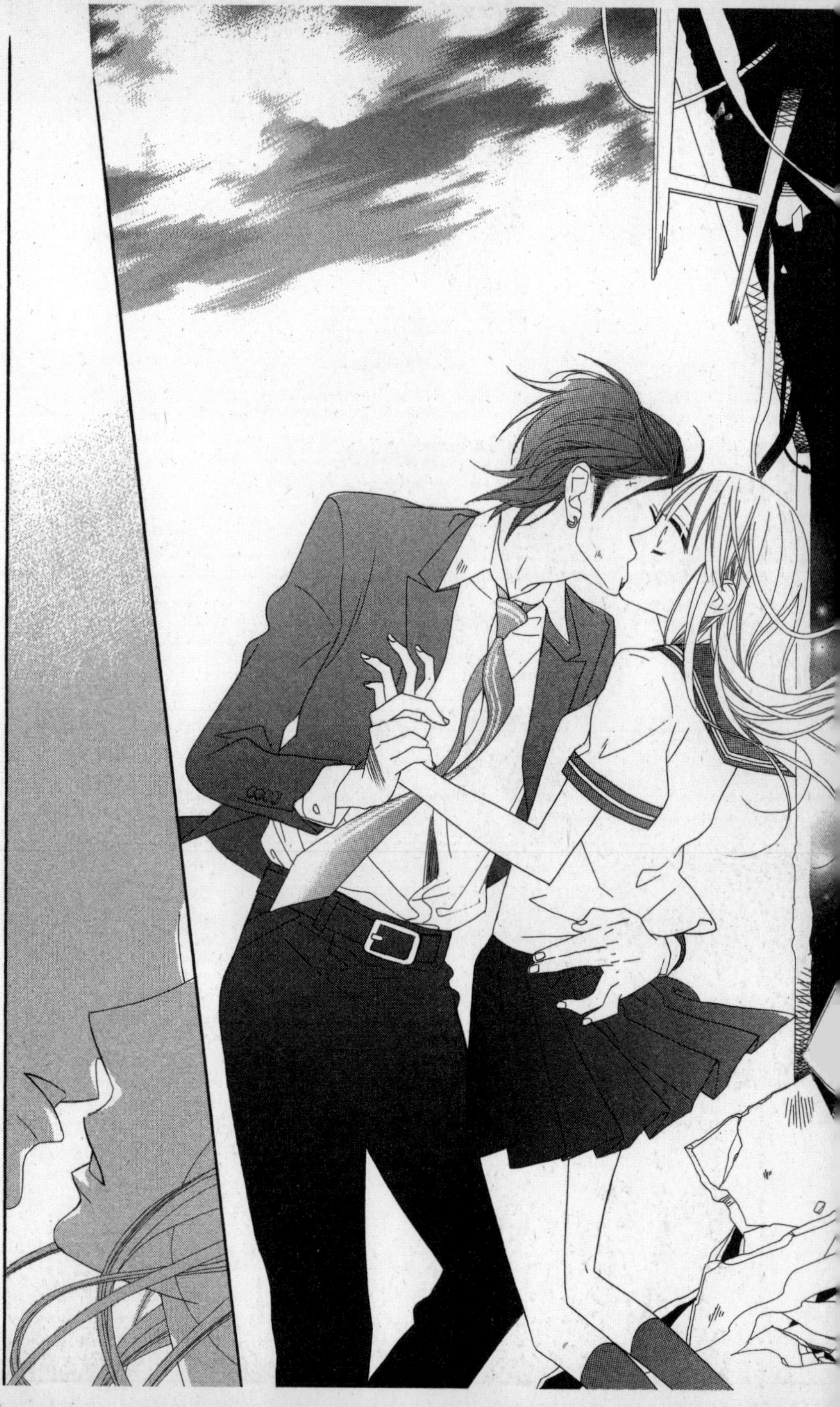

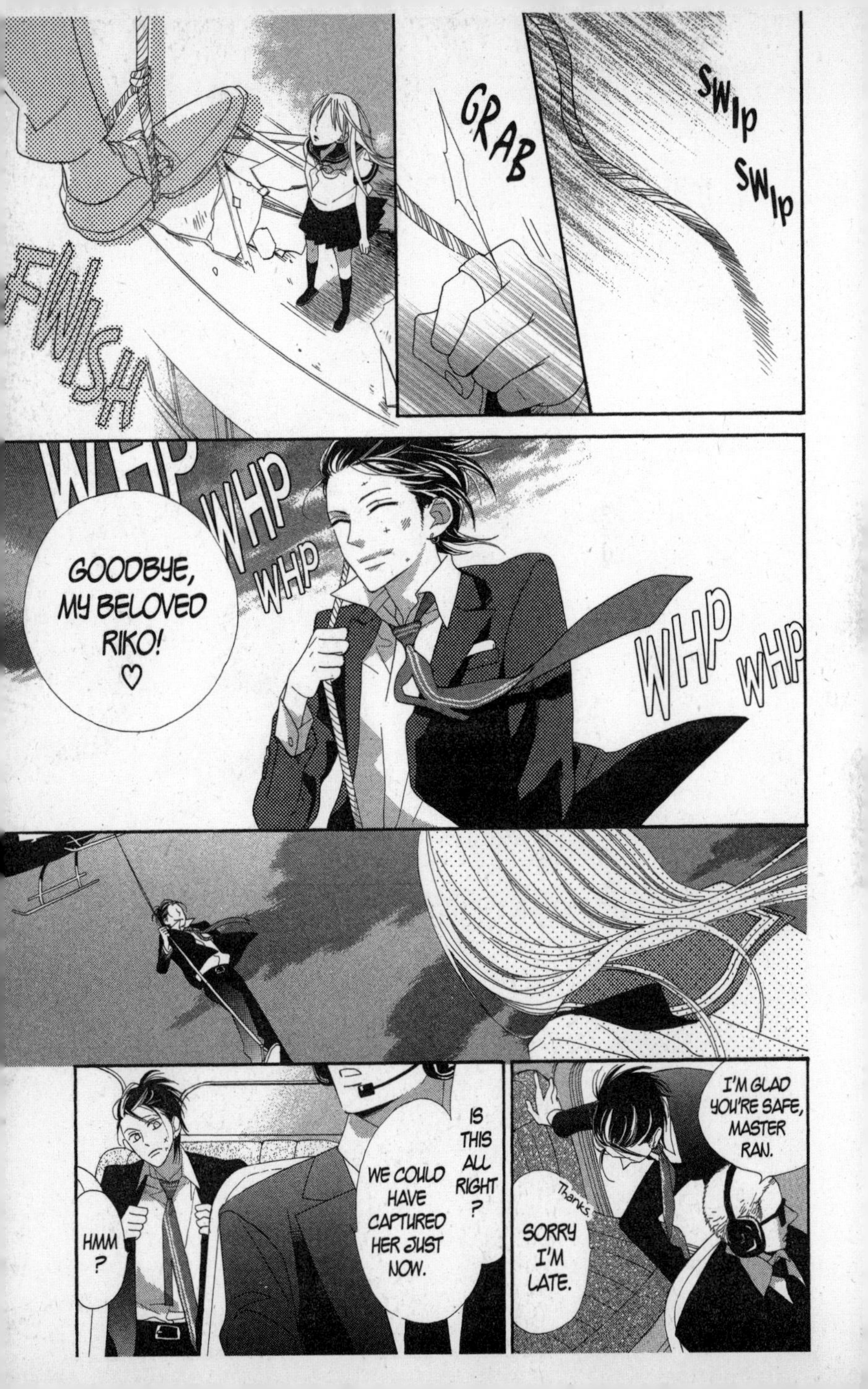
SWIP
SWIP
GRAB
FWISH
WHP
WHP
WHP
WHP
WHP
GOODBYE, MY BELOVED RIKO! ♡
I'M GLAD YOU'RE SAFE, MASTER RAN.
Thanks.
SORRY I'M LATE.
IS THIS ALL RIGHT?
WE COULD HAVE CAPTURED HER JUST NOW.
HMM?

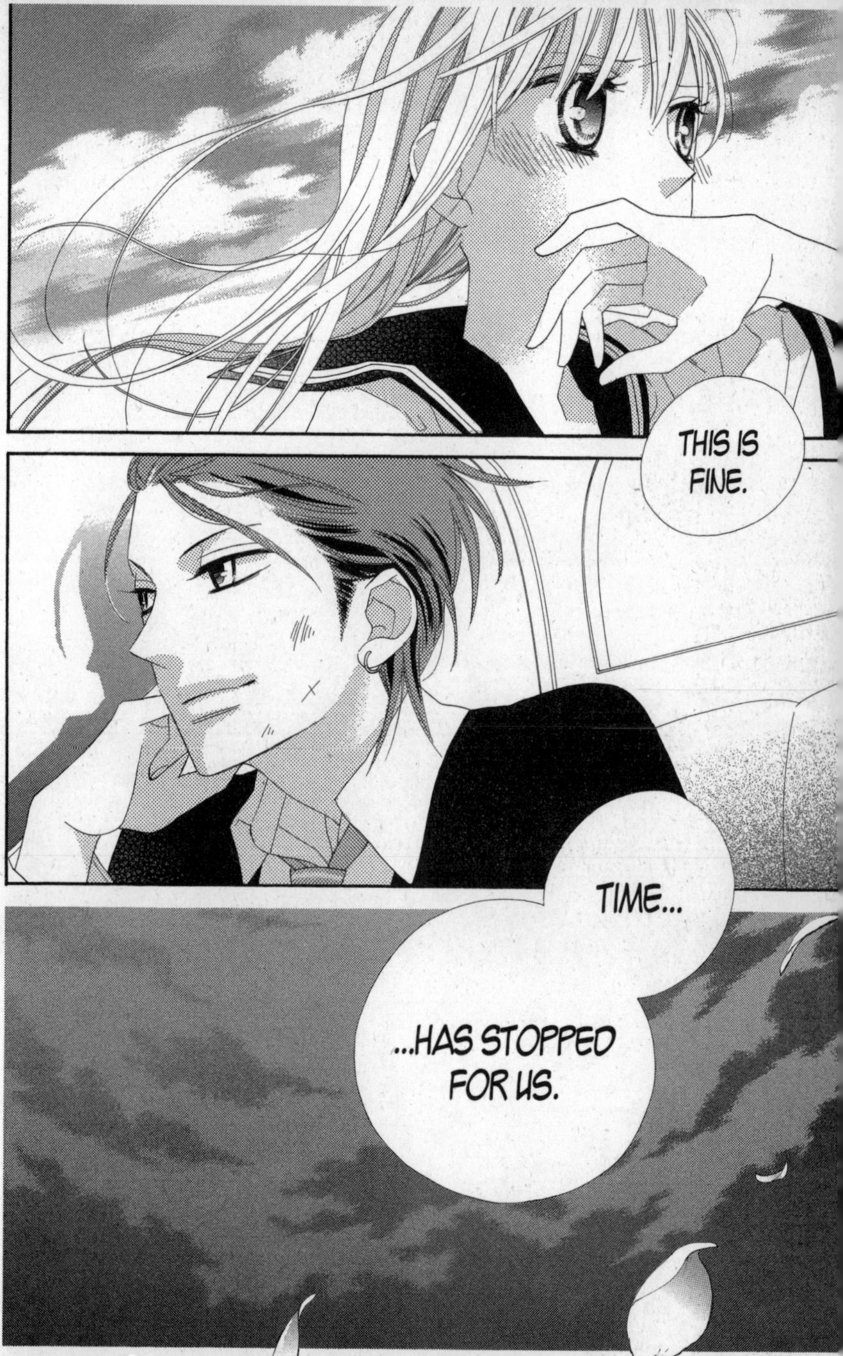
THIS IS FINE.
TIME...
...HAS STOPPED FOR US.

FLOWER IN A STORM CHAPTER 1 / END

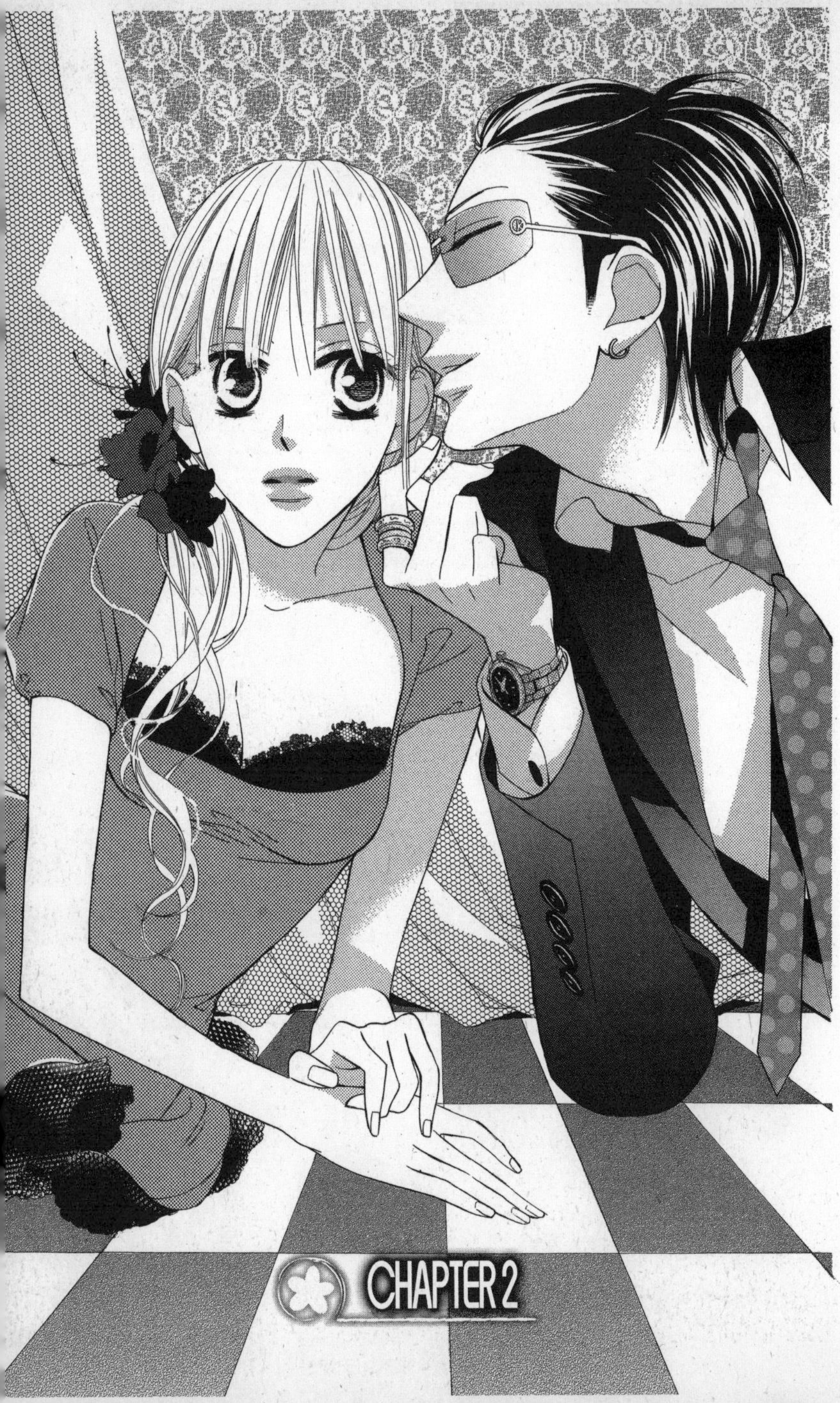
CHAPTER 2

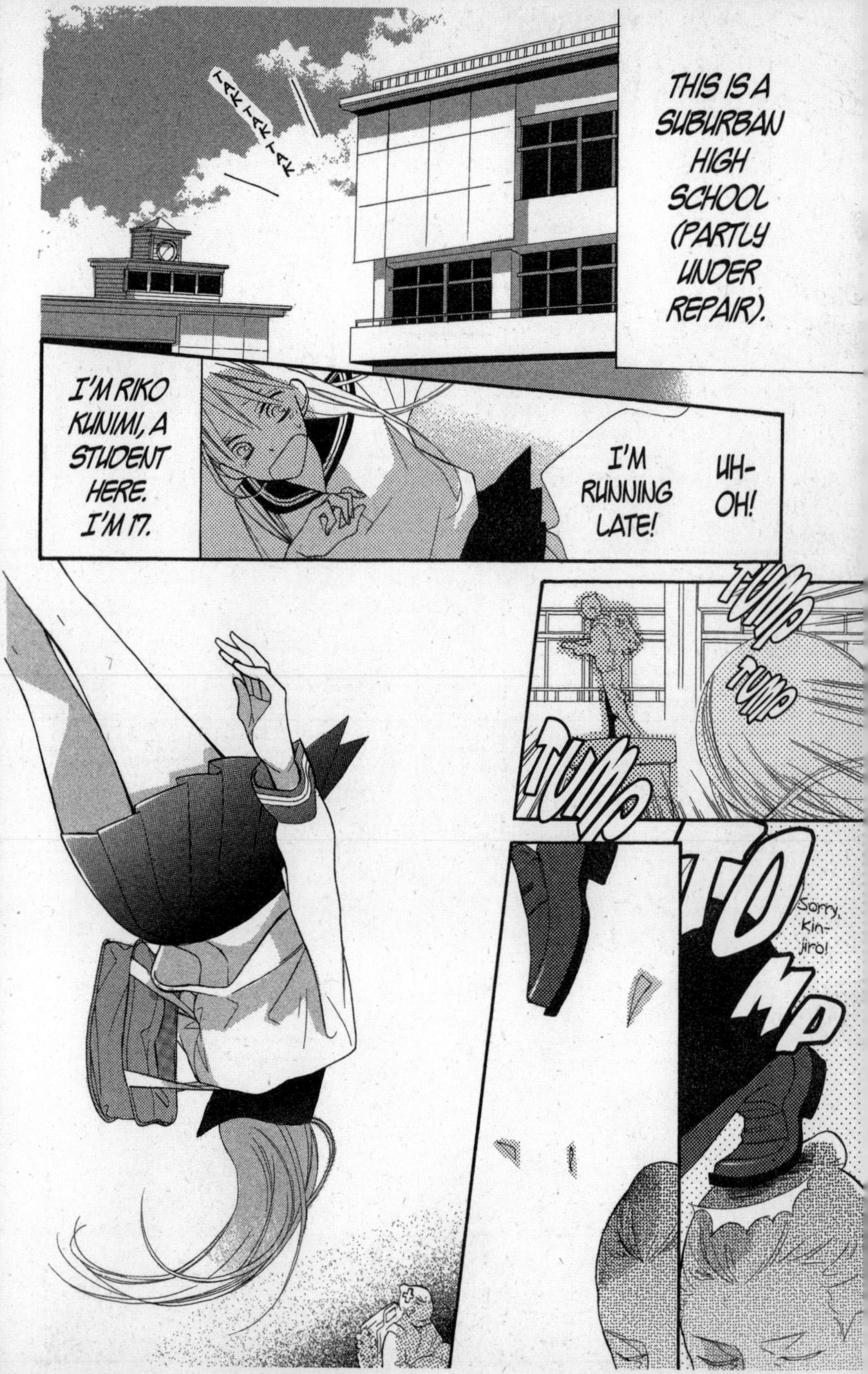
THIS IS A SUBURBAN HIGH SCHOOL (PARTLY UNDER REPAIR).
TAK TAK TAK TAK
UH-OH!
I'M RUNNING LATE!
I'M RIKO KUNIMI, A STUDENT HERE. I'M 17.
TUMP
TUMP
TUMP
TOMP
Sorry, Kinjiro!

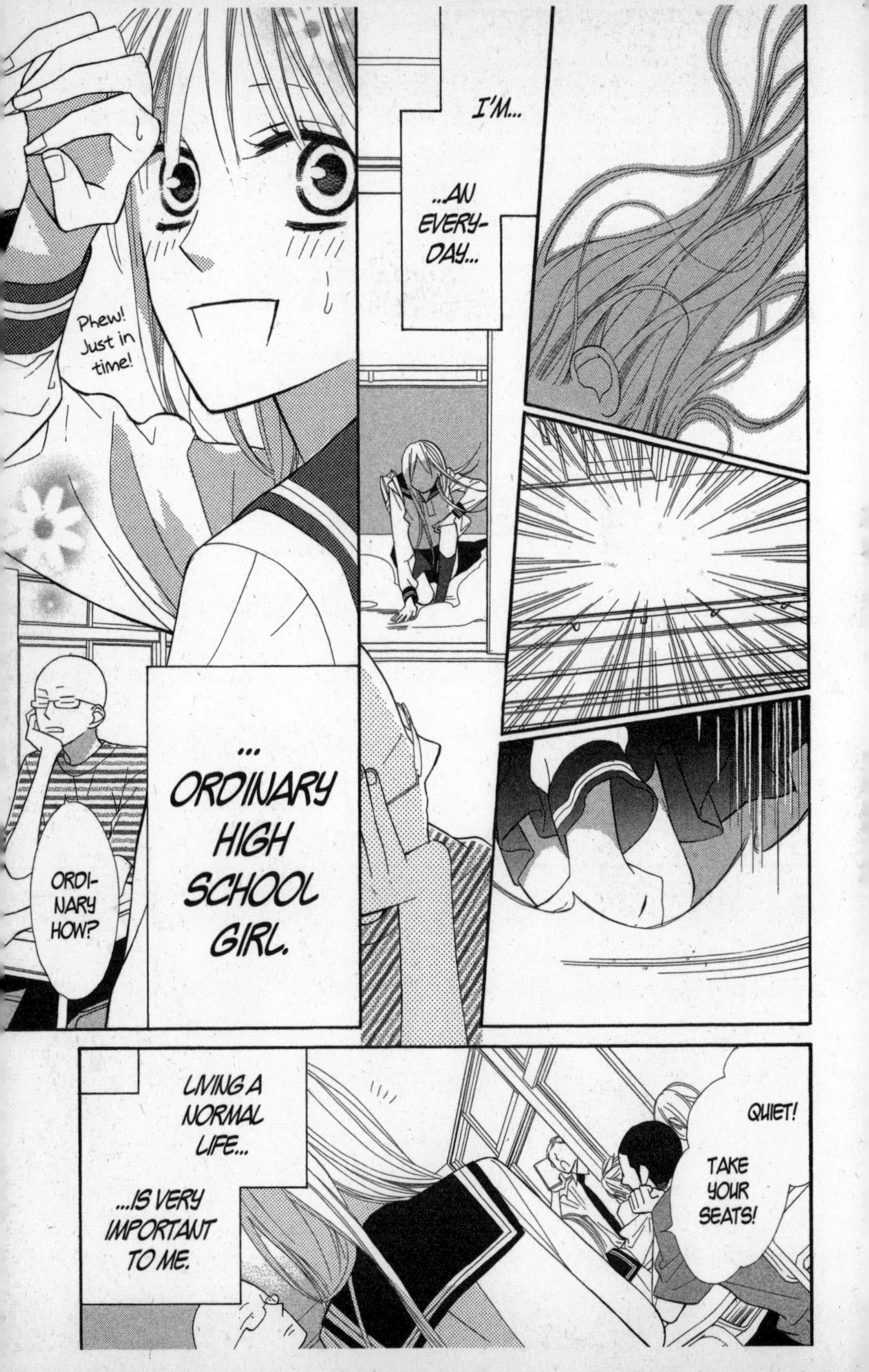
I'M...
...AN EVERY-DAY...
...ORDINARY HIGH SCHOOL GIRL.
Phew! Just in time!
ORDI-NARY HOW?
QUIET!
TAKE YOUR SEATS!
LIVING A NORMAL LIFE...
...IS VERY IMPORTANT TO ME.

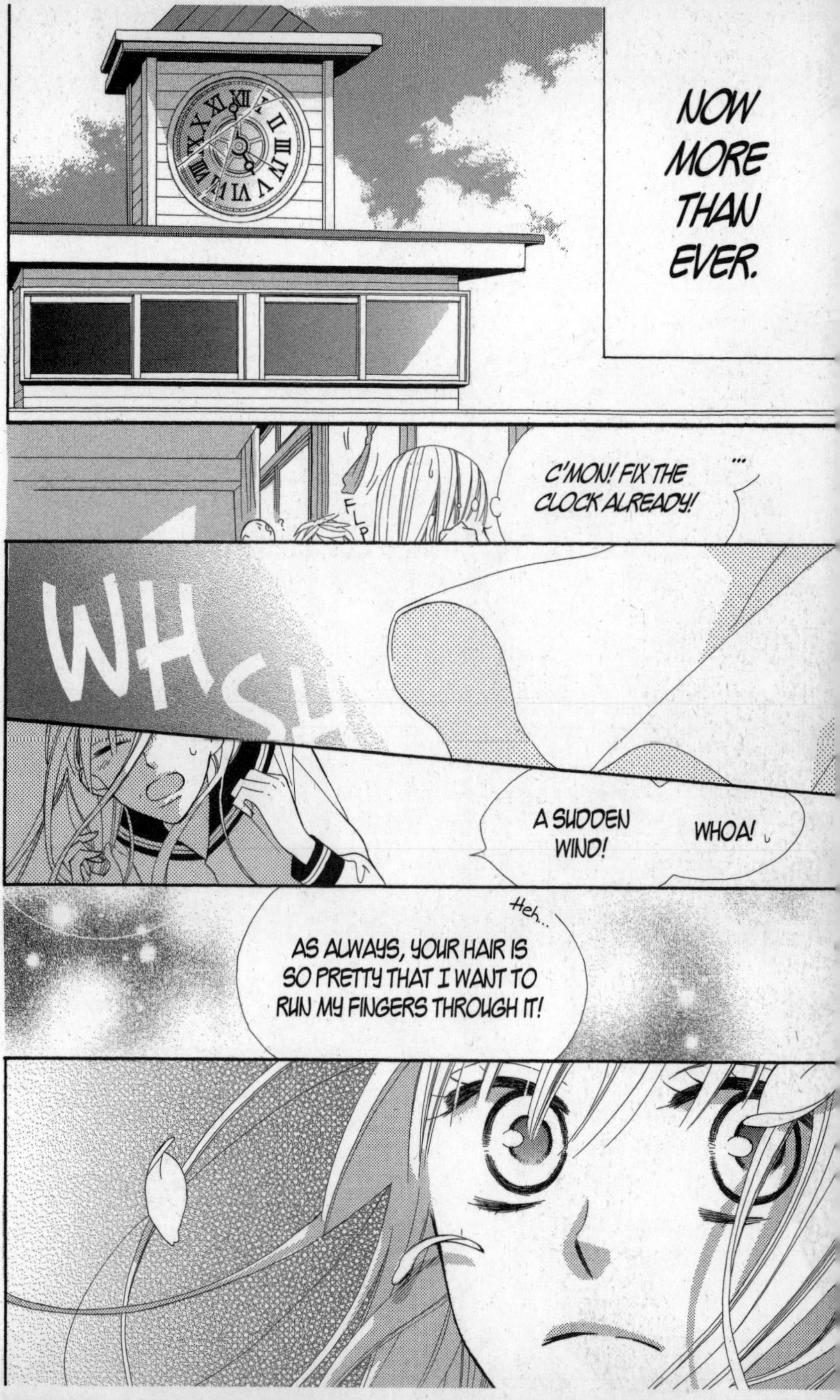
NOW MORE THAN EVER.
...
C'MON! FIX THE CLOCK ALREADY!
FLP
WHSH
WHOA!
A SUDDEN WIND!
Heh...
AS ALWAYS, YOUR HAIR IS SO PRETTY THAT I WANT TO RUN MY FINGERS THROUGH IT!

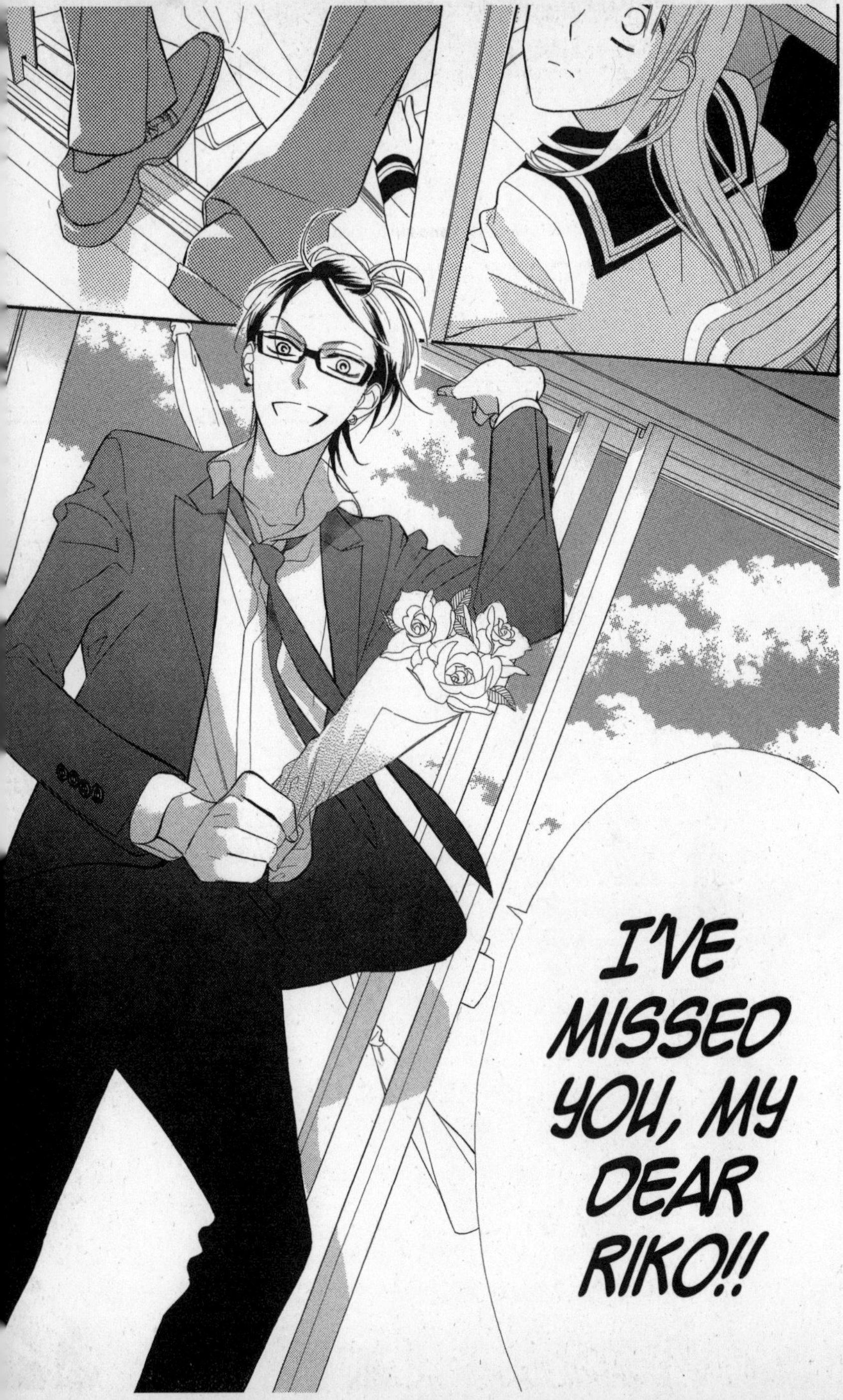
I'VE MISSED YOU, MY DEAR RIKO!!

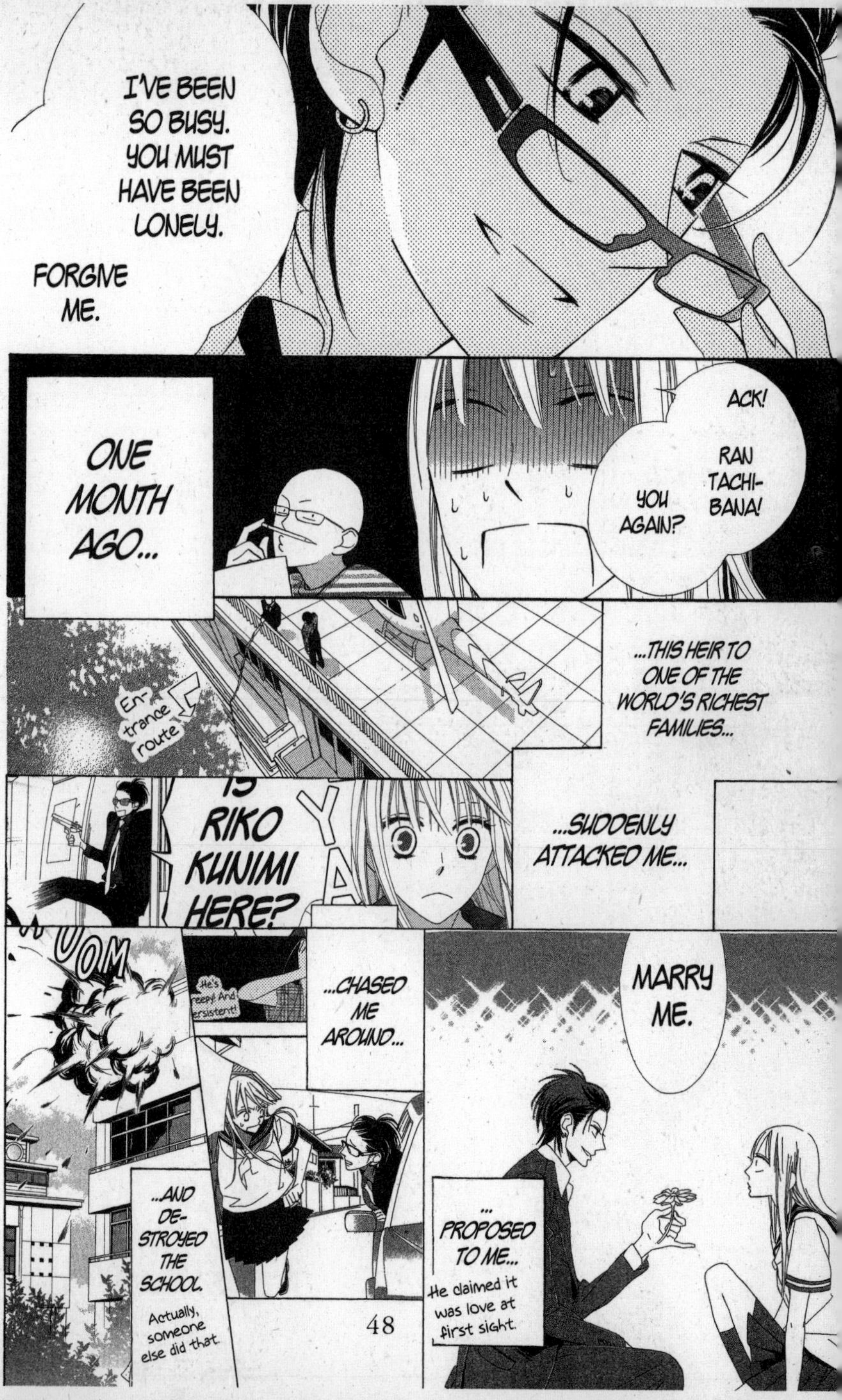
I'VE BEEN SO BUSY. YOU MUST HAVE BEEN LONELY.
FORGIVE ME.
ACK!
RAN TACHIBANA!
YOU AGAIN?
ONE MONTH AGO...
...THIS HEIR TO ONE OF THE WORLD'S RICHEST FAMILIES...
En-trance route
...SUDDENLY ATTACKED ME...
IS RIKO KUNIMI HERE?
YA
MARRY ME.
...PROPOSED TO ME...
He claimed it was love at first sight.
...CHASED ME AROUND...
He's reepy! And ersistent!
UOM
...AND DE-STROYED THE SCHOOL.
Actually, someone else did that.

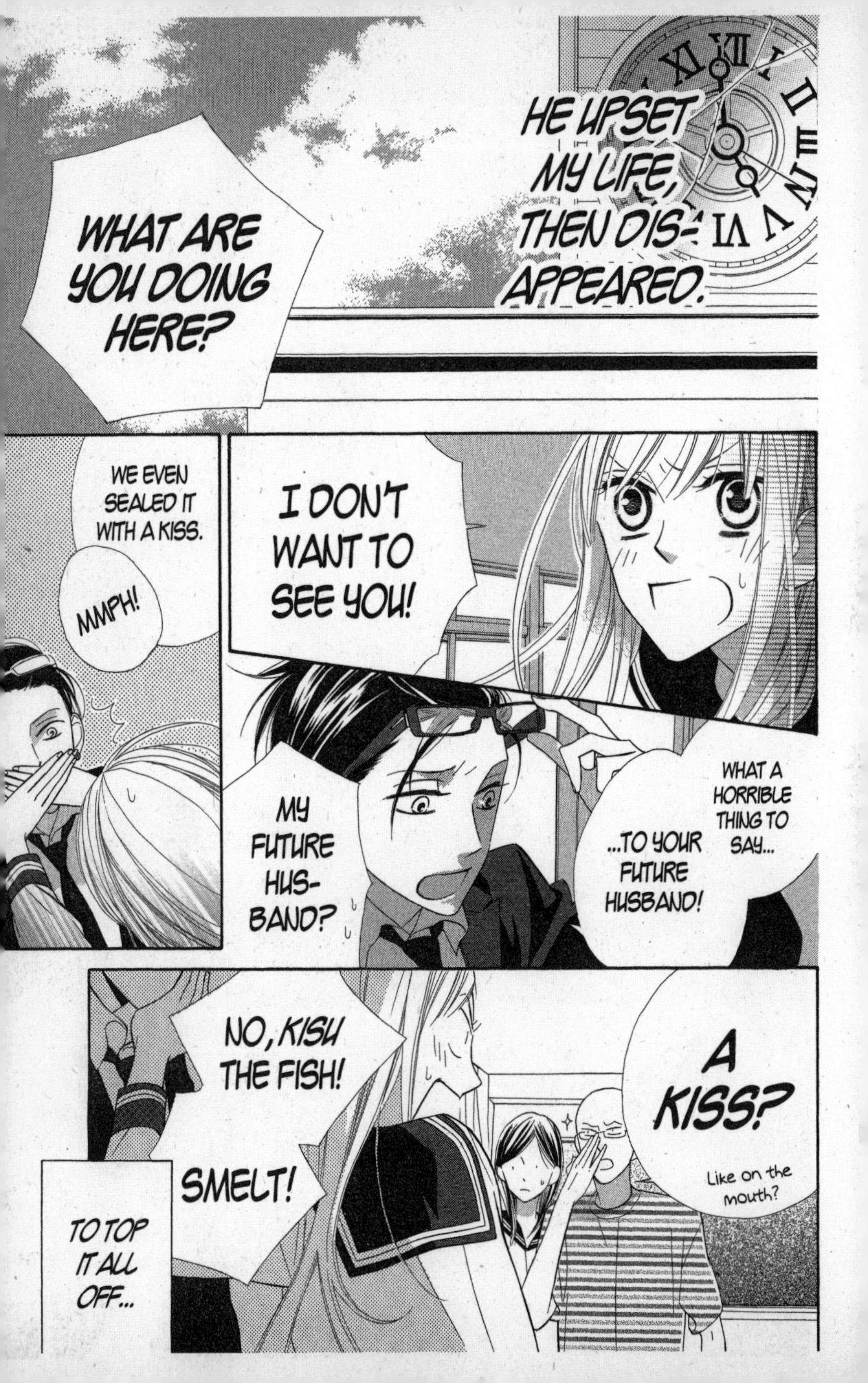
HE UPSET MY LIFE, THEN DIS-APPEARED.
WHAT ARE YOU DOING HERE?
I DON'T WANT TO SEE YOU!
WHAT A HORRIBLE THING TO SAY...
...TO YOUR FUTURE HUSBAND!
MY FUTURE HUS-BAND?
WE EVEN SEALED IT WITH A KISS.
MMPH!
A KISS?
Like on the mouth?
NO, KISU THE FISH!
SMELT!
TO TOP IT ALL OFF...

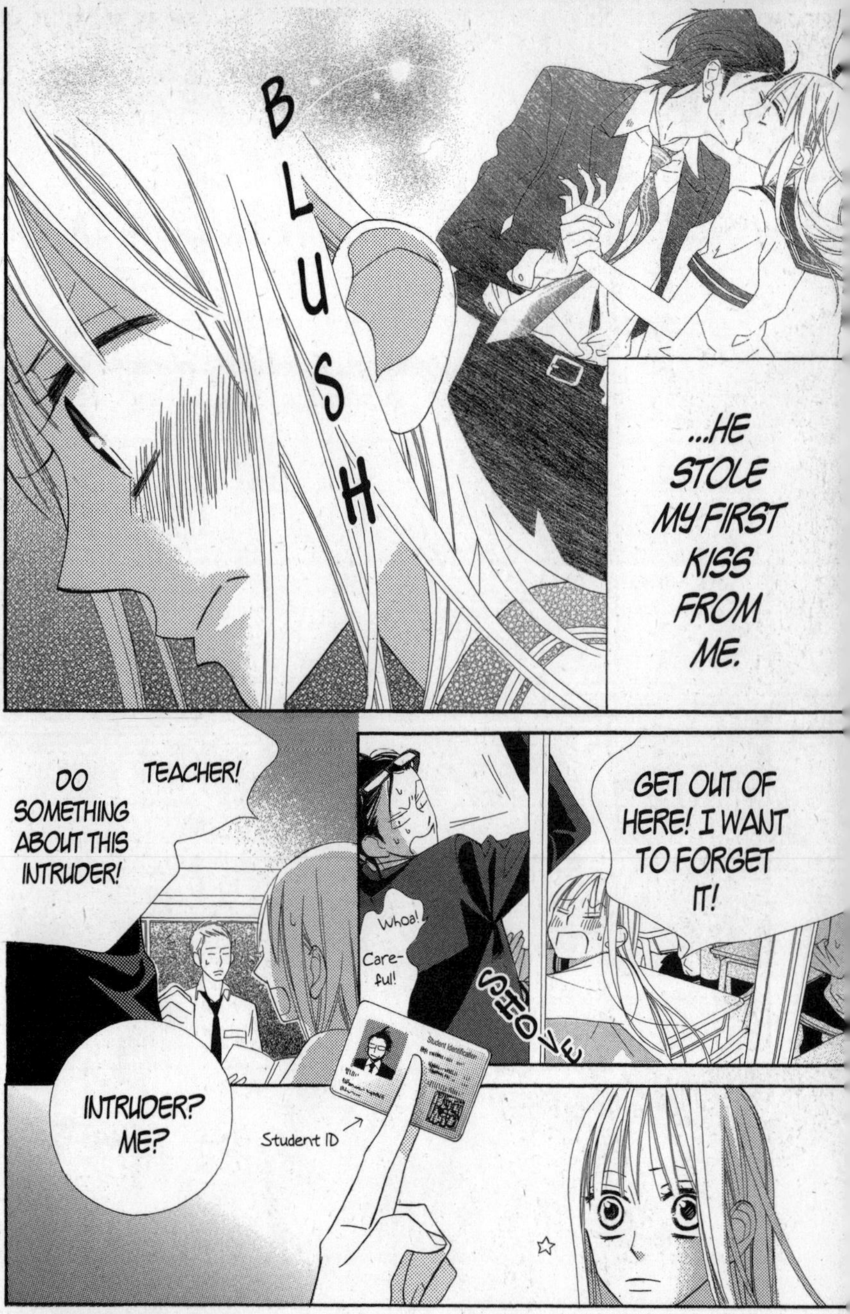
...HE STOLE MY FIRST KISS FROM ME.
BLUSH
GET OUT OF HERE! I WANT TO FORGET IT!
Whoa!
Care-ful!
SHOVE
TEACHER!
DO SOMETHING ABOUT THIS INTRUDER!
INTRUDER? ME?
Student Identification
Student ID

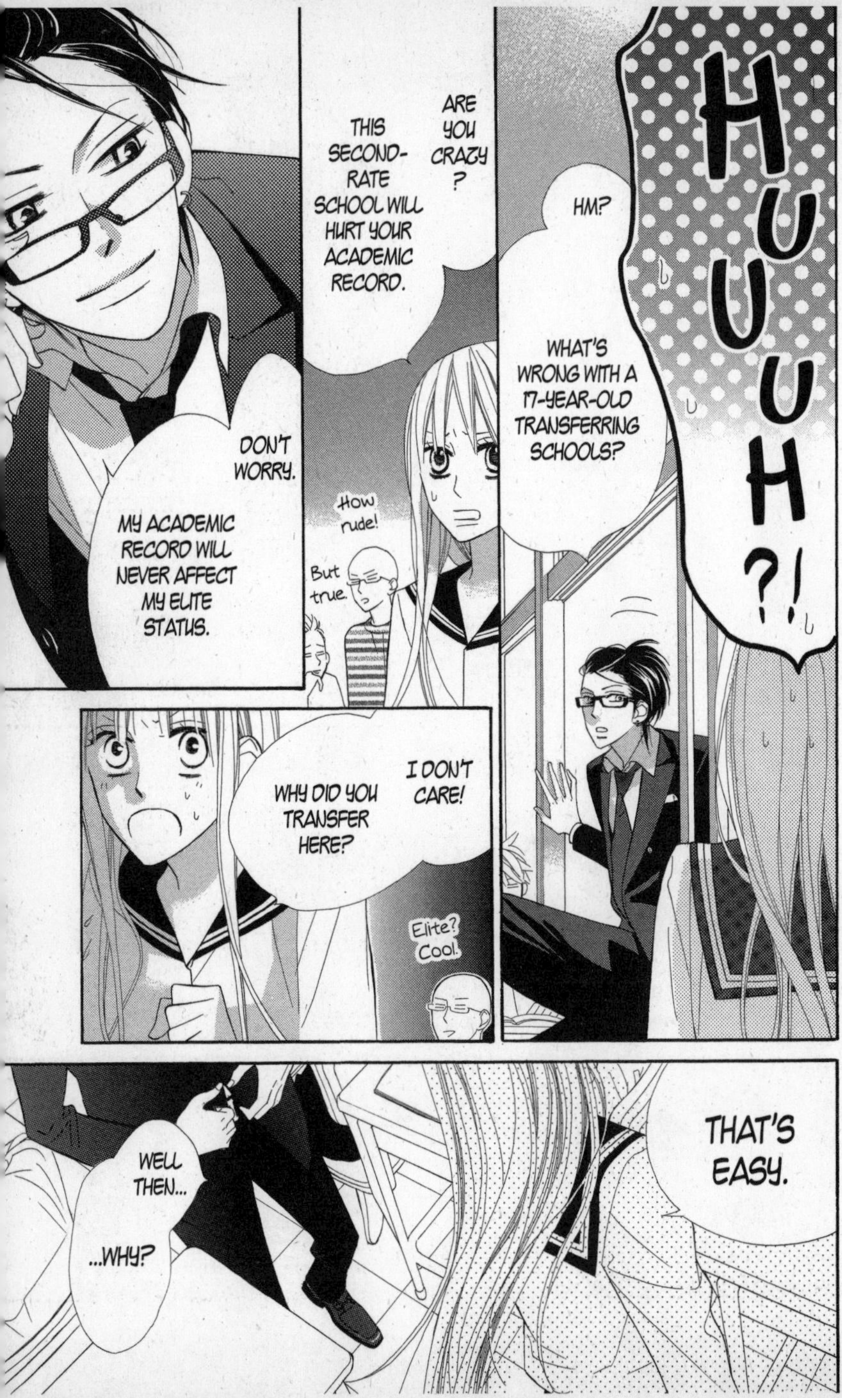
HUUUUH?!
HM?
WHAT'S WRONG WITH A 17-YEAR-OLD TRANSFERRING SCHOOLS?
ARE YOU CRAZY?
THIS SECOND-RATE SCHOOL WILL HURT YOUR ACADEMIC RECORD.
How rude!
But true.
DON'T WORRY.
MY ACADEMIC RECORD WILL NEVER AFFECT MY ELITE STATUS.
I DON'T CARE!
WHY DID YOU TRANSFER HERE?
Elite? Cool.
THAT'S EASY.
WELL THEN...
...WHY?

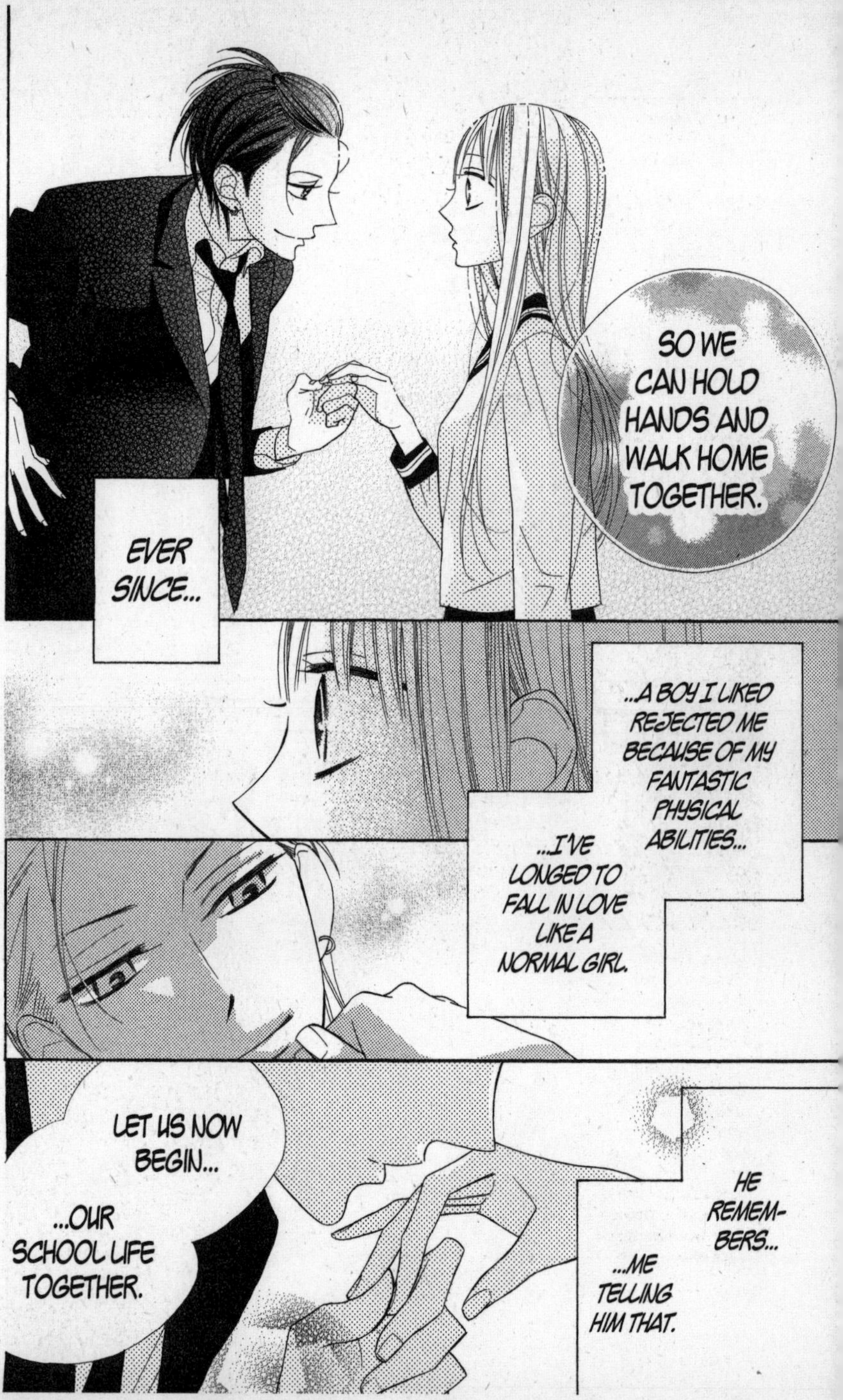
SO WE CAN HOLD HANDS AND WALK HOME TOGETHER.
EVER SINCE...
...A BOY I LIKED REJECTED ME BECAUSE OF MY FANTASTIC PHYSICAL ABILITIES...
...I'VE LONGED TO FALL IN LOVE LIKE A NORMAL GIRL.
HE REMEM-BERS...
...ME TELLING HIM THAT.
LET US NOW BEGIN...
...OUR SCHOOL LIFE TOGETHER.

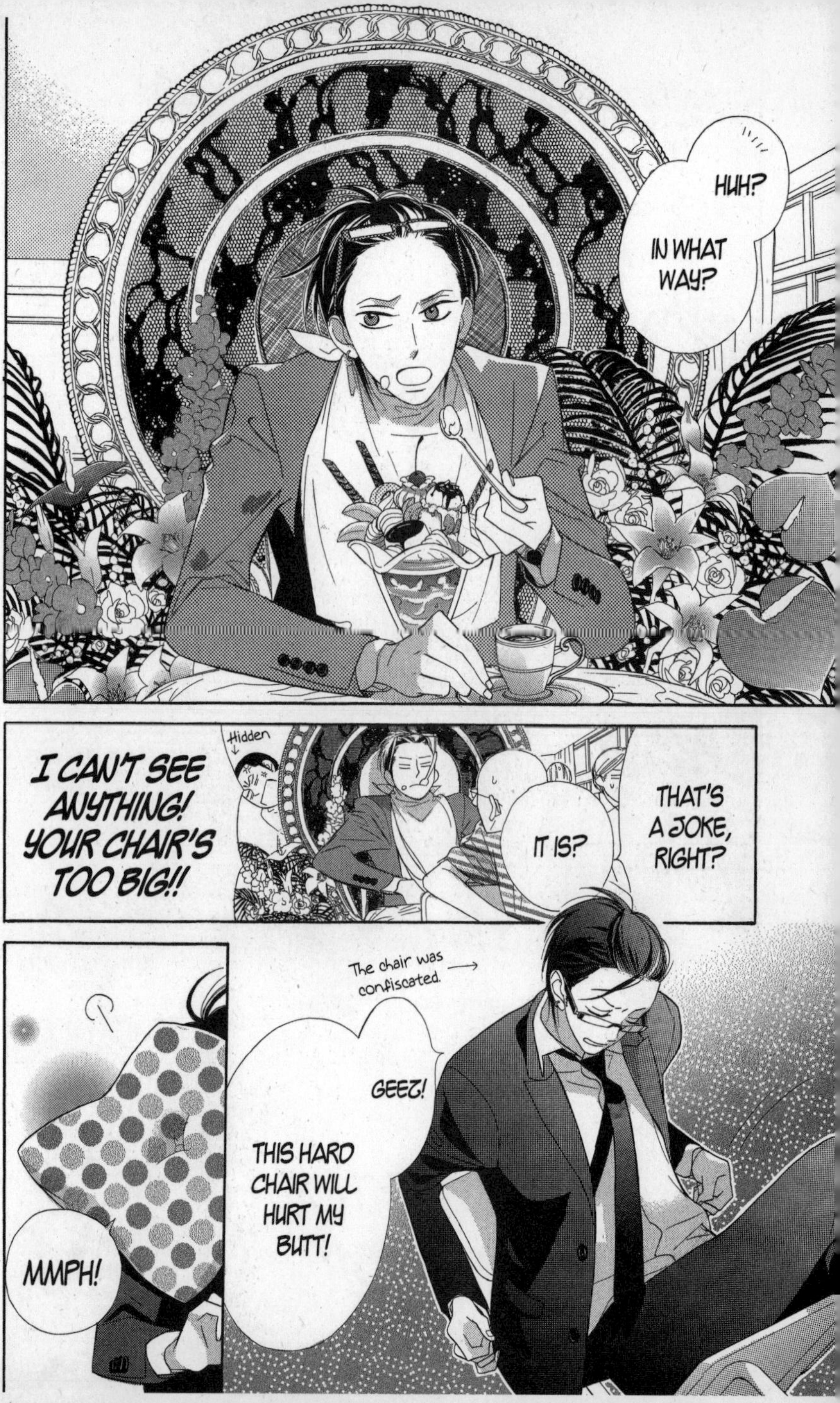
HUH?
IN WHAT WAY?
THAT'S A JOKE, RIGHT?
IT IS?
Hidden
I CAN'T SEE ANYTHING! YOUR CHAIR'S TOO BIG!!
The chair was confiscated.
GEEZ!
THIS HARD CHAIR WILL HURT MY BUTT!
MMPH!

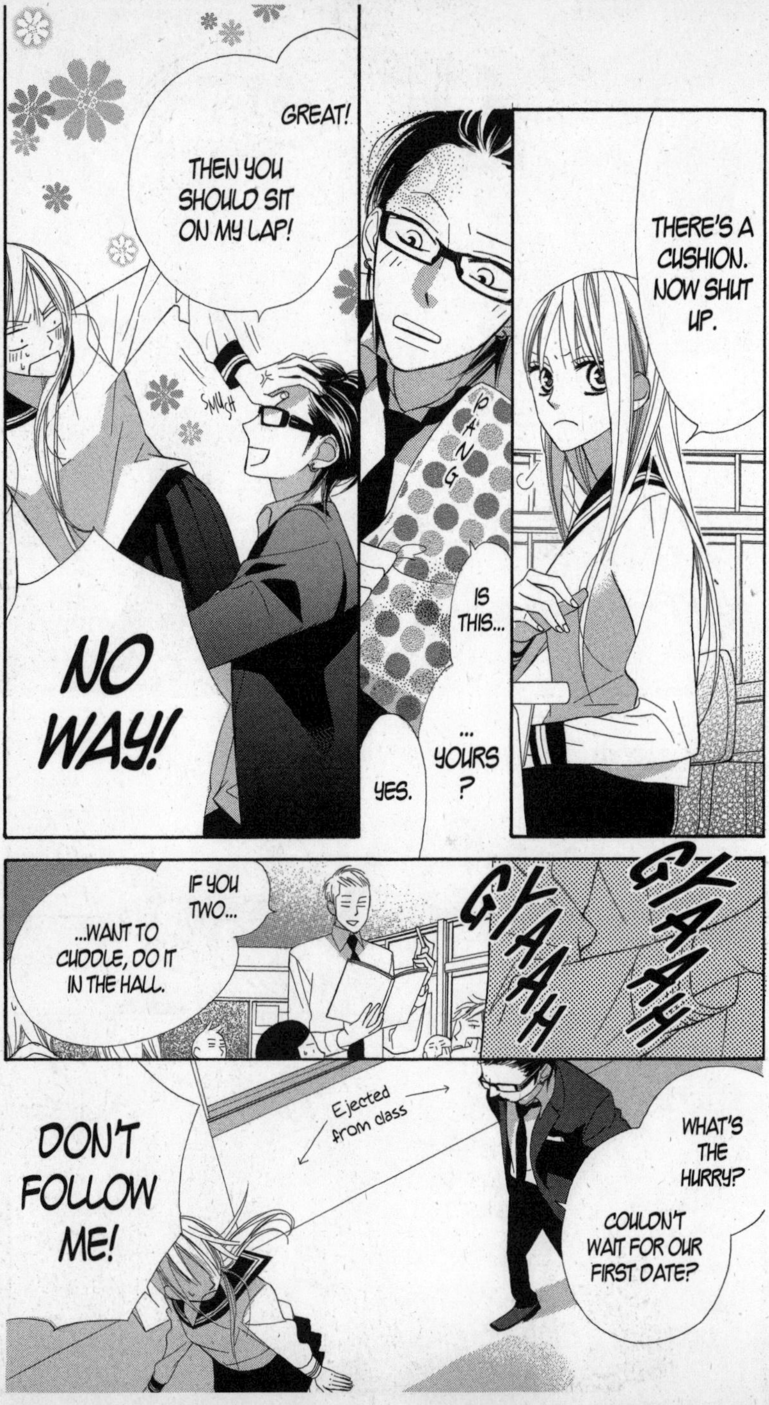
THERE'S A CUSHION. NOW SHUT UP.
PANG
IS THIS...
...YOURS?
YES.
GREAT!
THEN YOU SHOULD SIT ON MY LAP!
SMUSH
NO WAY!
GYAAAH
GYAAAH
IF YOU TWO...
...WANT TO CUDDLE, DO IT IN THE HALL.
WHAT'S THE HURRY?
COULDN'T WAIT FOR OUR FIRST DATE?
Ejected from class
DON'T FOLLOW ME!

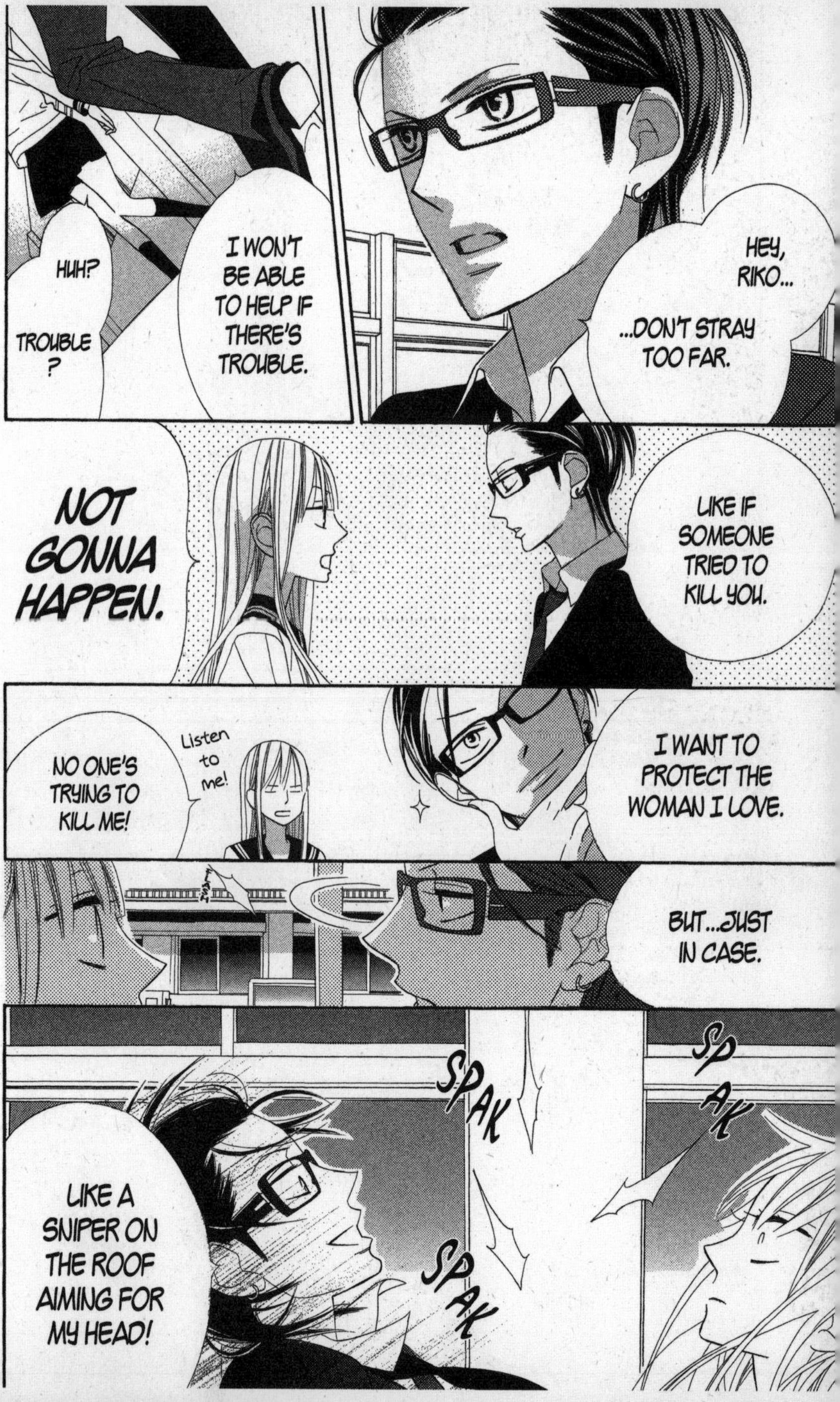
HEY, RIKO...
...DON'T STRAY TOO FAR.
I WON'T BE ABLE TO HELP IF THERE'S TROUBLE.
HUH?
TROUBLE?
LIKE IF SOMEONE TRIED TO KILL YOU.
NOT GONNA HAPPEN.
I WANT TO PROTECT THE WOMAN I LOVE.
Listen to me!
NO ONE'S TRYING TO KILL ME!
BUT...JUST IN CASE.
SPAK
SPAK
SPAK
LIKE A SNIPER ON THE ROOF AIMING FOR MY HEAD!

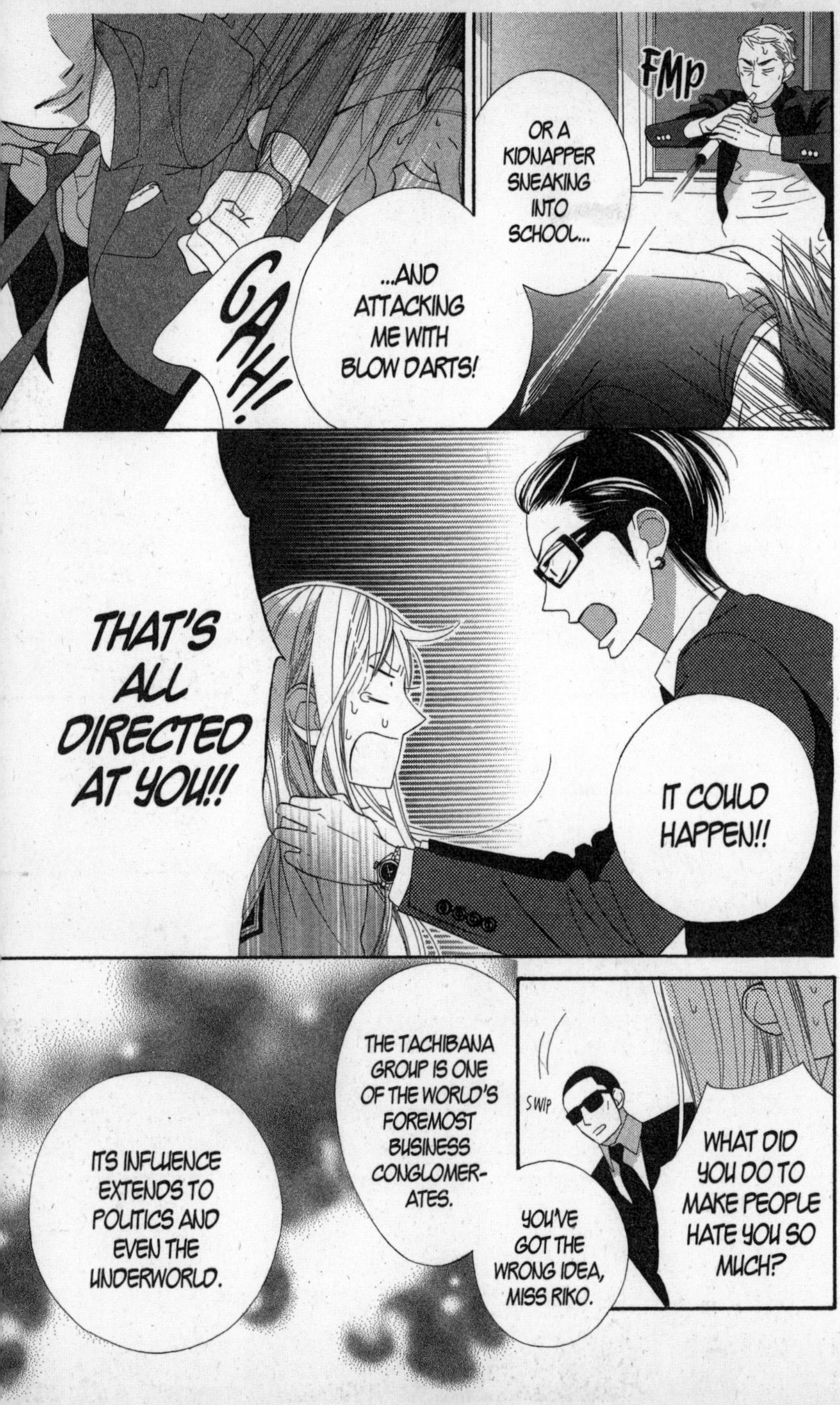
OR A KIDNAPPER SNEAKING INTO SCHOOL...
FMP
...AND ATTACKING ME WITH BLOW DARTS!
GAH!!
IT COULD HAPPEN!!
THAT'S ALL DIRECTED AT YOU!!
WHAT DID YOU DO TO MAKE PEOPLE HATE YOU SO MUCH?
SWIP
YOU'VE GOT THE WRONG IDEA, MISS RIKO.
THE TACHIBANA GROUP IS ONE OF THE WORLD'S FOREMOST BUSINESS CONGLOMER-ATES.
ITS INFLUENCE EXTENDS TO POLITICS AND EVEN THE UNDERWORLD.

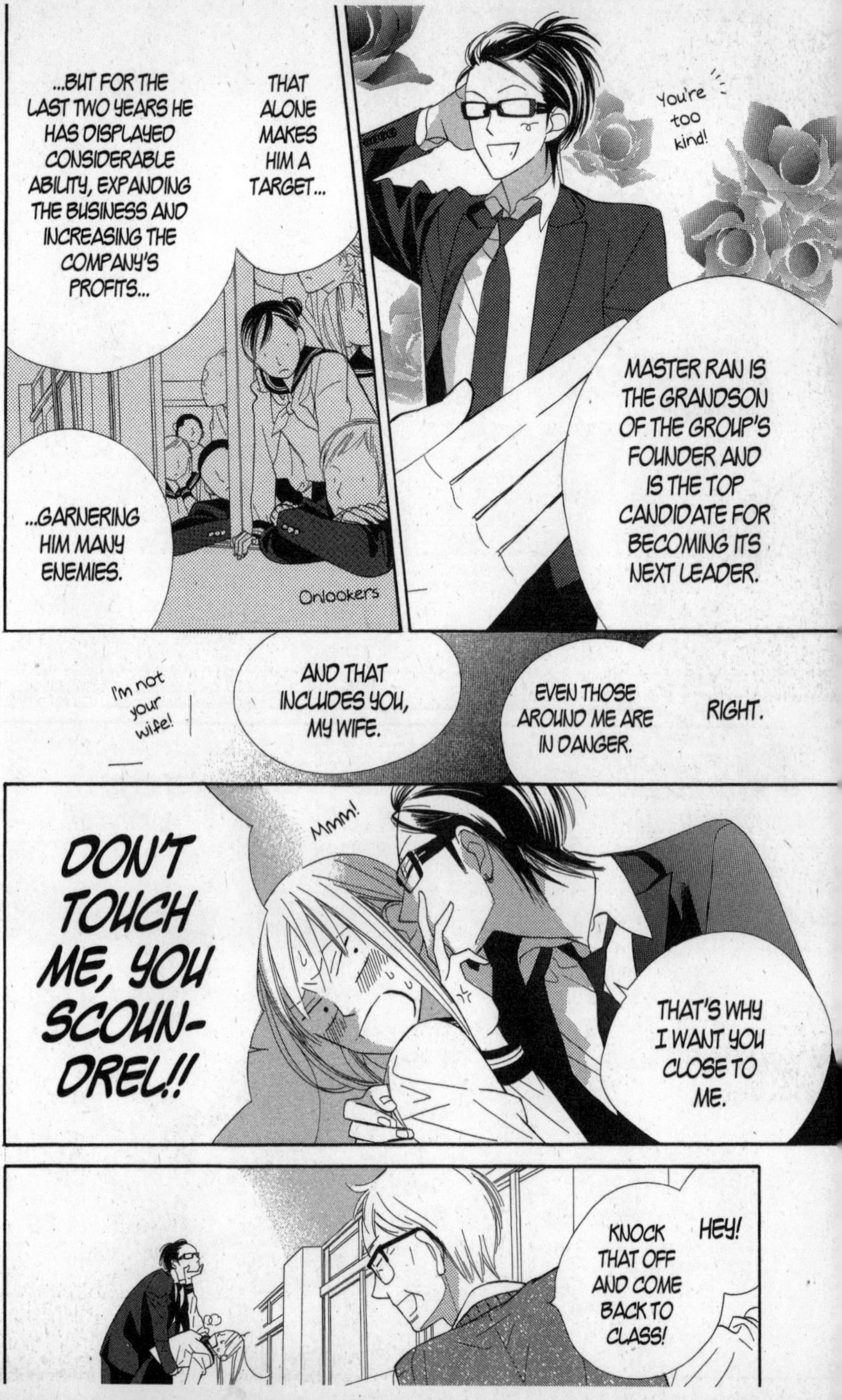
You're too kind!
MASTER RAN IS THE GRANDSON OF THE GROUP'S FOUNDER AND IS THE TOP CANDIDATE FOR BECOMING ITS NEXT LEADER.
THAT ALONE MAKES HIM A TARGET...
...BUT FOR THE LAST TWO YEARS HE HAS DISPLAYED CONSIDERABLE ABILITY, EXPANDING THE BUSINESS AND INCREASING THE COMPANY'S PROFITS...
...GARNERING HIM MANY ENEMIES.
Onlookers
RIGHT.
EVEN THOSE AROUND ME ARE IN DANGER.
AND THAT INCLUDES YOU, MY WIFE.
I'm not your wife!
THAT'S WHY I WANT YOU CLOSE TO ME.
Mmm!
DON'T TOUCH ME, YOU SCOUN-DREL!!
HEY!
KNOCK THAT OFF AND COME BACK TO CLASS!

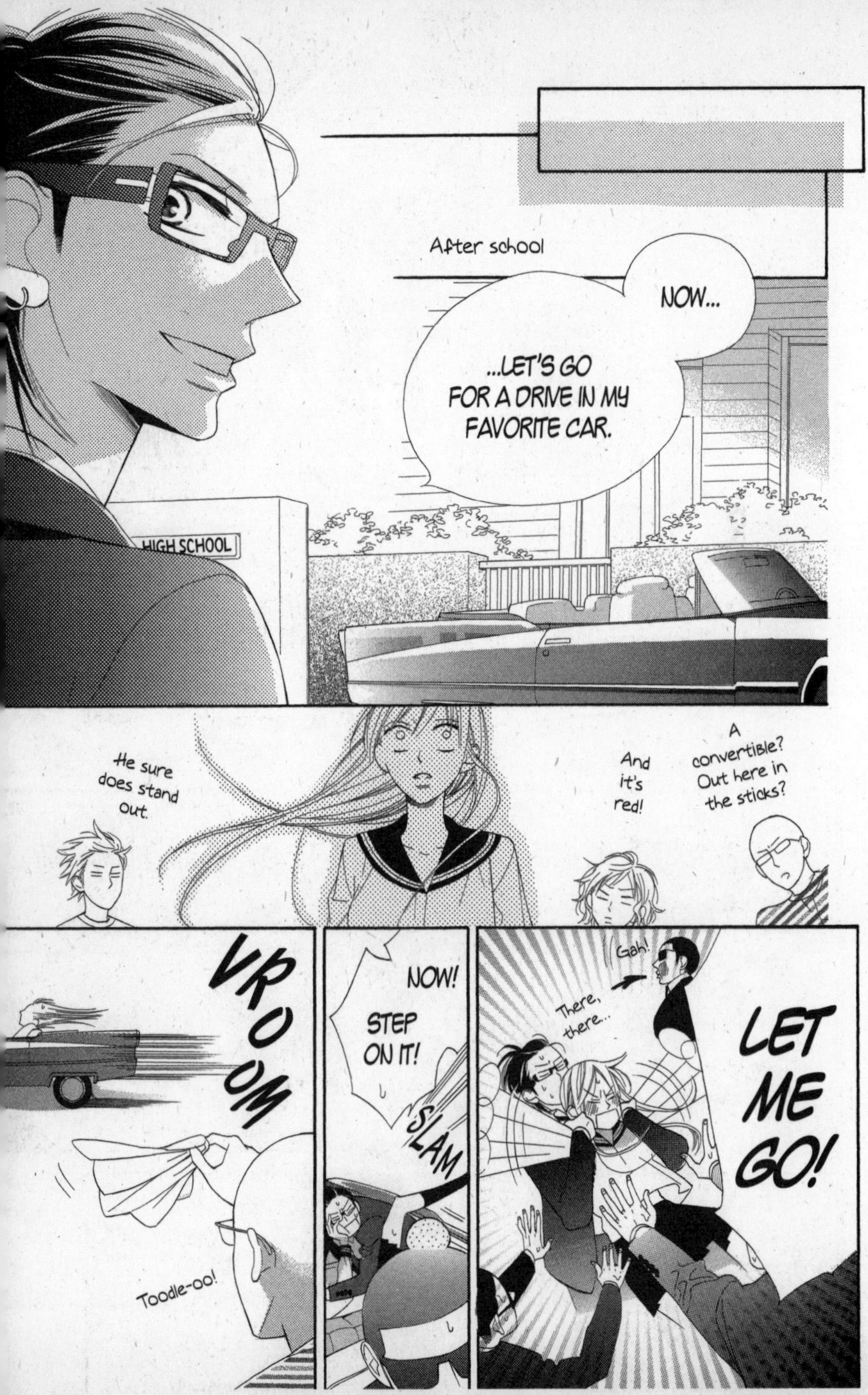
After school
NOW...
...LET'S GO FOR A DRIVE IN MY FAVORITE CAR.
HIGH SCHOOL
A convertible? Out here in the sticks?
And it's red!
He sure does stand out.
Gah!
There, there...
LET ME GO!
NOW! STEP ON IT!
SLAM
VROOM
Toodle-oo!

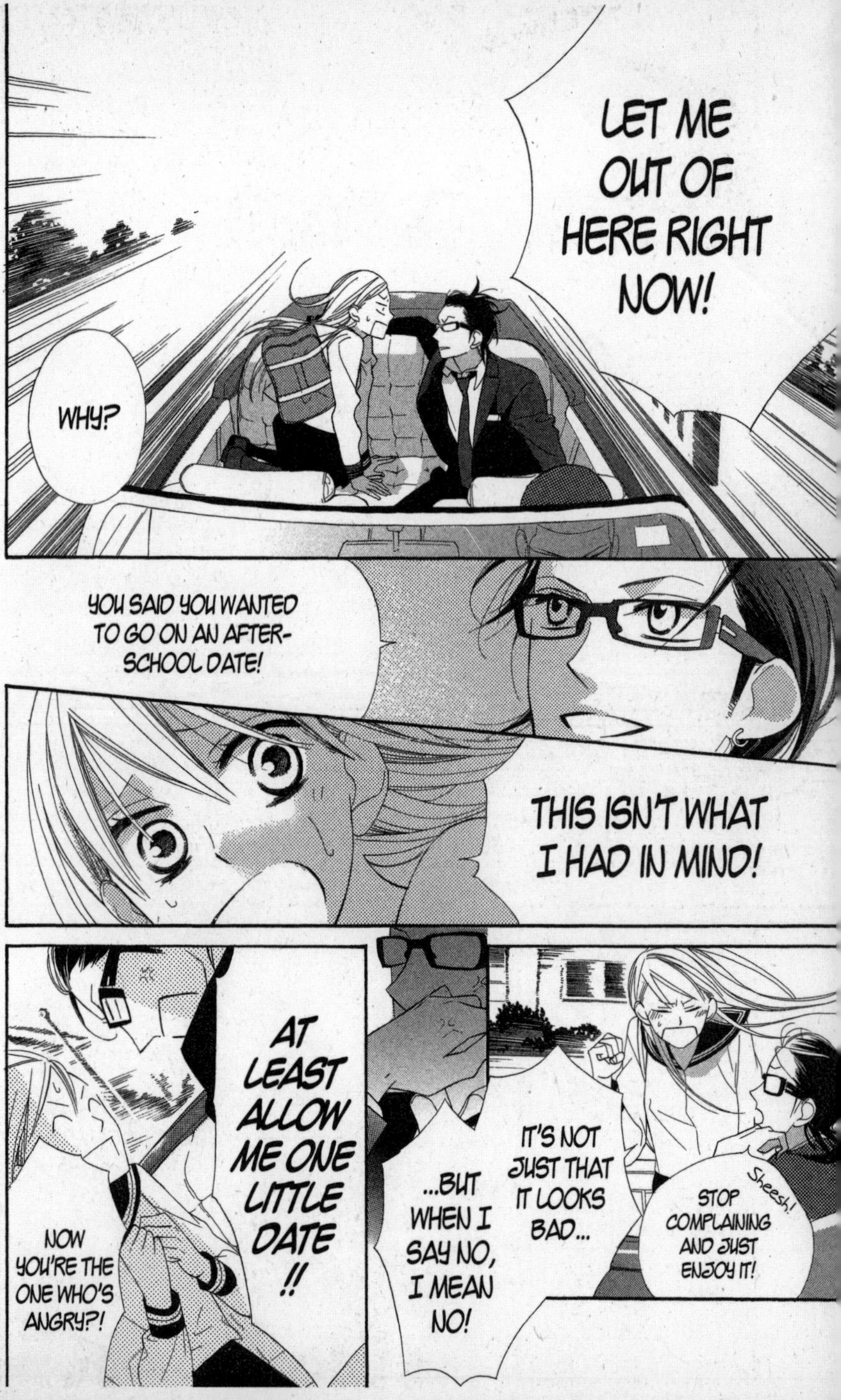
LET ME OUT OF HERE RIGHT NOW!
WHY?
YOU SAID YOU WANTED TO GO ON AN AFTER-SCHOOL DATE!
THIS ISN'T WHAT I HAD IN MIND!
Sheesh!
STOP COMPLAINING AND JUST ENJOY IT!
IT'S NOT JUST THAT IT LOOKS BAD...
...BUT WHEN I SAY NO, I MEAN NO!
AT LEAST ALLOW ME ONE LITTLE DATE !!
NOW YOU'RE THE ONE WHO'S ANGRY?!

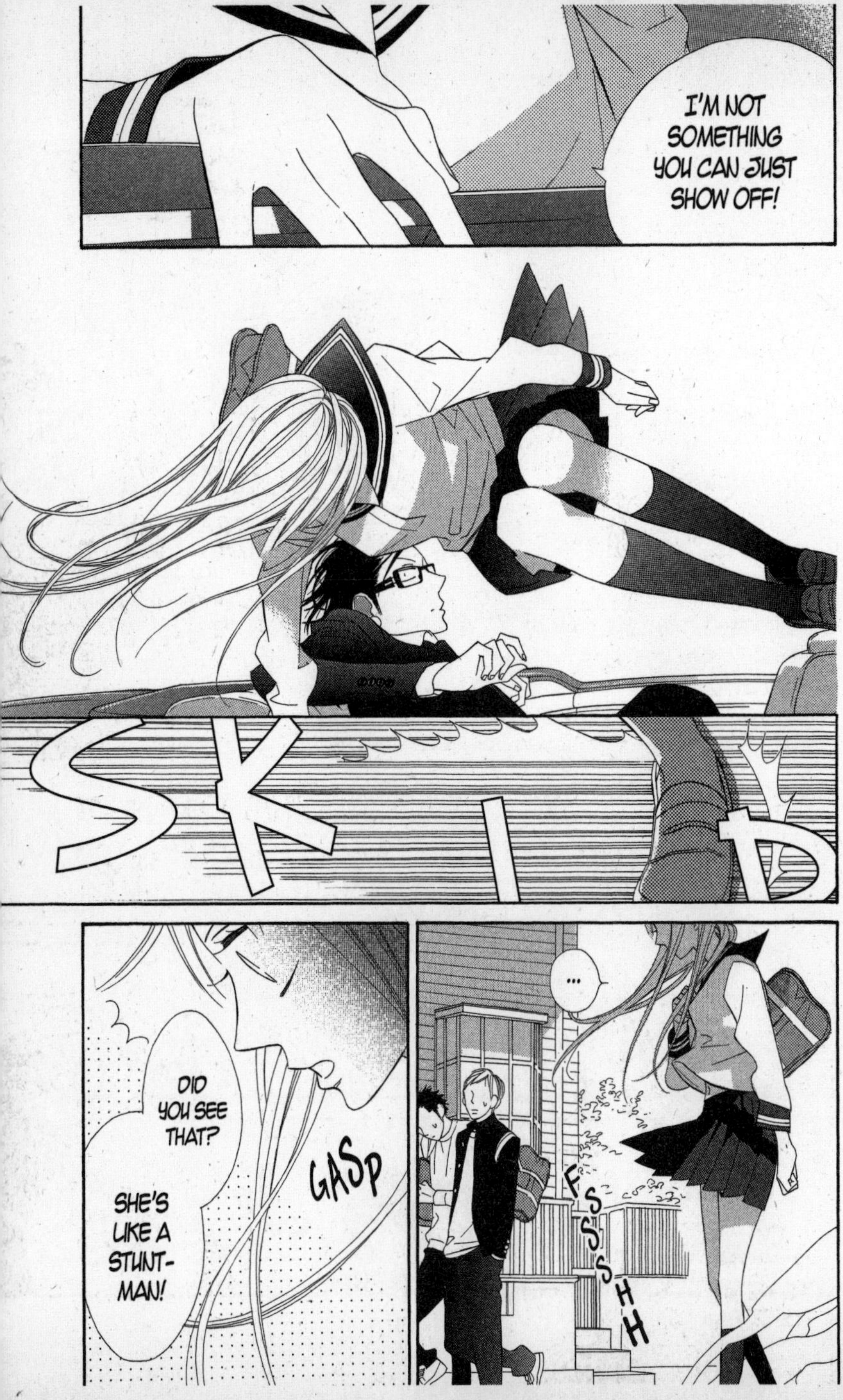
I'M NOT SOMETHING YOU CAN JUST SHOW OFF!
SKID
...
FSSSHH
DID YOU SEE THAT?
SHE'S LIKE A STUNT-MAN!
GASP

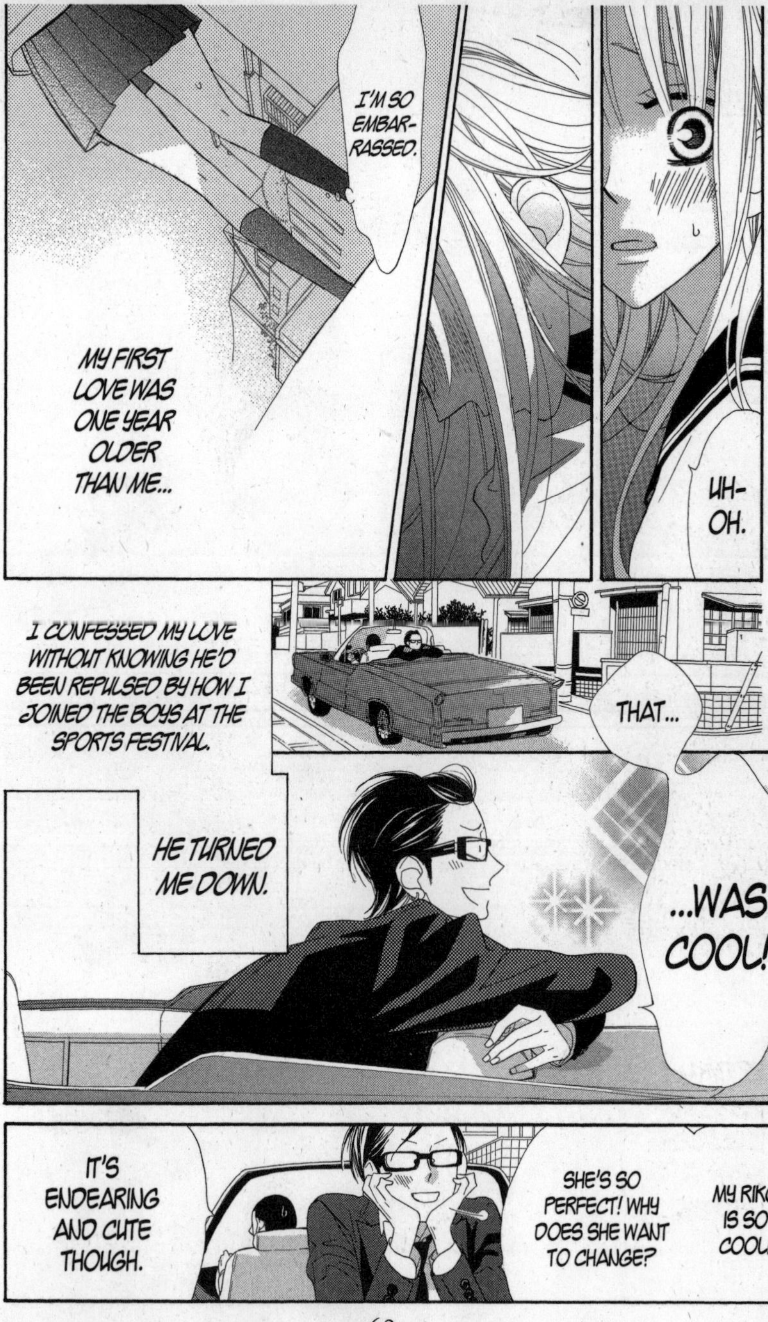
UH-OH.
I'M SO EMBARRASSED.
MY FIRST LOVE WAS ONE YEAR OLDER THAN ME...
THAT...
I CONFESSED MY LOVE WITHOUT KNOWING HE'D BEEN REPULSED BY HOW I JOINED THE BOYS AT THE SPORTS FESTIVAL.
...WAS COOL!
HE TURNED ME DOWN.
MY RIKO IS SO COOL!
SHE'S SO PERFECT! WHY DOES SHE WANT TO CHANGE?
IT'S ENDEARING AND CUTE THOUGH.

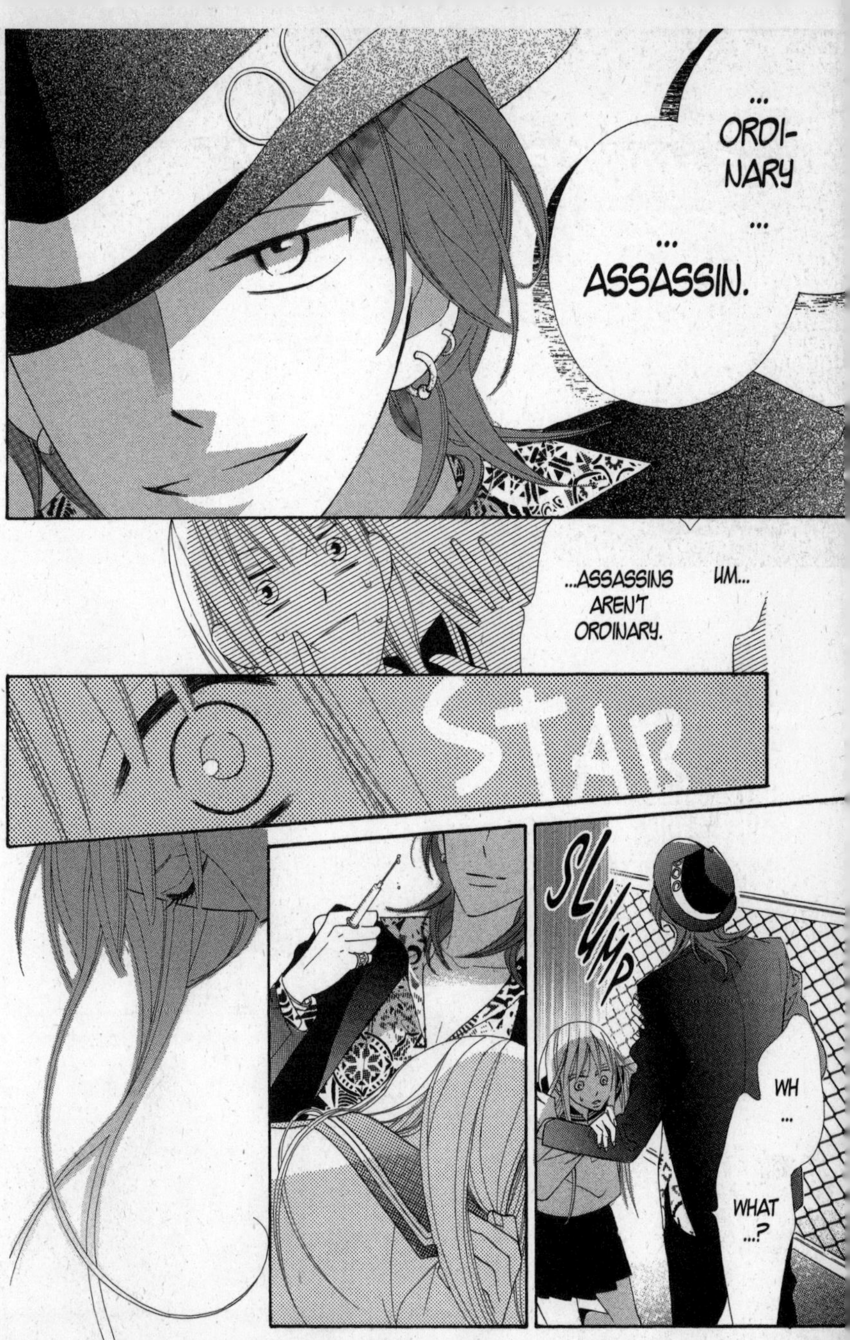
... ORDI- NARY ... ... ASSASSIN.
UM...
...ASSASSINS AREN'T ORDINARY.
STAB
SLUMP
WH ... WHAT ...?

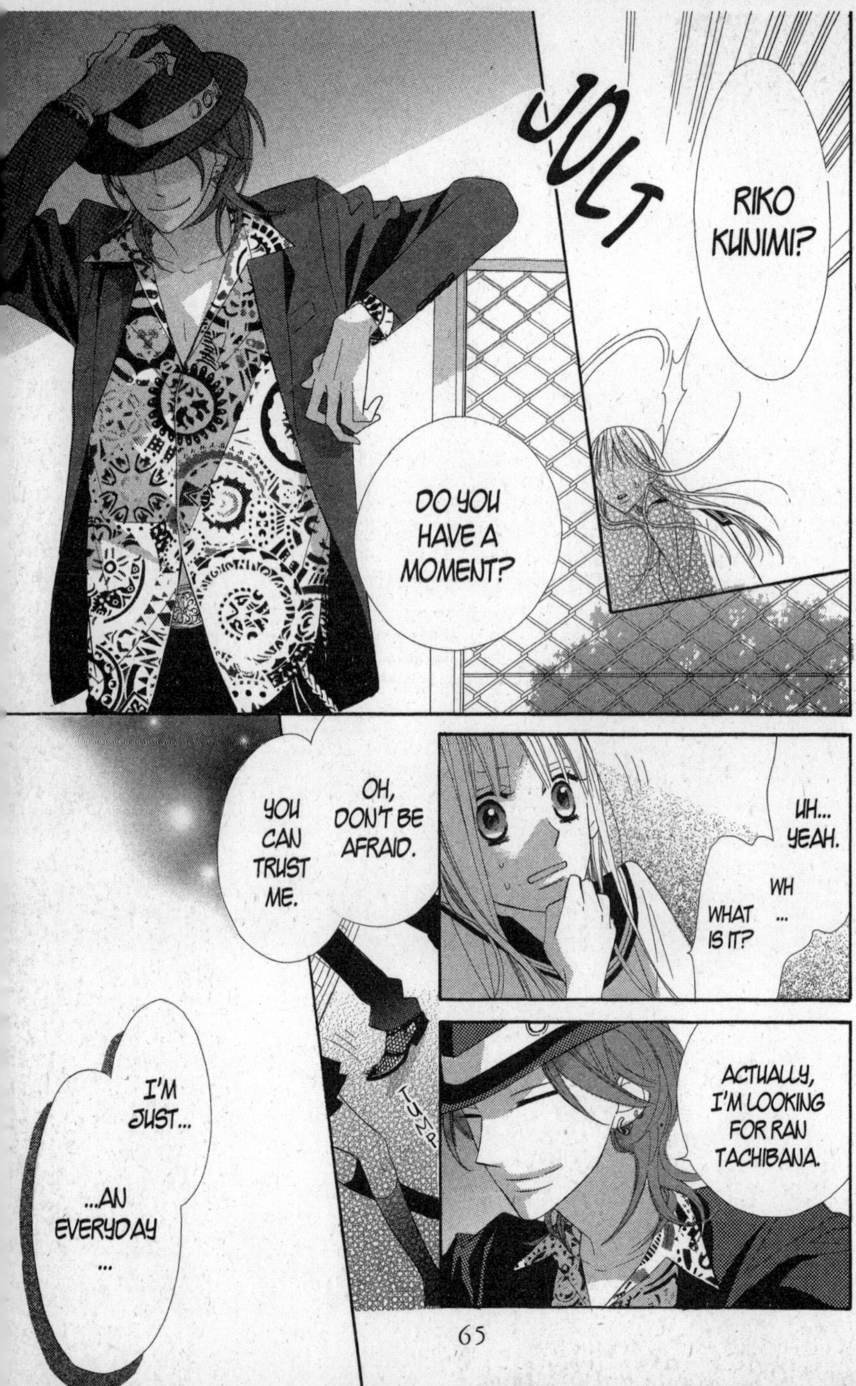
JOLT
RIKO KUNIMI?
DO YOU HAVE A MOMENT?
UH... YEAH.
WH... WHAT IS IT?
OH, DON'T BE AFRAID.
YOU CAN TRUST ME.
ACTUALLY, I'M LOOKING FOR RAN TACHIBANA.
TUMP
I'M JUST...
...AN EVERYDAY ...

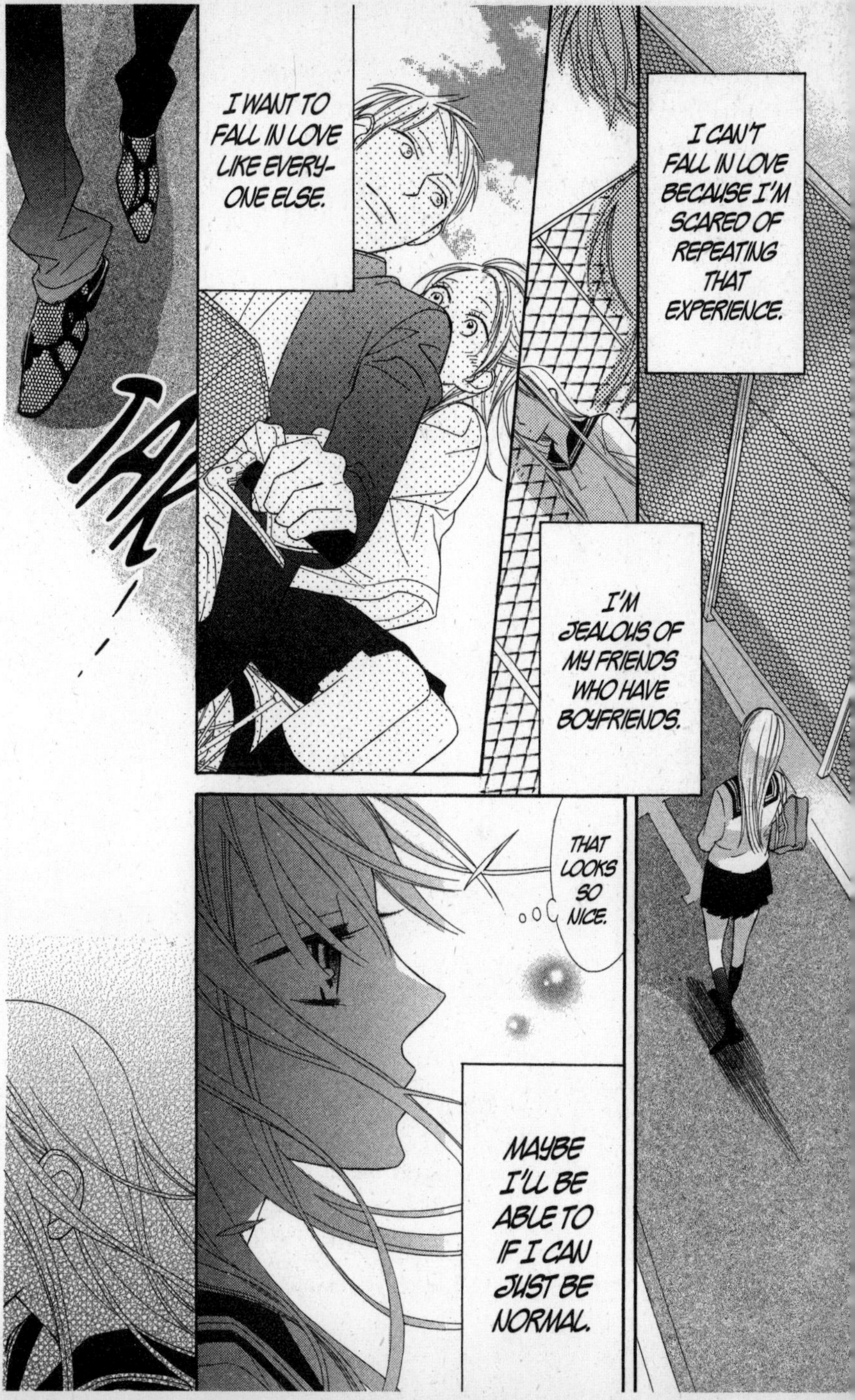
I CAN'T FALL IN LOVE BECAUSE I'M SCARED OF REPEATING THAT EXPERIENCE.
I'M JEALOUS OF MY FRIENDS WHO HAVE BOYFRIENDS.
I WANT TO FALL IN LOVE LIKE EVERY-ONE ELSE.
TAK
THAT LOOKS SO NICE.
MAYBE I'LL BE ABLE TO IF I CAN JUST BE NORMAL.

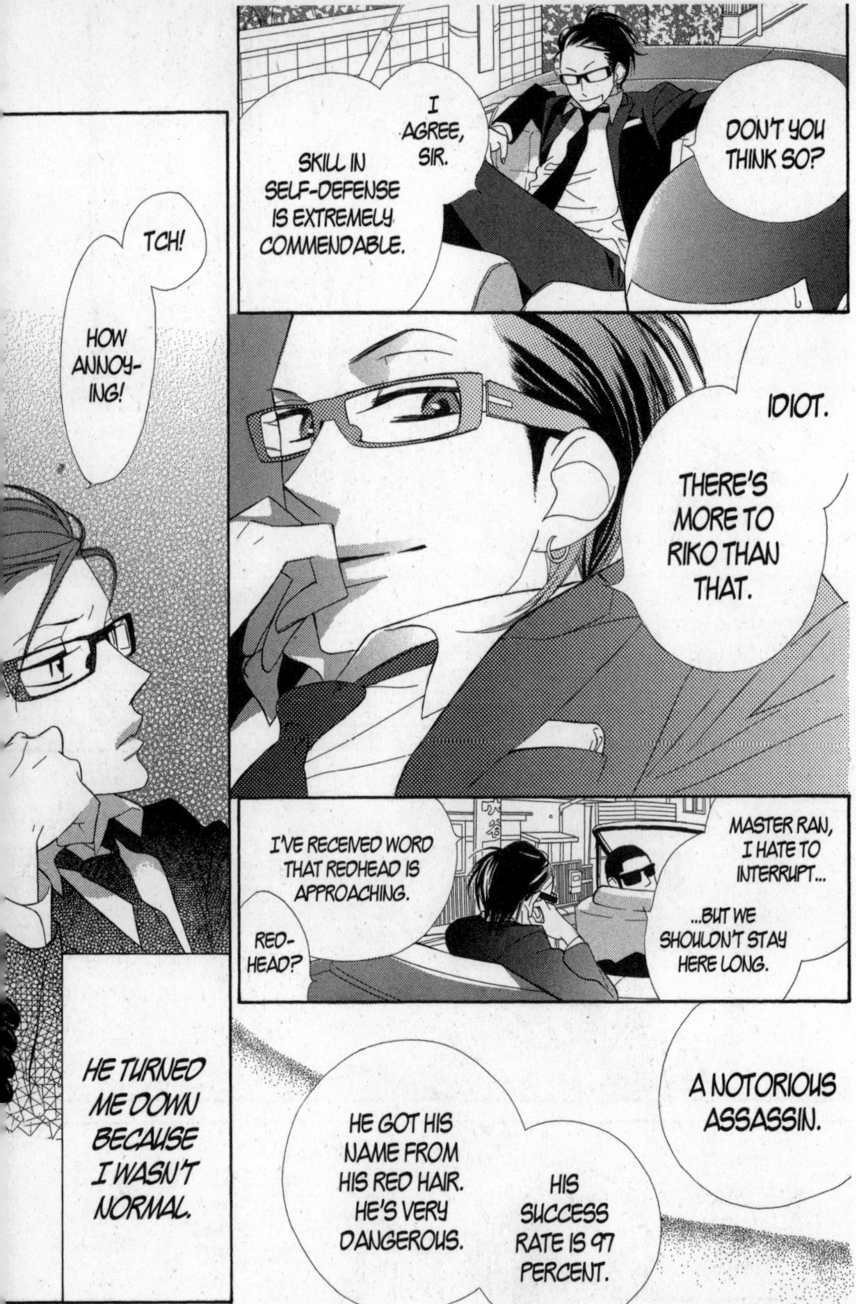
DON'T YOU THINK SO?
I AGREE, SIR.
SKILL IN SELF-DEFENSE IS EXTREMELY COMMENDABLE.
IDIOT.
THERE'S MORE TO RIKO THAN THAT.
TCH!
HOW ANNOY-ING!
HE TURNED ME DOWN BECAUSE I WASN'T NORMAL.
MASTER RAN, I HATE TO INTERRUPT...
...BUT WE SHOULDN'T STAY HERE LONG.
I'VE RECEIVED WORD THAT REDHEAD IS APPROACHING.
RED-HEAD?
A NOTORIOUS ASSASSIN.
HE GOT HIS NAME FROM HIS RED HAIR. HE'S VERY DANGEROUS.
HIS SUCCESS RATE IS 97 PERCENT.

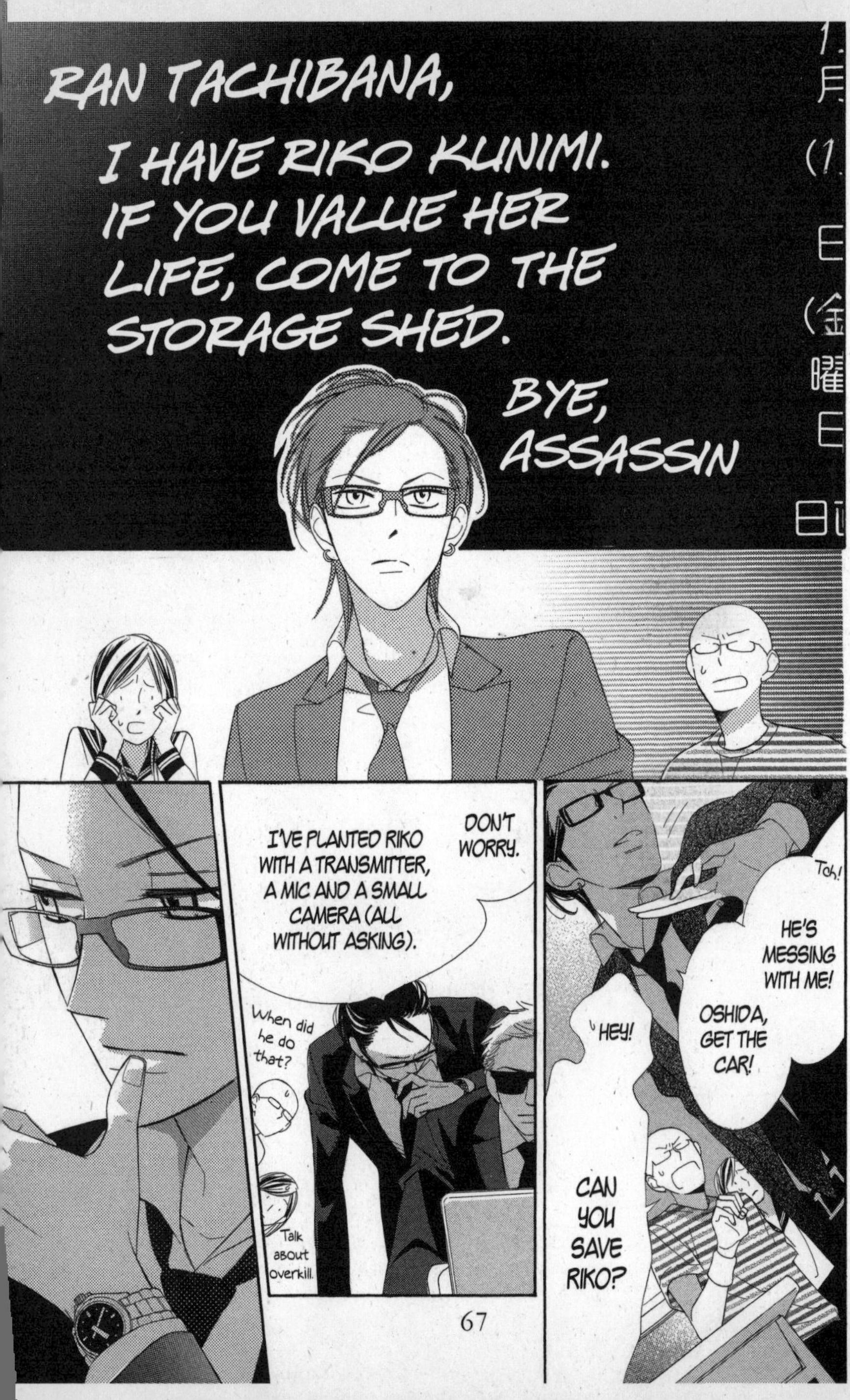
RAN TACHIBANA,
I HAVE RIKO KUNIMI. IF YOU VALUE HER LIFE, COME TO THE STORAGE SHED.
BYE, ASSASSIN
Tch!
HE'S MESSING WITH ME!
OSHIDA, GET THE CAR!
HEY!
CAN YOU SAVE RIKO?
DON'T WORRY.
I'VE PLANTED RIKO WITH A TRANSMITTER, A MIC AND A SMALL CAMERA (ALL WITHOUT ASKING).
When did he do that?
Talk about overkill.

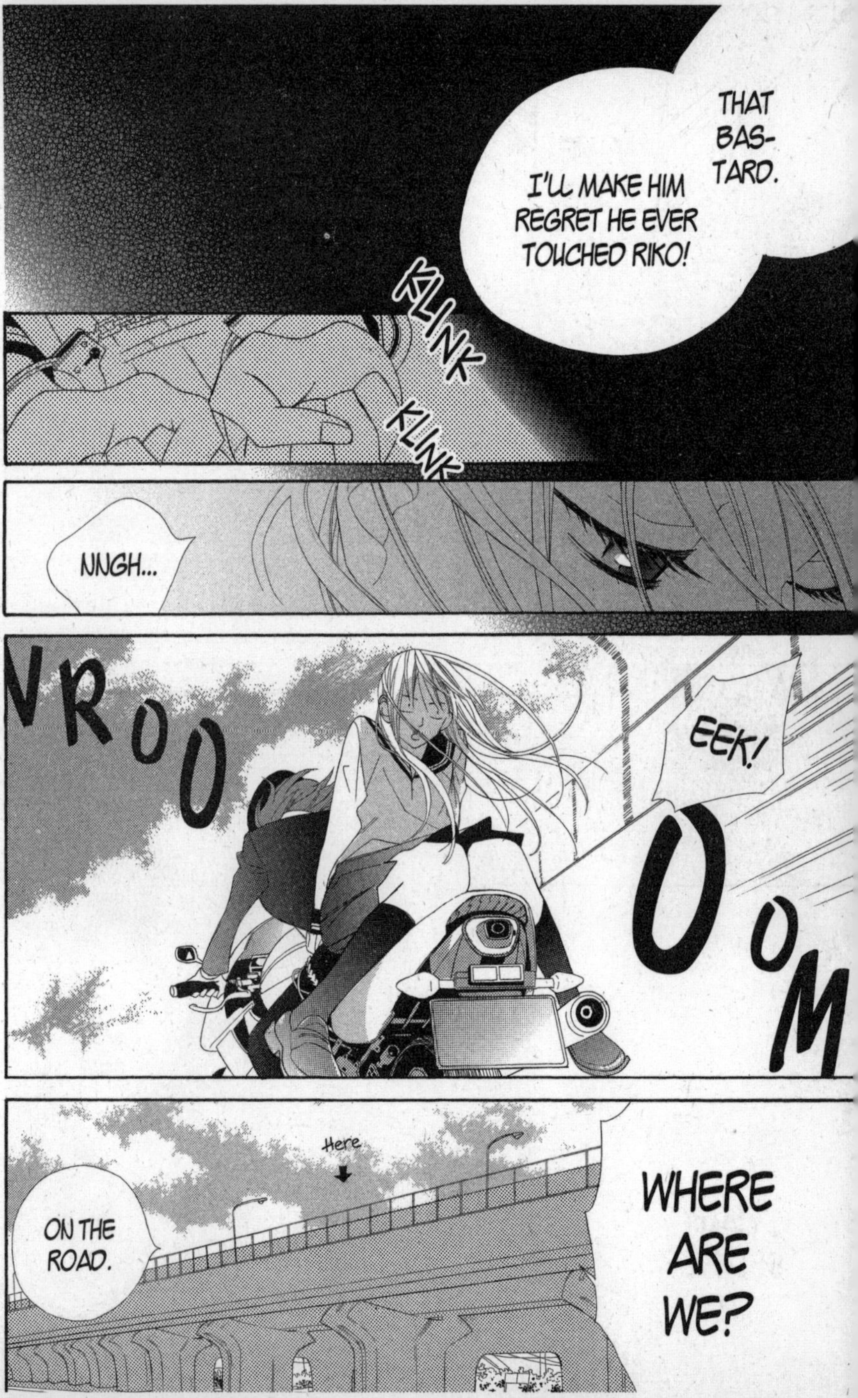
THAT BAS-TARD.
I'LL MAKE HIM REGRET HE EVER TOUCHED RIKO!
KLINK KLINK
NNGH...
EEK!
VROOOOOM
WHERE ARE WE?
Here
ON THE ROAD.

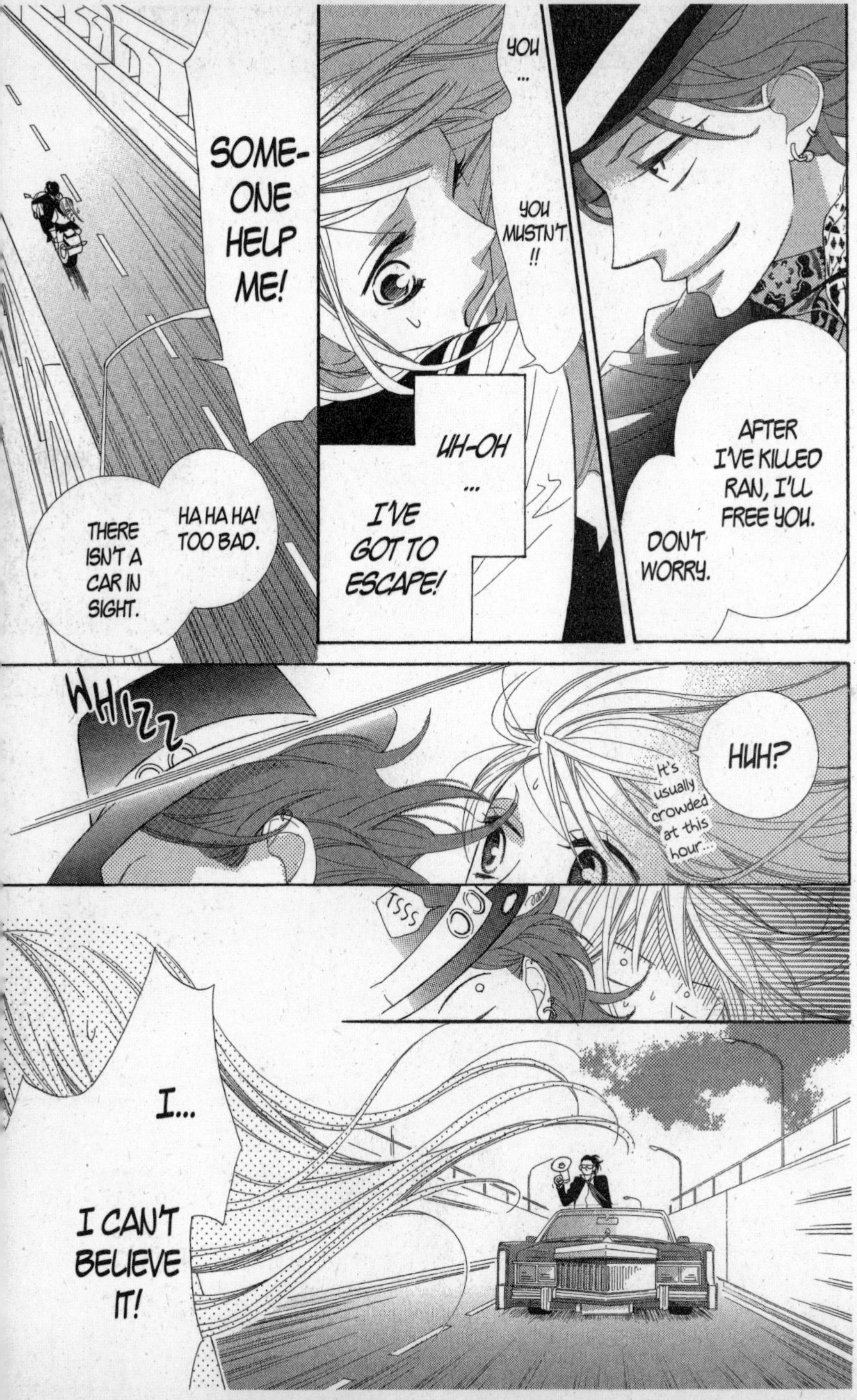
AFTER I'VE KILLED RAN, I'LL FREE YOU.
DON'T WORRY.
YOU ...
YOU MUSTN'T !!
UH-OH ...
I'VE GOT TO ESCAPE!
SOME-ONE HELP ME!
HA HA HA! TOO BAD.
THERE ISN'T A CAR IN SIGHT.
HUH?
It's usually crowded at this hour...
WHIZZ
TSSS
I...
I CAN'T BELIEVE IT!

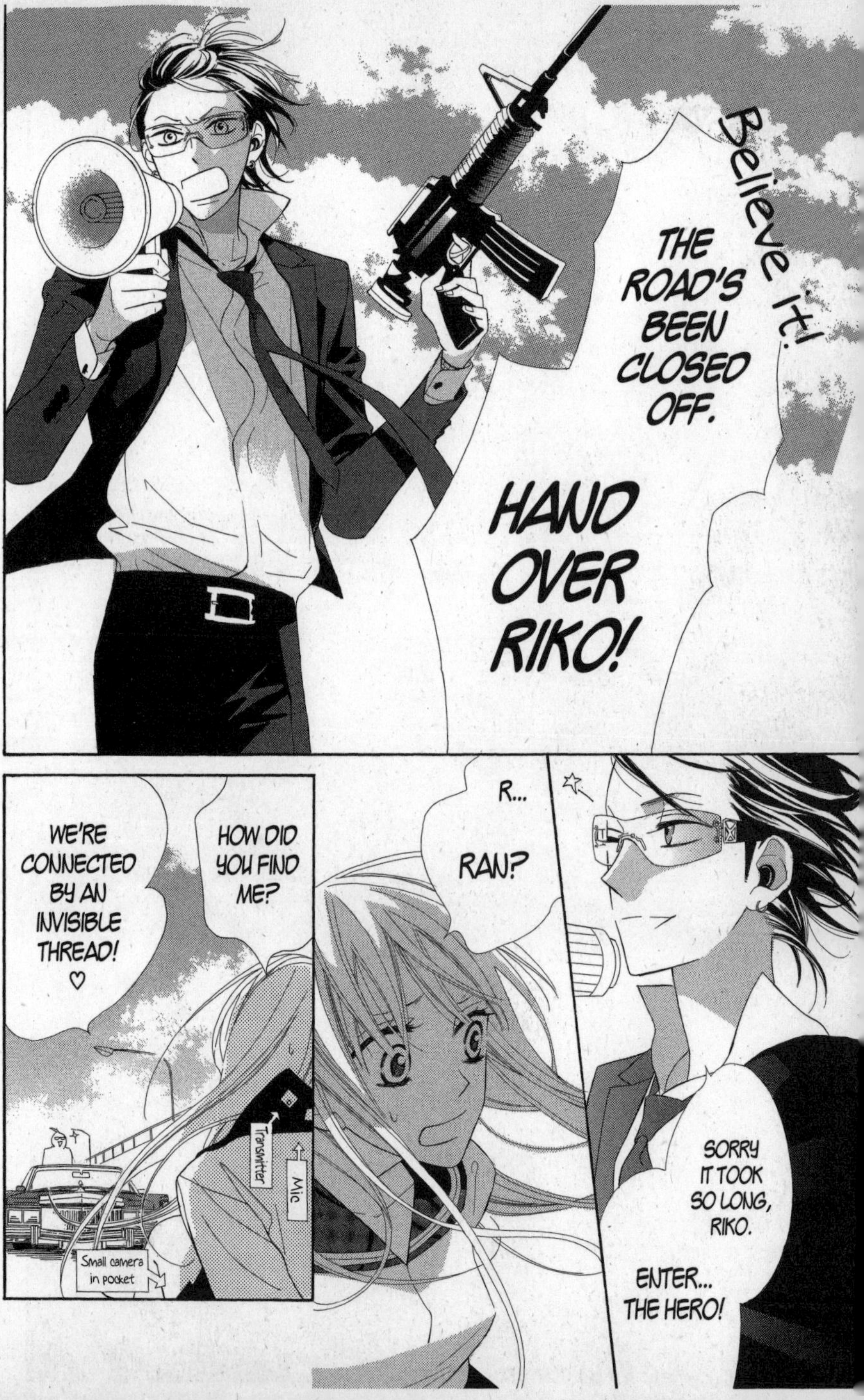
Believe it!
THE ROAD'S BEEN CLOSED OFF.
HAND OVER RIKO!
R...
RAN?
SORRY IT TOOK SO LONG, RIKO.
ENTER... THE HERO!
HOW DID YOU FIND ME?
WE'RE CONNECTED BY AN INVISIBLE THREAD! ♡
Transmitter
Mic
Small camera in pocket

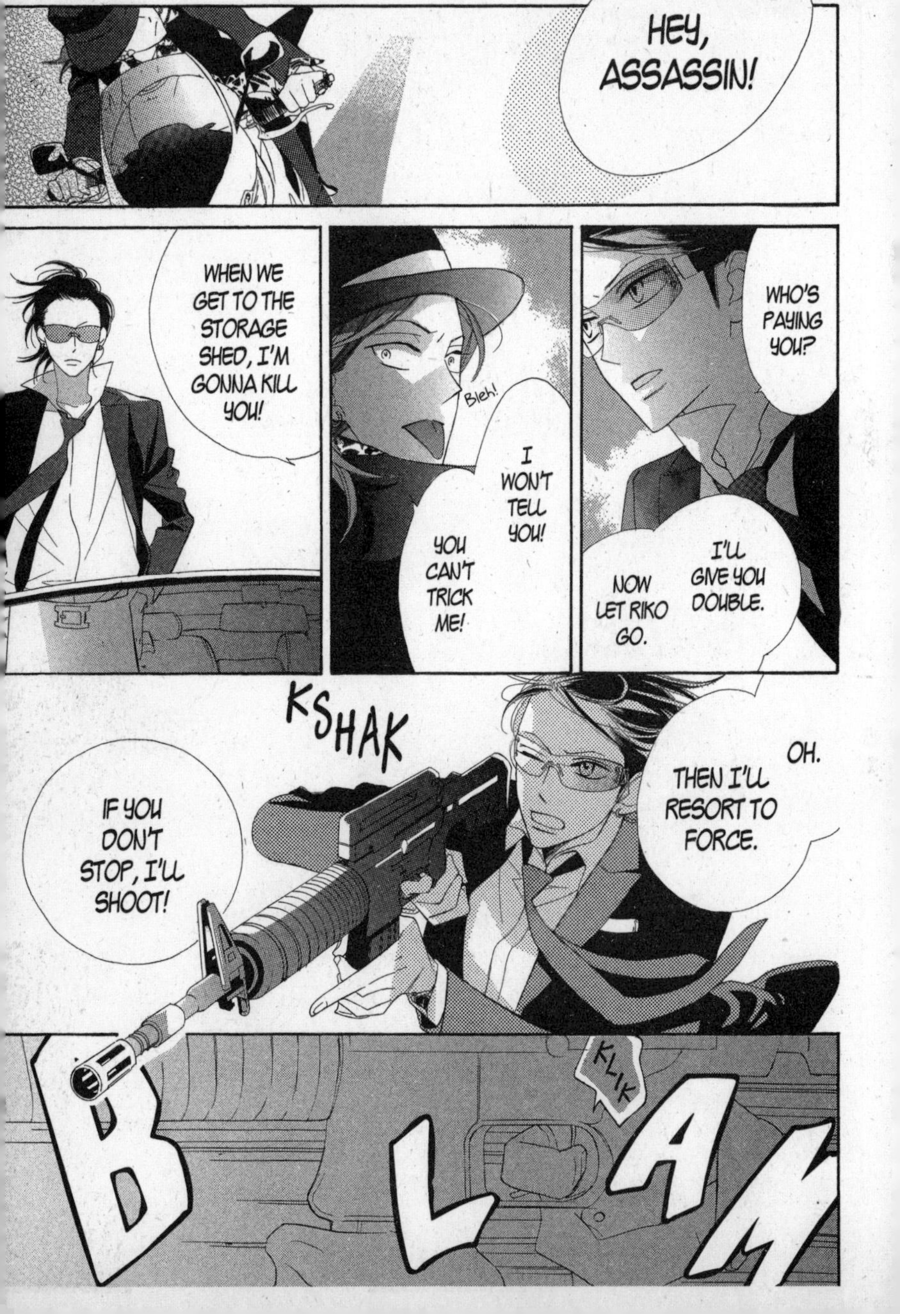
HEY, ASSASSIN!
WHO'S PAYING YOU?
I'LL GIVE YOU DOUBLE.
NOW LET RIKO GO.
Bleh!
I WON'T TELL YOU!
YOU CAN'T TRICK ME!
WHEN WE GET TO THE STORAGE SHED, I'M GONNA KILL YOU!
OH.
THEN I'LL RESORT TO FORCE.
KSHAK
IF YOU DON'T STOP, I'LL SHOOT!
KLIK
BLAM

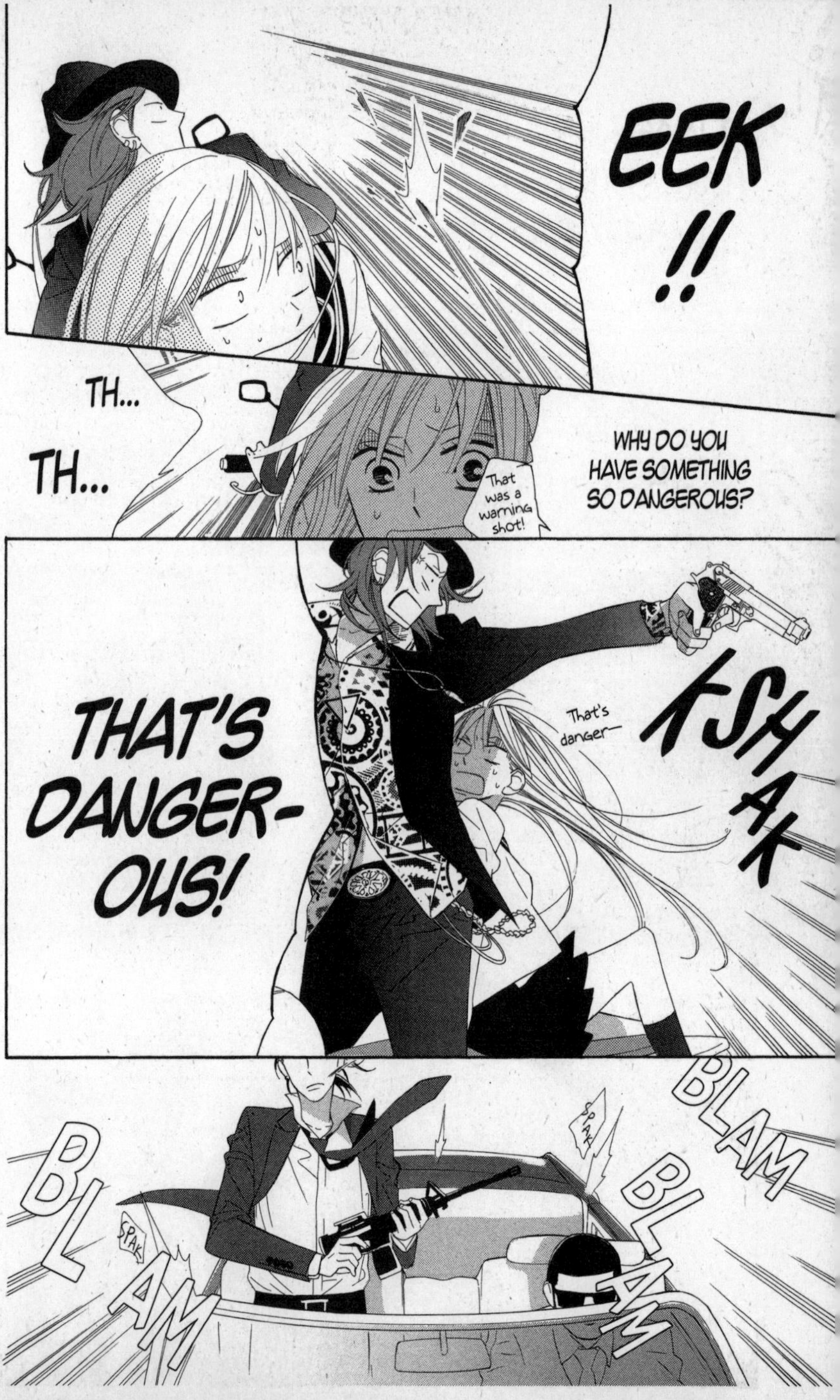
EEK!!
WHY DO YOU HAVE SOMETHING SO DANGEROUS?
That was a warning shot!
TH...
TH...
KSHAK
That's danger—
THAT'S DANGER-OUS!
BLAM
BLAM
SPAK
BLAM
BLAM
SPAK

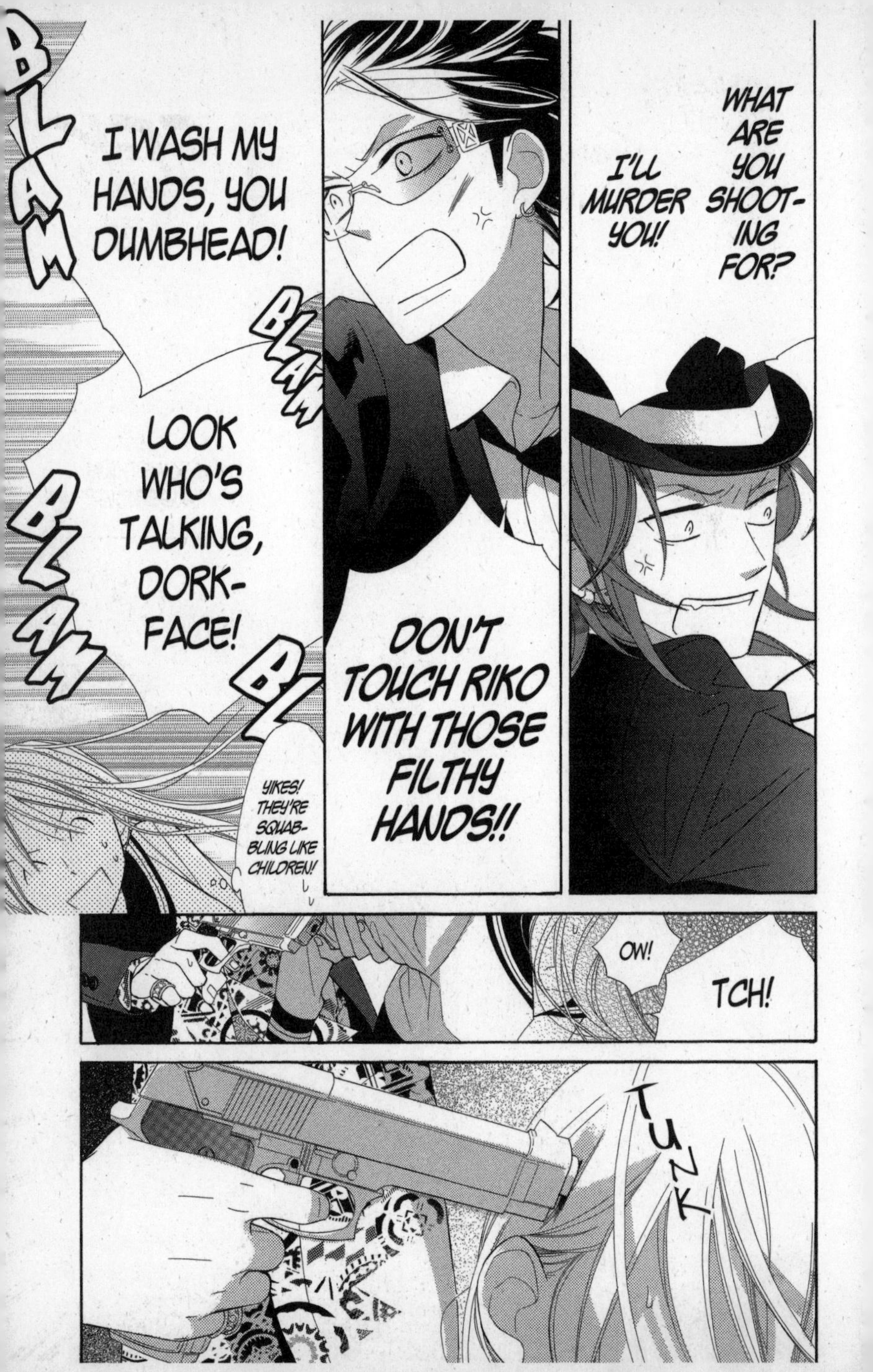
WHAT ARE YOU SHOOT-ING FOR?
I'LL MURDER YOU!
DON'T TOUCH RIKO WITH THOSE FILTHY HANDS!!
I WASH MY HANDS, YOU DUMBHEAD!
BLAM
BLAM
LOOK WHO'S TALKING, DORK-FACE!
BLAM
BL
YIKES! THEY'RE SQUAB-BLING LIKE CHILDREN!
TCH!
OW!
TUNK

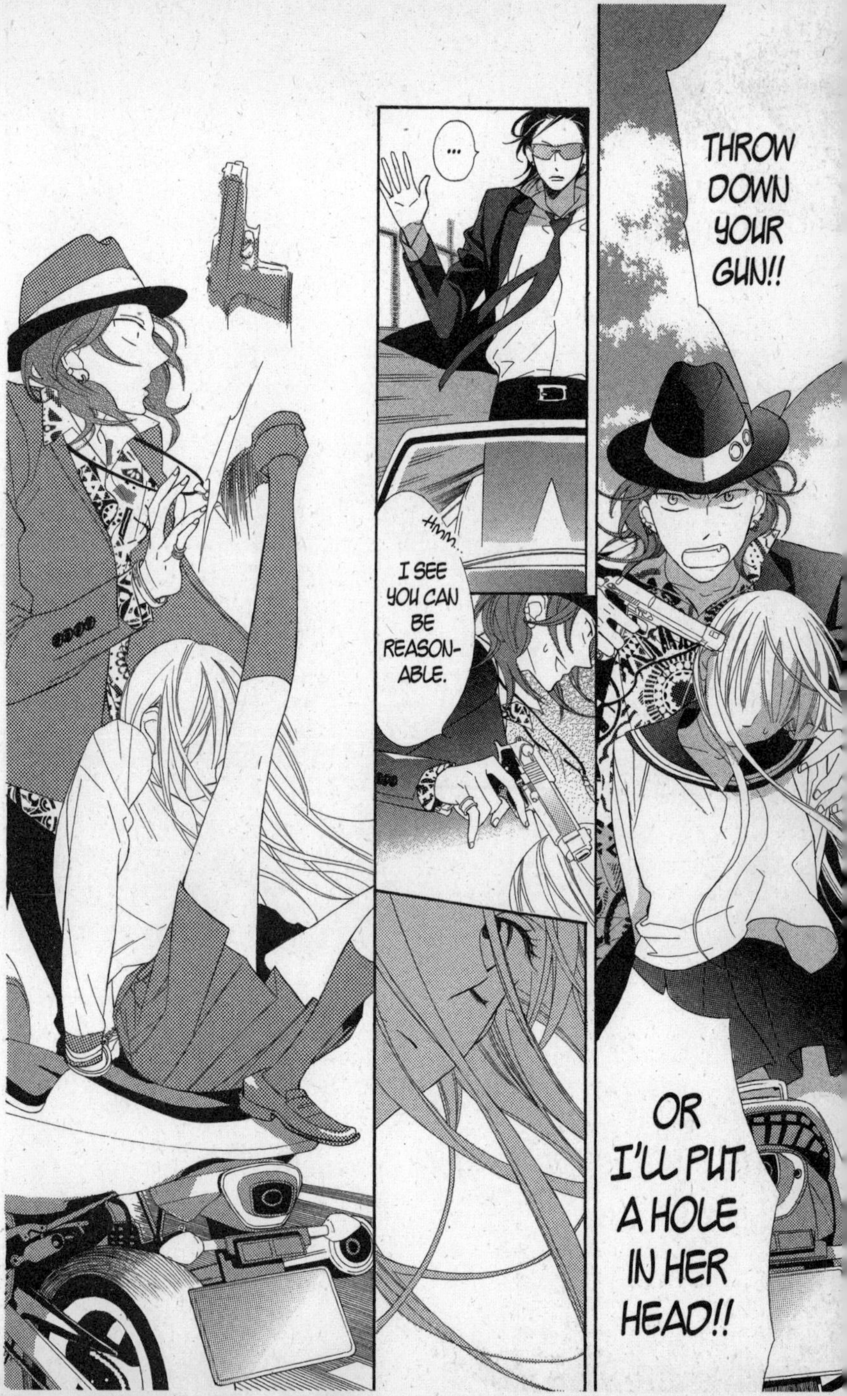
THROW DOWN YOUR GUN!!
OR I'LL PUT A HOLE IN HER HEAD!!
...
Hmm..
I SEE YOU CAN BE REASON-ABLE.

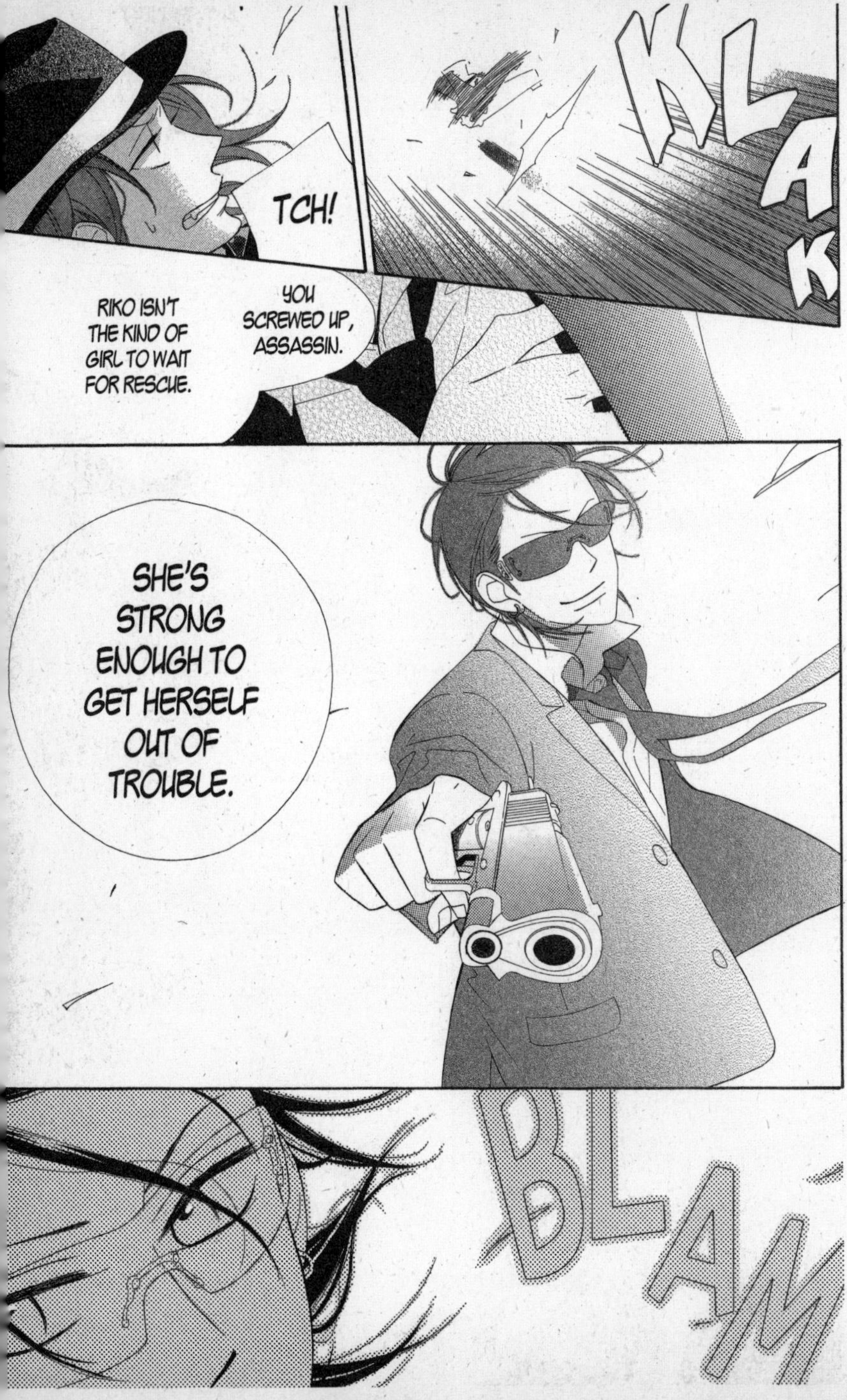
KLAK
TCH!
YOU SCREWED UP, ASSASSIN.
RIKO ISN'T THE KIND OF GIRL TO WAIT FOR RESCUE.
SHE'S STRONG ENOUGH TO GET HERSELF OUT OF TROUBLE.
BLAM

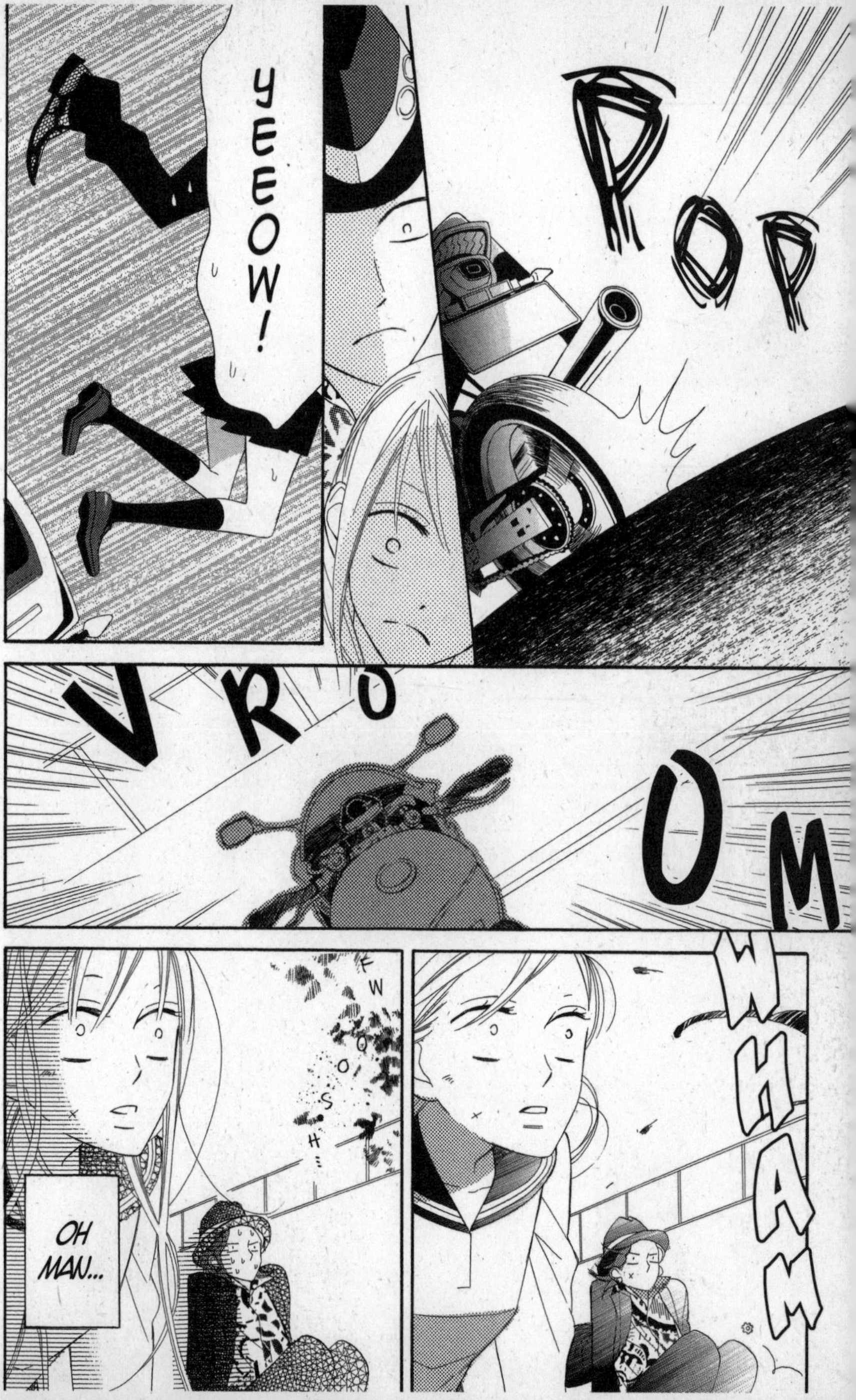
POP
YEEOW!
VROOM
WHAM
FWOOSH...
OH MAN...

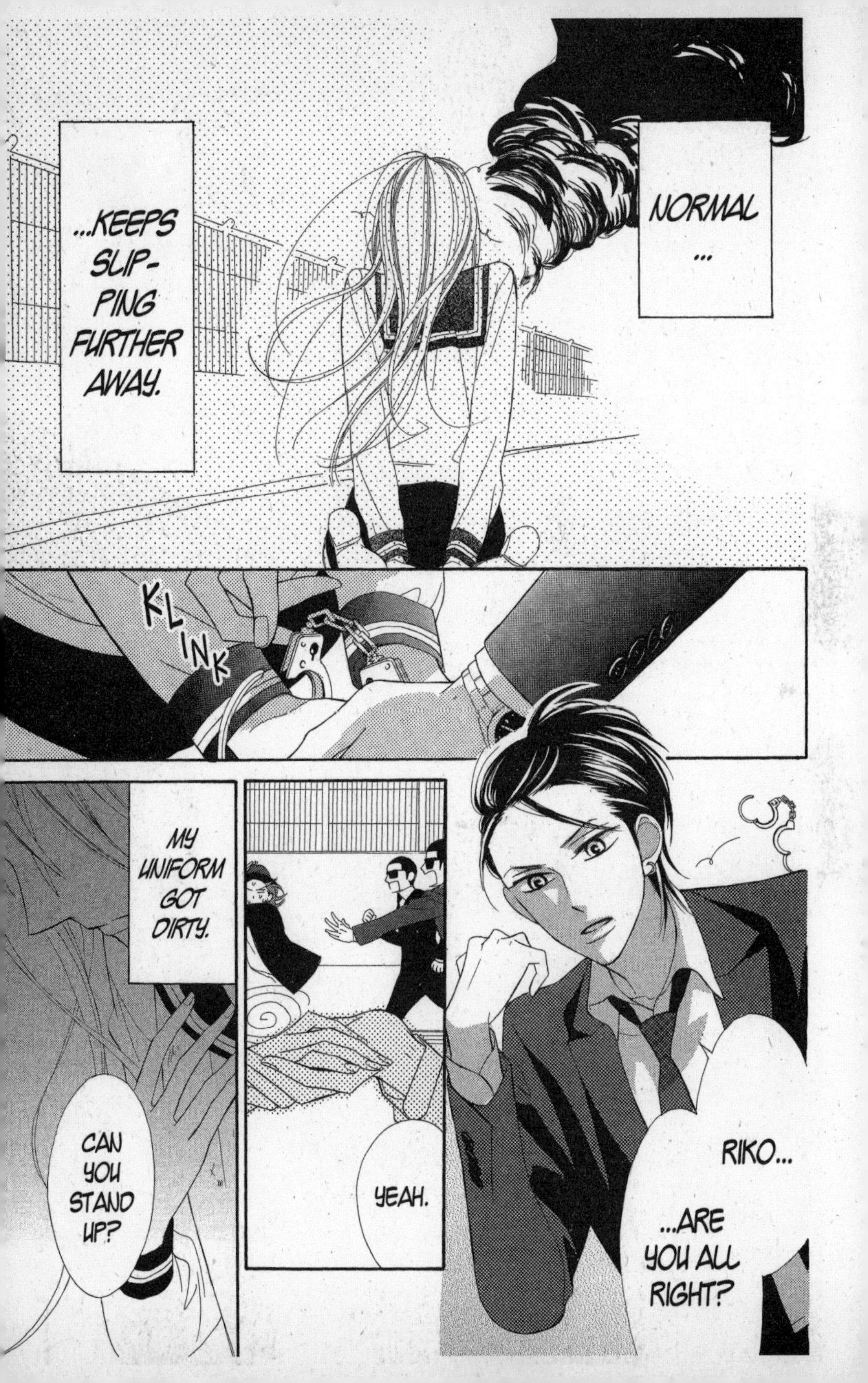
NORMAL...
...KEEPS SLIPPING FURTHER AWAY.
KLINK
RIKO...
...ARE YOU ALL RIGHT?
MY UNIFORM GOT DIRTY.
YEAH.
CAN YOU STAND UP?

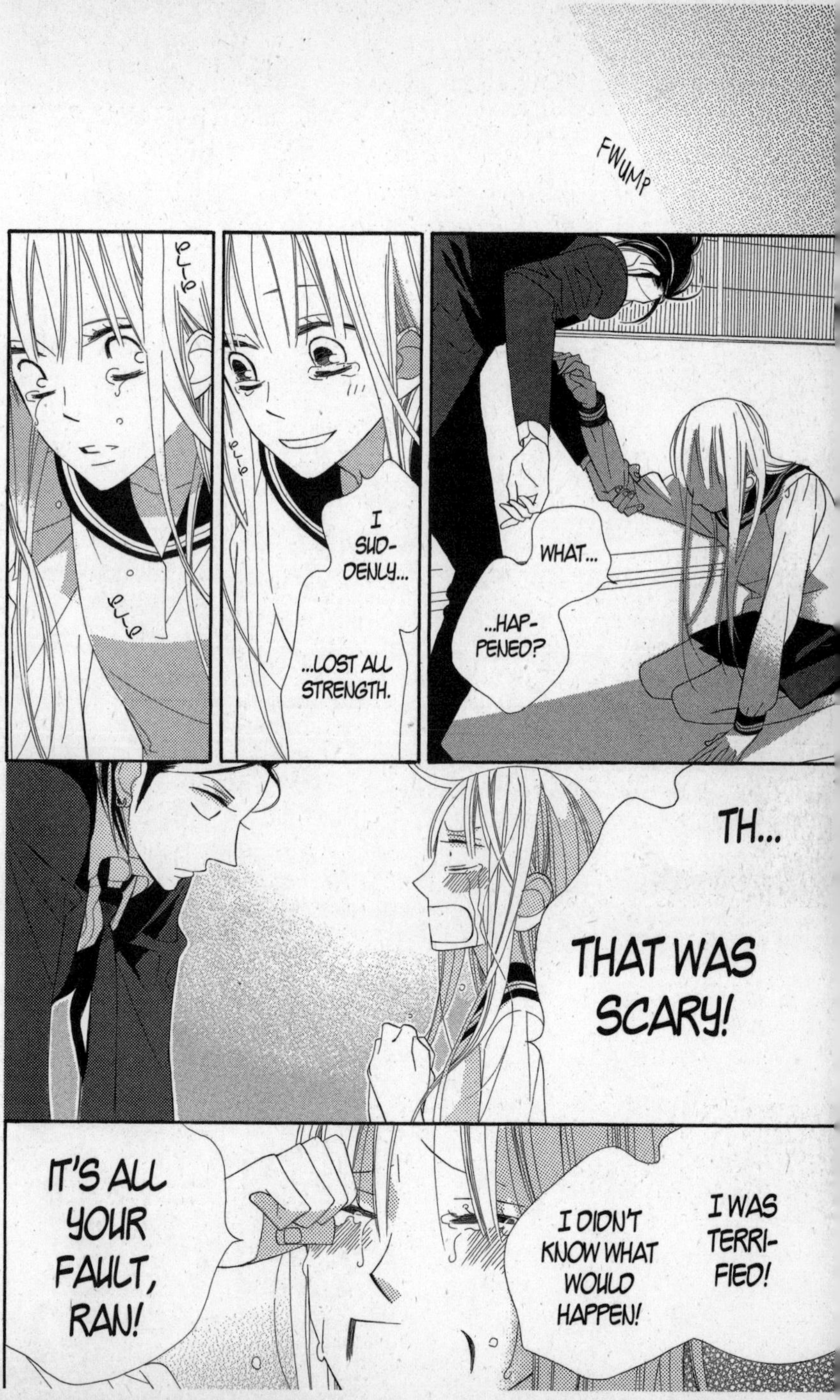
FWUMP
WHAT...
...HAPPENED?
I SUDDENLY...
...LOST ALL STRENGTH.
TH...
THAT WAS SCARY!
I WAS TERRIFIED!
I DIDN'T KNOW WHAT WOULD HAPPEN!
IT'S ALL YOUR FAULT, RAN!

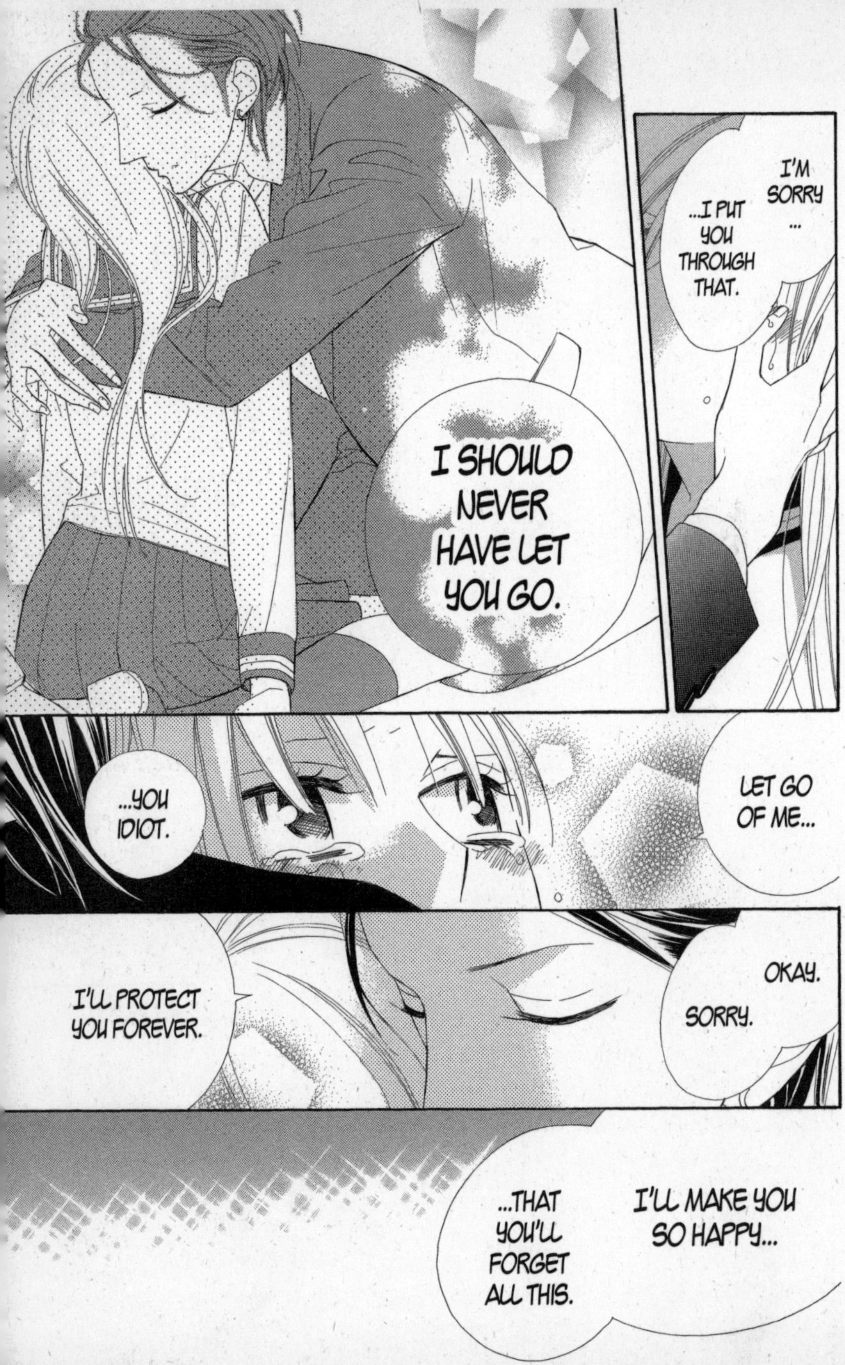
I'M SORRY...
...I PUT YOU THROUGH THAT.
I SHOULD NEVER HAVE LET YOU GO.
LET GO OF ME...
...YOU IDIOT.
OKAY.
SORRY.
I'LL PROTECT YOU FOREVER.
I'LL MAKE YOU SO HAPPY...
...THAT YOU'LL FORGET ALL THIS.

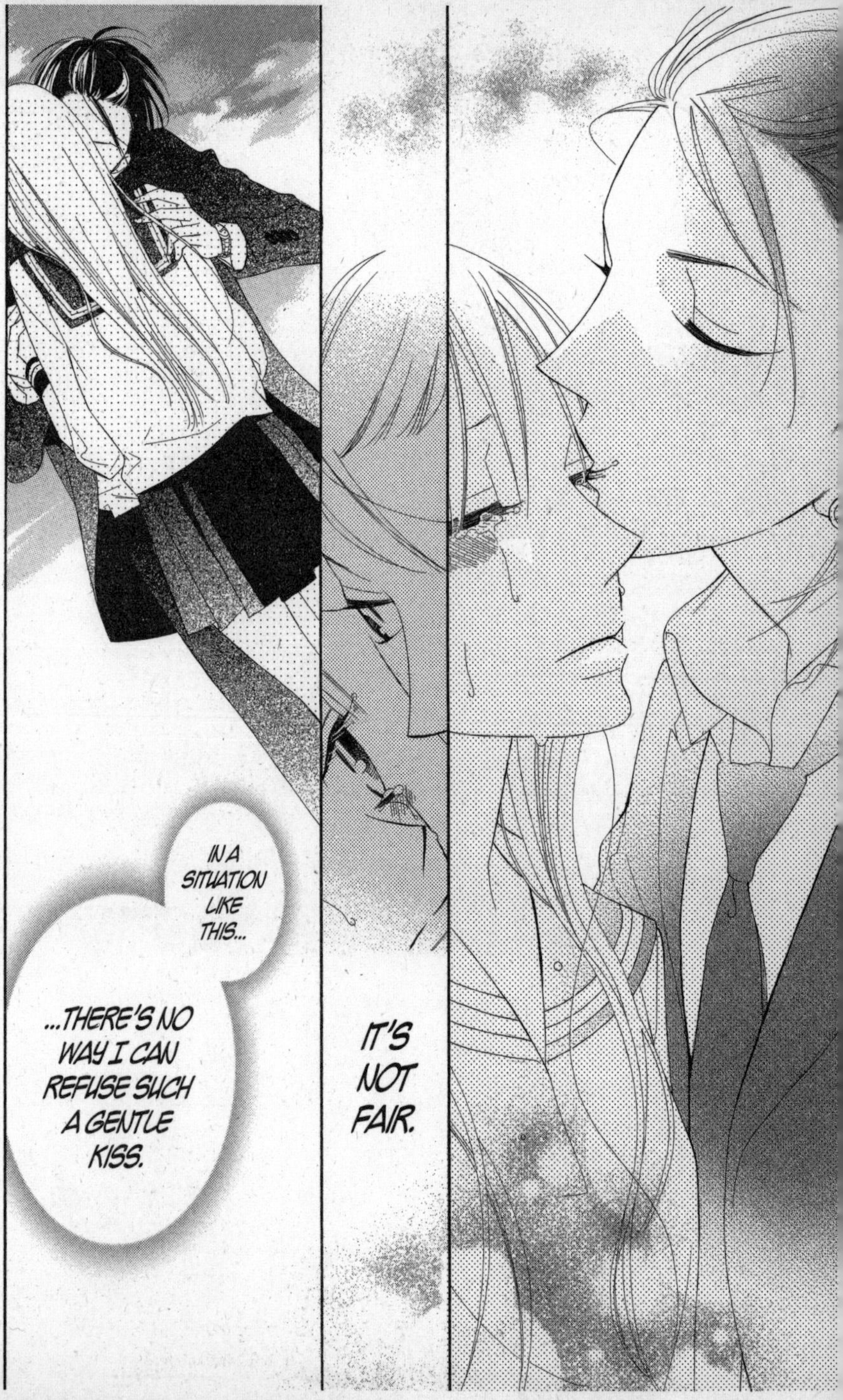
IN A SITUATION LIKE THIS...
...THERE'S NO WAY I CAN REFUSE SUCH A GENTLE KISS.
IT'S NOT FAIR.

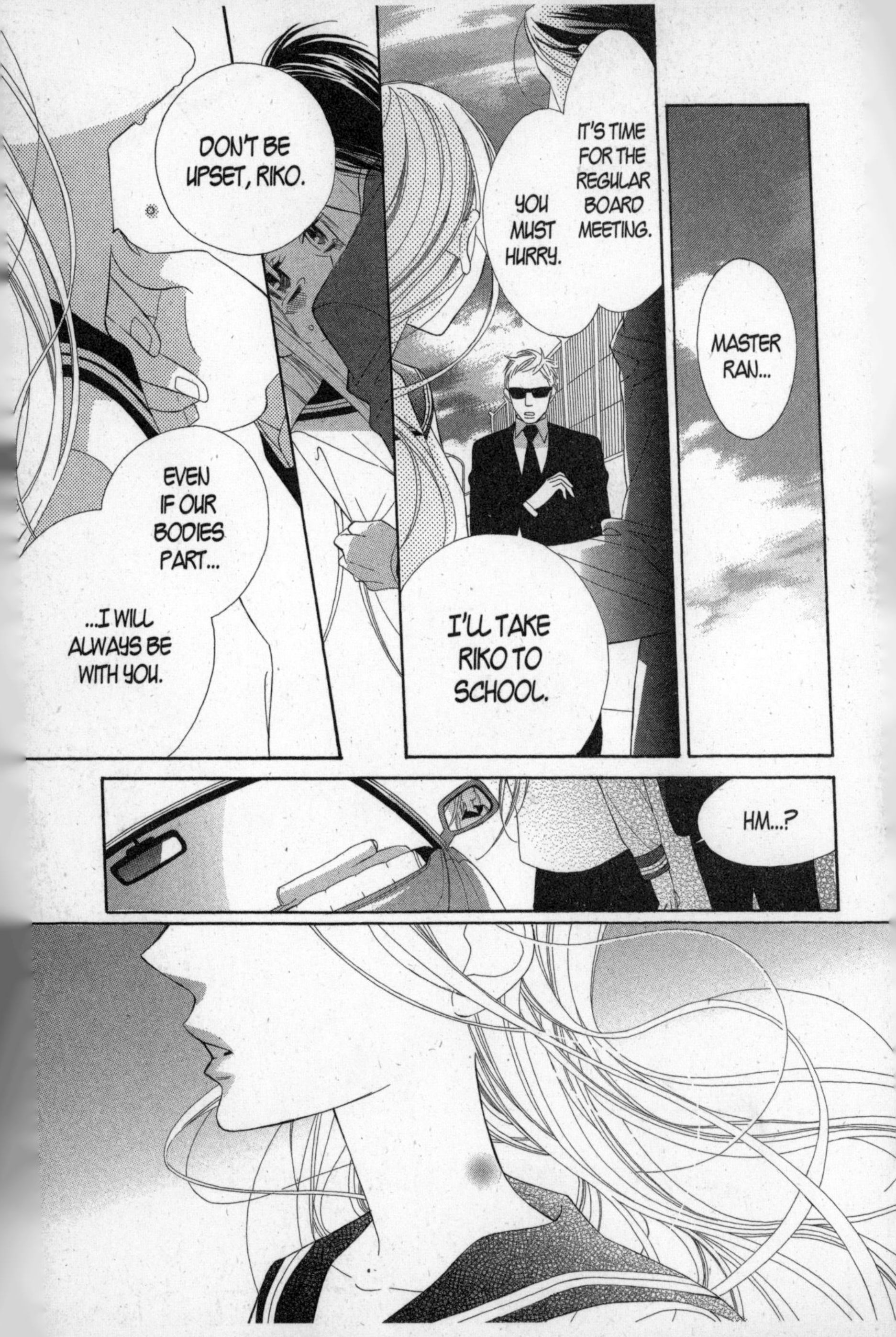
MASTER RAN...
IT'S TIME FOR THE REGULAR BOARD MEETING.
YOU MUST HURRY.
I'LL TAKE RIKO TO SCHOOL.
DON'T BE UPSET, RIKO.
EVEN IF OUR BODIES PART...
...I WILL ALWAYS BE WITH YOU.
HM...?

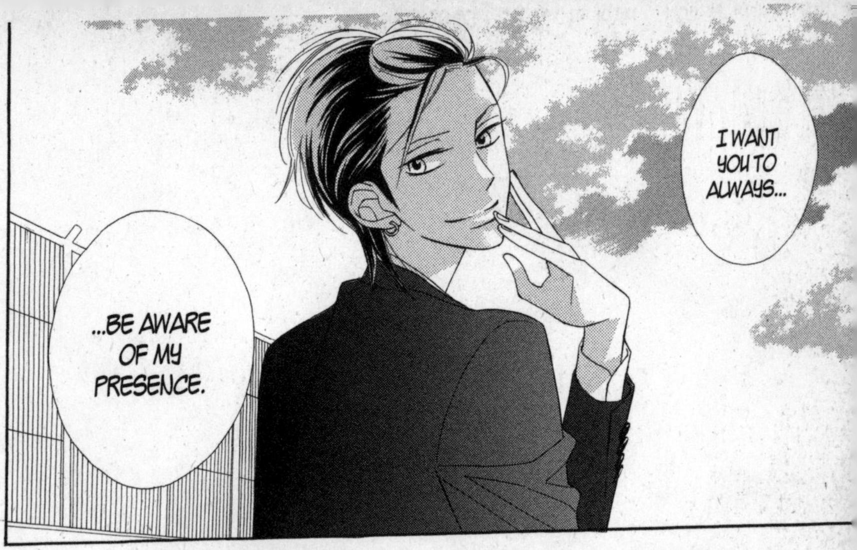
I WANT YOU TO ALWAYS...
...BE AWARE OF MY PRESENCE.

HIS KISS SWEPT THROUGH ME LIKE A STORM...

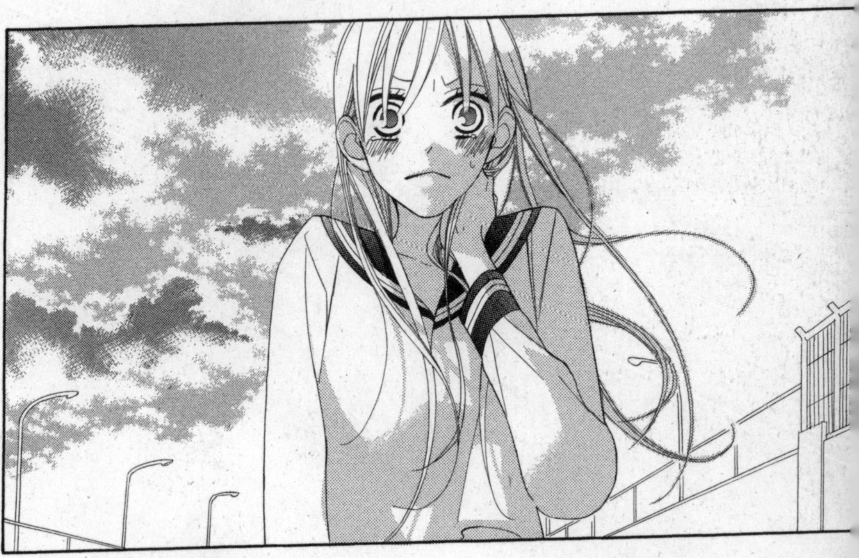

...LEAVING A MARK THAT WOULD NEVER FADE.

FLOWER IN A STORM CHAPTER 2 / END

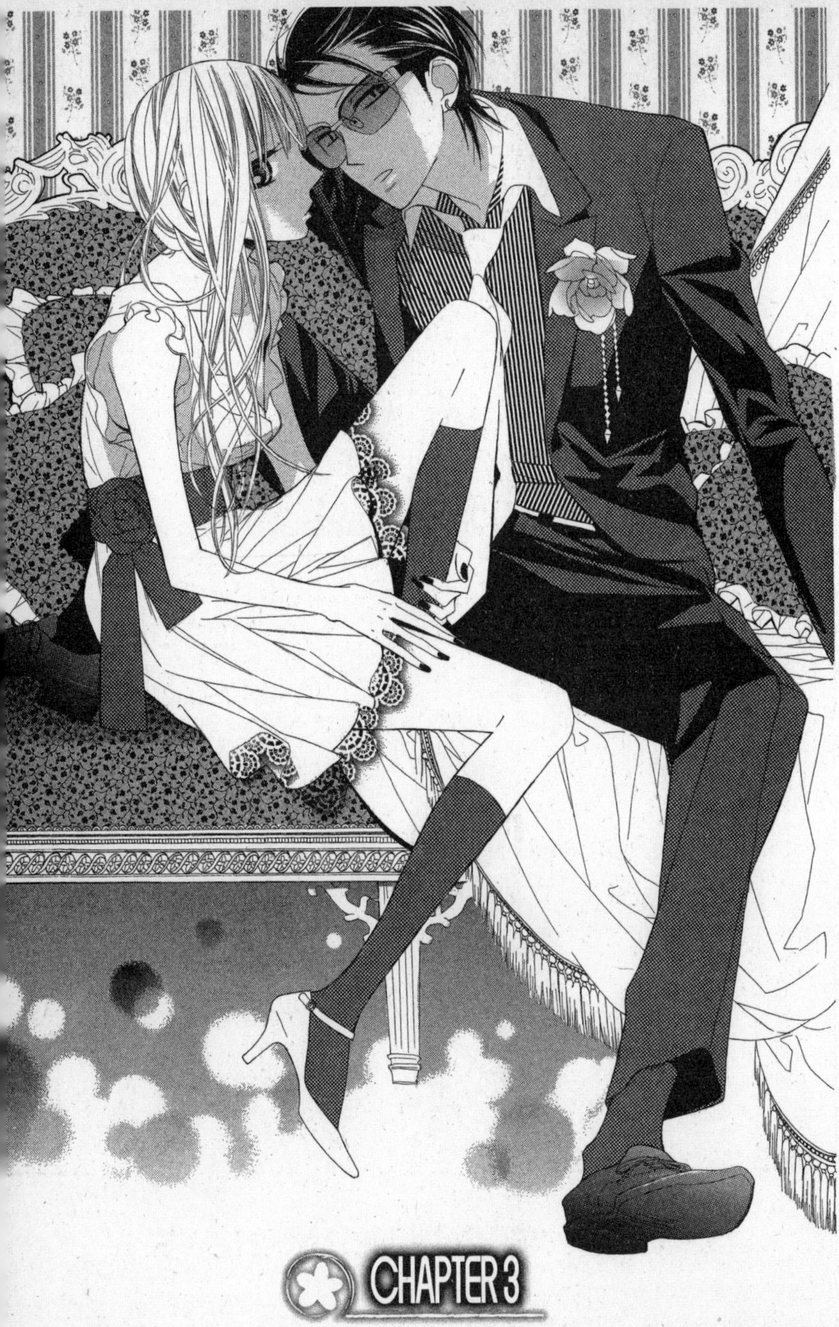

CHAPTER 3

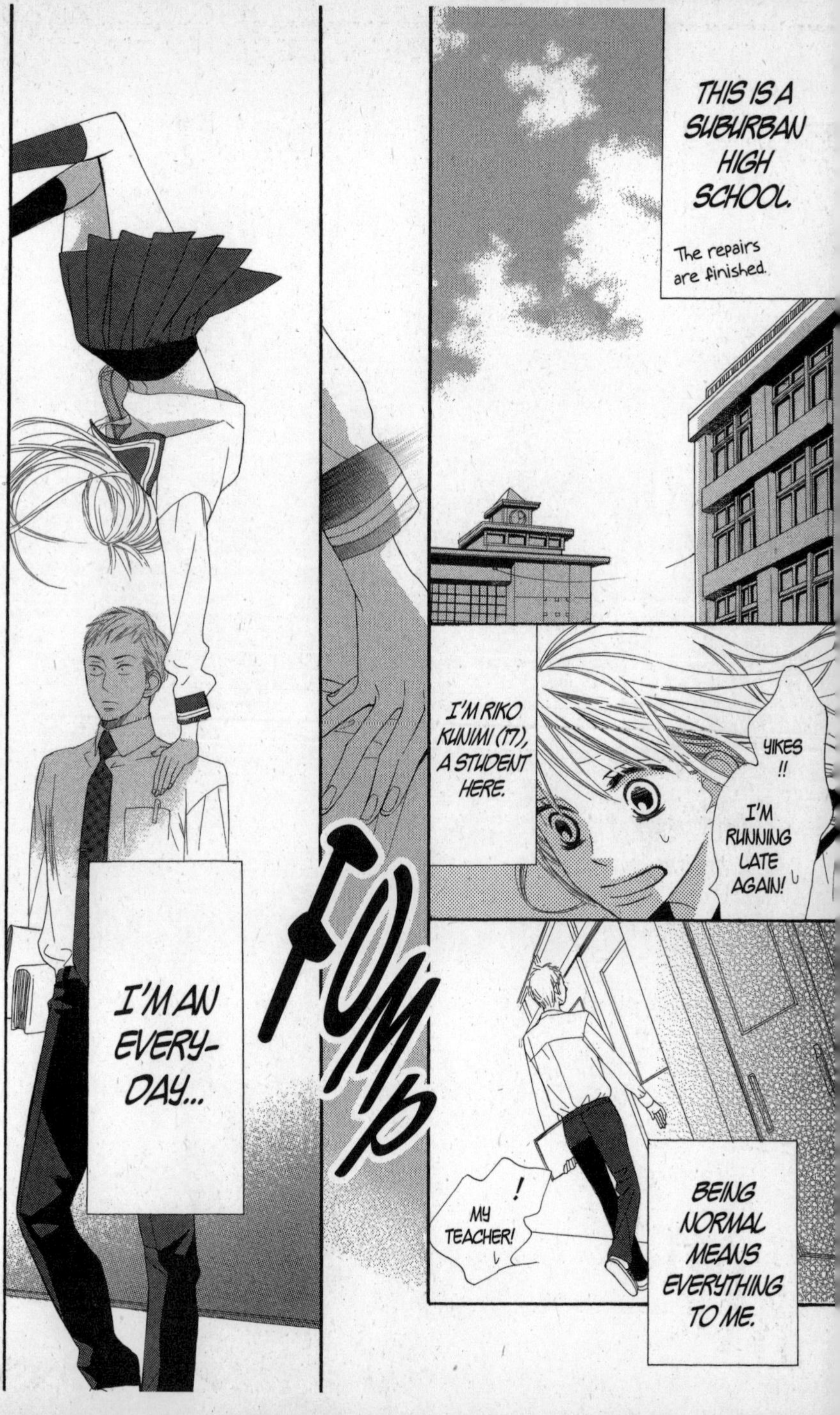
THIS IS A SUBURBAN HIGH SCHOOL.
The repairs are finished.
YIKES !!
I'M RUNNING LATE AGAIN!
I'M RIKO KUNIMI (17), A STUDENT HERE.
BEING NORMAL MEANS EVERYTHING TO ME.
! MY TEACHER!
FOMP
I'M AN EVERY-DAY...

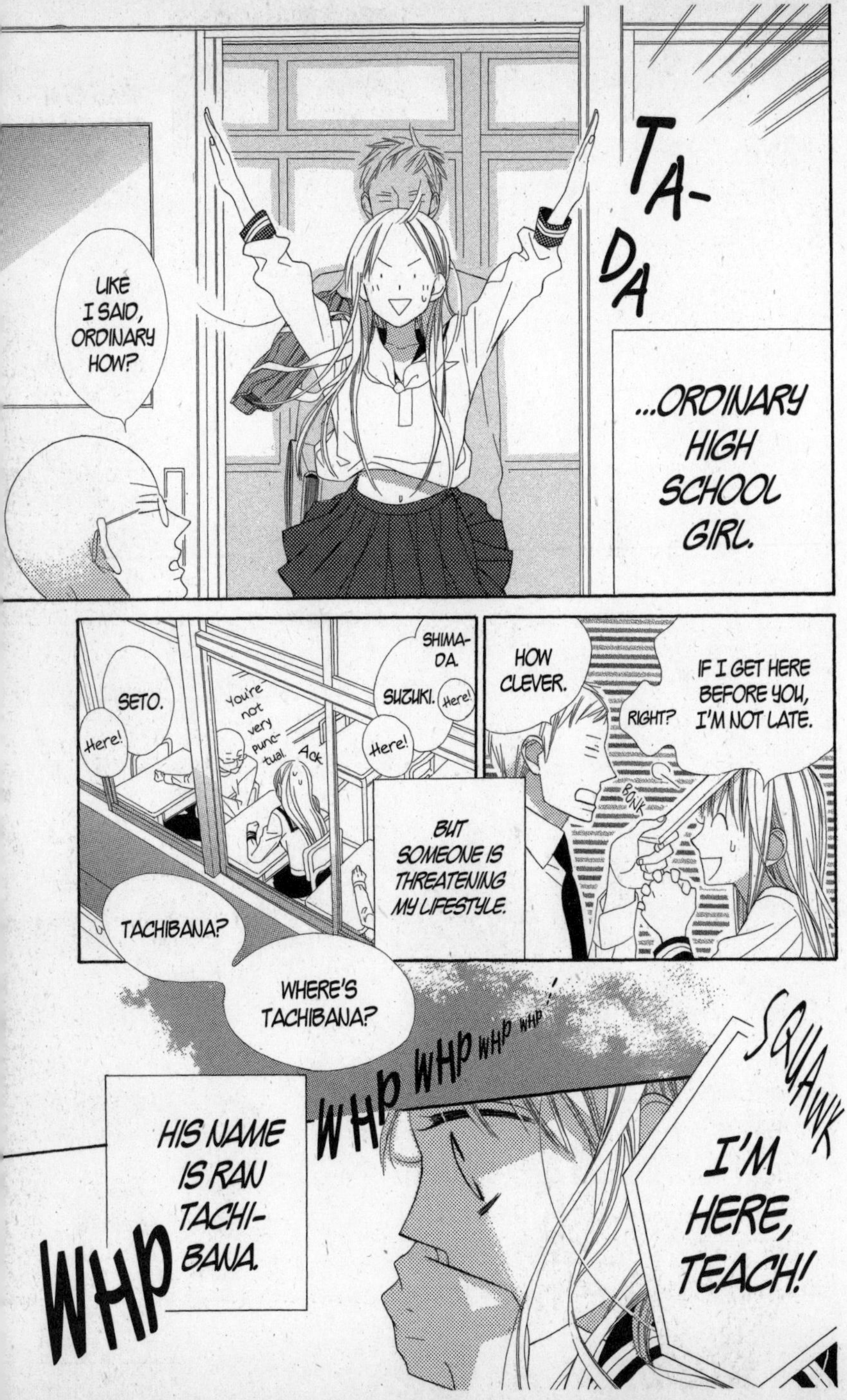

TA-DA
...ORDINARY HIGH SCHOOL GIRL.
LIKE I SAID, ORDINARY HOW?
IF I GET HERE BEFORE YOU, I'M NOT LATE.
RIGHT?
BONK
HOW CLEVER.
SHIMA-DA.
Here!
SUZUKI.
Here!
SETO.
Here!
You're not very punc-tual.
Ack
BUT SOMEONE IS THREATENING MY LIFESTYLE.
TACHIBANA?
WHERE'S TACHIBANA?
SQUAWK
I'M HERE, TEACH!
WHP WHP WHP WHP WHP
HIS NAME IS RAN TACHI-BANA.
WHP

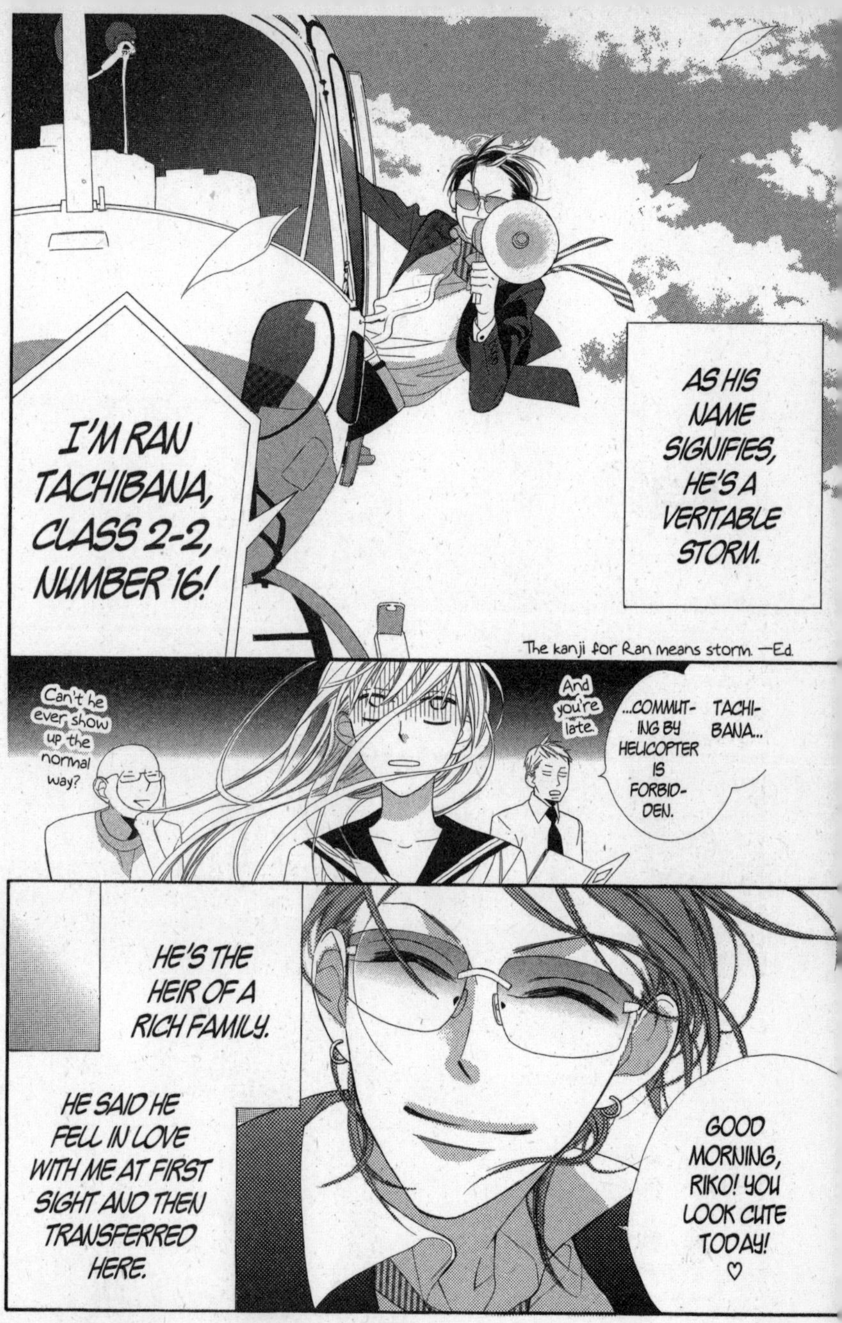
AS HIS NAME SIGNIFIES, HE'S A VERITABLE STORM.
I'M RAN TACHIBANA, CLASS 2-2, NUMBER 16!
The kanji for Ran means storm. —Ed.
TACHIBANA...
...COMMUTING BY HELICOPTER IS FORBIDDEN.
And you're late.
Can't he ever show up the normal way?
HE'S THE HEIR OF A RICH FAMILY.
GOOD MORNING, RIKO! YOU LOOK CUTE TODAY! ♡
HE SAID HE FELL IN LOVE WITH ME AT FIRST SIGHT AND THEN TRANSFERRED HERE.

Character Profile Part 3

Chiaki

Age 17 5' 8-1/2"

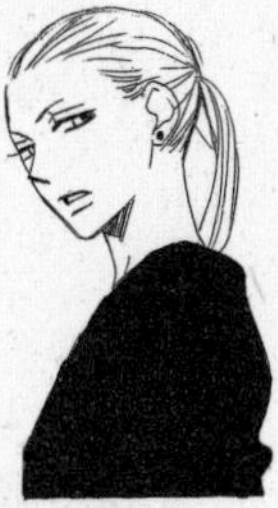

I needed to put in a rival for Ran, and after a long struggle I came up with Chiaki. It's too bad I couldn't have him appear more often. He's sort of a sad individual.

Class President

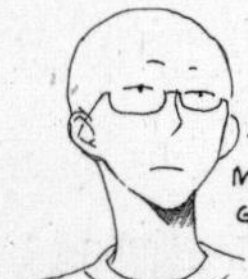
I am the true man in Glass-es.

For some reason, he's very knowledge-able. He isn't bald—he shaves his head.

Their silhouettes are almost identical.

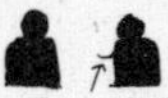
This one's Chiaki.

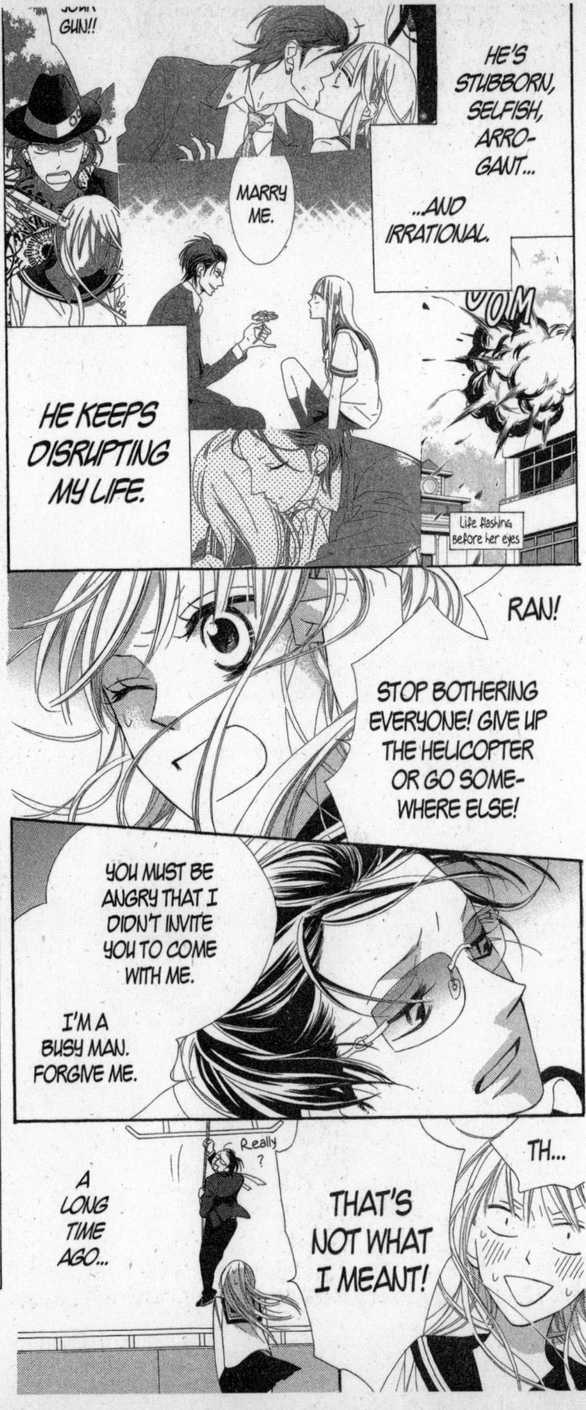
HE'S STUBBORN, SELFISH, ARRO-GANT...
...AND IRRATIONAL.
MARRY ME.
GUN!!
HE KEEPS DISRUPTING MY LIFE.
Life flashing before her eyes
RAN!
STOP BOTHERING EVERYONE! GIVE UP THE HELICOPTER OR GO SOME-WHERE ELSE!
YOU MUST BE ANGRY THAT I DIDN'T INVITE YOU TO COME WITH ME.
I'M A BUSY MAN. FORGIVE ME.
TH...
THAT'S NOT WHAT I MEANT!
Really?
A LONG TIME AGO...

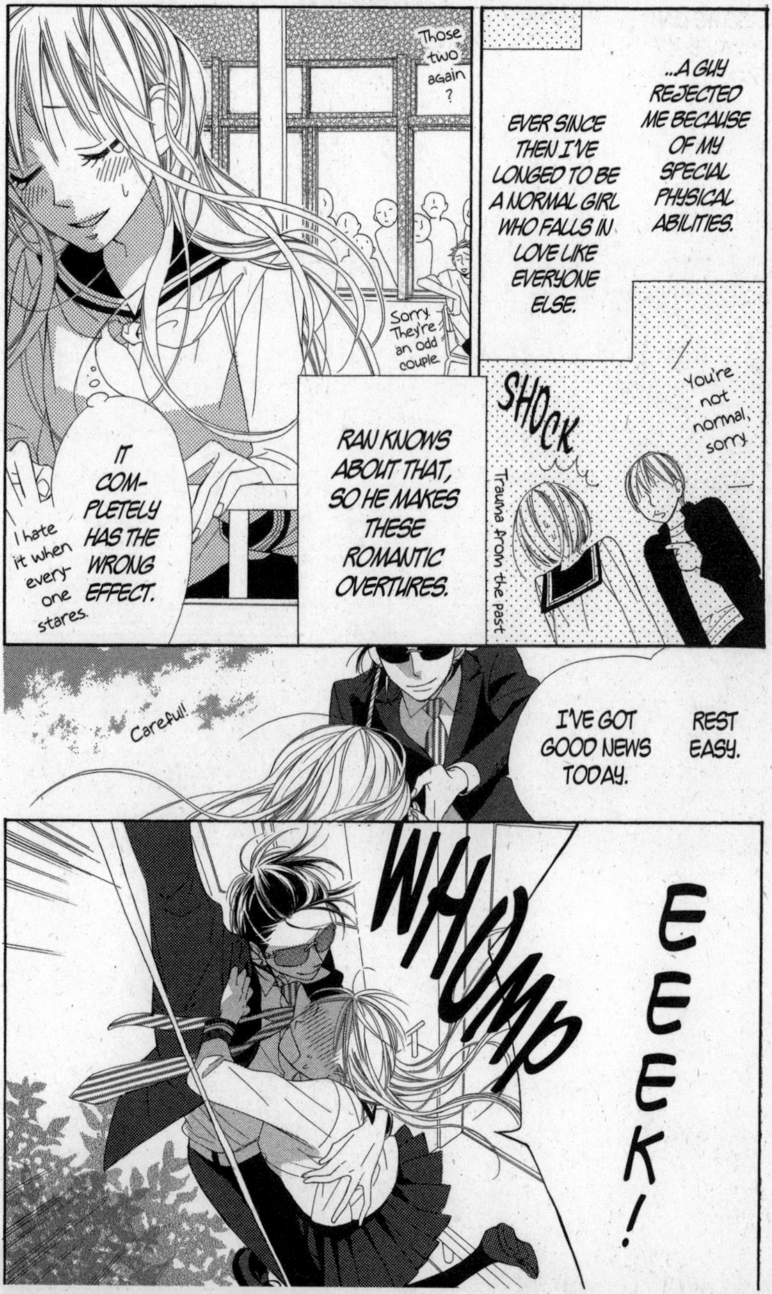
...A GUY REJECTED ME BECAUSE OF MY SPECIAL PHYSICAL ABILITIES.
EVER SINCE THEN I'VE LONGED TO BE A NORMAL GIRL WHO FALLS IN LOVE LIKE EVERYONE ELSE.
You're not normal, sorry.
SHOCK
Trauma from the past
Those two again?
Sorry. They're an odd couple.
RAN KNOWS ABOUT THAT, SO HE MAKES THESE ROMANTIC OVERTURES.
IT COM-PLETELY HAS THE WRONG EFFECT.
I hate it when every-one stares.
REST EASY.
I'VE GOT GOOD NEWS TODAY.
Careful!
EEEK!
WHOMP

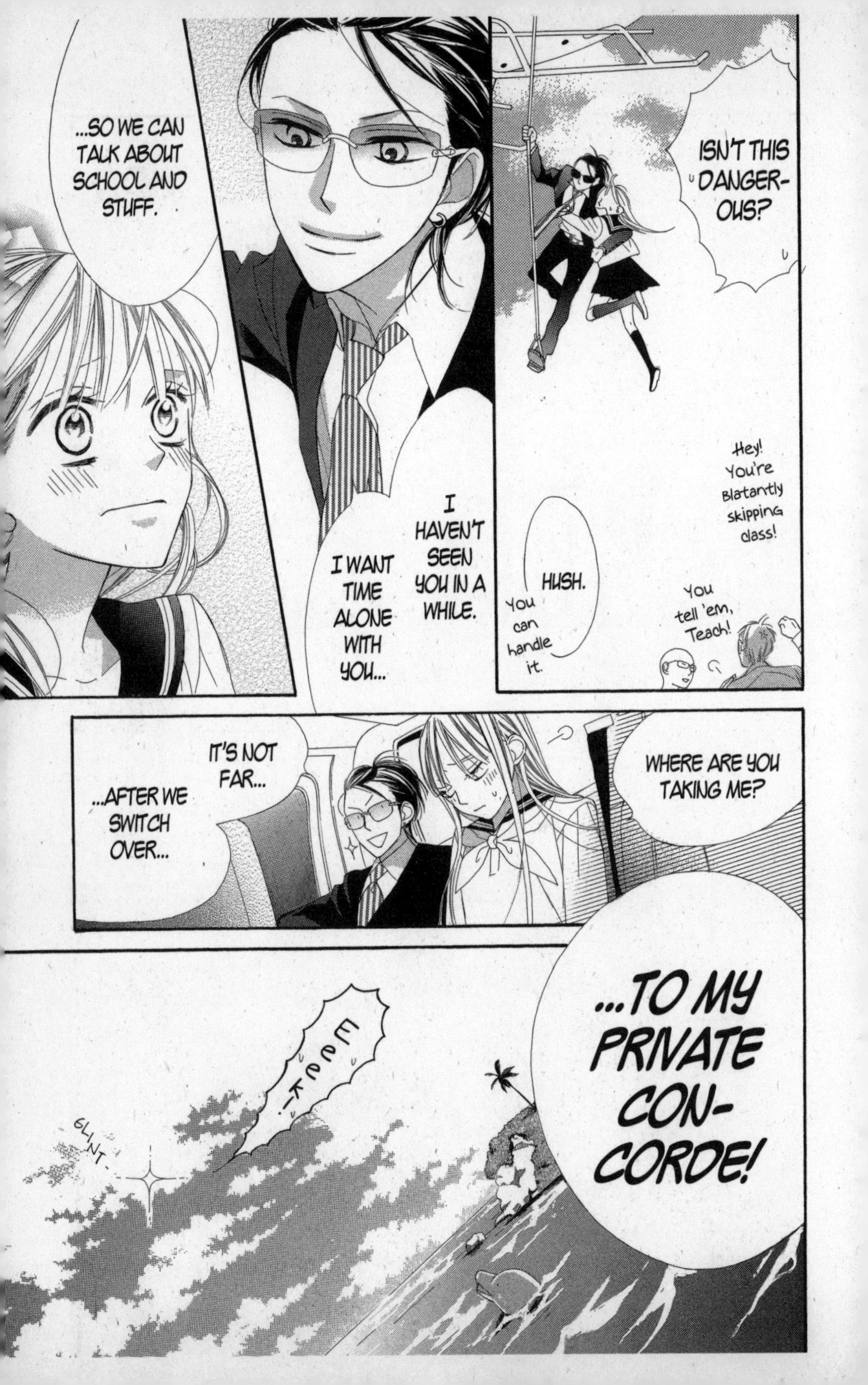
ISN'T THIS DANGER-OUS?
Hey! You're Blatantly skipping class!
You tell 'em, Teach!
HUSH.
You can handle it.
I HAVEN'T SEEN YOU IN A WHILE.
I WANT TIME ALONE WITH YOU...
...SO WE CAN TALK ABOUT SCHOOL AND STUFF.
WHERE ARE YOU TAKING ME?
IT'S NOT FAR...
...AFTER WE SWITCH OVER...
...TO MY PRIVATE CON-CORDE!
Eeek!
GLINT

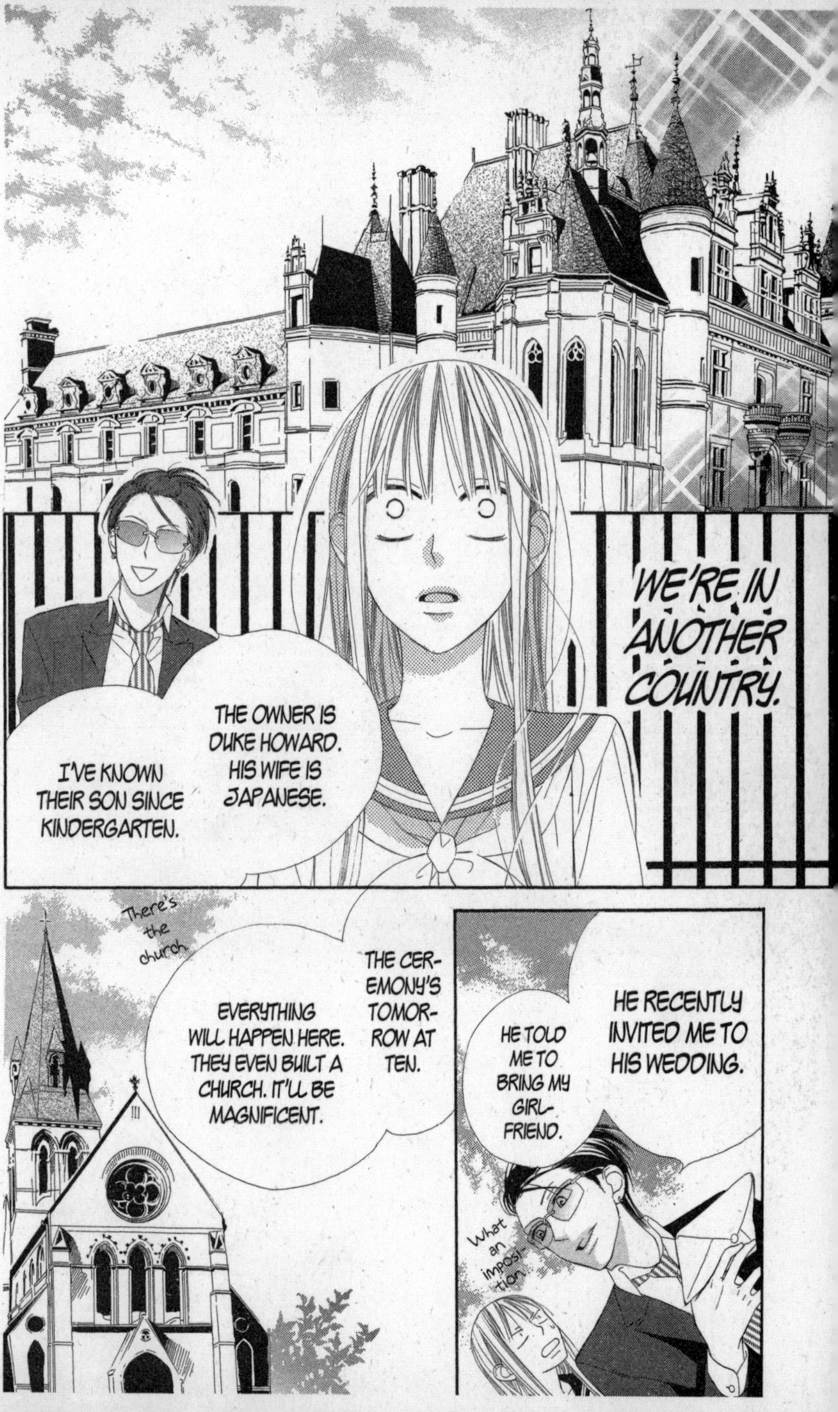
WE'RE IN ANOTHER COUNTRY.
THE OWNER IS DUKE HOWARD. HIS WIFE IS JAPANESE.
I'VE KNOWN THEIR SON SINCE KINDERGARTEN.
HE RECENTLY INVITED ME TO HIS WEDDING.
HE TOLD ME TO BRING MY GIRL-FRIEND.
What an imposi-tion.
THE CER-EMONY'S TOMOR-ROW AT TEN.
EVERYTHING WILL HAPPEN HERE. THEY EVEN BUILT A CHURCH. IT'LL BE MAGNIFICENT.
There's the church

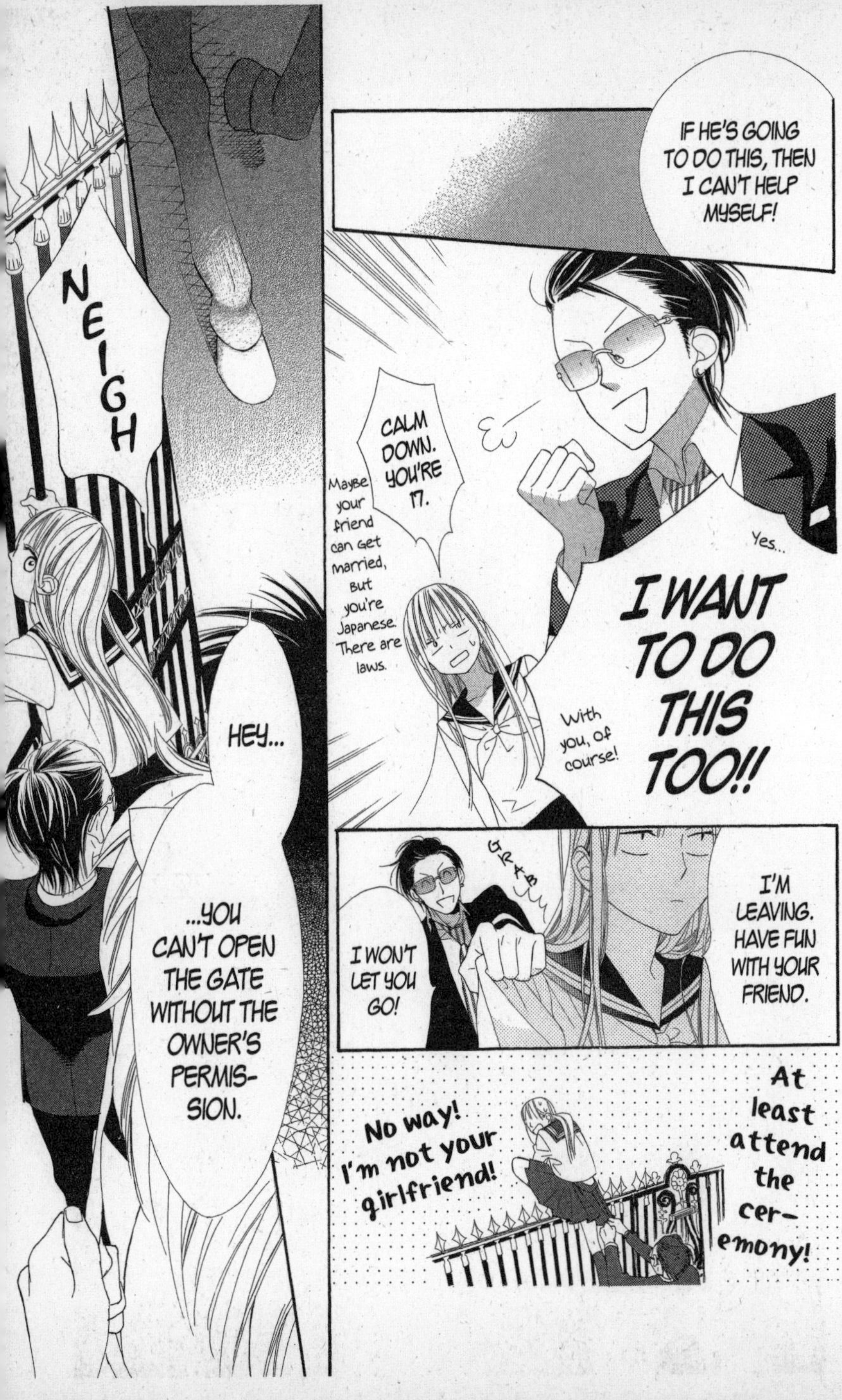
IF HE'S GOING TO DO THIS, THEN I CAN'T HELP MYSELF!
Yes...
I WANT TO DO THIS TOO!!
With you, of course!
CALM DOWN. YOU'RE 17.
Maybe your friend can get married, but you're Japanese. There are laws.
I'M LEAVING. HAVE FUN WITH YOUR FRIEND.
GRAB
I WON'T LET YOU GO!
At least attend the cer-emony!
No way! I'm not your girlfriend!
NEIGH
HEY...
...YOU CAN'T OPEN THE GATE WITHOUT THE OWNER'S PERMIS-SION.

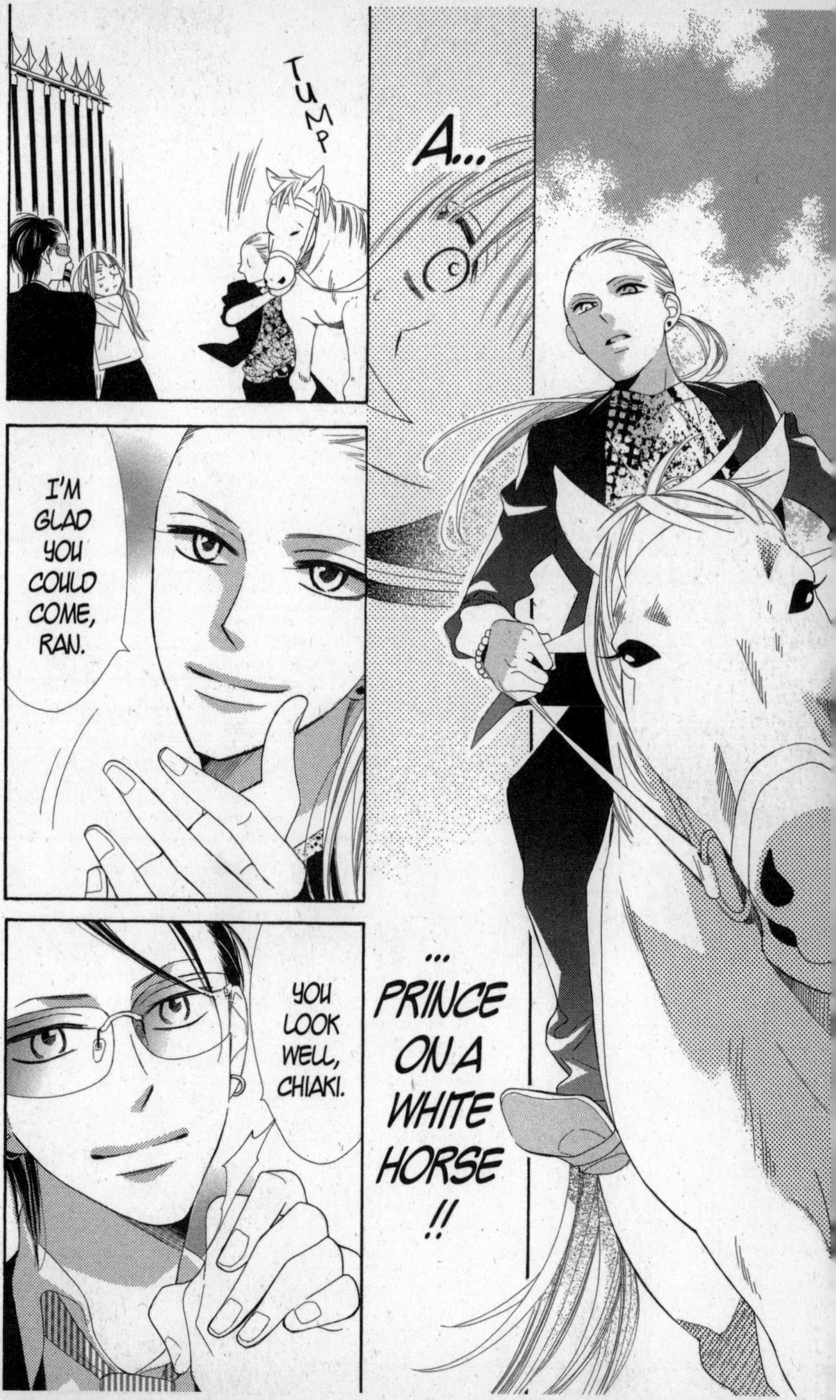
A...
...PRINCE ON A WHITE HORSE!!
TUMP
I'M GLAD YOU COULD COME, RAN.
YOU LOOK WELL, CHIAKI.

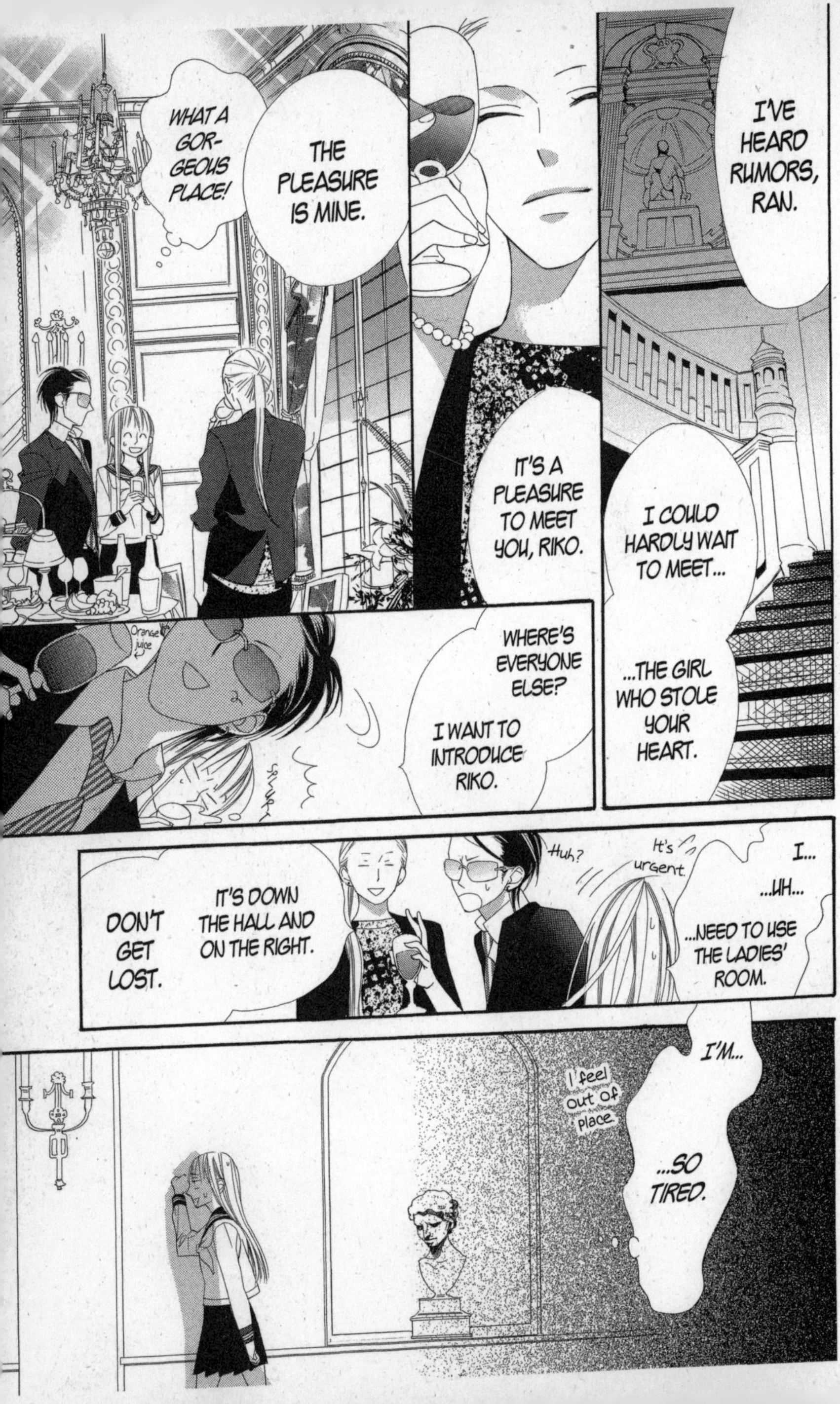
I'VE HEARD RUMORS, RAN.
I COULD HARDLY WAIT TO MEET...
...THE GIRL WHO STOLE YOUR HEART.
IT'S A PLEASURE TO MEET YOU, RIKO.
THE PLEASURE IS MINE.
WHAT A GORGEOUS PLACE!
WHERE'S EVERYONE ELSE?
I WANT TO INTRODUCE RIKO.
Orange juice
I...
...UH...
...NEED TO USE THE LADIES' ROOM.
It's urgent.
Huh?
IT'S DOWN THE HALL AND ON THE RIGHT.
DON'T GET LOST.
I'M...
...SO TIRED.
I feel out of place.

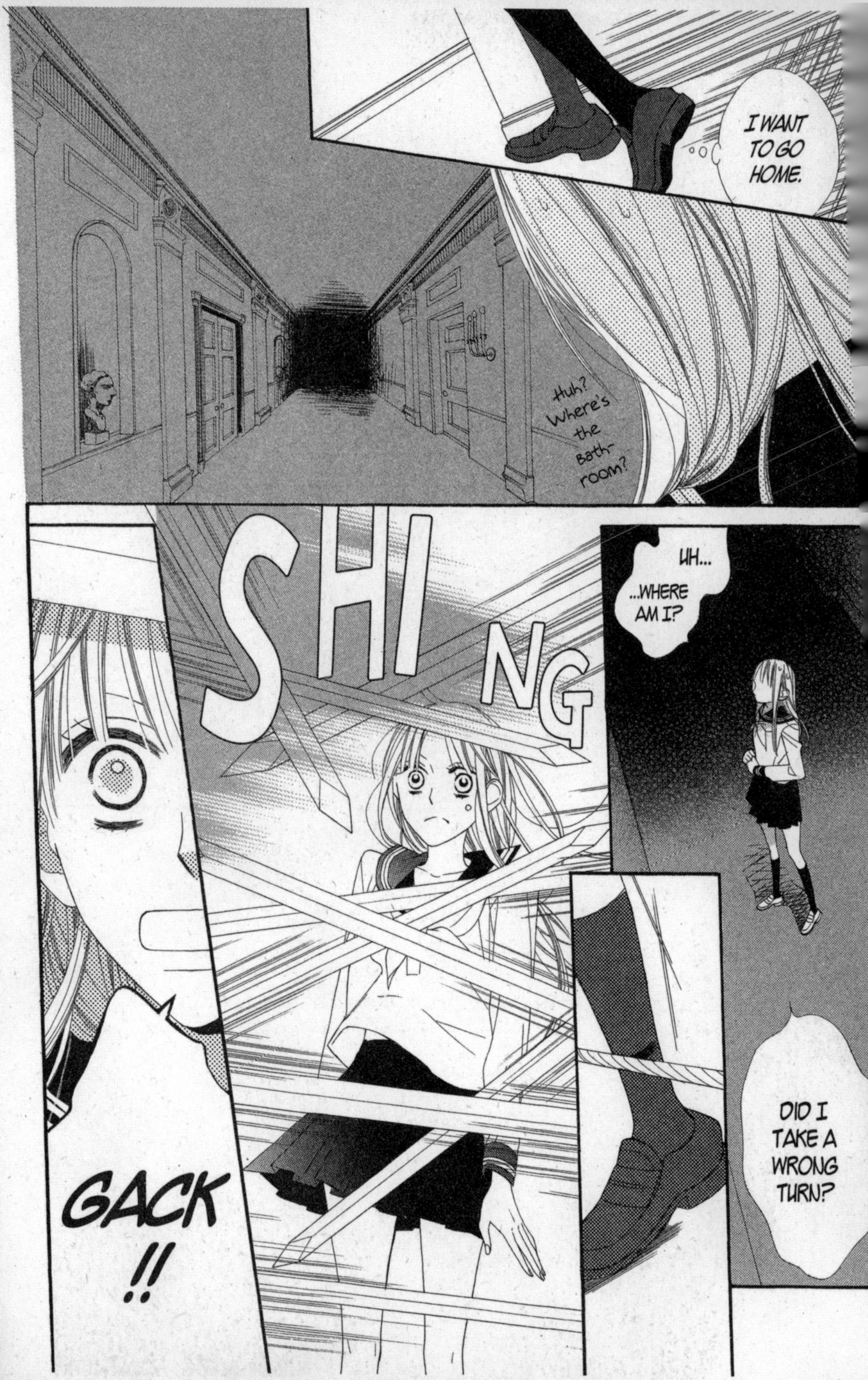
I WANT TO GO HOME.
Huh? Where's the bath-room?
UH...
...WHERE AM I?
DID I TAKE A WRONG TURN?
SHING
GACK!!

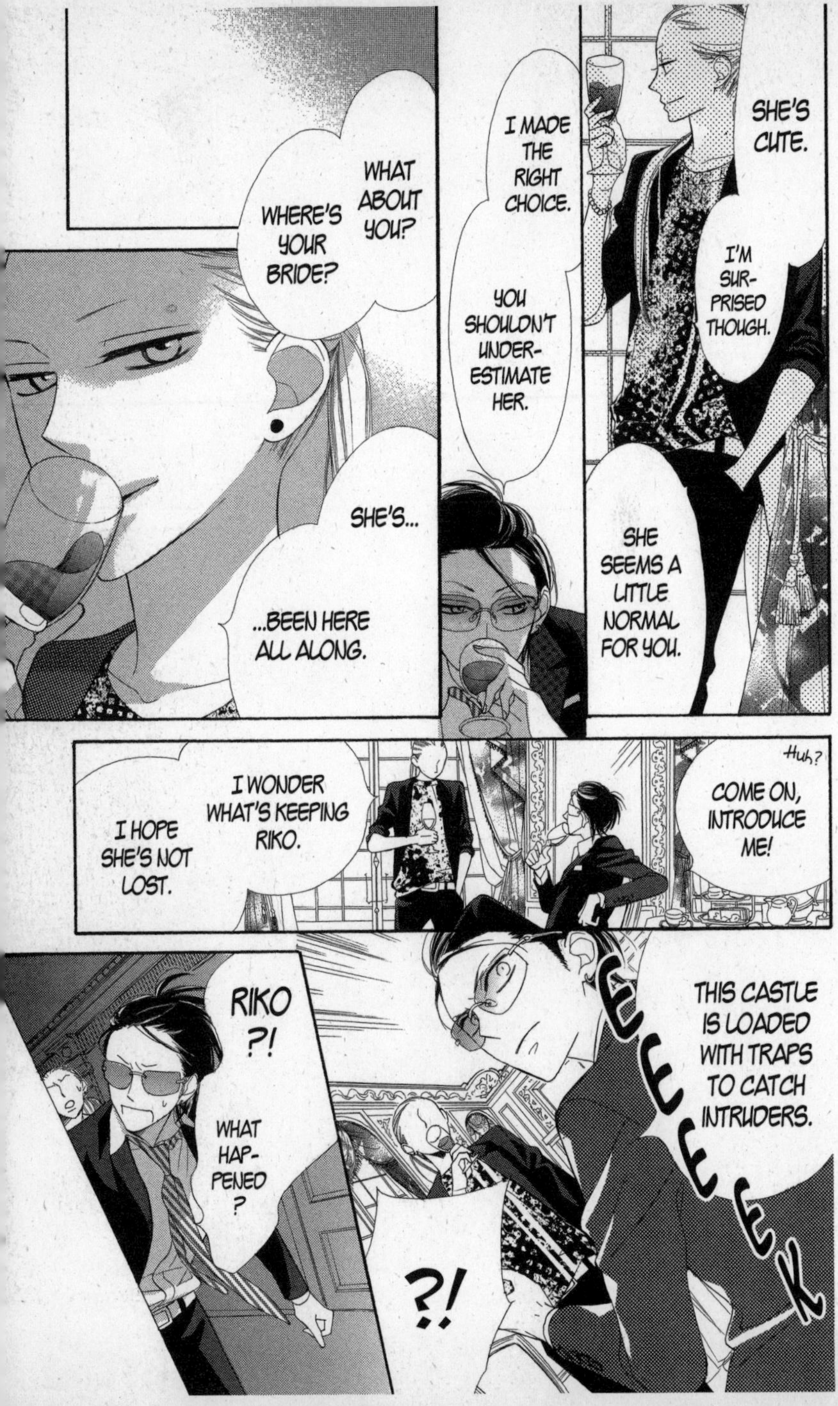
SHE'S CUTE.
I'M SURPRISED THOUGH.
SHE SEEMS A LITTLE NORMAL FOR YOU.
I MADE THE RIGHT CHOICE.
YOU SHOULDN'T UNDERESTIMATE HER.
WHAT ABOUT YOU?
WHERE'S YOUR BRIDE?
SHE'S...
...BEEN HERE ALL ALONG.
Huh?
COME ON, INTRODUCE ME!
I WONDER WHAT'S KEEPING RIKO.
I HOPE SHE'S NOT LOST.
THIS CASTLE IS LOADED WITH TRAPS TO CATCH INTRUDERS.
EEEEEEK
?!
RIKO?!
WHAT HAPPENED?

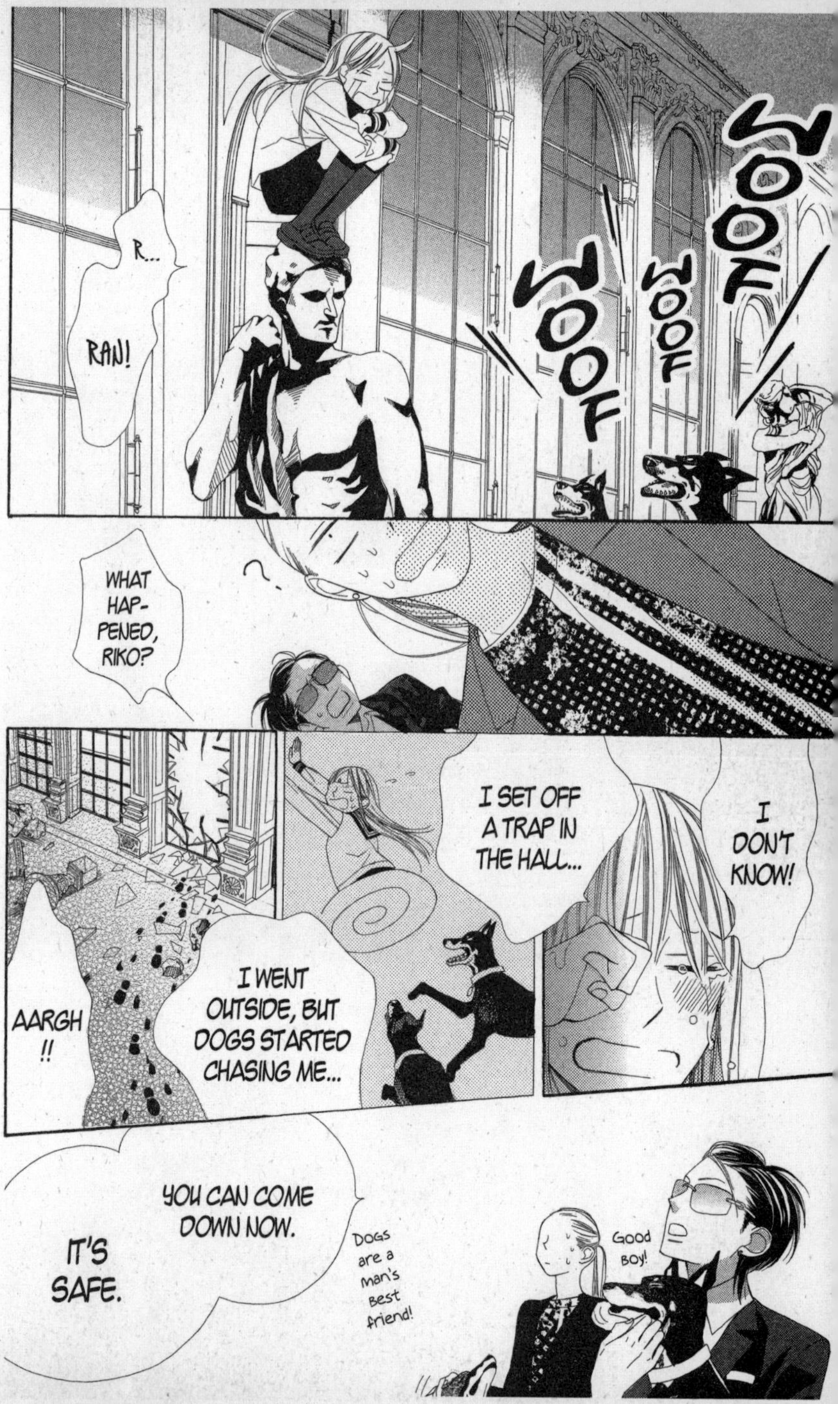
WOOF
WOOF
WOOF
R... RAN!
WHAT HAP-PENED, RIKO?
I DON'T KNOW!
I SET OFF A TRAP IN THE HALL...
I WENT OUTSIDE, BUT DOGS STARTED CHASING ME...
AARGH!!
Good boy!
Dogs are a man's best friend!
YOU CAN COME DOWN NOW.
IT'S SAFE.

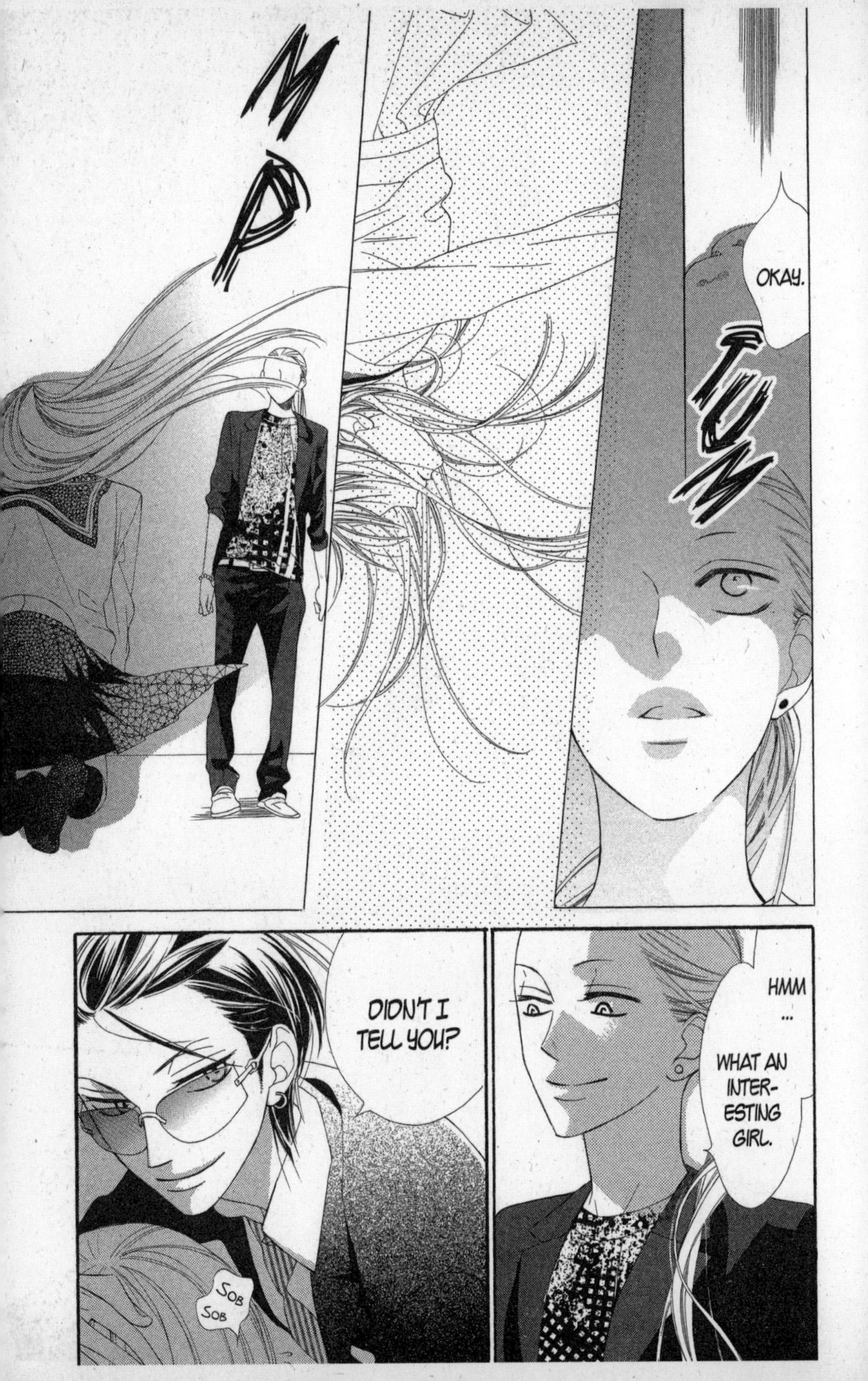
OKAY.
TUM
MP
HMM ... WHAT AN INTER-ESTING GIRL.
DIDN'T I TELL YOU?
SOB SOB

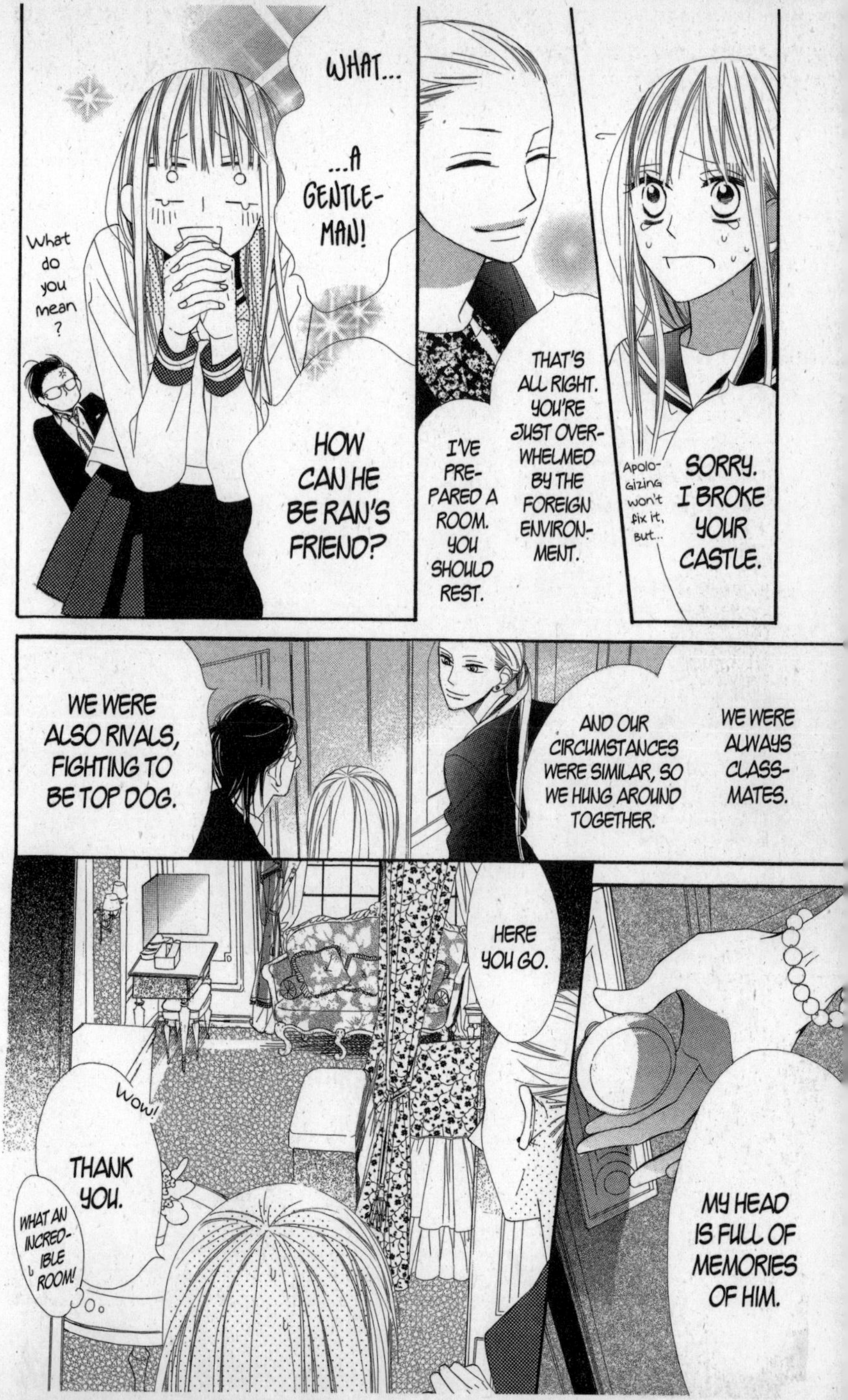
SORRY. I BROKE YOUR CASTLE.
Apologizing won't fix it, but...
THAT'S ALL RIGHT. YOU'RE JUST OVERWHELMED BY THE FOREIGN ENVIRONMENT.
I'VE PREPARED A ROOM. YOU SHOULD REST.
WHAT...
...A GENTLEMAN!
HOW CAN HE BE RAN'S FRIEND?
What do you mean?
WE WERE ALWAYS CLASSMATES.
AND OUR CIRCUMSTANCES WERE SIMILAR, SO WE HUNG AROUND TOGETHER.
WE WERE ALSO RIVALS, FIGHTING TO BE TOP DOG.
MY HEAD IS FULL OF MEMORIES OF HIM.
HERE YOU GO.
Wow!
THANK YOU.
WHAT AN INCREDIBLE ROOM!

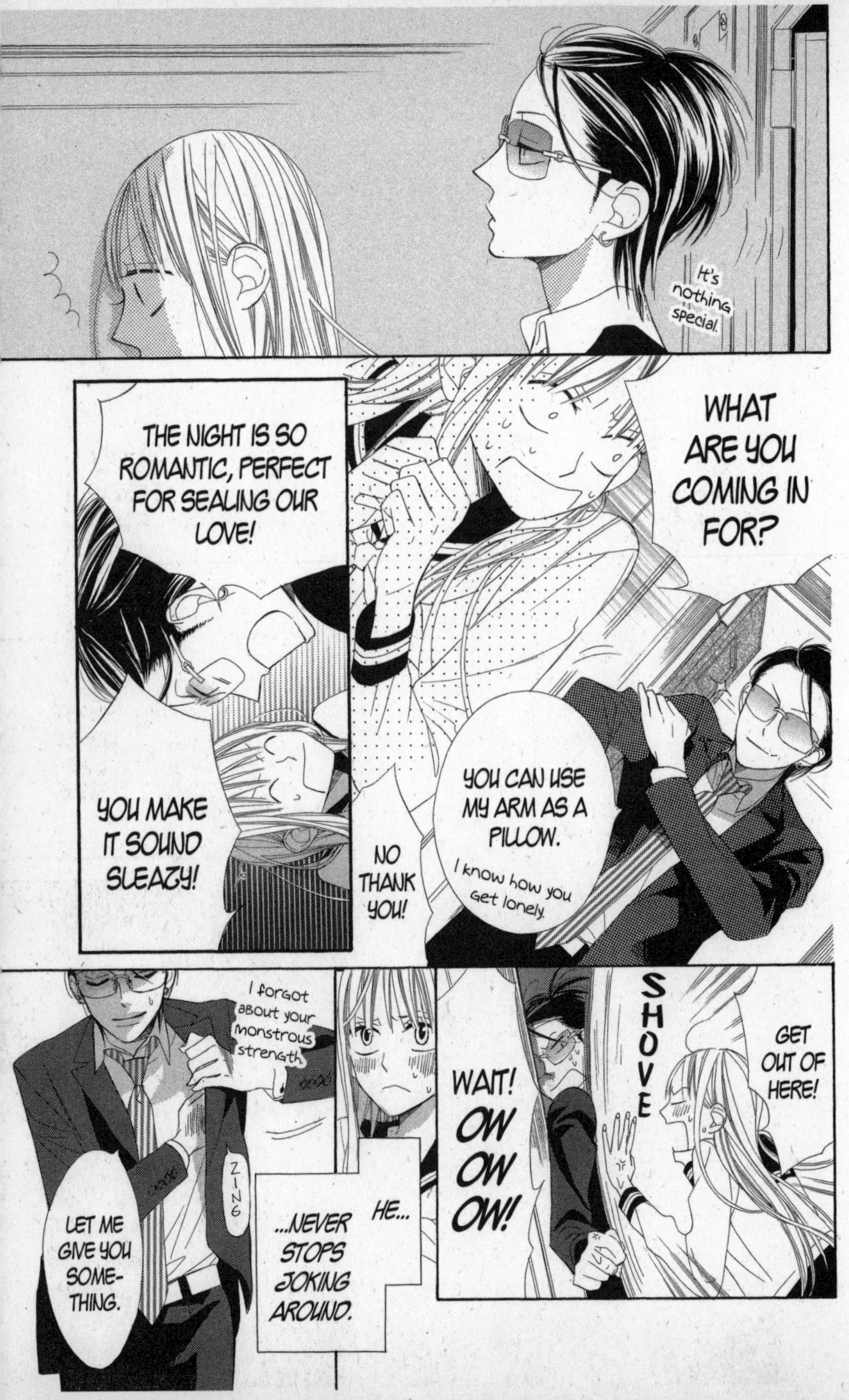
It's nothing special.
WHAT ARE YOU COMING IN FOR?
YOU CAN USE MY ARM AS A PILLOW.
I know how you get lonely.
NO THANK YOU!
THE NIGHT IS SO ROMANTIC, PERFECT FOR SEALING OUR LOVE!
YOU MAKE IT SOUND SLEAZY!
GET OUT OF HERE!
SHOVE
WAIT! OW OW OW!
HE...
...NEVER STOPS JOKING AROUND.
I forgot about your monstrous strength.
ZING
LET ME GIVE YOU SOME-THING.

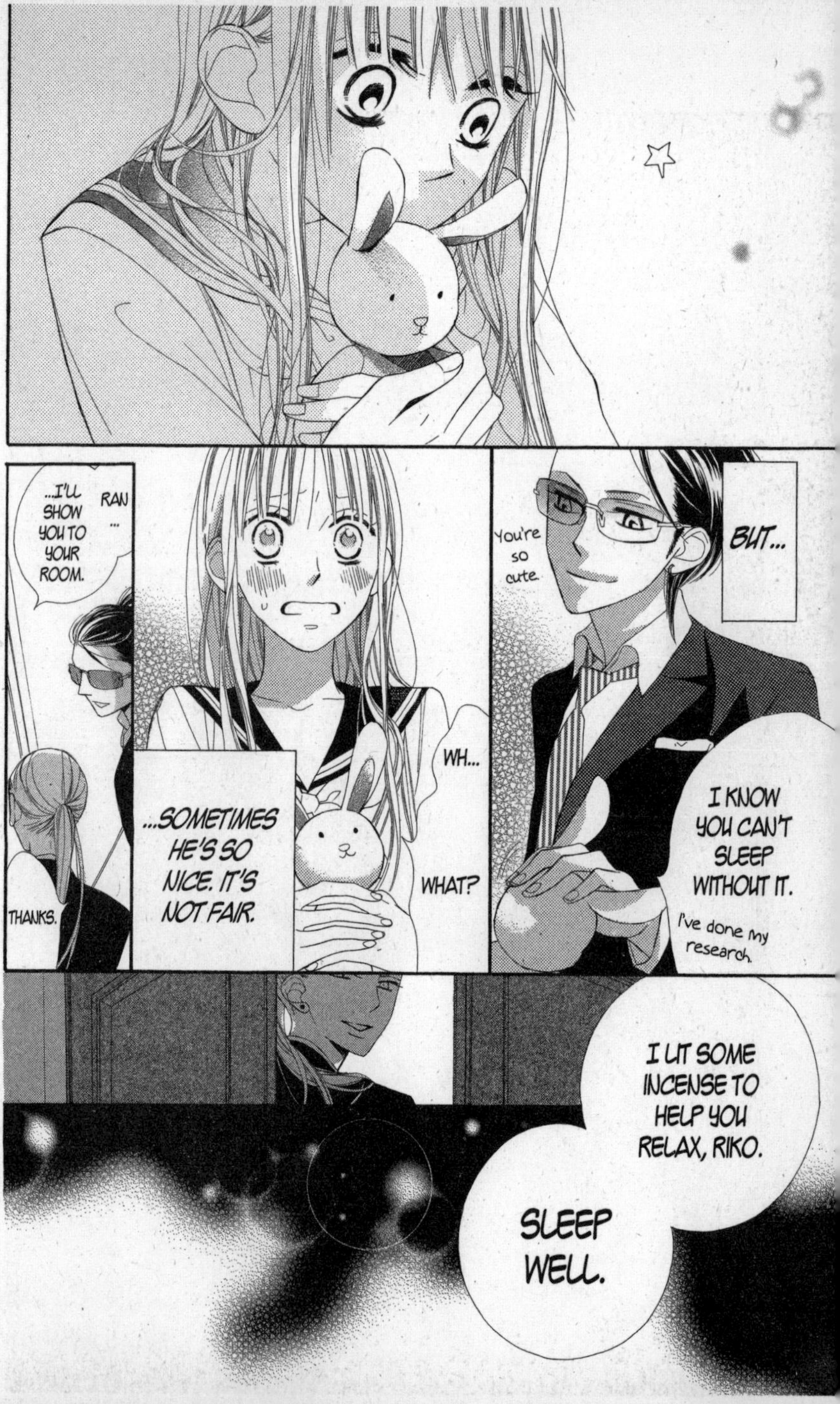
BUT...
You're so cute.
I KNOW YOU CAN'T SLEEP WITHOUT IT.
I've done my research.
WH...
WHAT?
...SOMETIMES HE'S SO NICE. IT'S NOT FAIR.
RAN...
...I'LL SHOW YOU TO YOUR ROOM.
THANKS.
I LIT SOME INCENSE TO HELP YOU RELAX, RIKO.
SLEEP WELL.

MM....?

DID SOMEONE COME IN?

FLICKR

HM?

I'M AWAKE...

...BUT I CAN'T MOVE.

KREAK

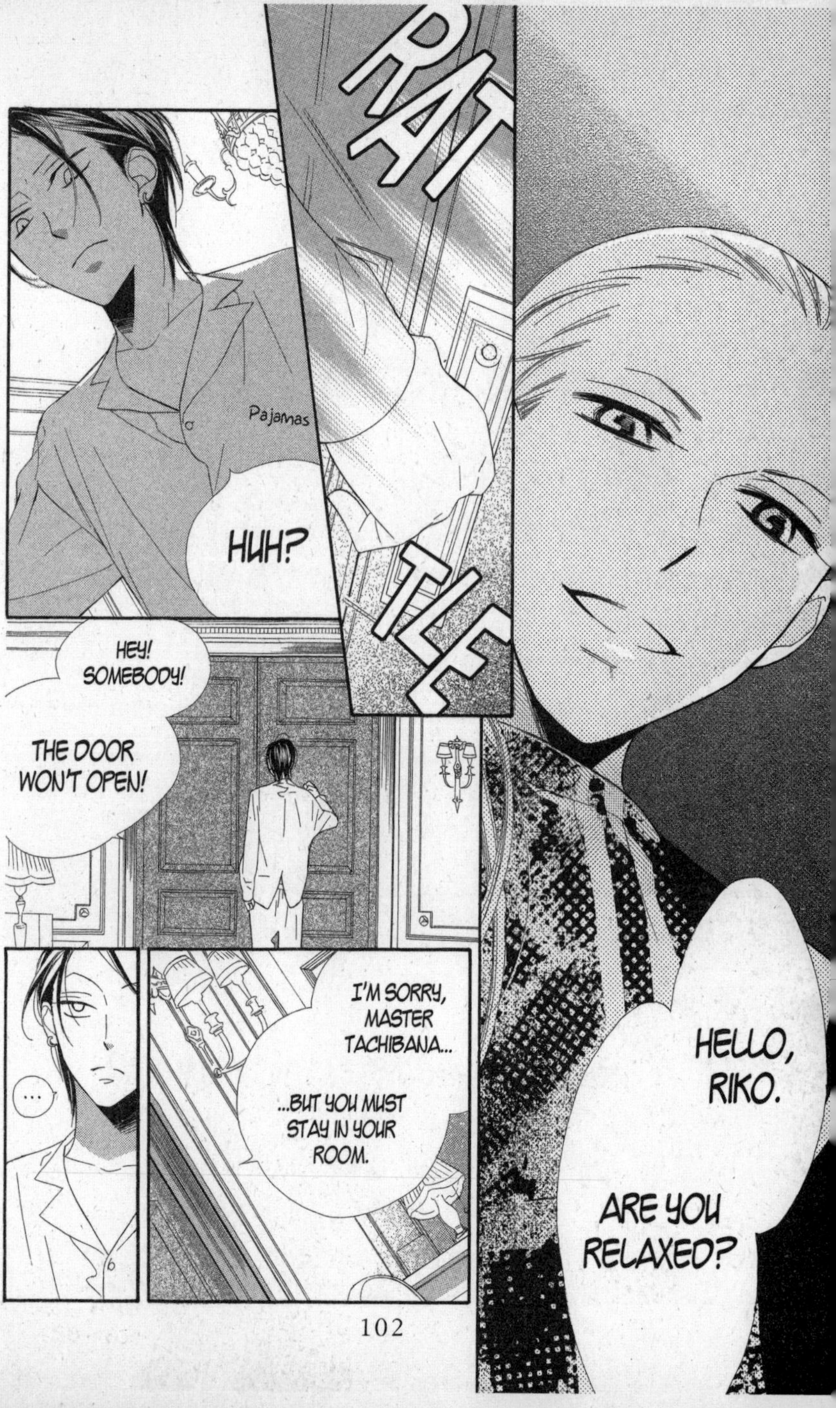
RATTLE
Pajamas
HUH?
HEY! SOMEBODY!
THE DOOR WON'T OPEN!
I'M SORRY, MASTER TACHIBANA...
...BUT YOU MUST STAY IN YOUR ROOM.
...
HELLO, RIKO.
ARE YOU RELAXED?

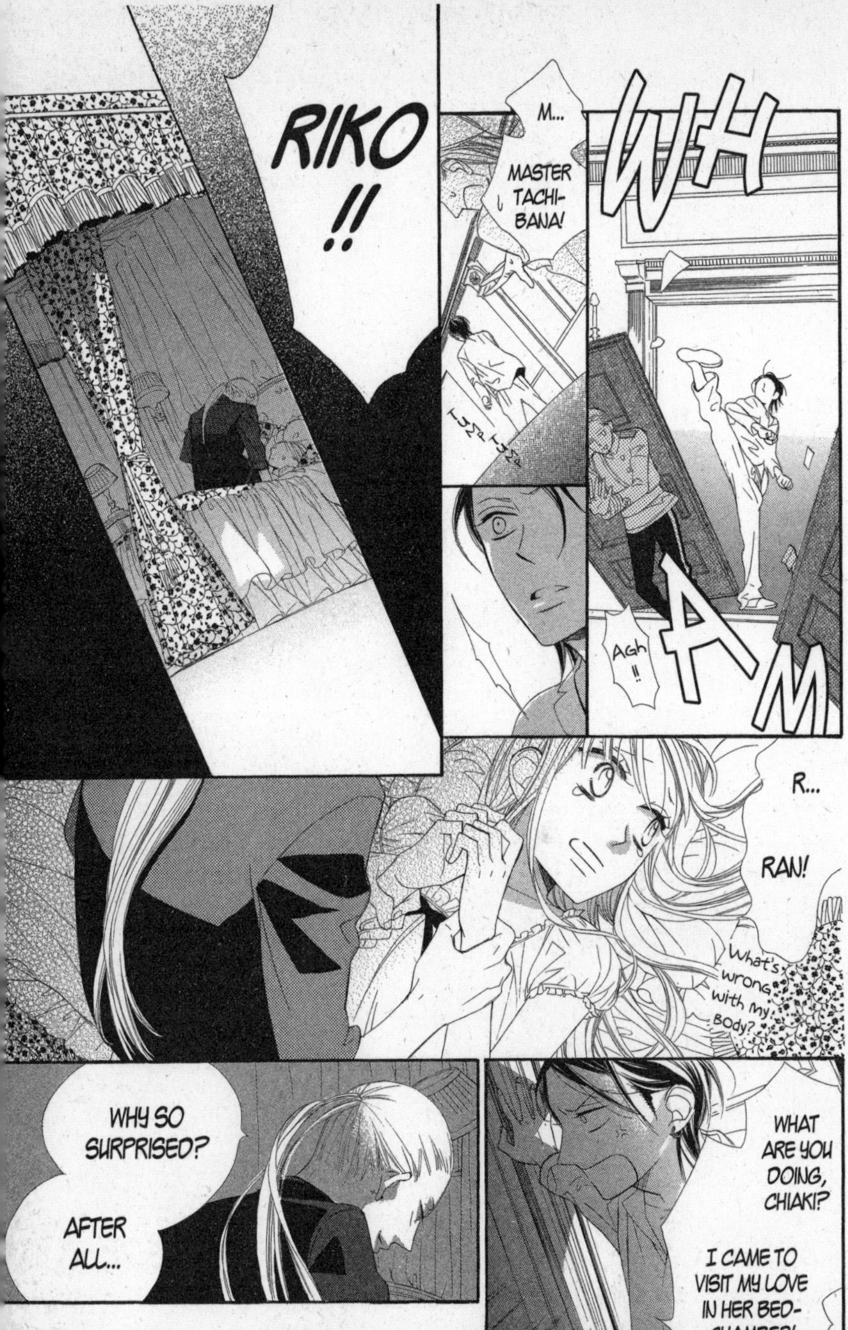
WH
AM
Agh!!
M...
MASTER TACHIBANA!
RIKO!!
R...
RAN!
What's wrong with my body?
WHAT ARE YOU DOING, CHIAKI?
I CAME TO VISIT MY LOVE IN HER BED-CHAMBER!
WHY SO SURPRISED?
AFTER ALL...

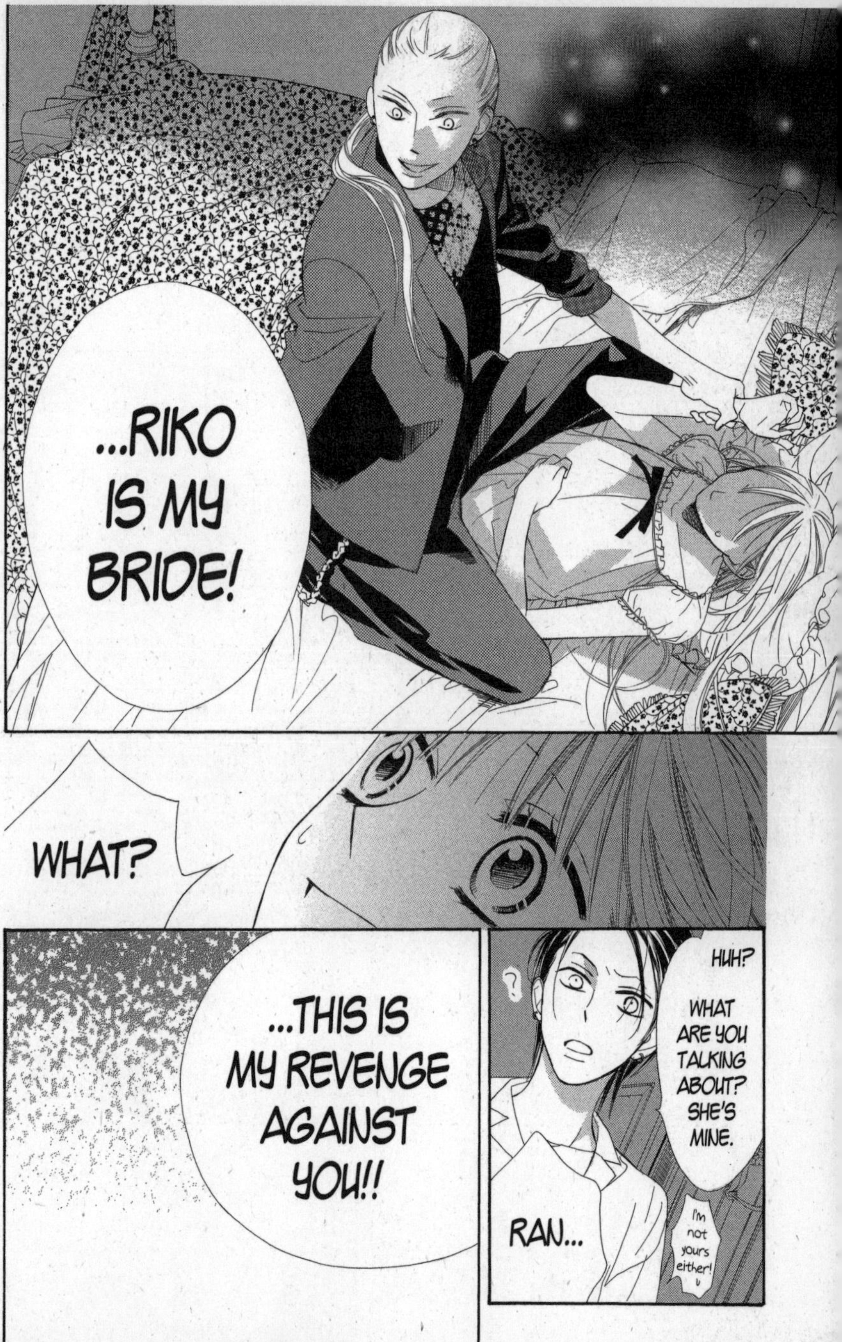
...RIKO IS MY BRIDE!
WHAT?
HUH?
WHAT ARE YOU TALKING ABOUT? SHE'S MINE.
I'm not yours either!
RAN...
...THIS IS MY REVENGE AGAINST YOU!!

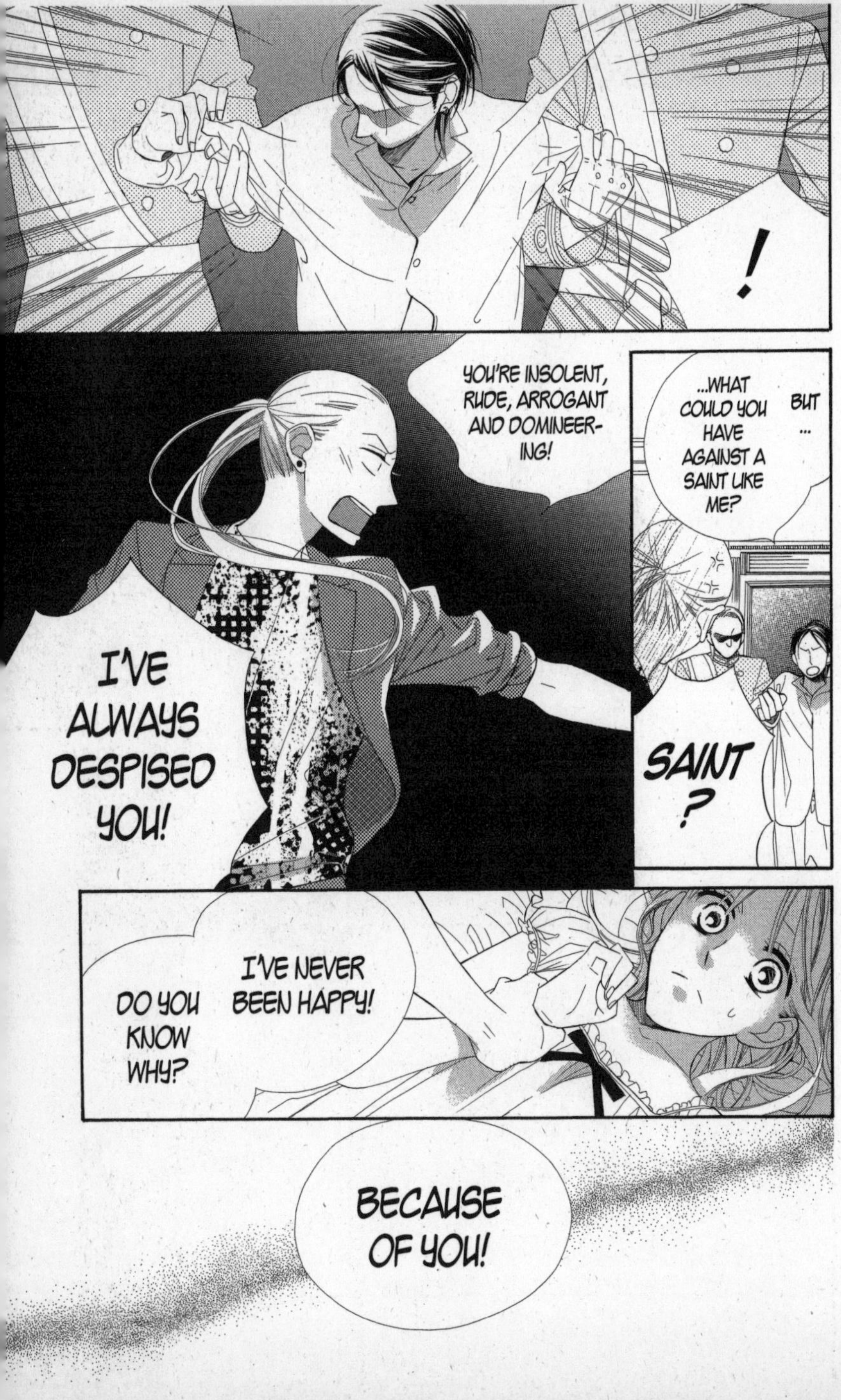
!
BUT ...
...WHAT COULD YOU HAVE AGAINST A SAINT LIKE ME?
SAINT?
YOU'RE INSOLENT, RUDE, ARROGANT AND DOMINEERING!
I'VE ALWAYS DESPISED YOU!
I'VE NEVER BEEN HAPPY!
DO YOU KNOW WHY?
BECAUSE OF YOU!

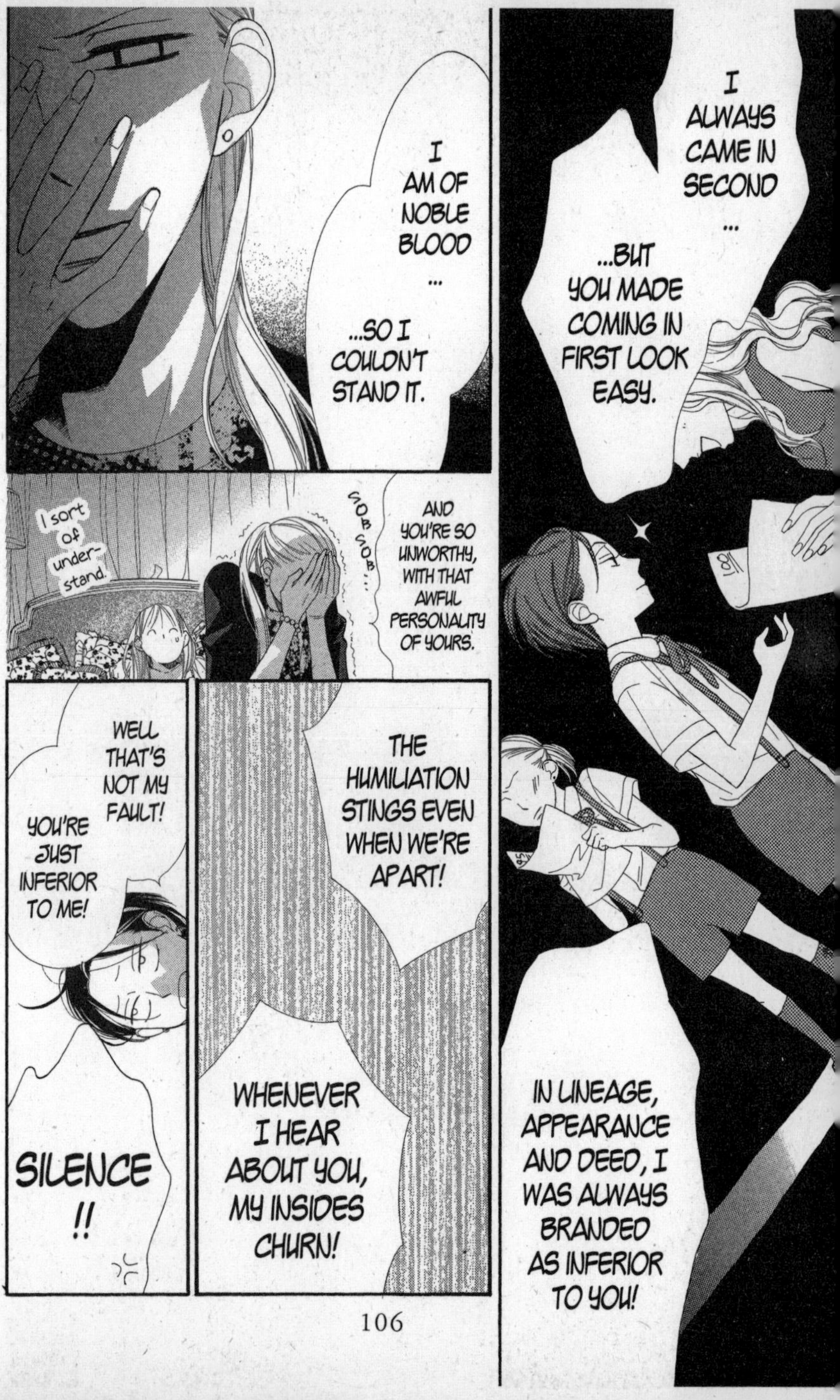
I ALWAYS CAME IN SECOND ...
...BUT YOU MADE COMING IN FIRST LOOK EASY.
IN LINEAGE, APPEARANCE AND DEED, I WAS ALWAYS BRANDED AS INFERIOR TO YOU!
I AM OF NOBLE BLOOD ...
...SO I COULDN'T STAND IT.
AND YOU'RE SO UNWORTHY, WITH THAT AWFUL PERSONALITY OF YOURS.
SOB SOB...
I sort of under-stand.
THE HUMILIATION STINGS EVEN WHEN WE'RE APART!
WHENEVER I HEAR ABOUT YOU, MY INSIDES CHURN!
WELL THAT'S NOT MY FAULT!
YOU'RE JUST INFERIOR TO ME!
SILENCE !!

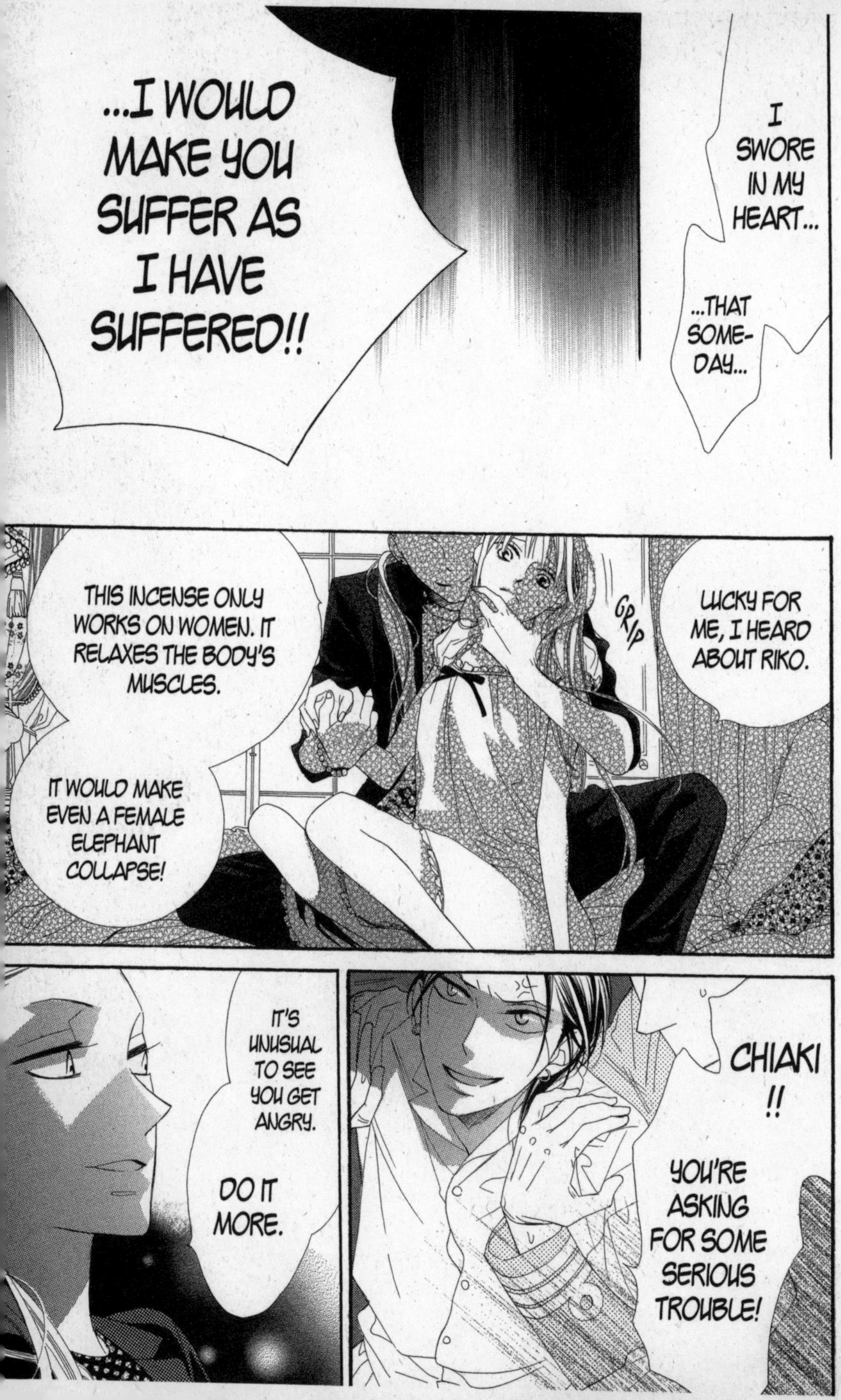
I SWORE IN MY HEART...
...THAT SOME-DAY...
...I WOULD MAKE YOU SUFFER AS I HAVE SUFFERED!!
LUCKY FOR ME, I HEARD ABOUT RIKO.
GRIP
THIS INCENSE ONLY WORKS ON WOMEN. IT RELAXES THE BODY'S MUSCLES.
IT WOULD MAKE EVEN A FEMALE ELEPHANT COLLAPSE!
CHIAKI !!
YOU'RE ASKING FOR SOME SERIOUS TROUBLE!
IT'S UNUSUAL TO SEE YOU GET ANGRY.
DO IT MORE.

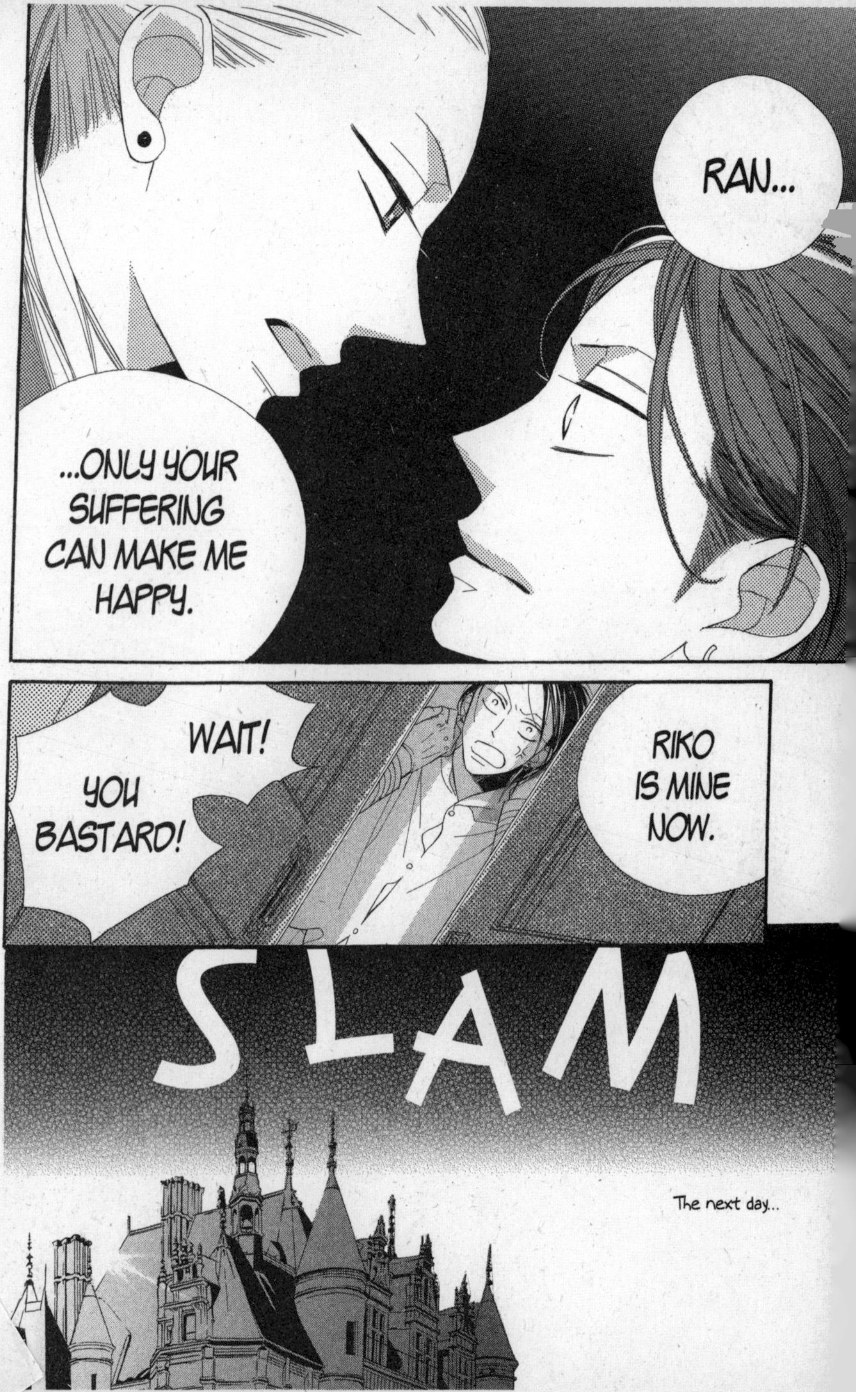
RAN...
...ONLY YOUR SUFFERING CAN MAKE ME HAPPY.
RIKO IS MINE NOW.
WAIT!
YOU BASTARD!
SLAM
The next day...

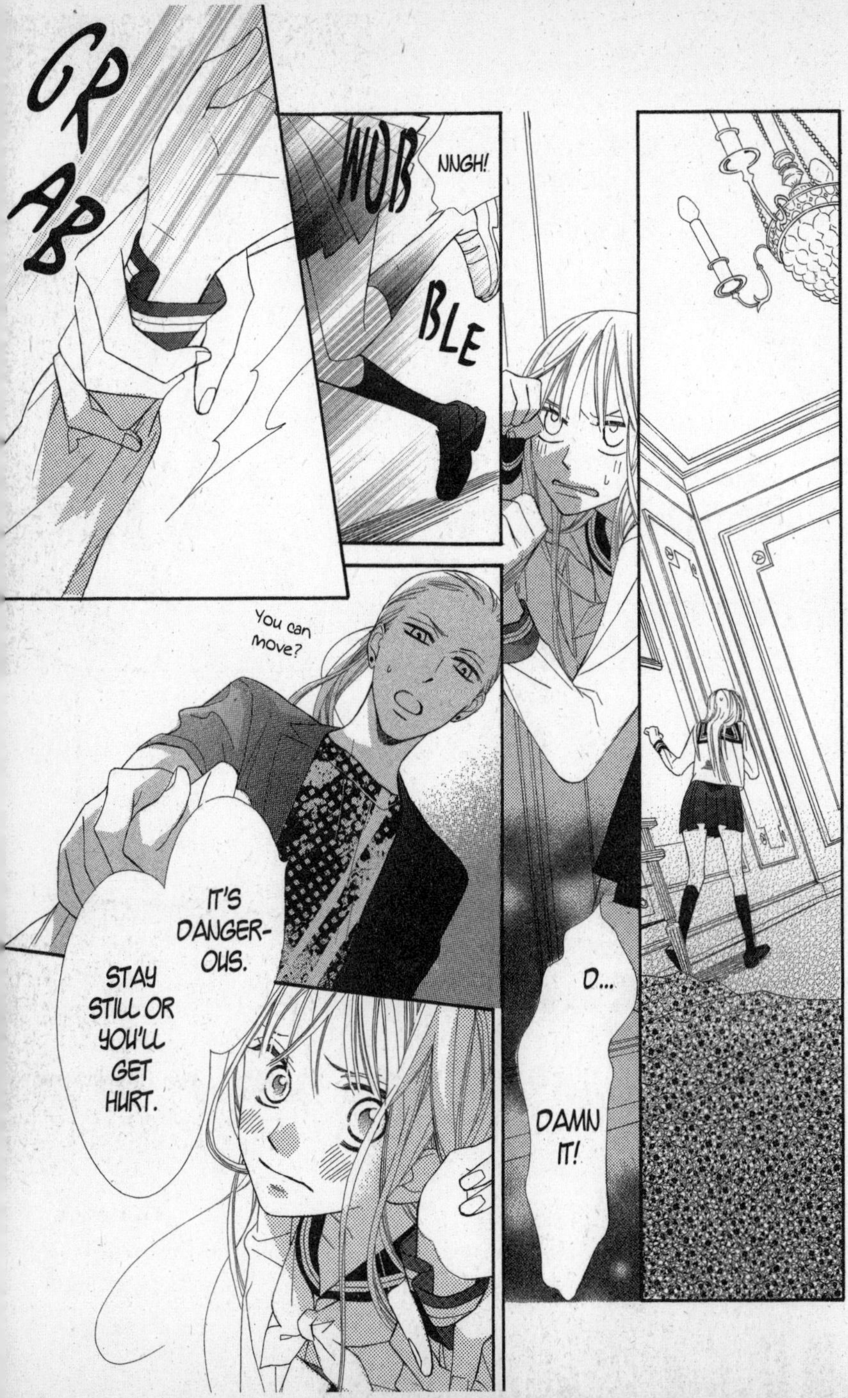
D...
DAMN IT!
WOBBLE
NNGH!
GRAB
You can move?
IT'S DANGER-OUS.
STAY STILL OR YOU'LL GET HURT.

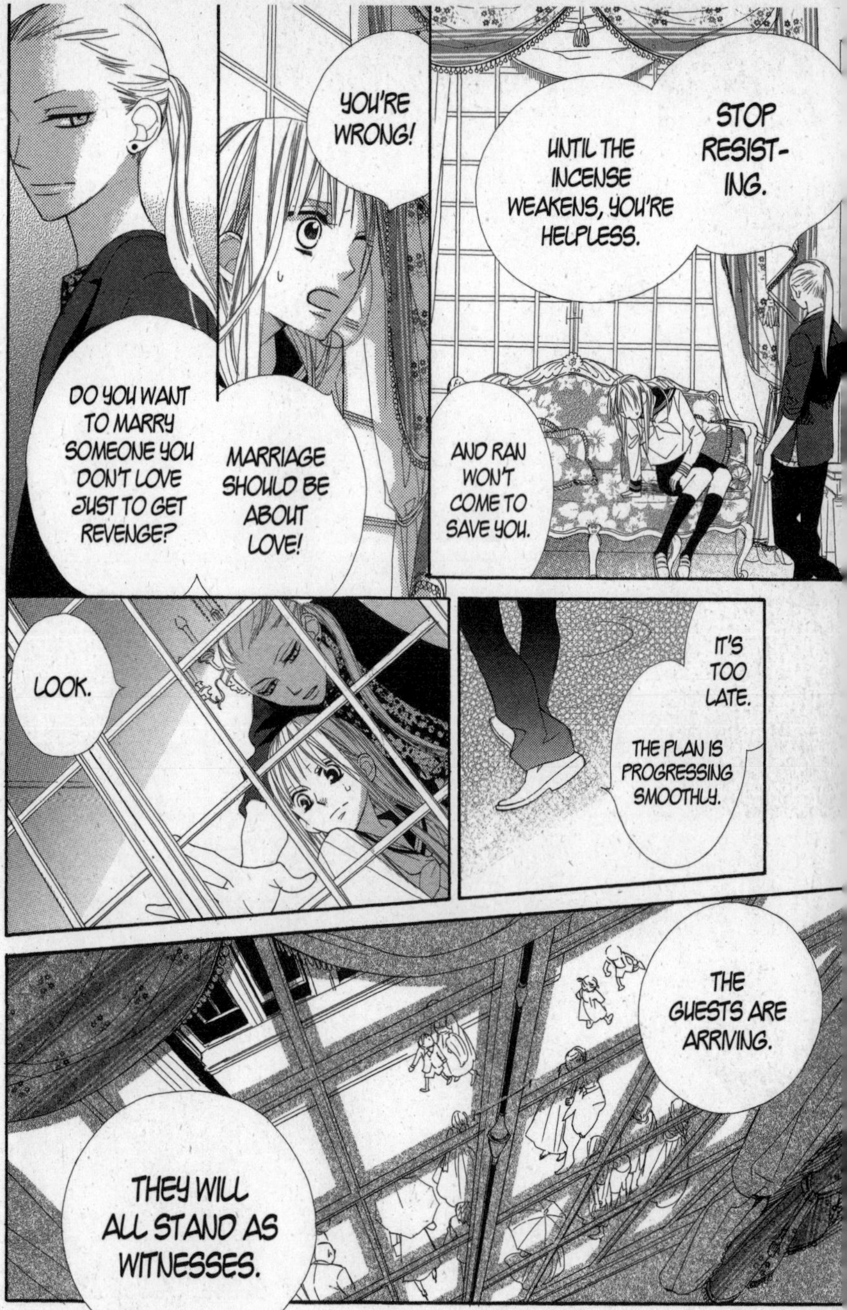
STOP RESIST-ING.
UNTIL THE INCENSE WEAKENS, YOU'RE HELPLESS.
AND RAN WON'T COME TO SAVE YOU.
YOU'RE WRONG!
MARRIAGE SHOULD BE ABOUT LOVE!
DO YOU WANT TO MARRY SOMEONE YOU DON'T LOVE JUST TO GET REVENGE?
IT'S TOO LATE.
THE PLAN IS PROGRESSING SMOOTHLY.
LOOK.
THE GUESTS ARE ARRIVING.
THEY WILL ALL STAND AS WITNESSES.

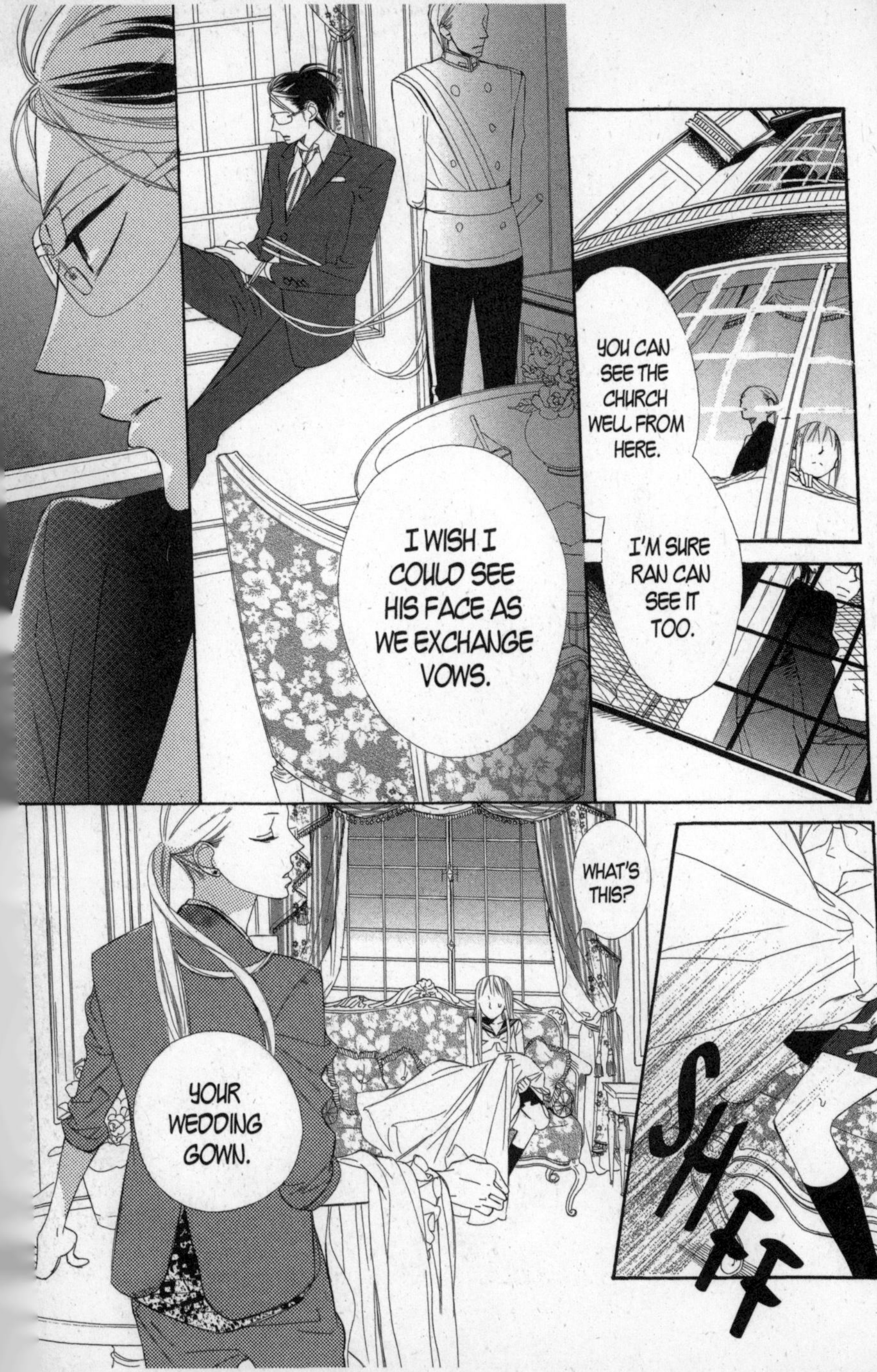
YOU CAN SEE THE CHURCH WELL FROM HERE.
I'M SURE RAN CAN SEE IT TOO.
I WISH I COULD SEE HIS FACE AS WE EXCHANGE VOWS.
SHFF
WHAT'S THIS?
YOUR WEDDING GOWN.

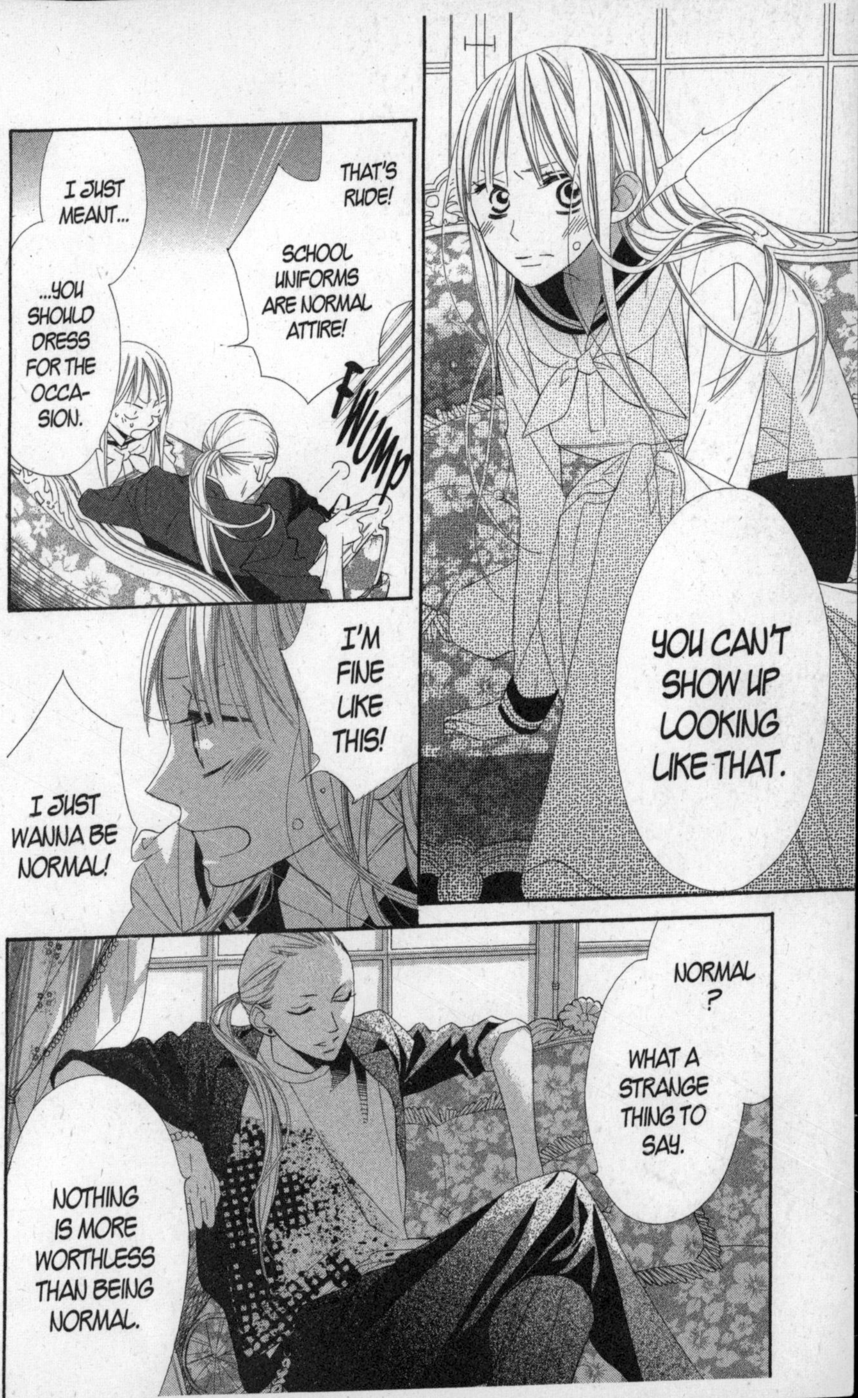
YOU CAN'T SHOW UP LOOKING LIKE THAT.
THAT'S RUDE!
SCHOOL UNIFORMS ARE NORMAL ATTIRE!
FWUMP
I JUST MEANT...
...YOU SHOULD DRESS FOR THE OCCASION.
I'M FINE LIKE THIS!
I JUST WANNA BE NORMAL!
NORMAL?
WHAT A STRANGE THING TO SAY.
NOTHING IS MORE WORTHLESS THAN BEING NORMAL.

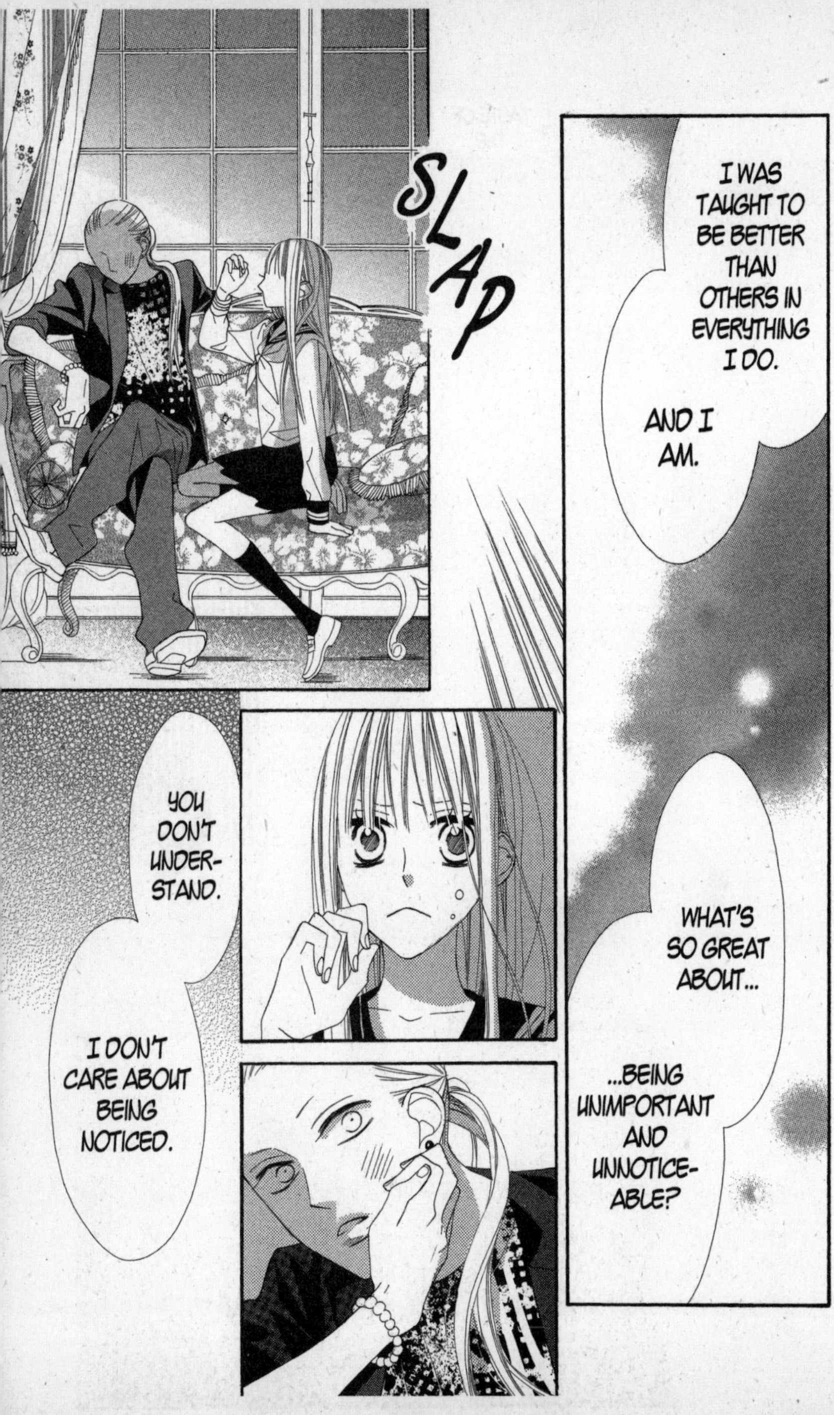
I WAS TAUGHT TO BE BETTER THAN OTHERS IN EVERYTHING I DO.
AND I AM.
WHAT'S SO GREAT ABOUT...
...BEING UNIMPORTANT AND UNNOTICE-ABLE?
SLAP
YOU DON'T UNDER-STAND.
I DON'T CARE ABOUT BEING NOTICED.

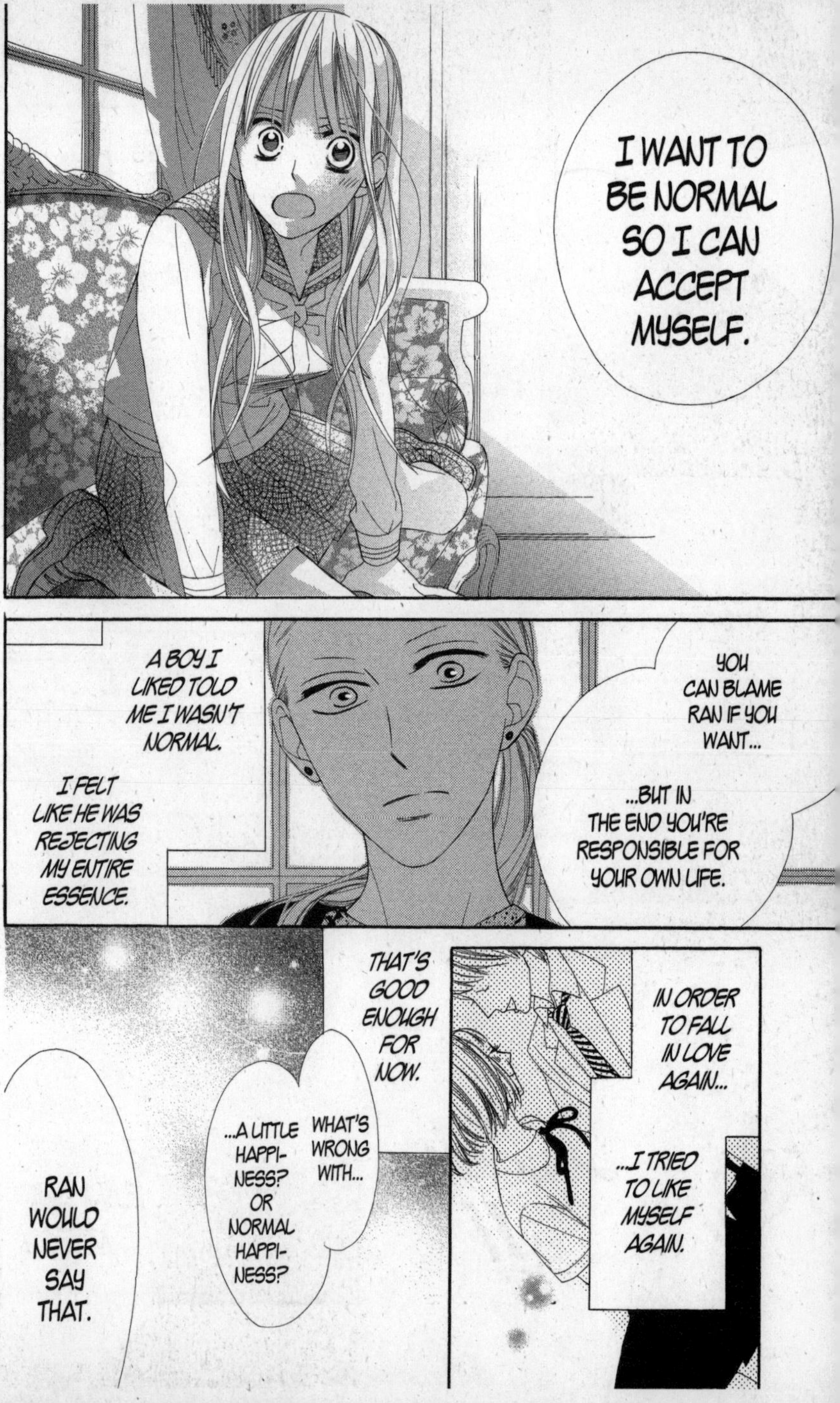
I WANT TO BE NORMAL SO I CAN ACCEPT MYSELF.
YOU CAN BLAME RAN IF YOU WANT...
...BUT IN THE END YOU'RE RESPONSIBLE FOR YOUR OWN LIFE.
A BOY I LIKED TOLD ME I WASN'T NORMAL.
I FELT LIKE HE WAS REJECTING MY ENTIRE ESSENCE.
IN ORDER TO FALL IN LOVE AGAIN...
...I TRIED TO LIKE MYSELF AGAIN.
THAT'S GOOD ENOUGH FOR NOW.
WHAT'S WRONG WITH...
...A LITTLE HAPPI-NESS? OR NORMAL HAPPI-NESS?
RAN WOULD NEVER SAY THAT.

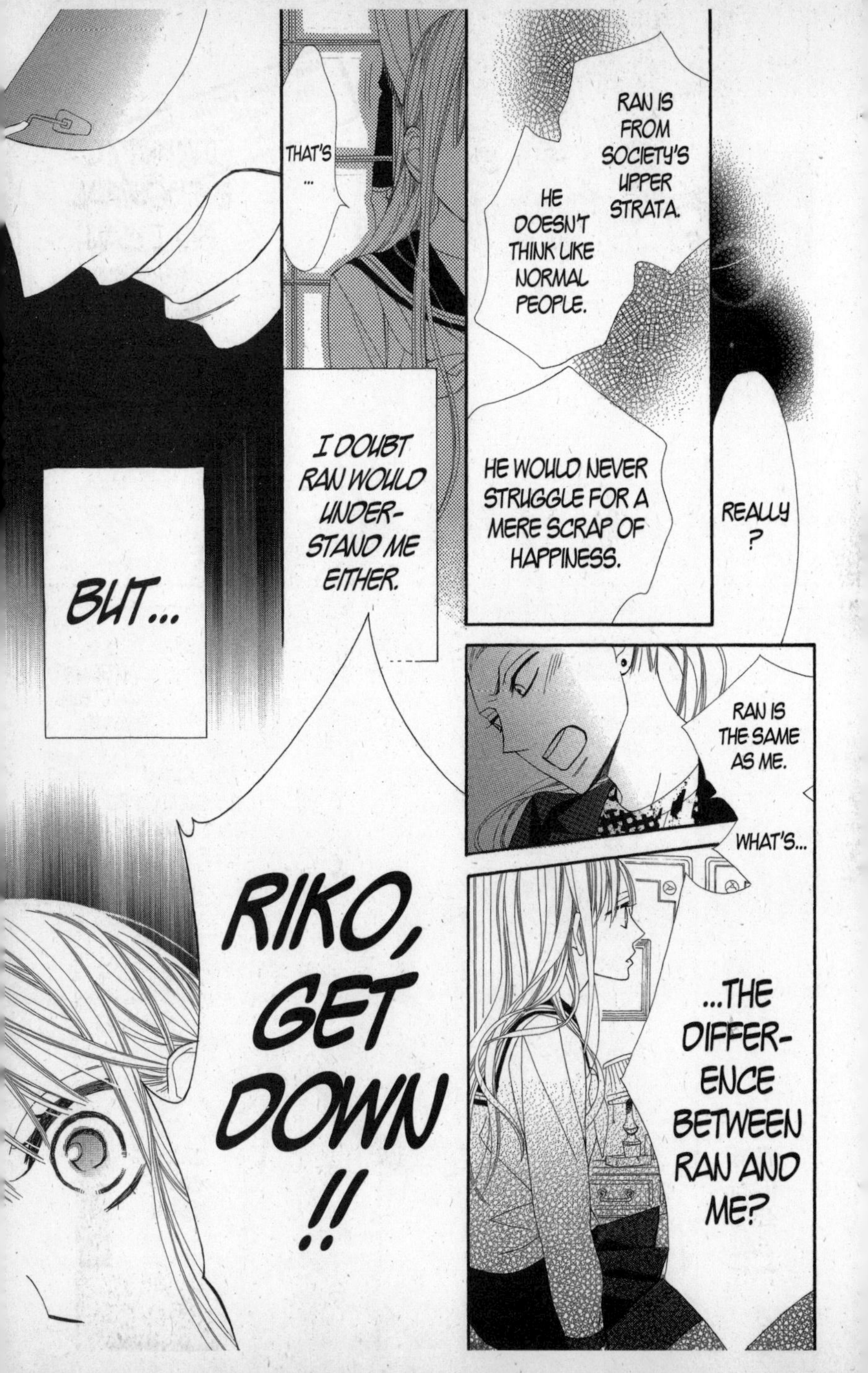
RAN IS FROM SOCIETY'S UPPER STRATA.
HE DOESN'T THINK LIKE NORMAL PEOPLE.
HE WOULD NEVER STRUGGLE FOR A MERE SCRAP OF HAPPINESS.
THAT'S ...
I DOUBT RAN WOULD UNDER-STAND ME EITHER.
BUT...
REALLY ?
RAN IS THE SAME AS ME.
WHAT'S...
...THE DIFFER-ENCE BETWEEN RAN AND ME?
RIKO, GET DOWN !!

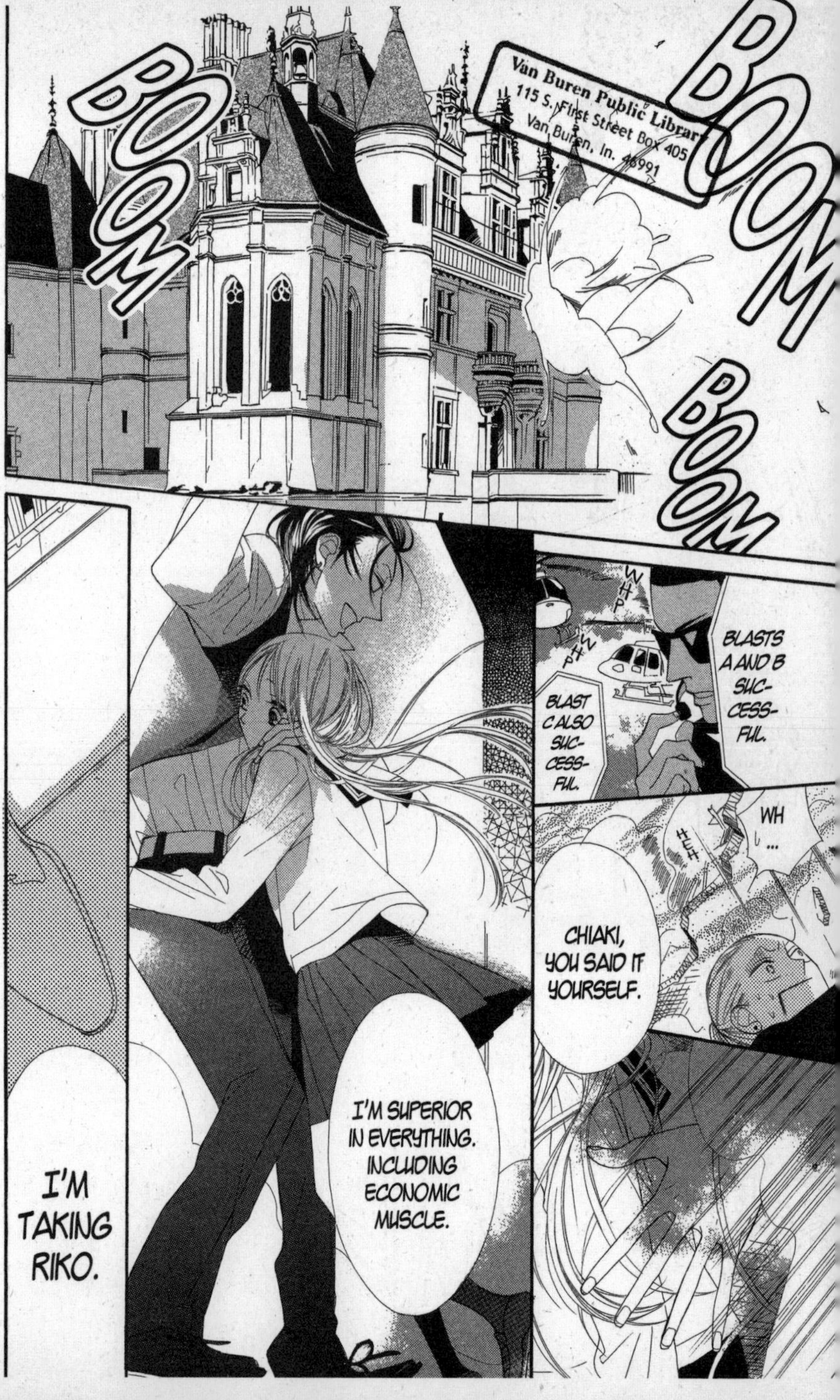
BOOM BOOM
BOOM
BOOM
WHP WHP
BLASTS A AND B SUCCESSFUL.
BLAST C ALSO SUCCESSFUL.
WH...
CHIAKI, YOU SAID IT YOURSELF.
I'M SUPERIOR IN EVERYTHING. INCLUDING ECONOMIC MUSCLE.
I'M TAKING RIKO.

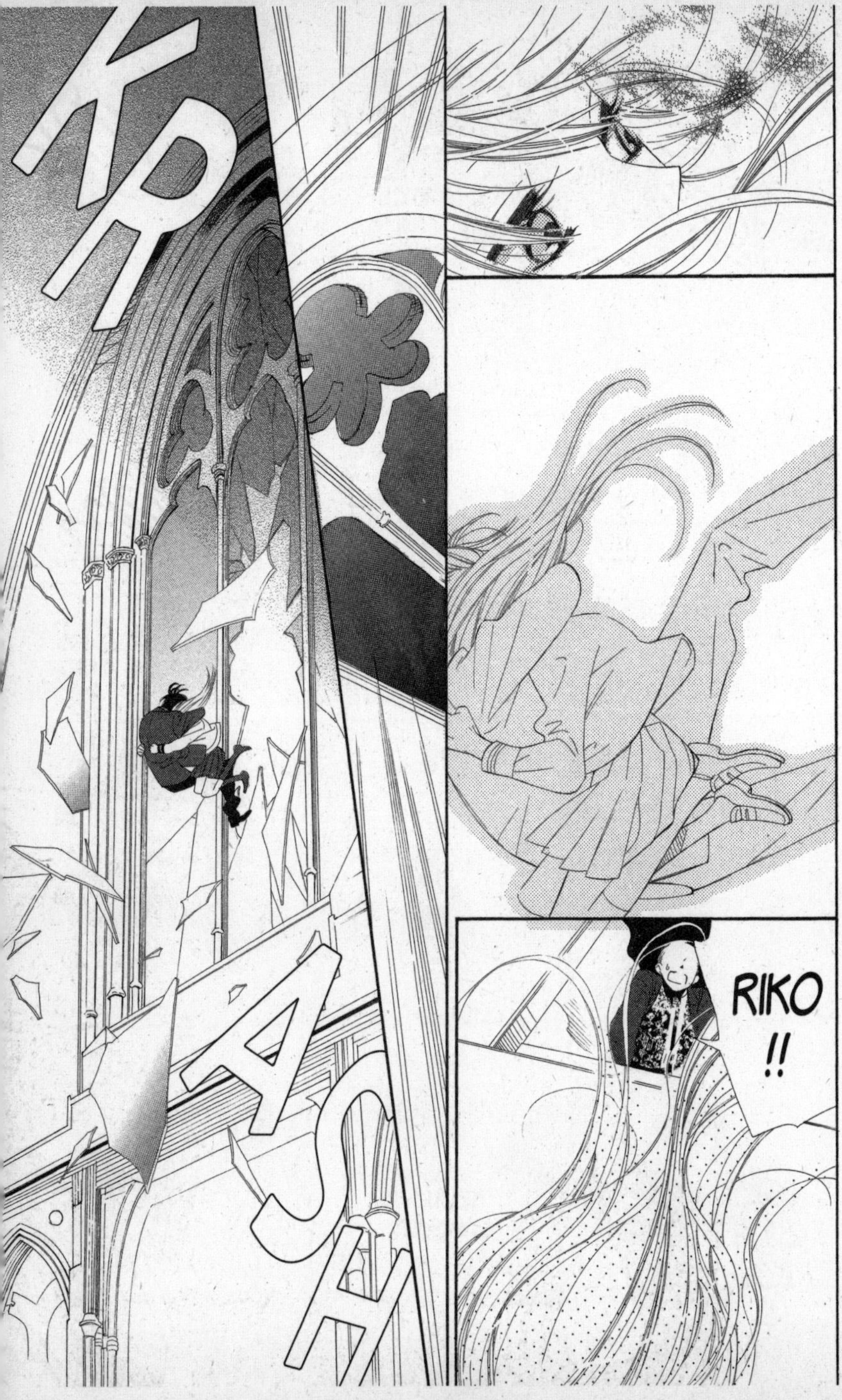
RIKO
!!
KRI
ASH

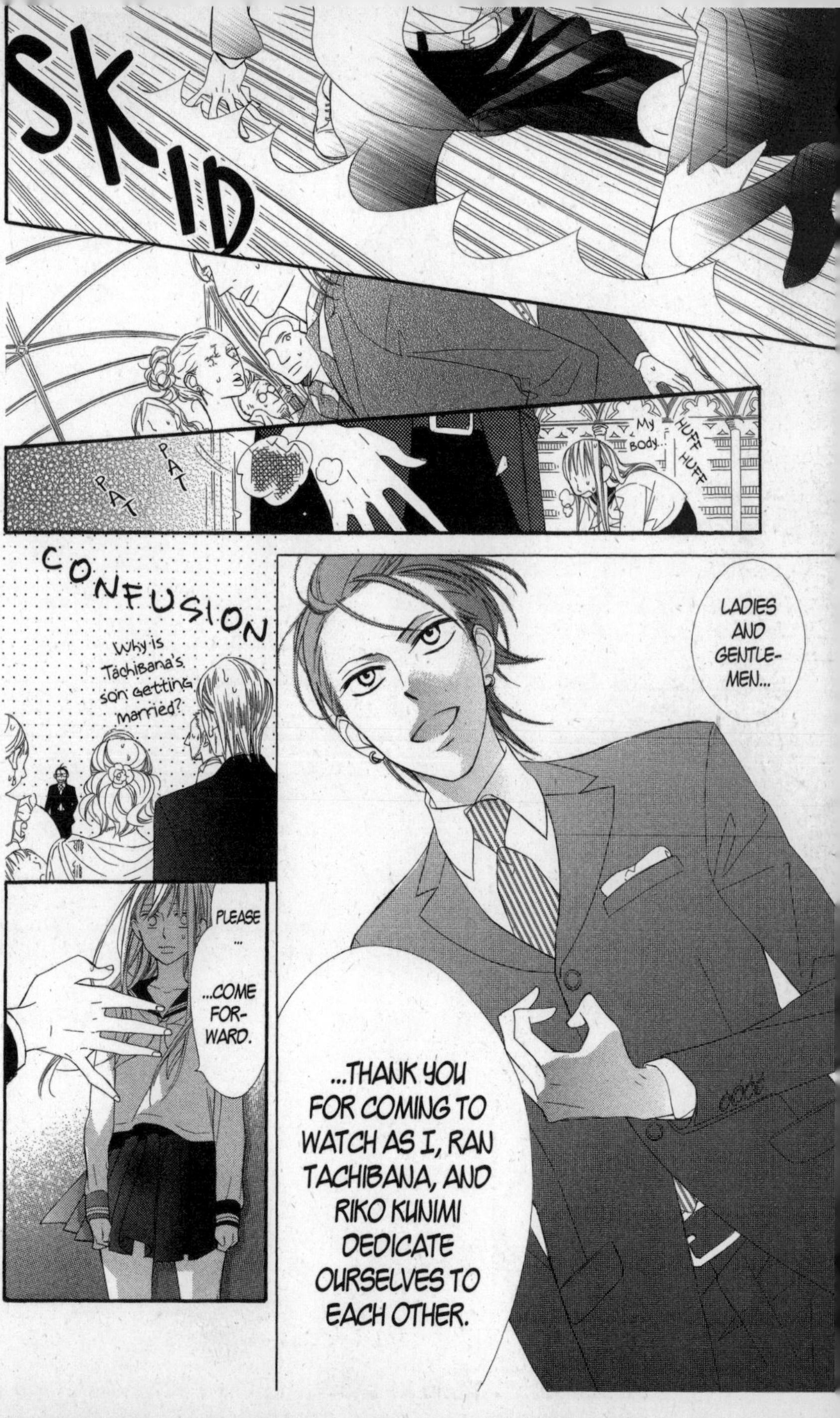
SKID
My body...
HUFF HUFF
PAT PAT
LADIES AND GENTLE-MEN...
...THANK YOU FOR COMING TO WATCH AS I, RAN TACHIBANA, AND RIKO KUNIMI DEDICATE OURSELVES TO EACH OTHER.
CONFUSION
Why is Tachibana's son getting married?
PLEASE ...
...COME FOR-WARD.

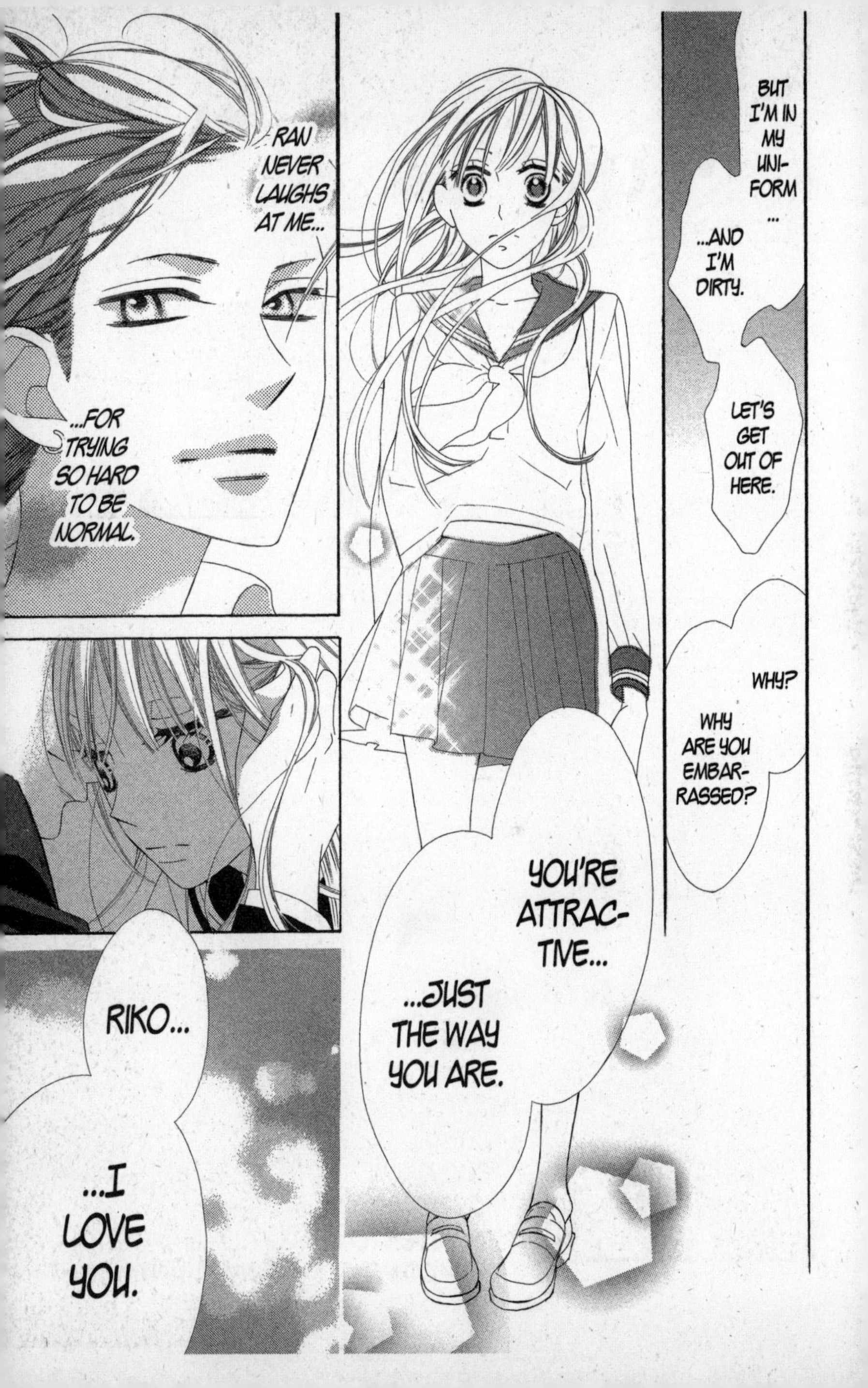
BUT I'M IN MY UNI-FORM...
...AND I'M DIRTY.
LET'S GET OUT OF HERE.
WHY?
WHY ARE YOU EMBAR-RASSED?
YOU'RE ATTRAC-TIVE...
...JUST THE WAY YOU ARE.
RAN NEVER LAUGHS AT ME...
...FOR TRYING SO HARD TO BE NORMAL.
RIKO...
...I LOVE YOU.

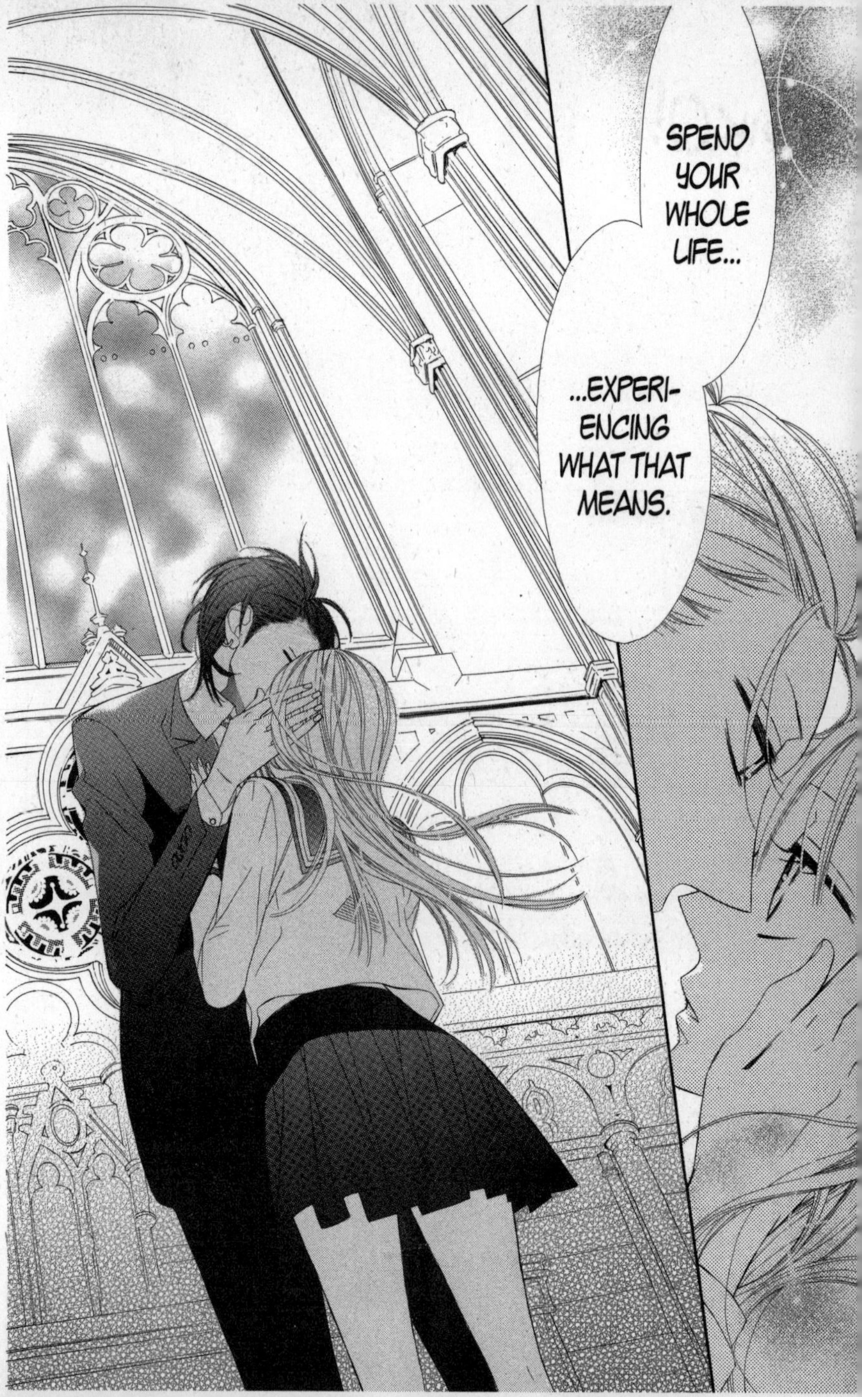
SPEND YOUR WHOLE LIFE...
...EXPERI-ENCING WHAT THAT MEANS.

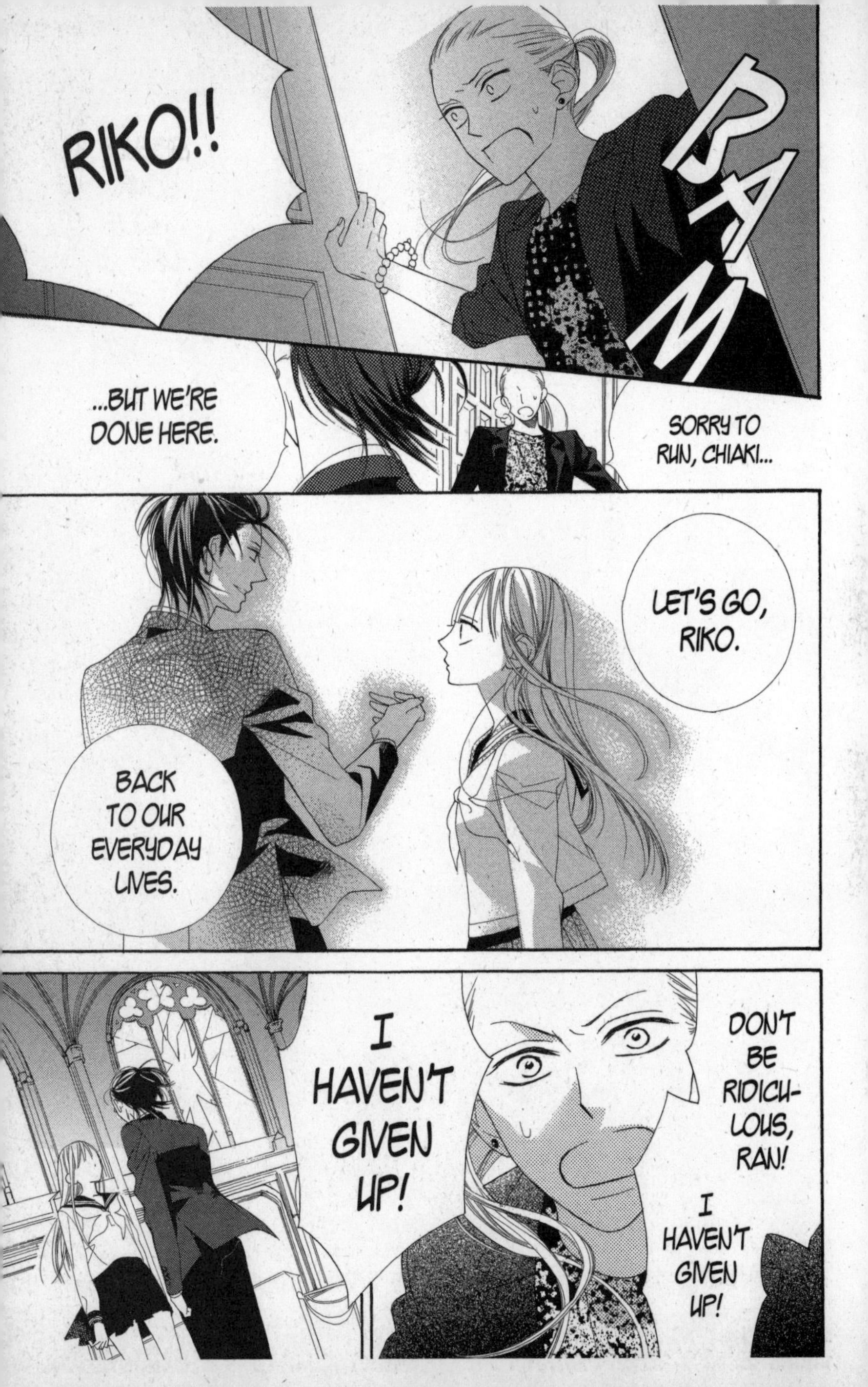
BAM
RIKO!!
SORRY TO RUN, CHIAKI...
...BUT WE'RE DONE HERE.
LET'S GO, RIKO.
BACK TO OUR EVERYDAY LIVES.
DON'T BE RIDICU-LOUS, RAN!
I HAVEN'T GIVEN UP!
I HAVEN'T GIVEN UP!

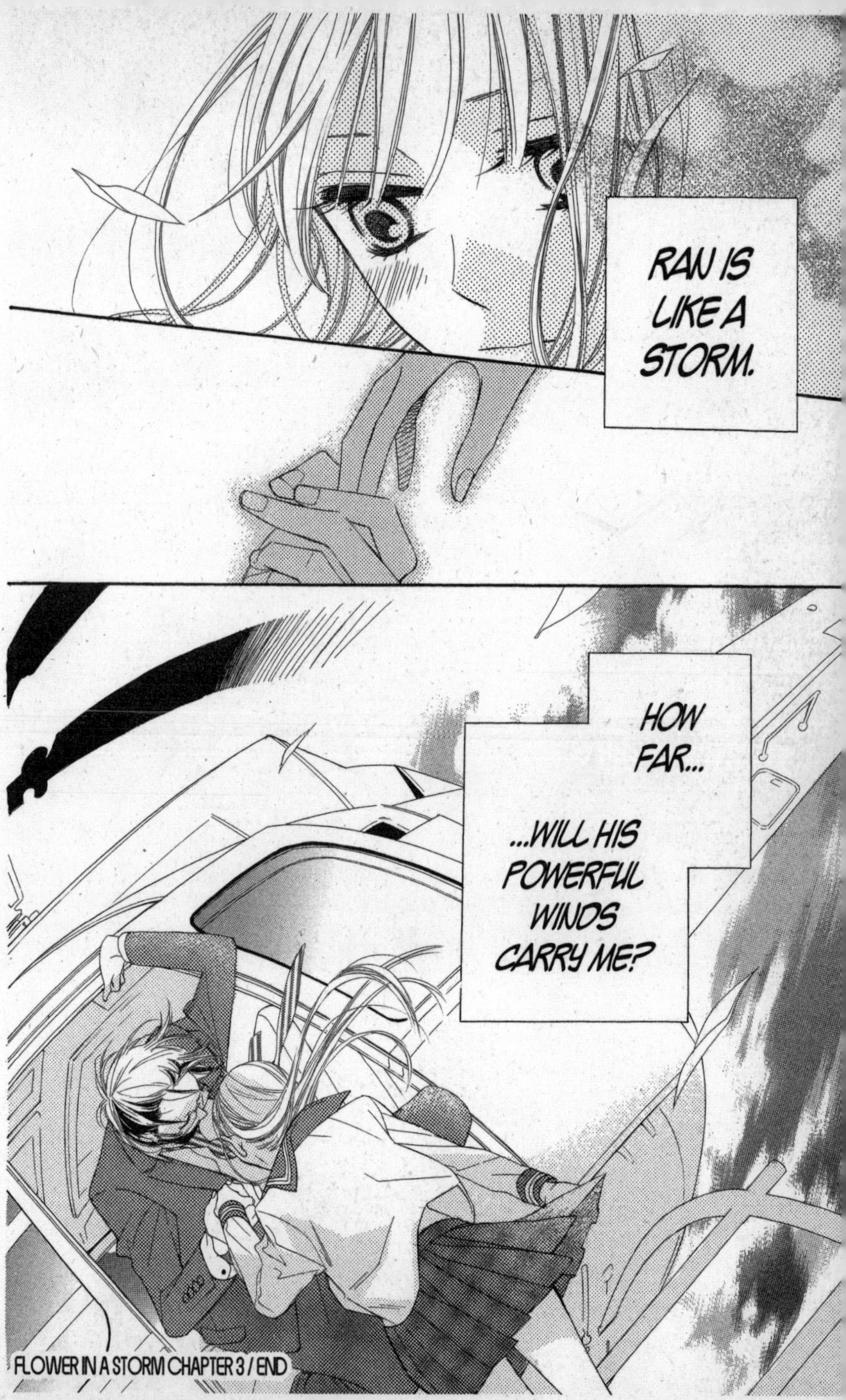
RAN IS LIKE A STORM.
HOW FAR...
...WILL HIS POWERFUL WINDS CARRY ME?
FLOWER IN A STORM CHAPTER 3 / END

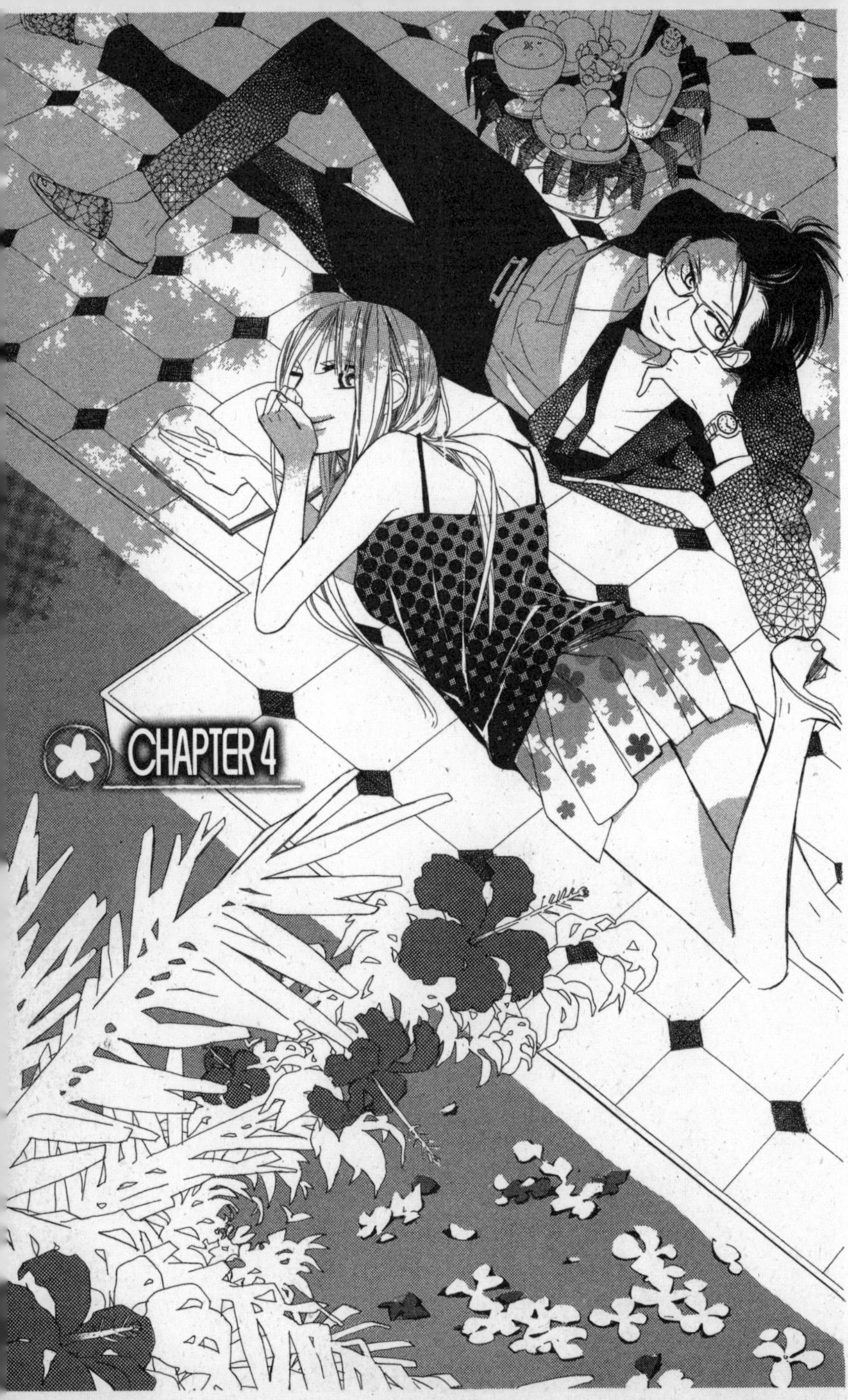
CHAPTER 4

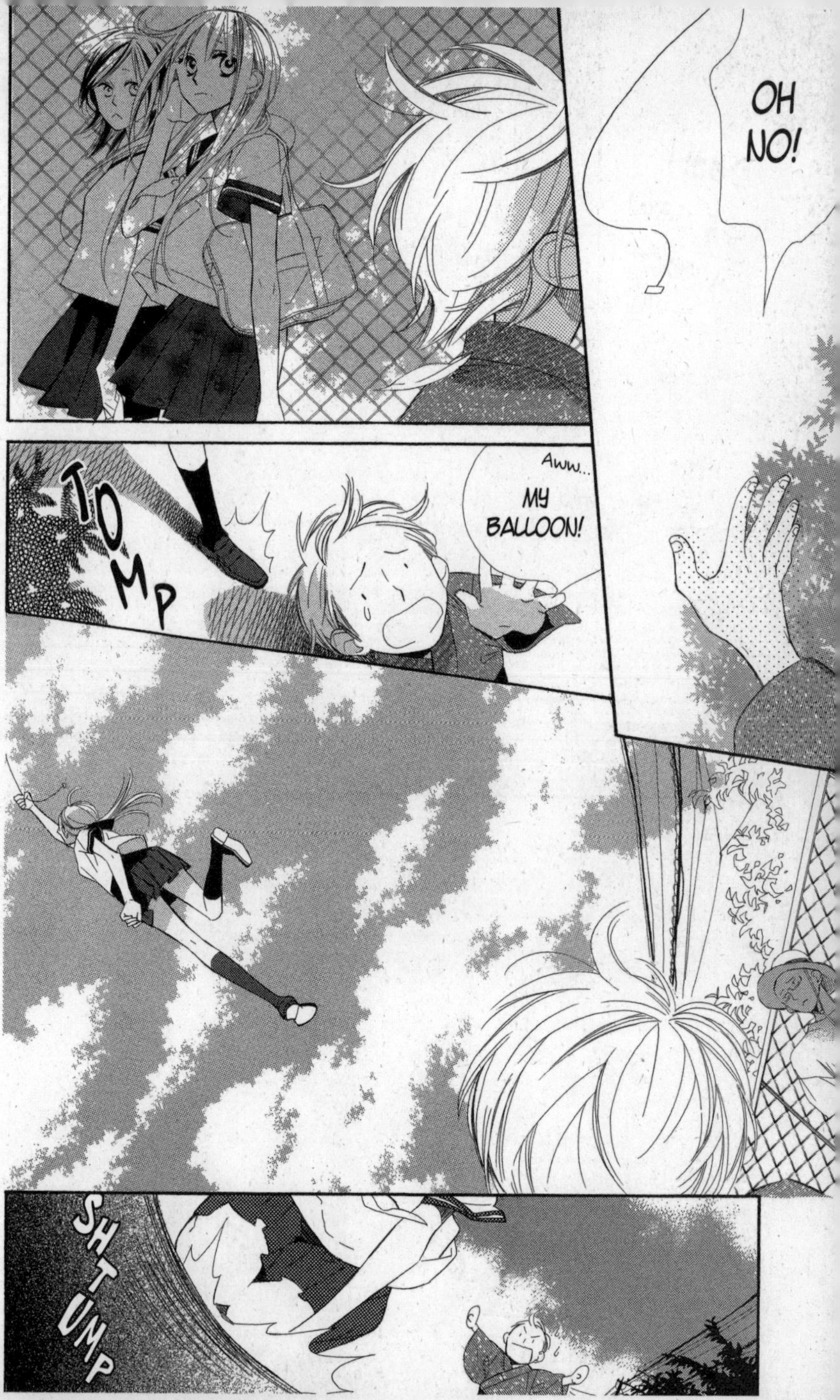
OH NO!
Aww...
MY BALLOON!
TOMP
SHTUMP

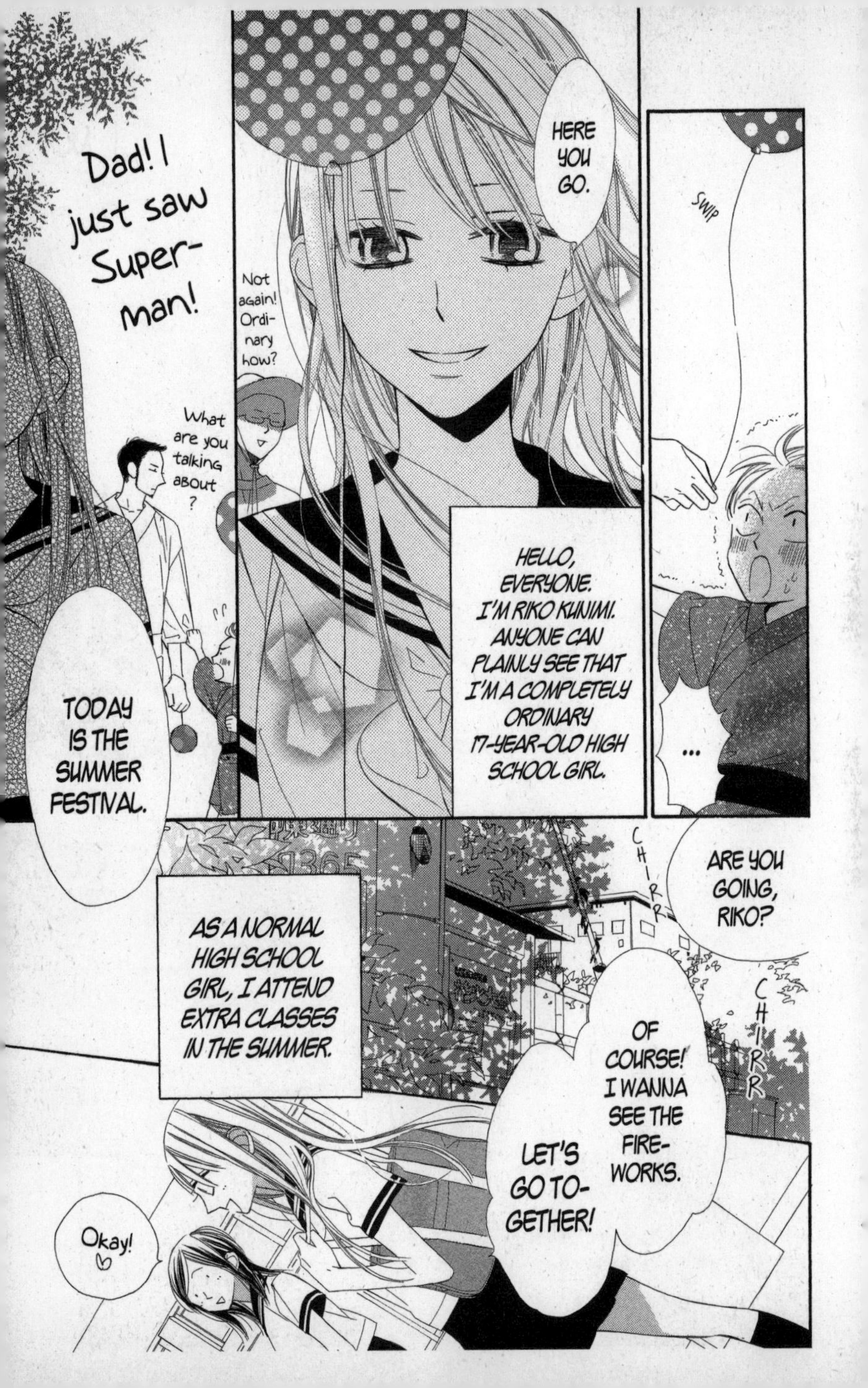
SWIP
...
HERE YOU GO.
HELLO, EVERYONE. I'M RIKO KUNIMI. ANYONE CAN PLAINLY SEE THAT I'M A COMPLETELY ORDINARY 17-YEAR-OLD HIGH SCHOOL GIRL.
Not again! Ordi-nary how?
Dad! I just saw Super-man!
What are you talking about?
TODAY IS THE SUMMER FESTIVAL.
CHIRR
ARE YOU GOING, RIKO?
AS A NORMAL HIGH SCHOOL GIRL, I ATTEND EXTRA CLASSES IN THE SUMMER.
CHIRR
OF COURSE! I WANNA SEE THE FIRE-WORKS.
LET'S GO TO-GETHER!
Okay!

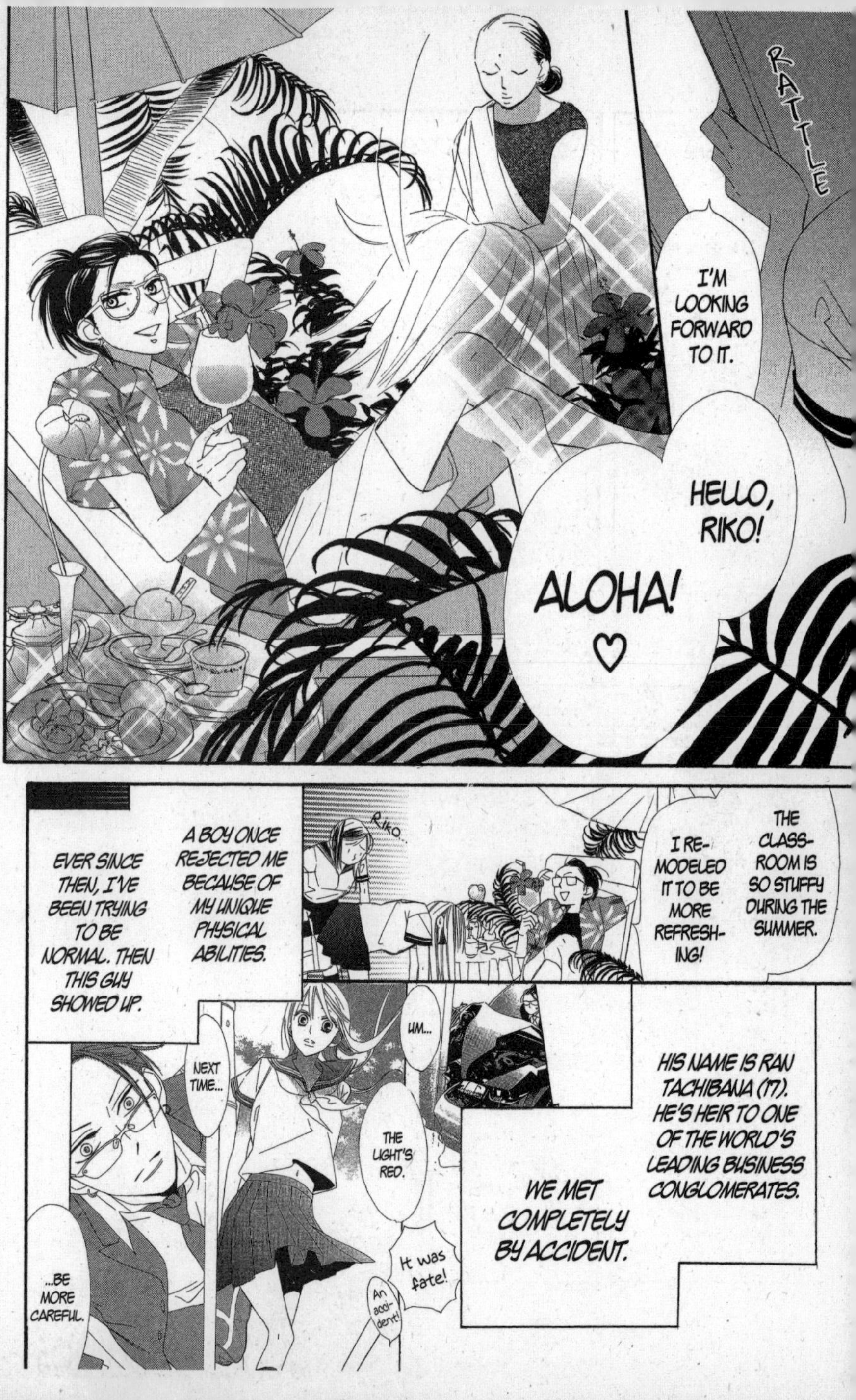
RATTLE
I'M LOOKING FORWARD TO IT.
HELLO, RIKO!
ALOHA! ♡
THE CLASSROOM IS SO STUFFY DURING THE SUMMER.
I REMODELED IT TO BE MORE REFRESHING!
RIKO...
A BOY ONCE REJECTED ME BECAUSE OF MY UNIQUE PHYSICAL ABILITIES.
EVER SINCE THEN, I'VE BEEN TRYING TO BE NORMAL. THEN THIS GUY SHOWED UP.
HIS NAME IS RAN TACHIBANA (17). HE'S HEIR TO ONE OF THE WORLD'S LEADING BUSINESS CONGLOMERATES.
WE MET COMPLETELY BY ACCIDENT.
UM...
NEXT TIME...
THE LIGHT'S RED.
It was fate!
An accident!
...BE MORE CAREFUL.

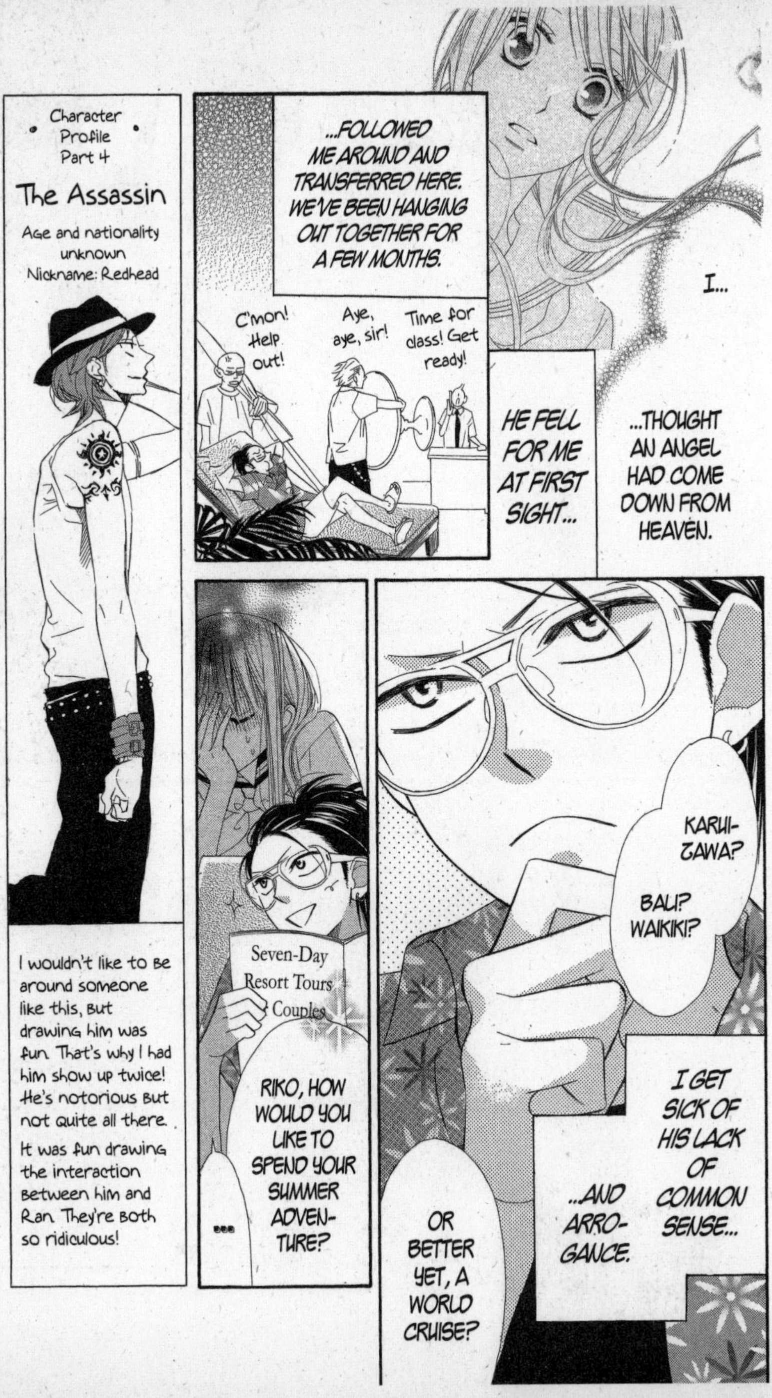
I...
...THOUGHT AN ANGEL HAD COME DOWN FROM HEAVEN.
HE FELL FOR ME AT FIRST SIGHT...
...FOLLOWED ME AROUND AND TRANSFERRED HERE. WE'VE BEEN HANGING OUT TOGETHER FOR A FEW MONTHS.
Time for class! Get ready!
Aye, aye, sir!
C'mon! Help out!
KARUI-ZAWA?
BALI? WAIKIKI?
I GET SICK OF HIS LACK OF COMMON SENSE...
...AND ARROGANCE.
OR BETTER YET, A WORLD CRUISE?
Seven-Day Resort Tours Couples
RIKO, HOW WOULD YOU LIKE TO SPEND YOUR SUMMER ADVENTURE?
...
Character Profile Part 4
The Assassin
Age and nationality unknown
Nickname: Redhead
I wouldn't like to be around someone like this, but drawing him was fun. That's why I had him show up twice! He's notorious but not quite all there.
It was fun drawing the interaction between him and Ran. They're both so ridiculous!

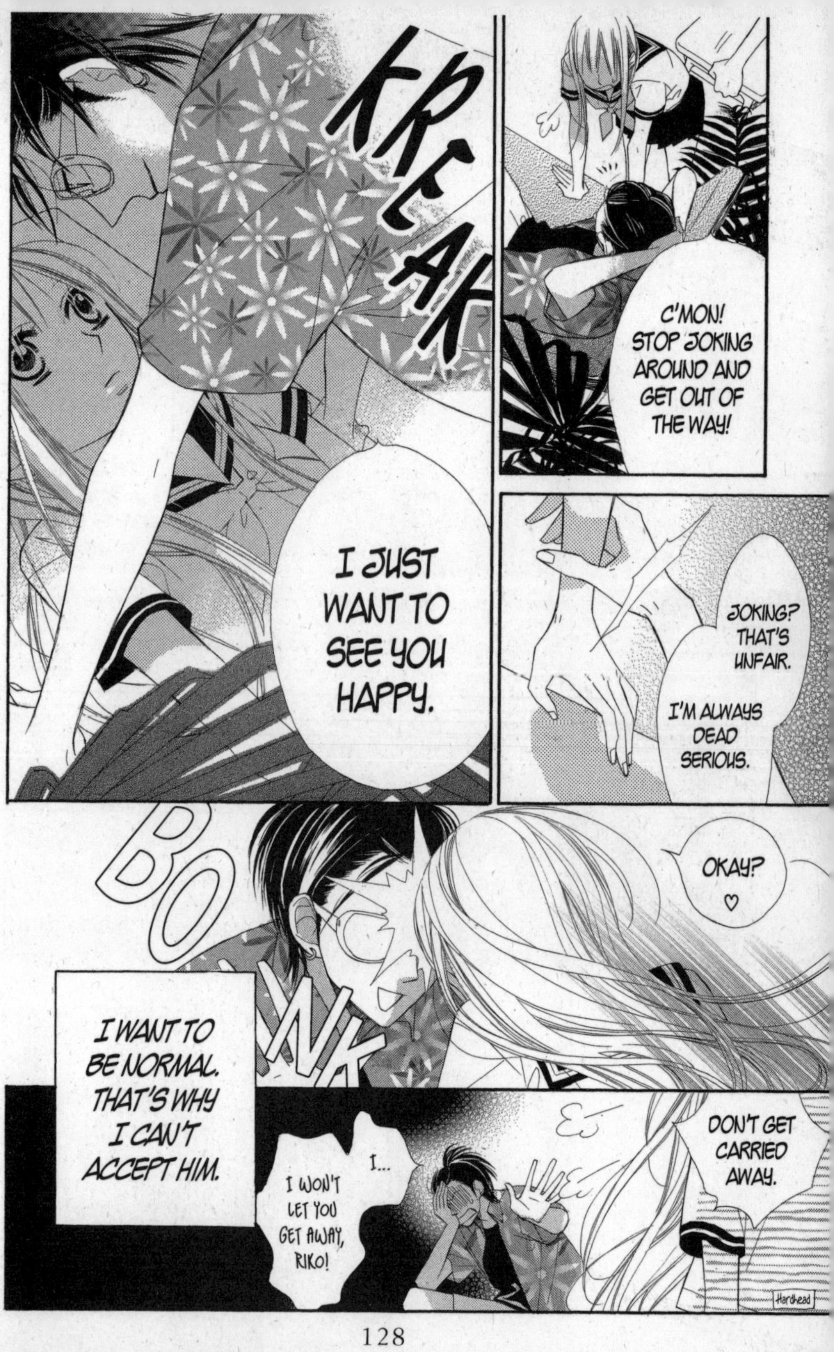
C'MON! STOP JOKING AROUND AND GET OUT OF THE WAY!
JOKING? THAT'S UNFAIR.
I'M ALWAYS DEAD SERIOUS.
KREAK
I JUST WANT TO SEE YOU HAPPY.
OKAY? ♥
BONK
I WANT TO BE NORMAL. THAT'S WHY I CAN'T ACCEPT HIM.
DON'T GET CARRIED AWAY.
I...
I WON'T LET YOU GET AWAY, RIKO!
Hardhead

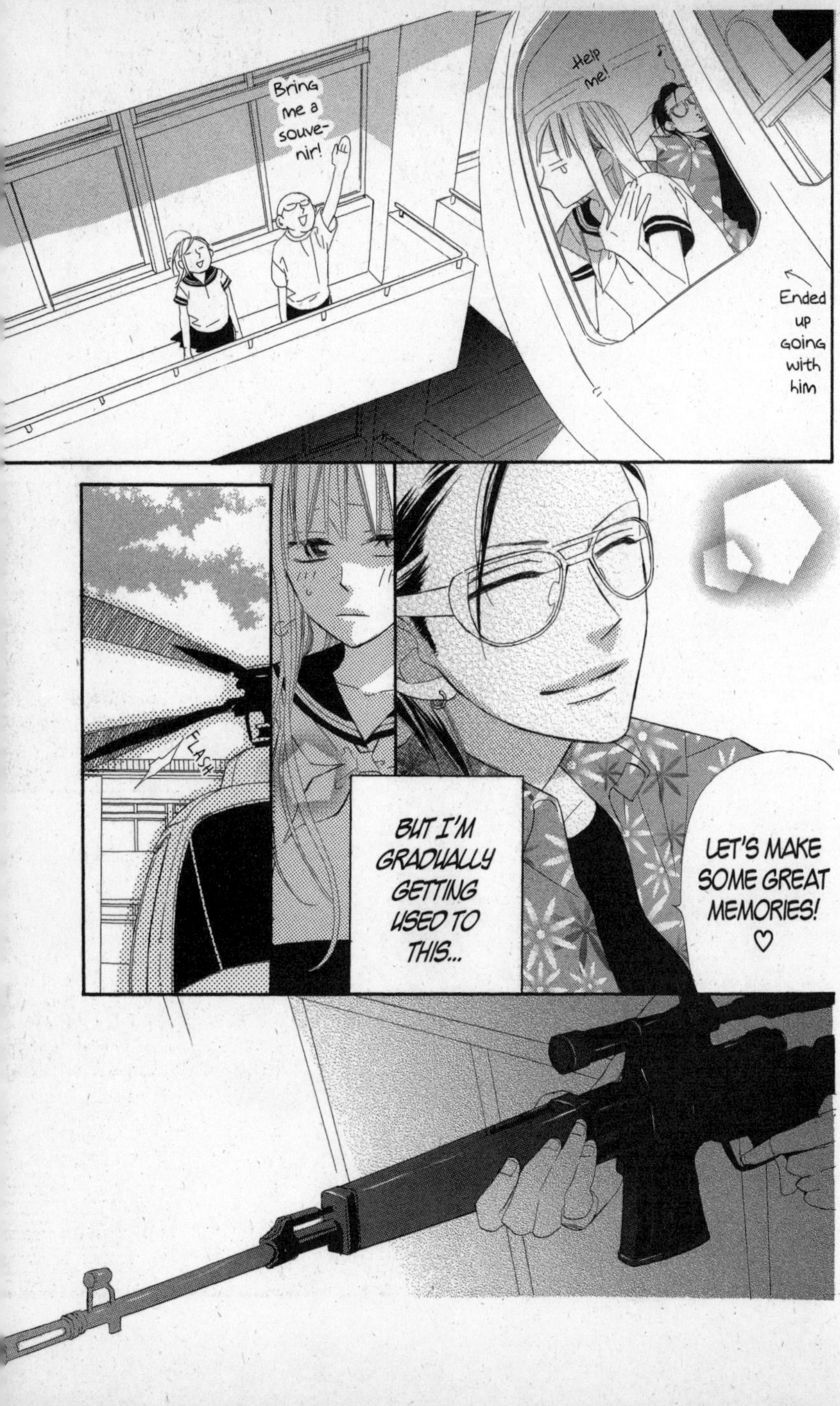
Help me!
Ended up going with him
Bring me a souvenir!
LET'S MAKE SOME GREAT MEMORIES! ♡
BUT I'M GRADUALLY GETTING USED TO THIS...
FLASH

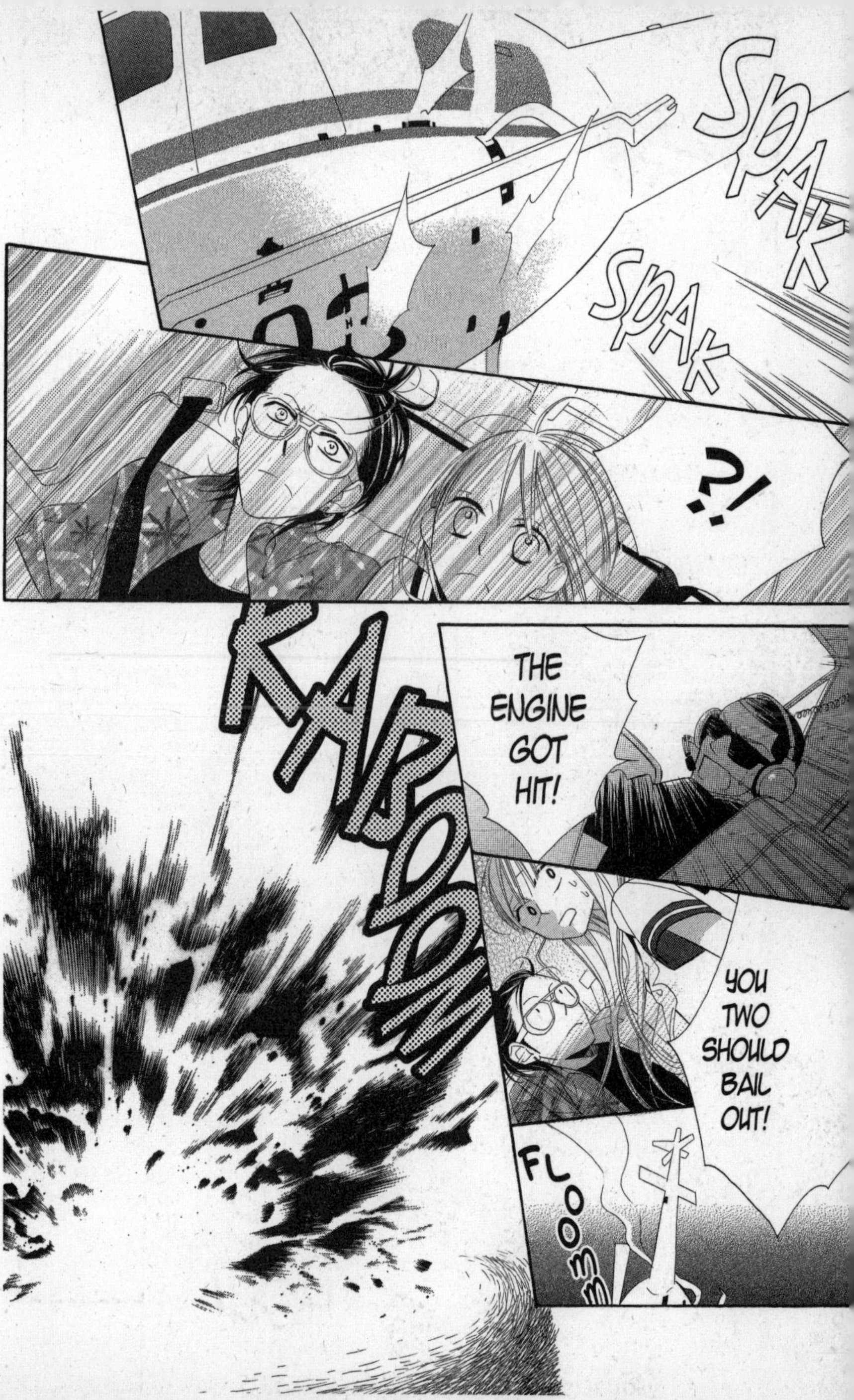
SPAK
SPAK
?!
THE ENGINE GOT HIT!
YOU TWO SHOULD BAIL OUT!
FLOOOM
KABOOM

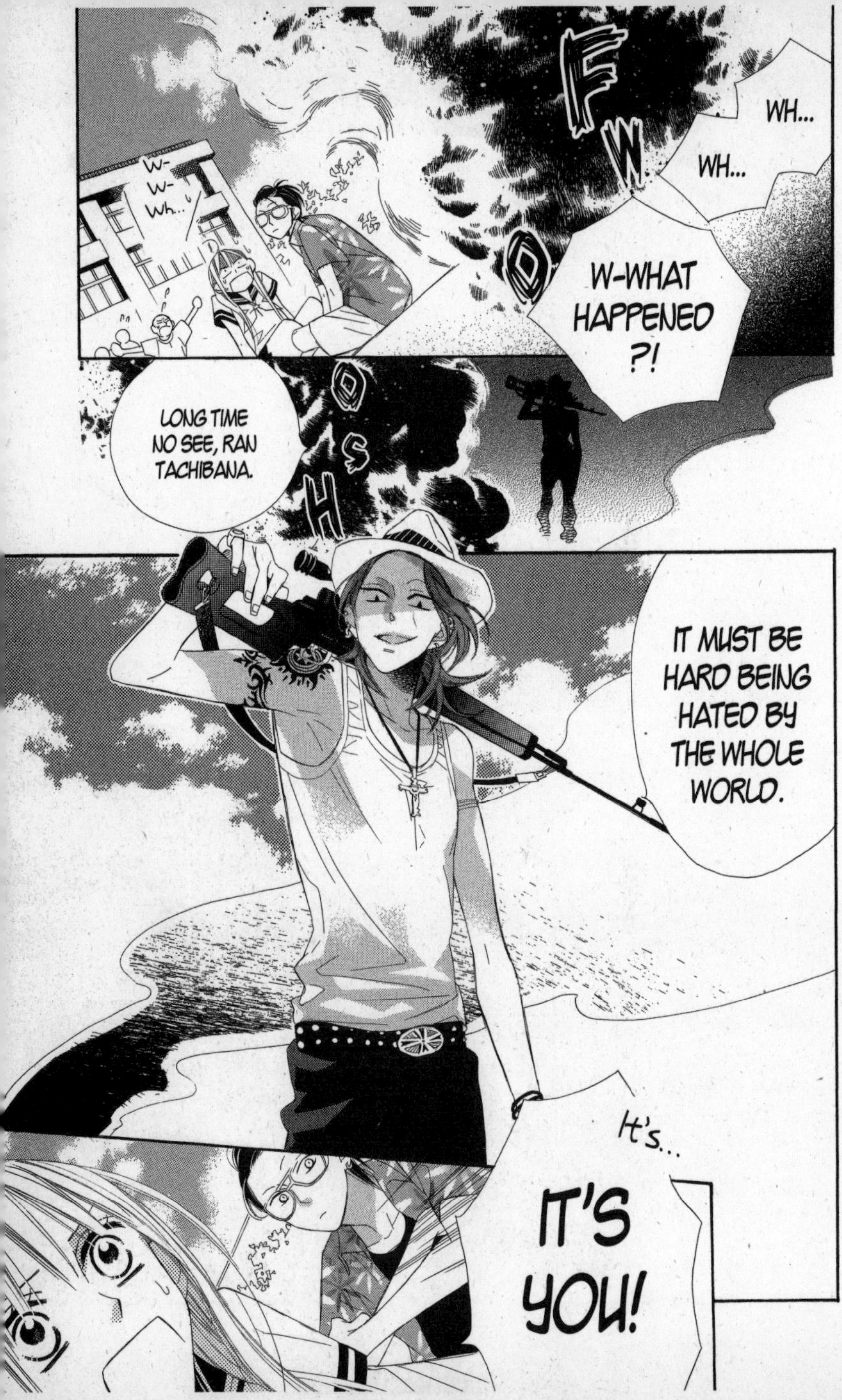
WH...
WH...
W-WHAT HAPPENED ?!
W- W- Wh...
FWOOSH
LONG TIME NO SEE, RAN TACHIBANA.
IT MUST BE HARD BEING HATED BY THE WHOLE WORLD.
It's...
IT'S YOU!

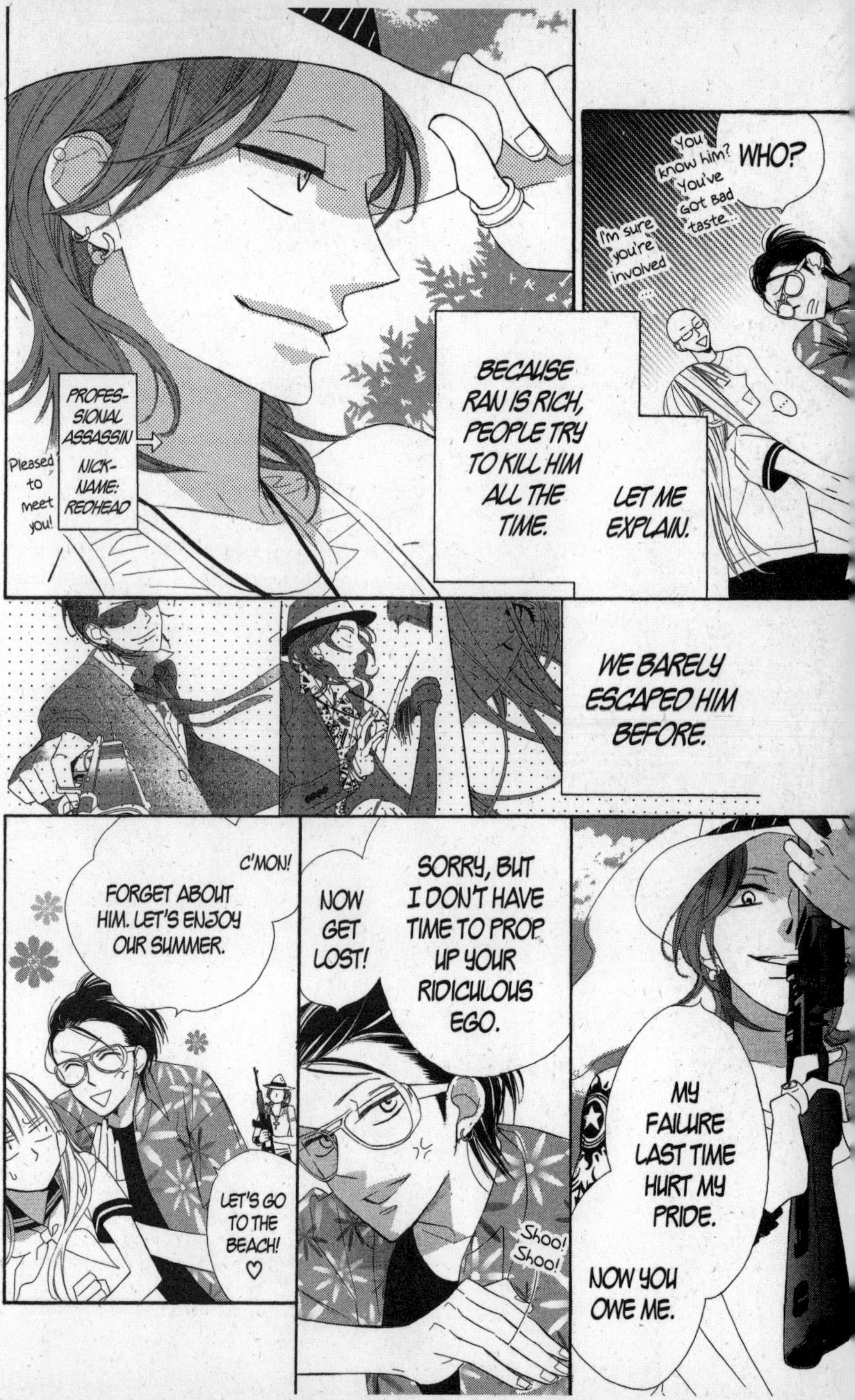
WHO?
You know him? You've Got bad taste...
I'm sure you're involved ...
...
LET ME EXPLAIN.
BECAUSE RAN IS RICH, PEOPLE TRY TO KILL HIM ALL THE TIME.
PROFES-SIONAL ASSASSIN
NICK-NAME: REDHEAD
Pleased to meet you!
WE BARELY ESCAPED HIM BEFORE.
MY FAILURE LAST TIME HURT MY PRIDE.
NOW YOU OWE ME.
SORRY, BUT I DON'T HAVE TIME TO PROP UP YOUR RIDICULOUS EGO.
NOW GET LOST!
Shoo! Shoo!
C'MON!
FORGET ABOUT HIM. LET'S ENJOY OUR SUMMER.
LET'S GO TO THE BEACH! ♡

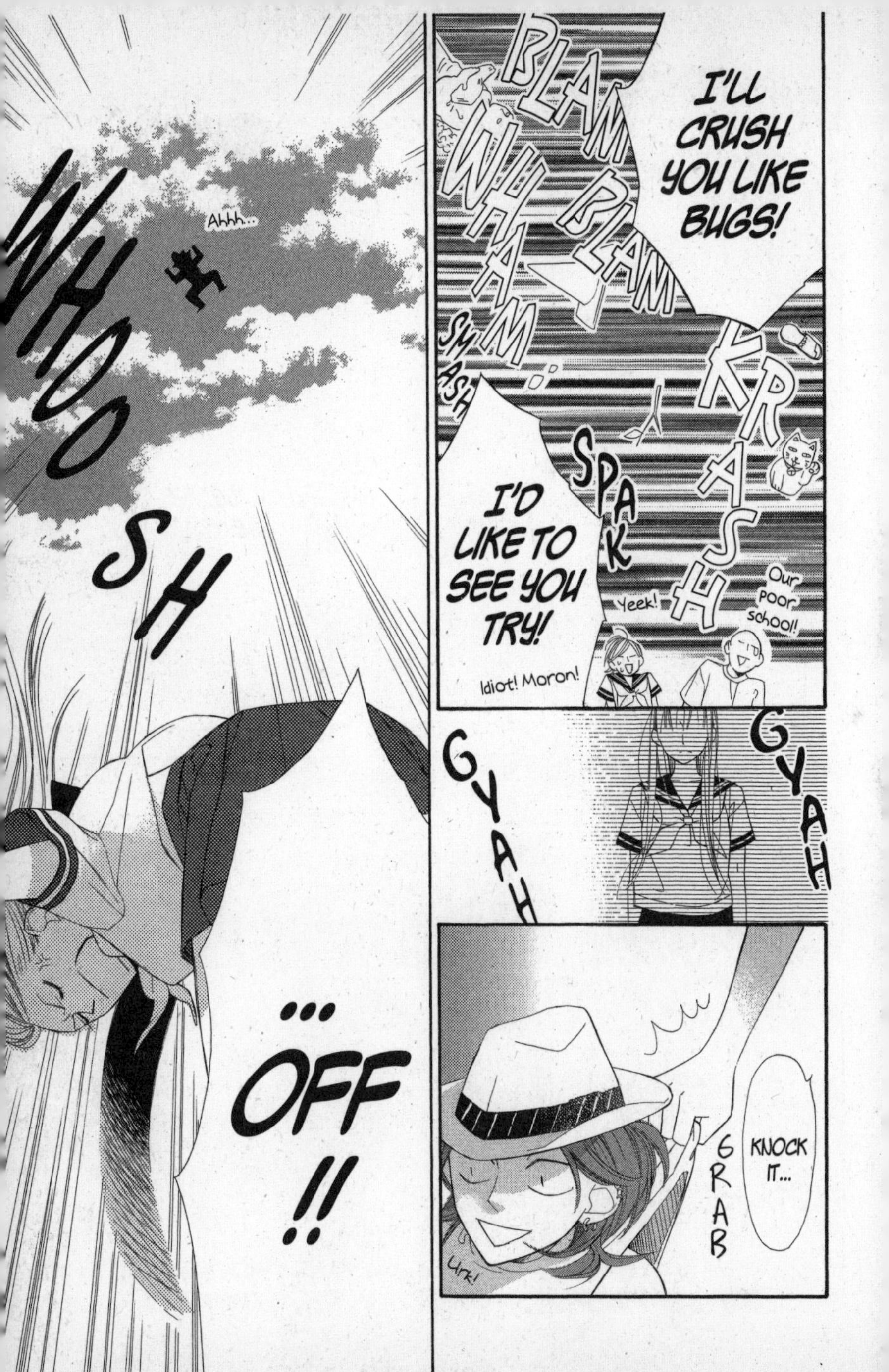
I'LL CRUSH YOU LIKE BUGS!
BLAM
BLAM
WHAM
SMASH
KRASH
SPAK
I'D LIKE TO SEE YOU TRY!
Our poor school!
Yeek!
Idiot! Moron!
GYAH
GYAH
KNOCK IT...
GRAB
Urk!
Ahhh...
WHOOOSH
...OFF!!

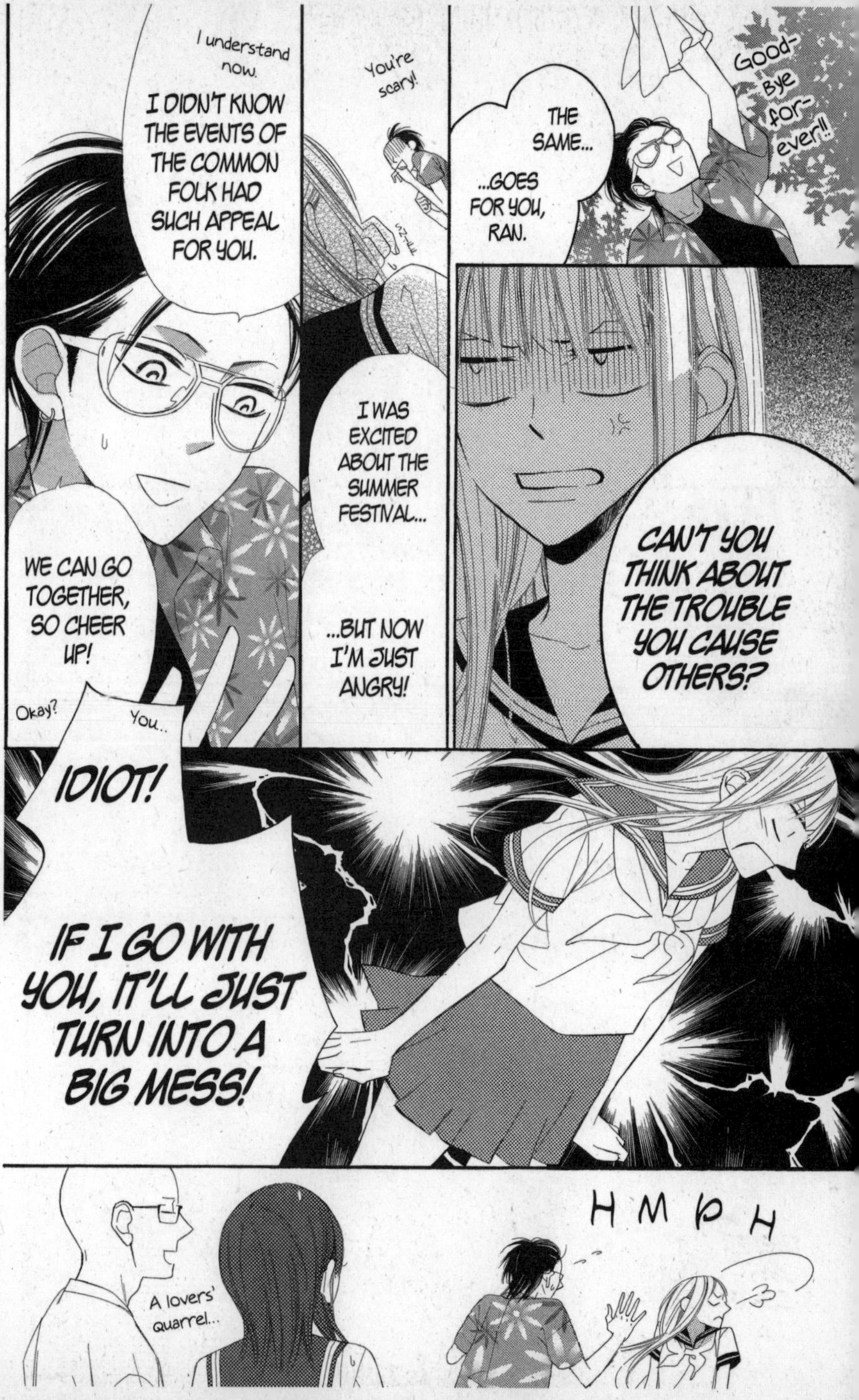
Good-bye for-ever!!
THE SAME...
...GOES FOR YOU, RAN.
CAN'T YOU THINK ABOUT THE TROUBLE YOU CAUSE OTHERS?
You're scary!
I WAS EXCITED ABOUT THE SUMMER FESTIVAL...
...BUT NOW I'M JUST ANGRY!
I understand now.
I DIDN'T KNOW THE EVENTS OF THE COMMON FOLK HAD SUCH APPEAL FOR YOU.
WE CAN GO TOGETHER, SO CHEER UP!
Okay?
You...
IDIOT!
IF I GO WITH YOU, IT'LL JUST TURN INTO A BIG MESS!
HMPH
A lovers' quarrel...

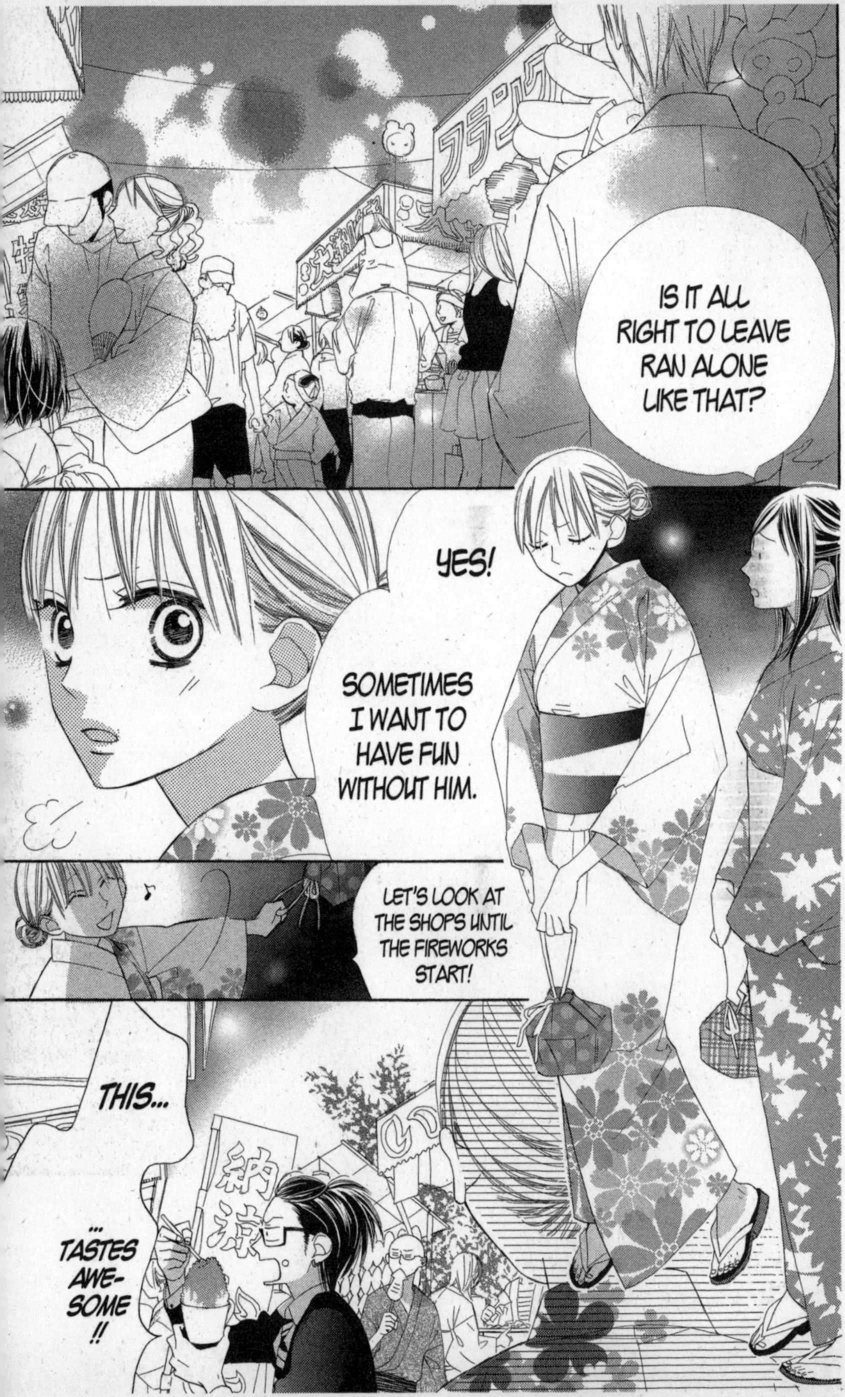
IS IT ALL RIGHT TO LEAVE RAN ALONE LIKE THAT?
YES!
SOMETIMES I WANT TO HAVE FUN WITHOUT HIM.
LET'S LOOK AT THE SHOPS UNTIL THE FIREWORKS START!
THIS...
...TASTES AWESOME!!

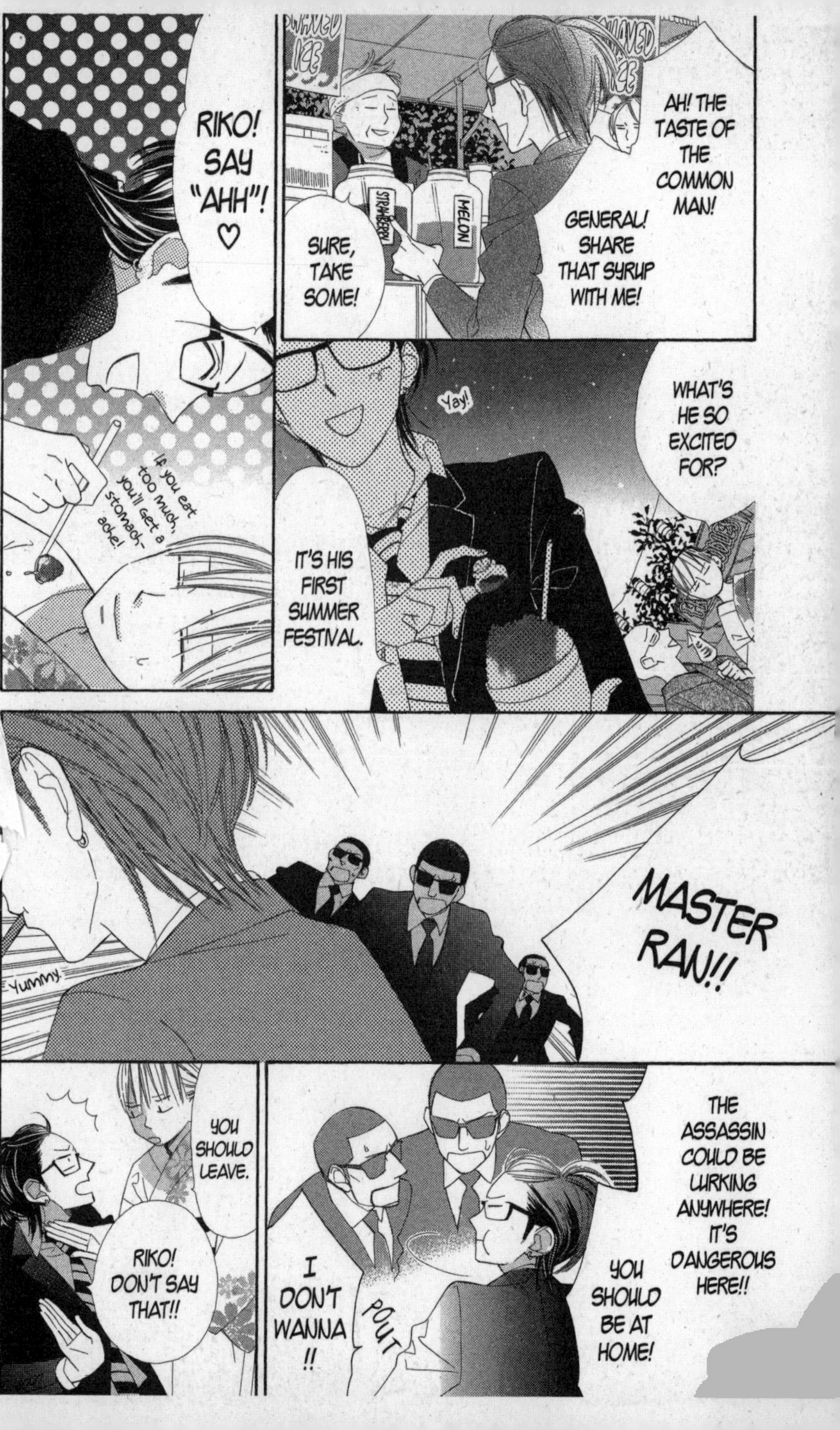
SHAVED ICE
SHAVED ICE
AH! THE TASTE OF THE COMMON MAN!
GENERAL! SHARE THAT SYRUP WITH ME!
STRAWBERRY
MELON
SURE, TAKE SOME!
WHAT'S HE SO EXCITED FOR?
Yay!
IT'S HIS FIRST SUMMER FESTIVAL.
RIKO! SAY "AHH"! ♡
If you eat too much, you'll get a stomach-ache!
MASTER RAN!!
Yummy.
THE ASSASSIN COULD BE LURKING ANYWHERE! IT'S DANGEROUS HERE!!
YOU SHOULD BE AT HOME!
POUT
I DON'T WANNA!!
YOU SHOULD LEAVE.
RIKO! DON'T SAY THAT!!

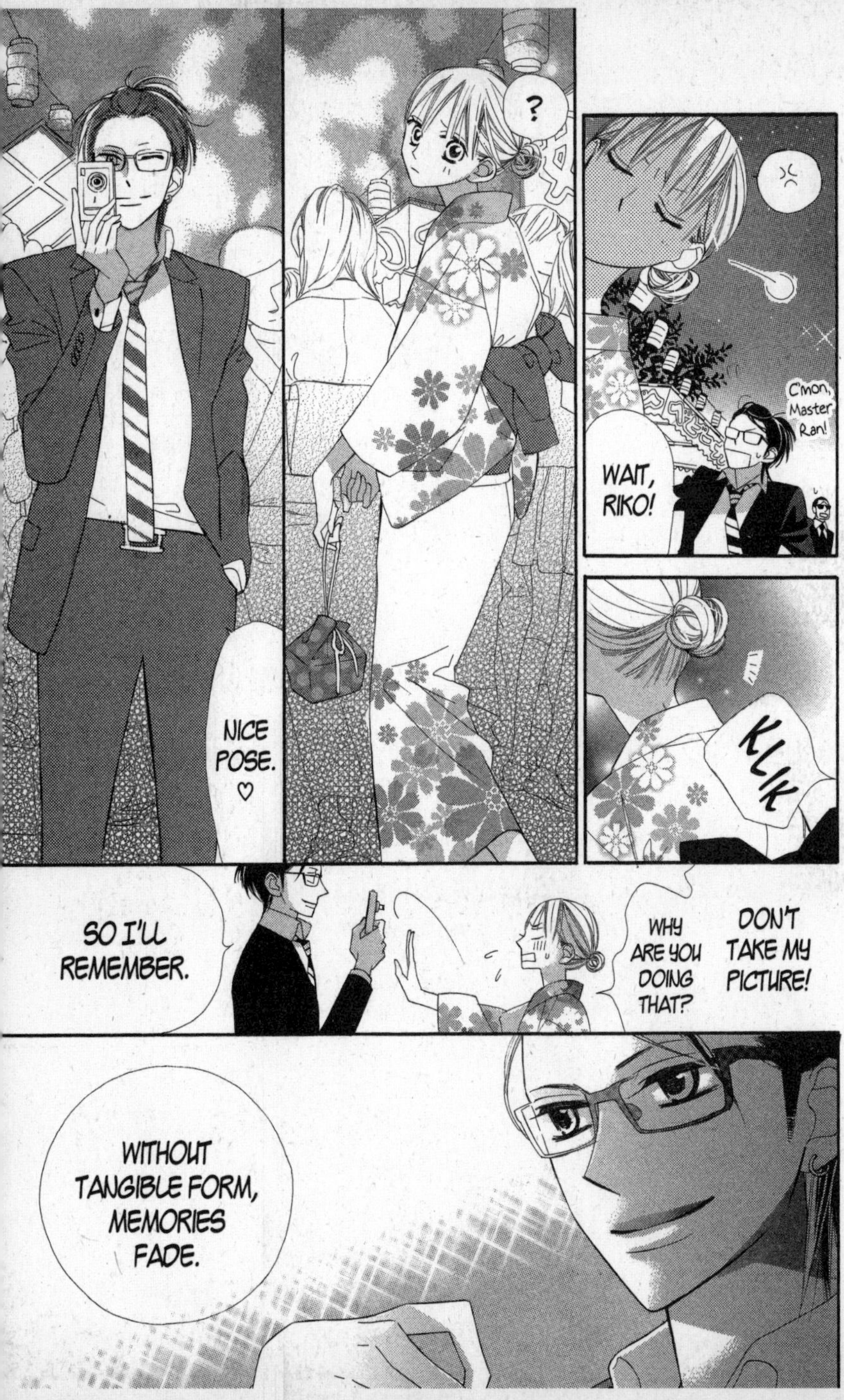
C'mon, Master Ran!
WAIT, RIKO!
KLIK
?
NICE POSE. ♡
DON'T TAKE MY PICTURE!
WHY ARE YOU DOING THAT?
SO I'LL REMEMBER.
WITHOUT TANGIBLE FORM, MEMORIES FADE.

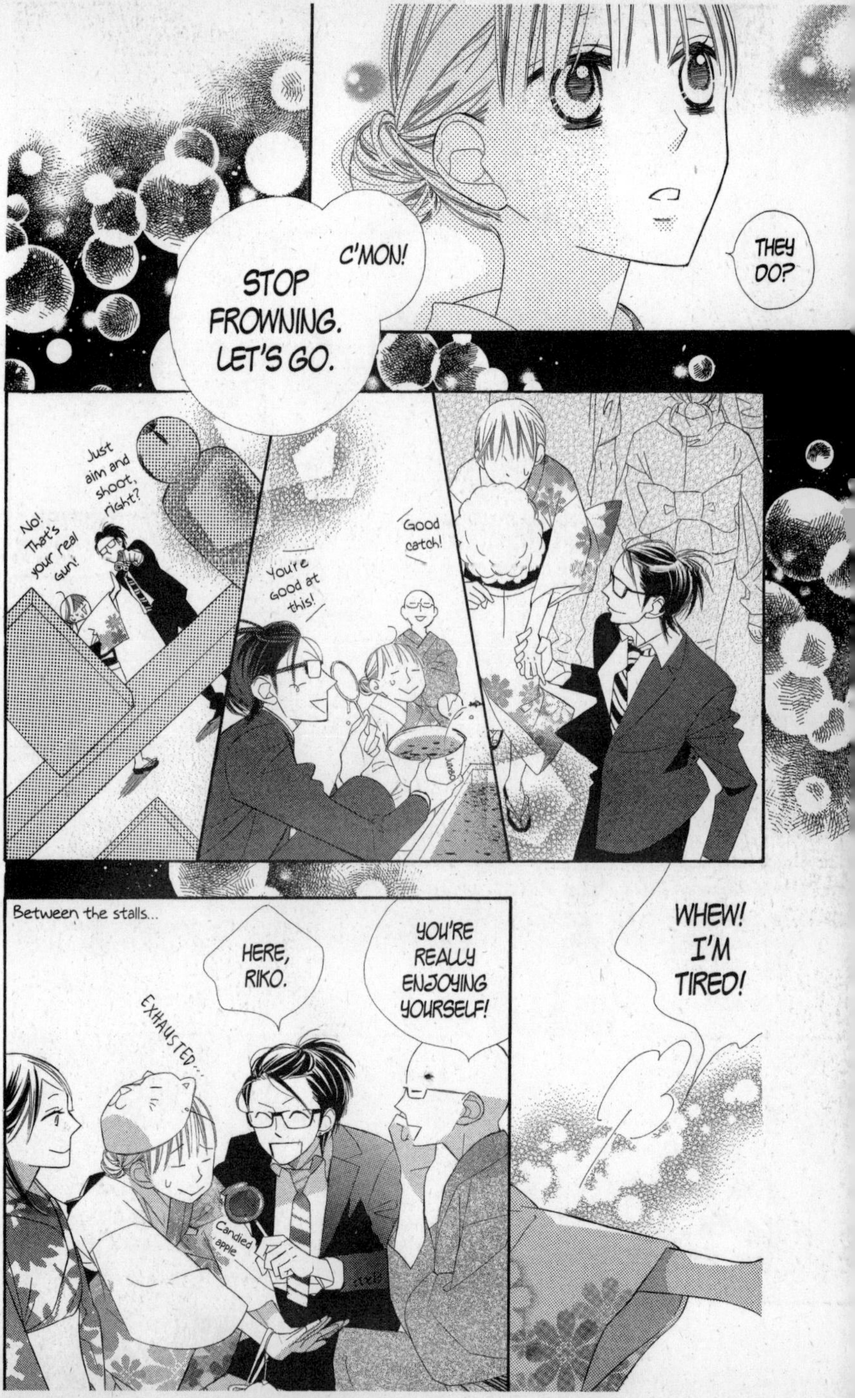
THEY DO?
C'MON!
STOP FROWNING. LET'S GO.
Good catch!
You're good at this!
Just aim and shoot, right?
No! That's your real gun!
WHEW! I'M TIRED!
Between the stalls...
YOU'RE REALLY ENJOYING YOURSELF!
HERE, RIKO.
EXHAUSTED...
Candied apple

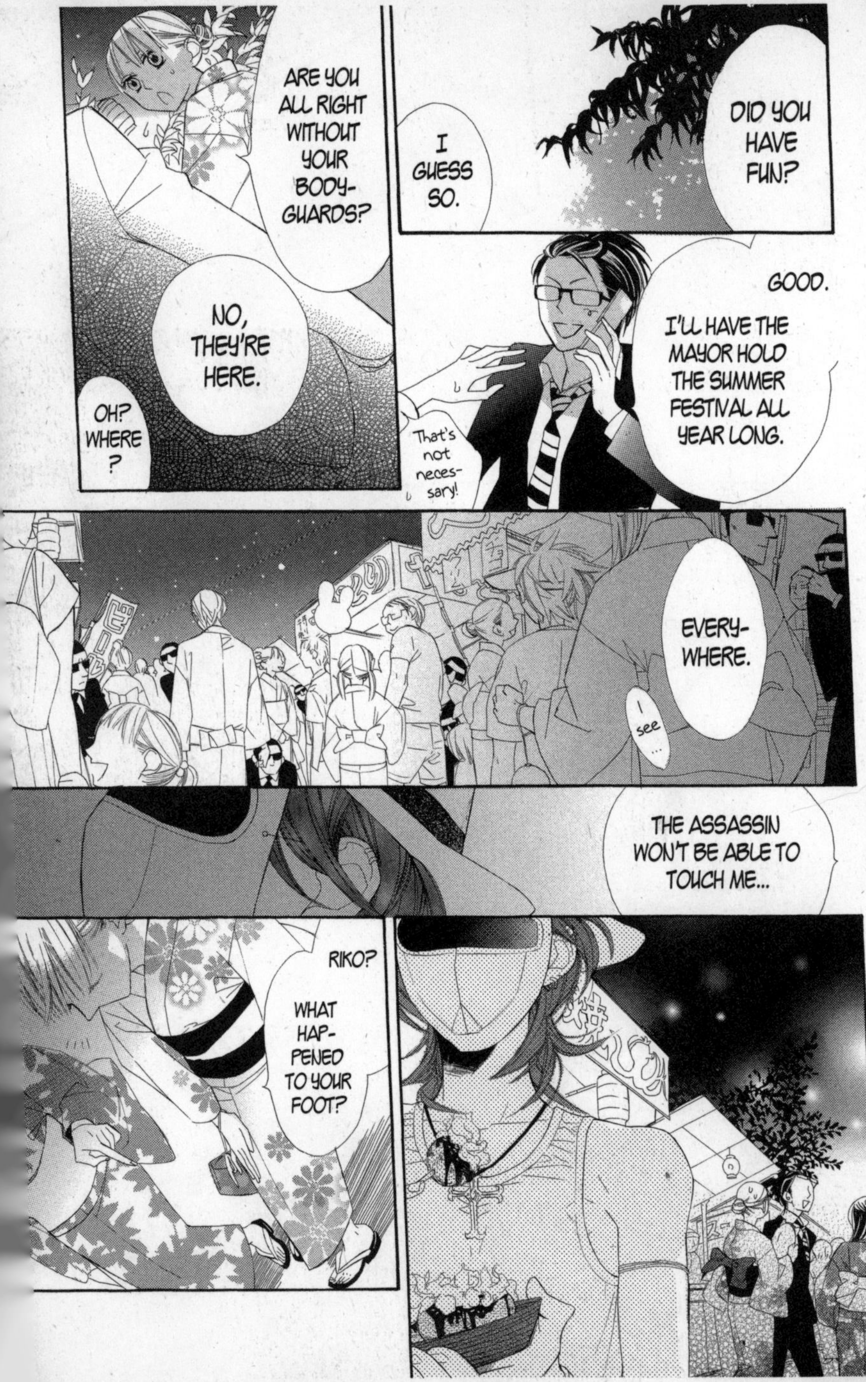
DID YOU HAVE FUN?
I GUESS SO.
GOOD.
I'LL HAVE THE MAYOR HOLD THE SUMMER FESTIVAL ALL YEAR LONG.
That's not neces-sary!
ARE YOU ALL RIGHT WITHOUT YOUR BODY-GUARDS?
NO, THEY'RE HERE.
OH? WHERE?
EVERY-WHERE.
I see...
THE ASSASSIN WON'T BE ABLE TO TOUCH ME...
RIKO?
WHAT HAP-PENED TO YOUR FOOT?

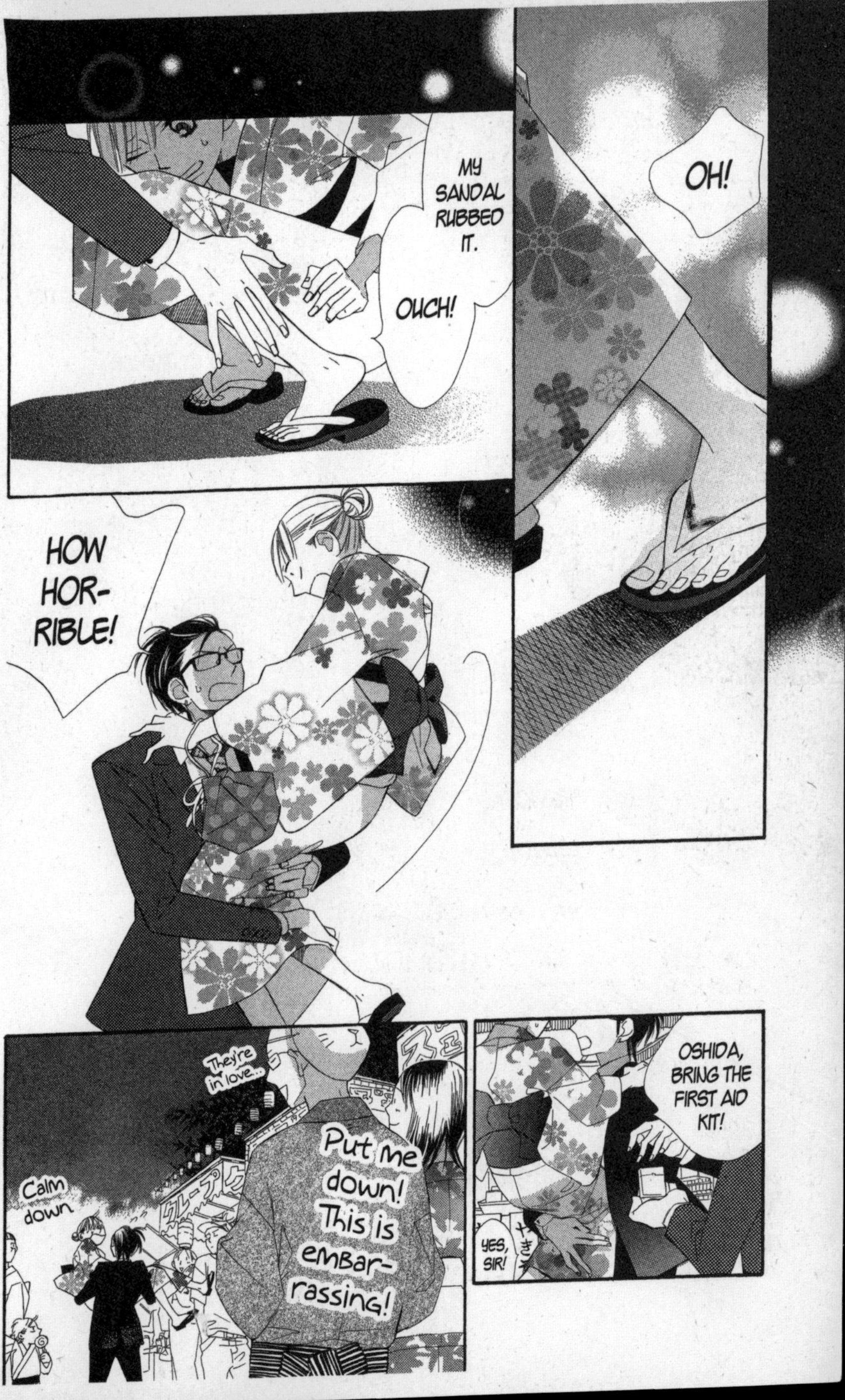
OH!
MY SANDAL RUBBED IT.
OUCH!
HOW HOR-RIBLE!
OSHIDA, BRING THE FIRST AID KIT!
YES, SIR!
They're in love...
Put me down! This is embar-rassing!
Calm down.

REST HERE A MOMENT.

THEN WE'LL GO WATCH THE FIREWORKS.

Sorry about this...

Your poor little feet

FIREWORKS ARE ESSENTIAL FOR SUMMER MEMORIES.

NO PARTICULAR REASON.

WHY ARE YOU SO OBSESSED WITH MEMORIES?

I JUST DON'T WANT TO REGRET ANYTHING.

Ouch !...

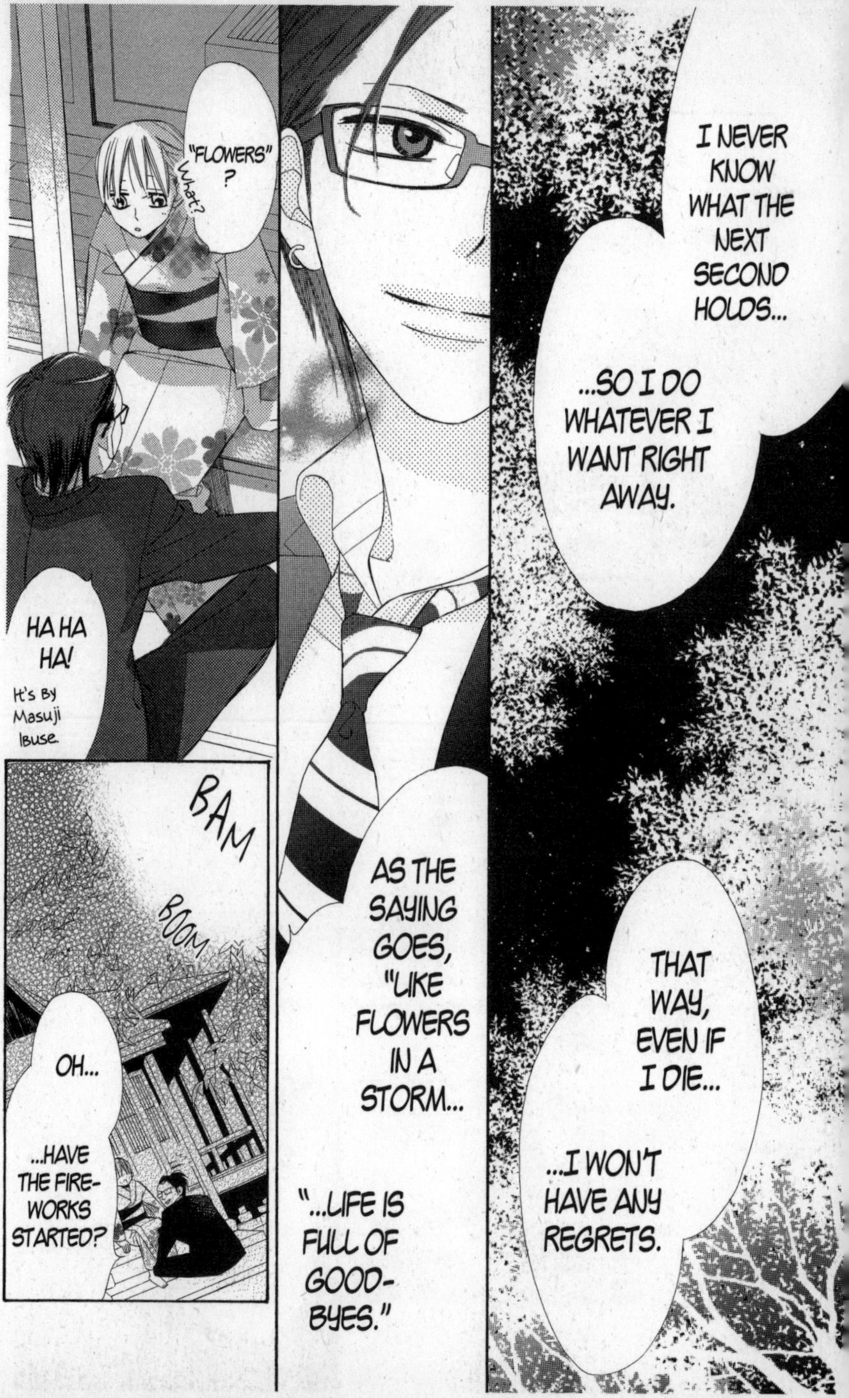
I NEVER KNOW WHAT THE NEXT SECOND HOLDS...
...SO I DO WHATEVER I WANT RIGHT AWAY.
THAT WAY, EVEN IF I DIE...
...I WON'T HAVE ANY REGRETS.
AS THE SAYING GOES, "LIKE FLOWERS IN A STORM...
"...LIFE IS FULL OF GOOD-BYES."
"FLOWERS"?
What?
HA HA HA!
It's By Masuji Ibuse.
BAM
BOOM
OH...
...HAVE THE FIRE-WORKS STARTED?

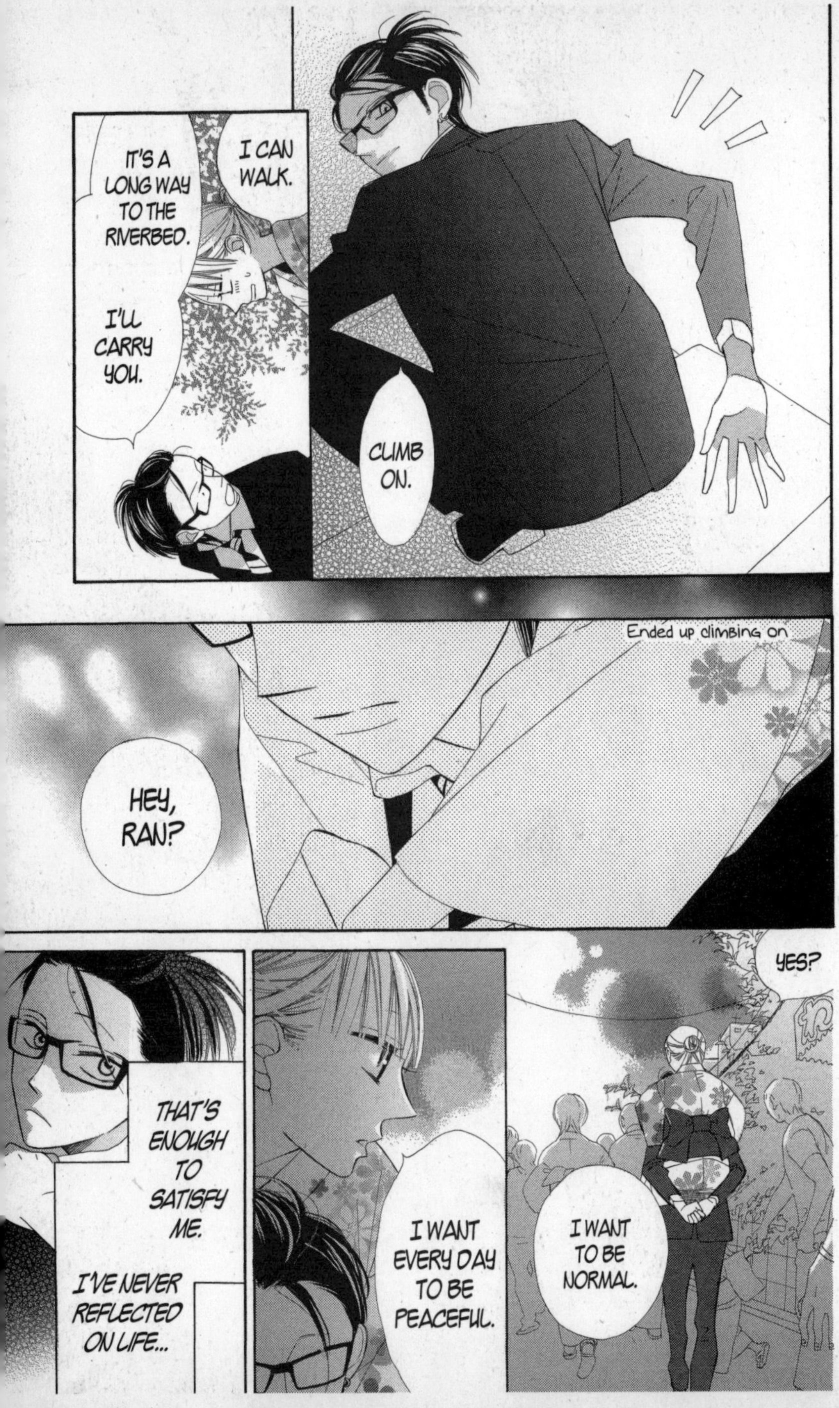
I CAN WALK.
IT'S A LONG WAY TO THE RIVERBED.
I'LL CARRY YOU.
CLIMB ON.
Ended up climbing on
HEY, RAN?
YES?
I WANT TO BE NORMAL.
I WANT EVERY DAY TO BE PEACEFUL.
THAT'S ENOUGH TO SATISFY ME.
I'VE NEVER REFLECTED ON LIFE...

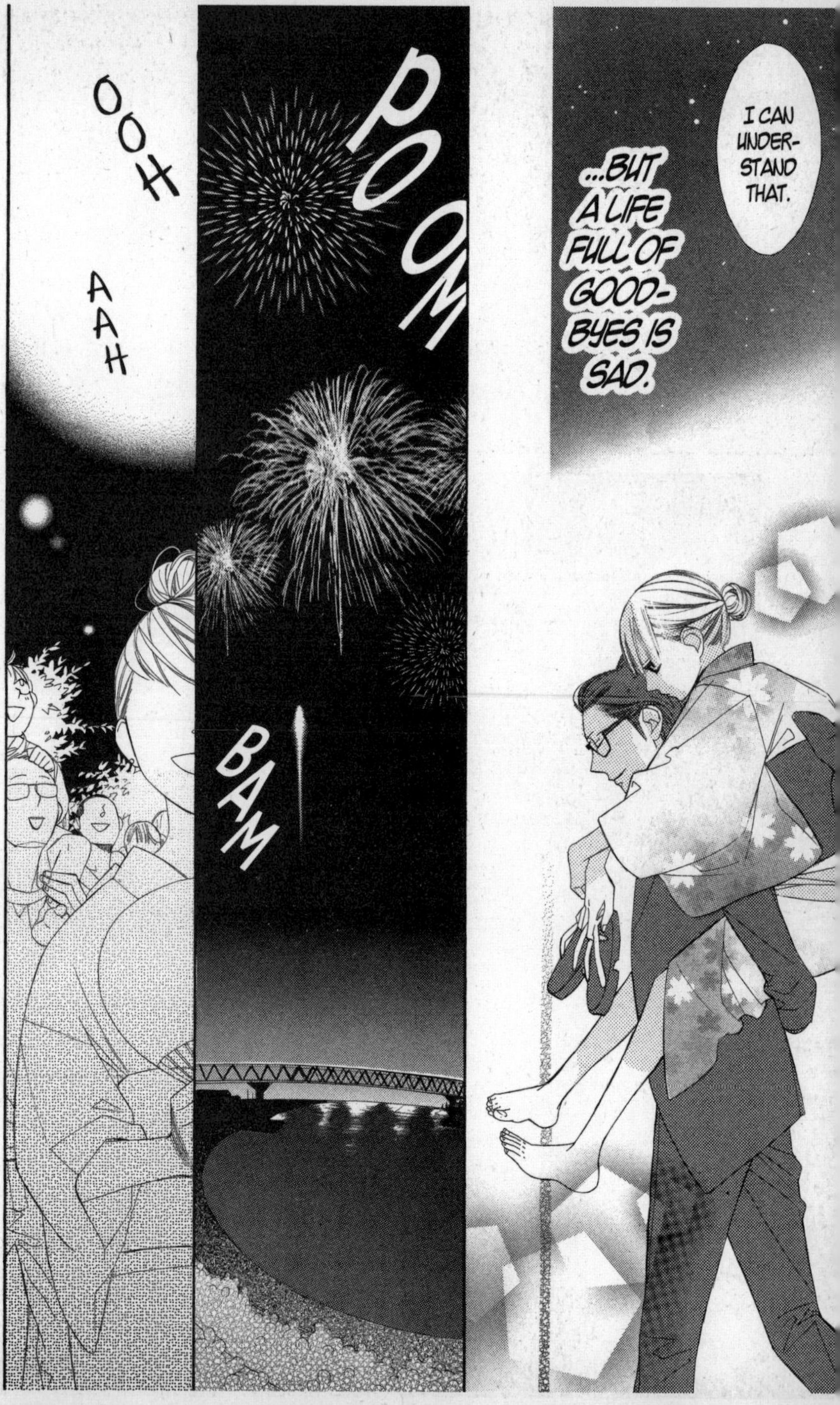
I CAN UNDER-STAND THAT.
...BUT A LIFE FULL OF GOOD-BYES IS SAD.
POOM
BAM
OOH
AAH

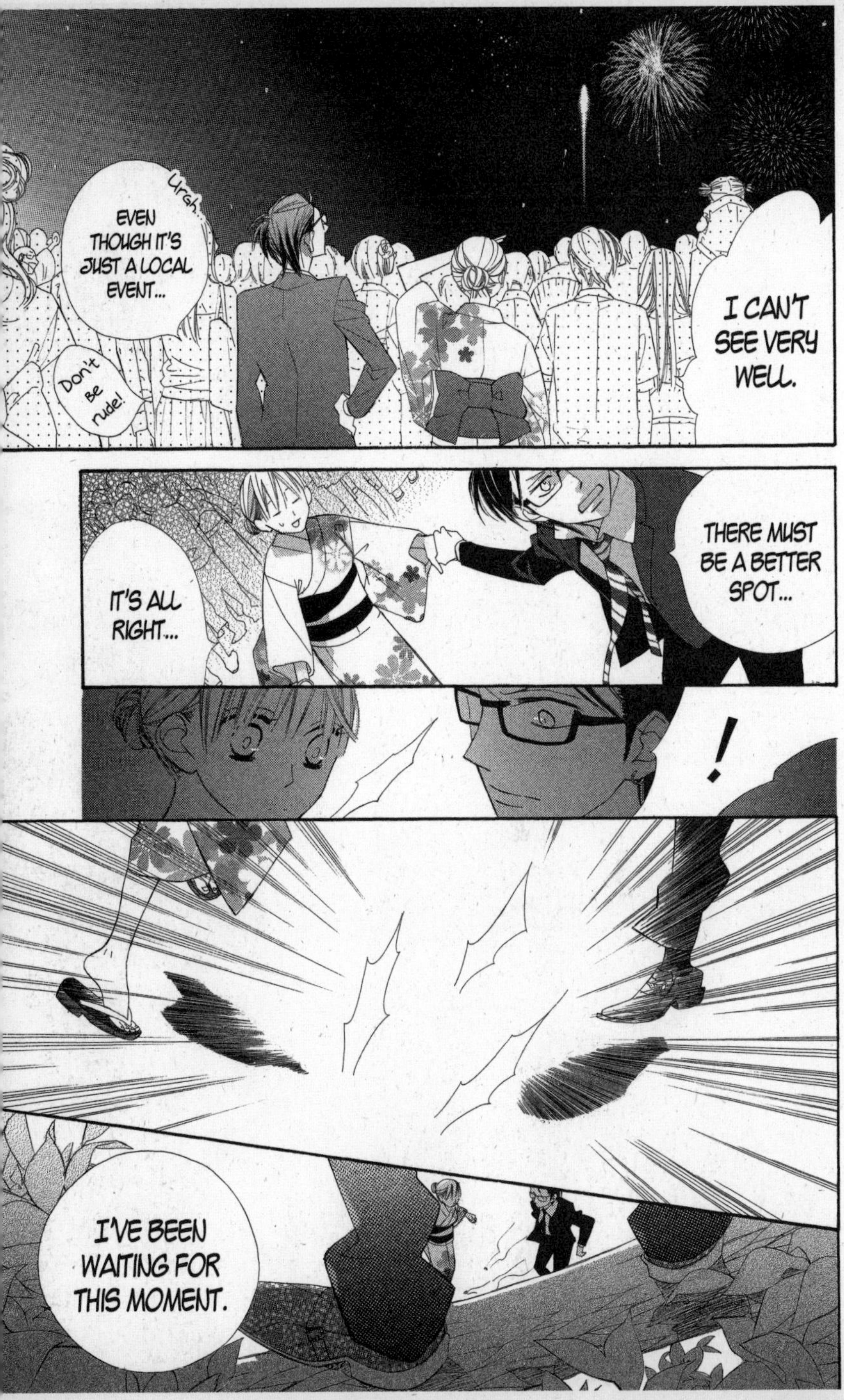

I CAN'T SEE VERY WELL.
Urgh...
EVEN THOUGH IT'S JUST A LOCAL EVENT...
Don't be rude!
THERE MUST BE A BETTER SPOT...
IT'S ALL RIGHT...
!
I'VE BEEN WAITING FOR THIS MOMENT.

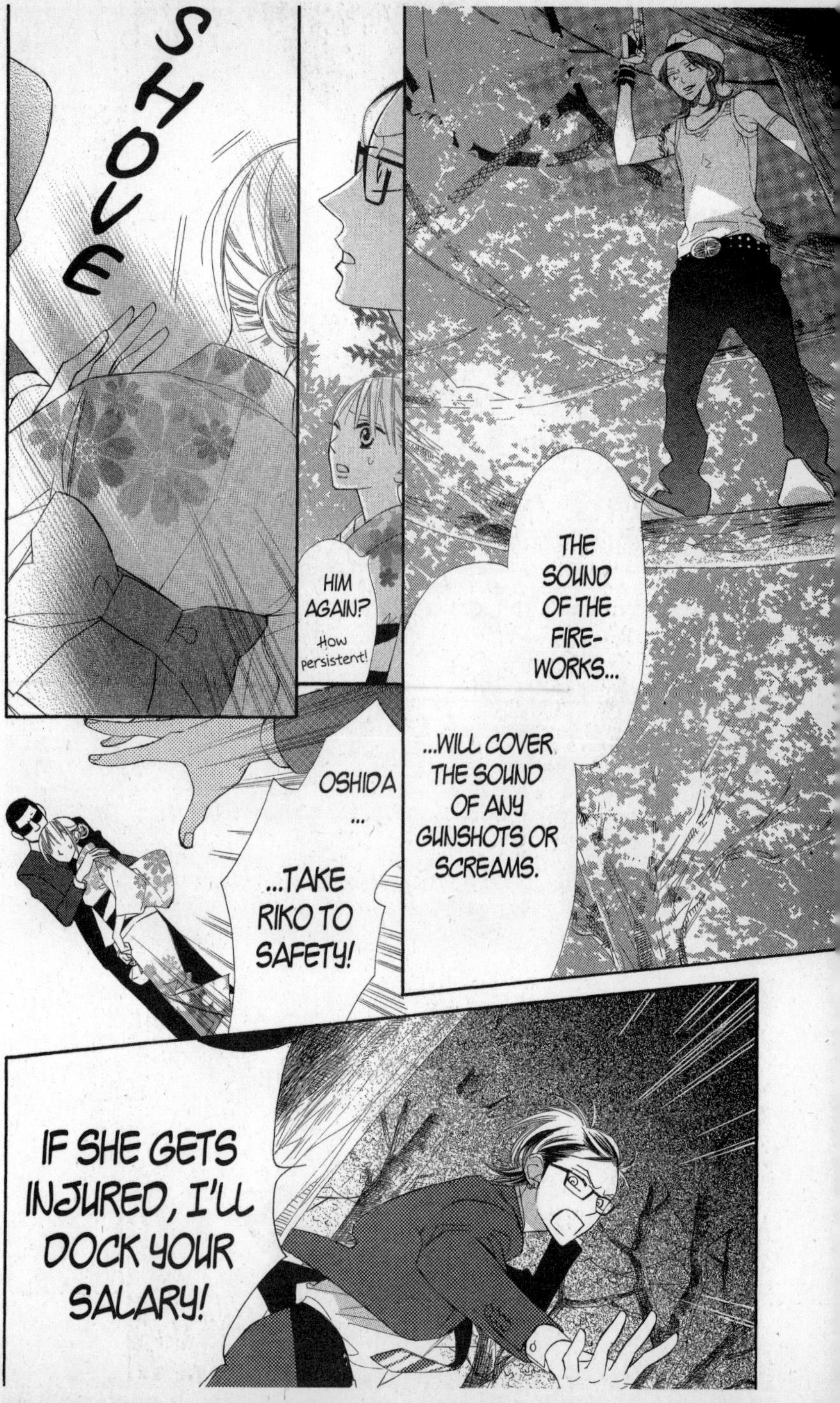
THE SOUND OF THE FIRE-WORKS...
...WILL COVER THE SOUND OF ANY GUNSHOTS OR SCREAMS.
HIM AGAIN?
How persistent!
SHOVE
OSHIDA...
...TAKE RIKO TO SAFETY!
IF SHE GETS INJURED, I'LL DOCK YOUR SALARY!

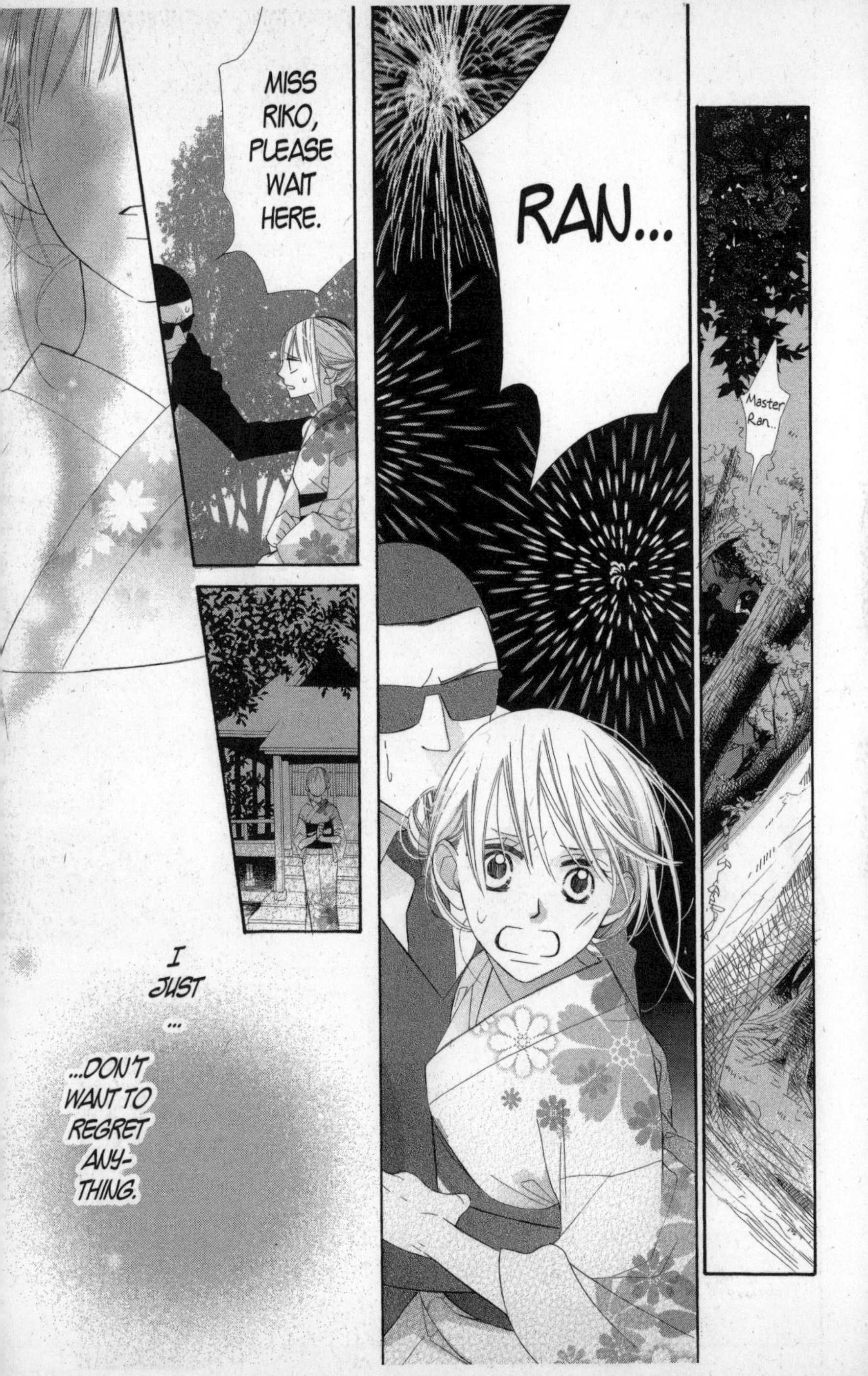
Master Ran..
RAN...
MISS RIKO, PLEASE WAIT HERE.
I JUST...
...DON'T WANT TO REGRET ANY-THING.

I DON'T WANT TO REGRET ANYTHING.

GIVE ME YOUR GUN.

WH AM

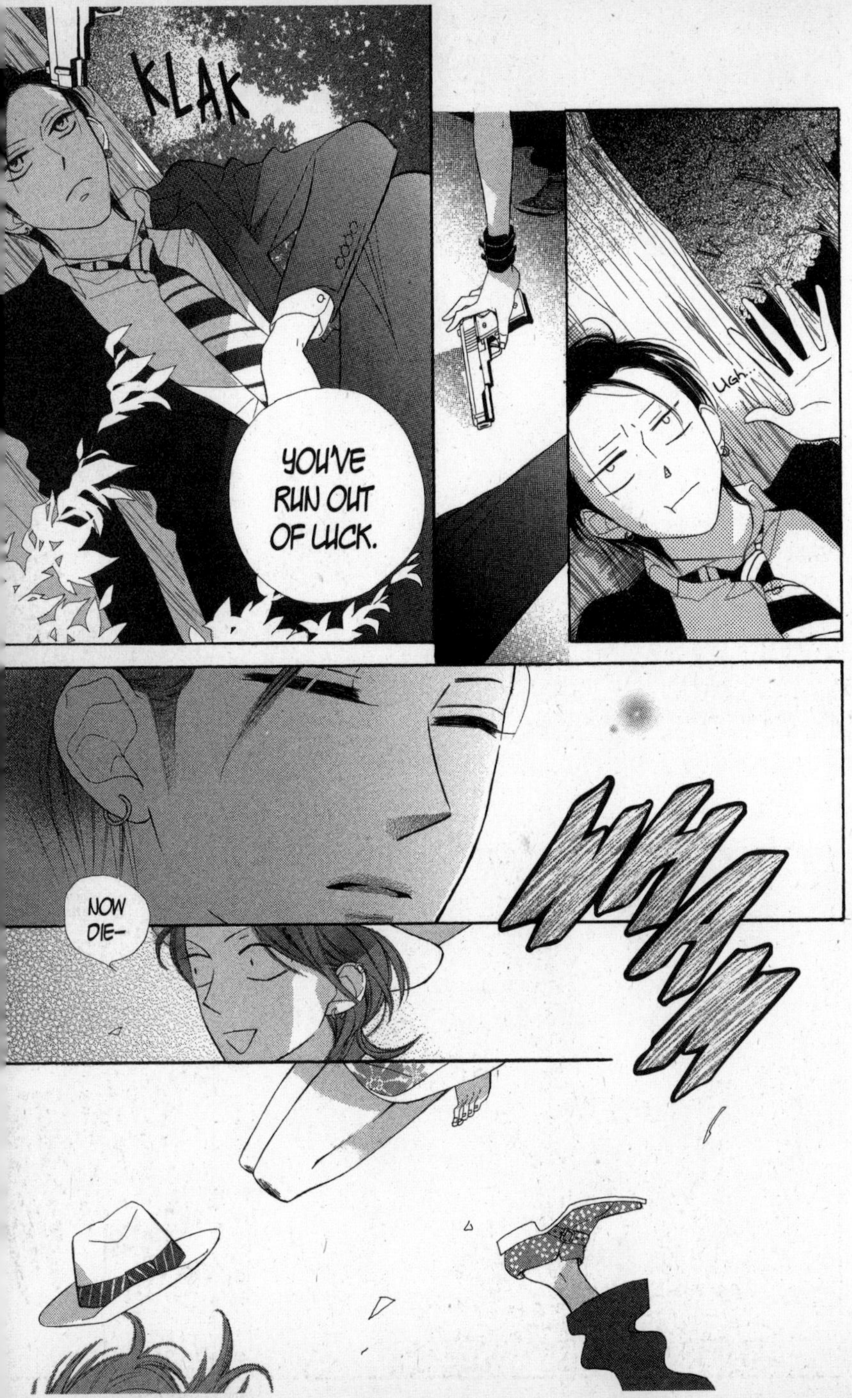
Ugh...
KLAK
YOU'VE RUN OUT OF LUCK.
NOW DIE–
WHAM

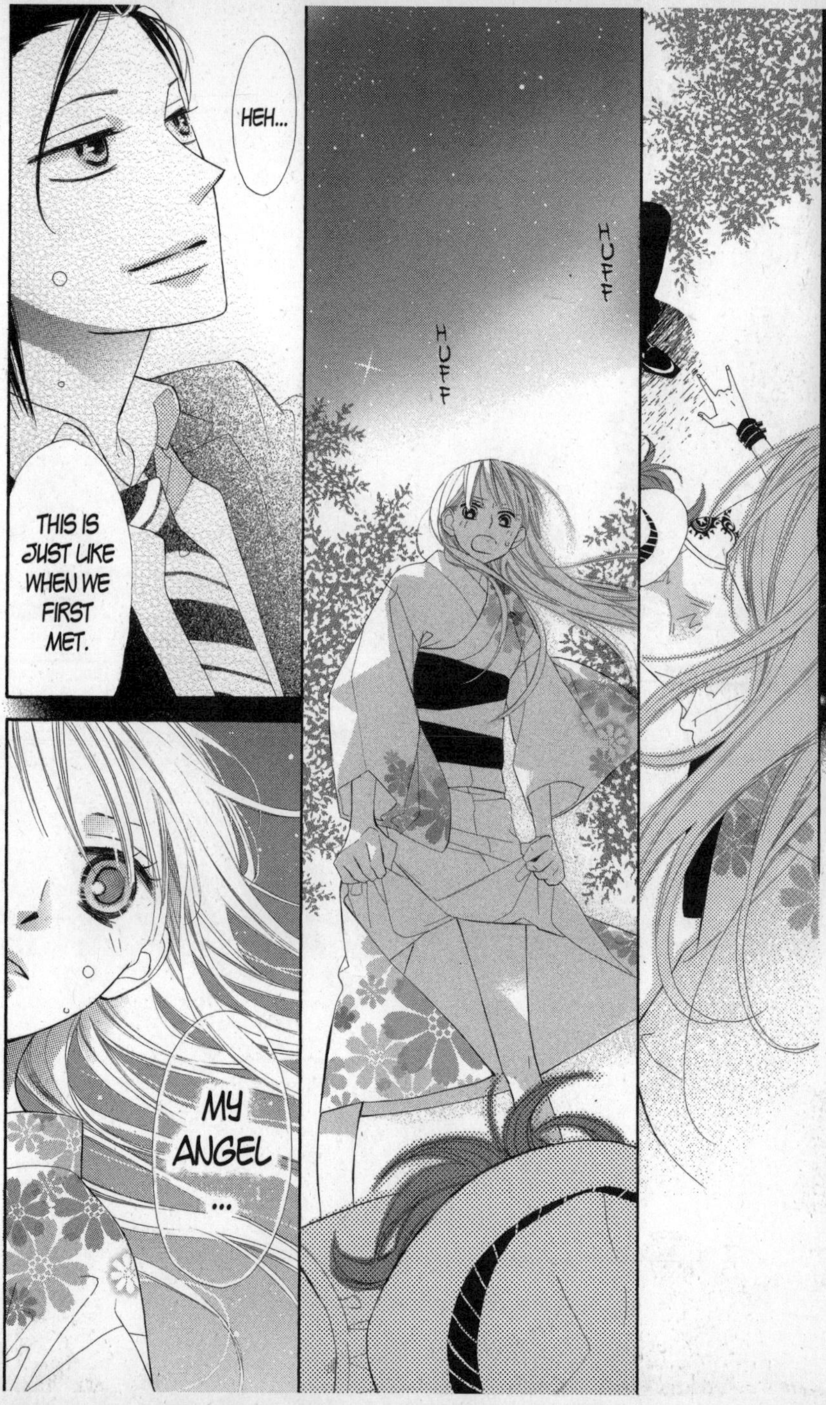
HUFF
HUFF
HEH...
THIS IS JUST LIKE WHEN WE FIRST MET.
MY ANGEL ...

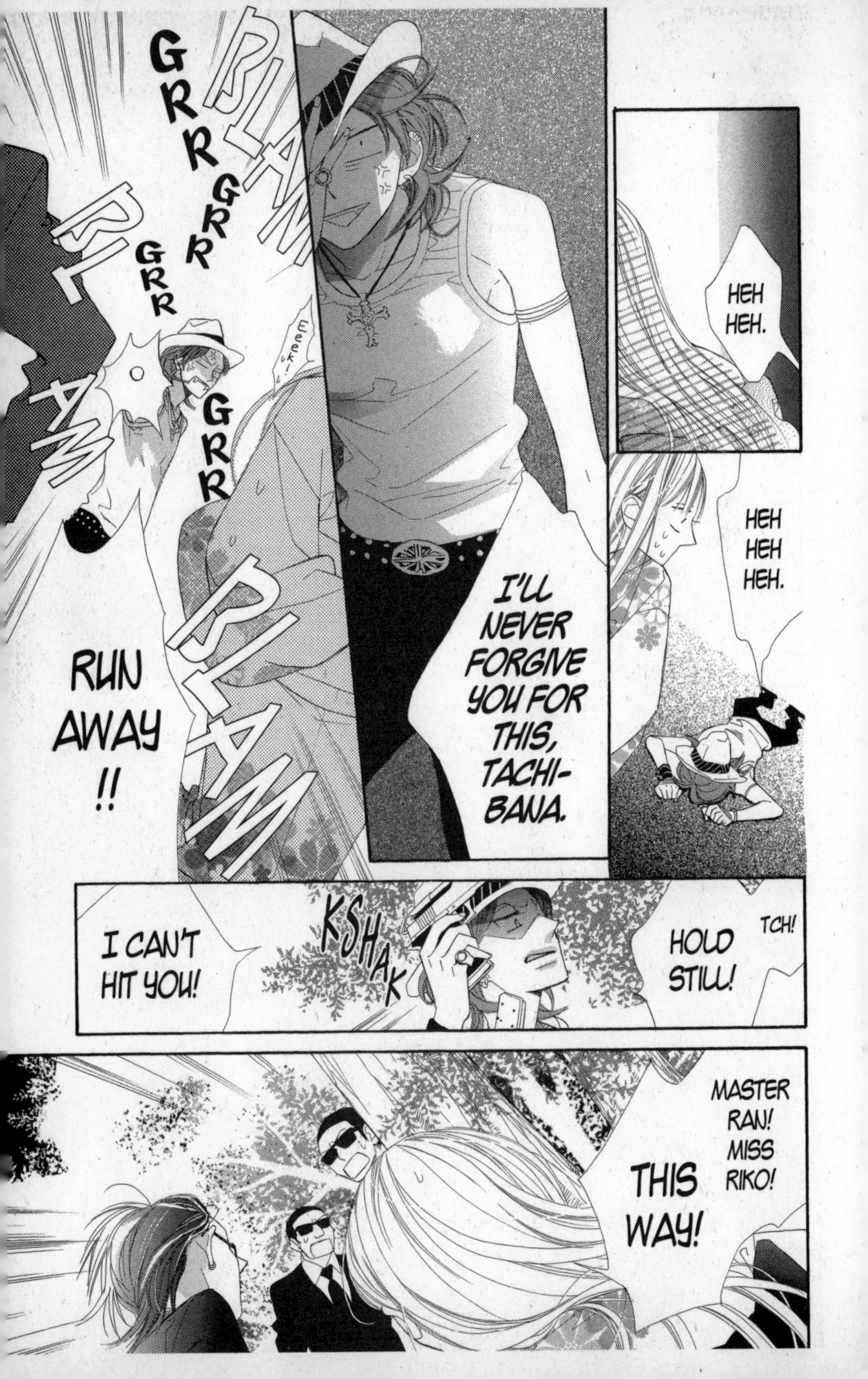
HEH HEH.
HEH HEH HEH.
I'LL NEVER FORGIVE YOU FOR THIS, TACHIBANA.
BLAM
GRR GRR
GRR
BLAM
GRR
Eeek!
BLAM
RUN AWAY!!
TCH!
HOLD STILL!
KSHAK
I CAN'T HIT YOU!
MASTER RAN! MISS RIKO!
THIS WAY!

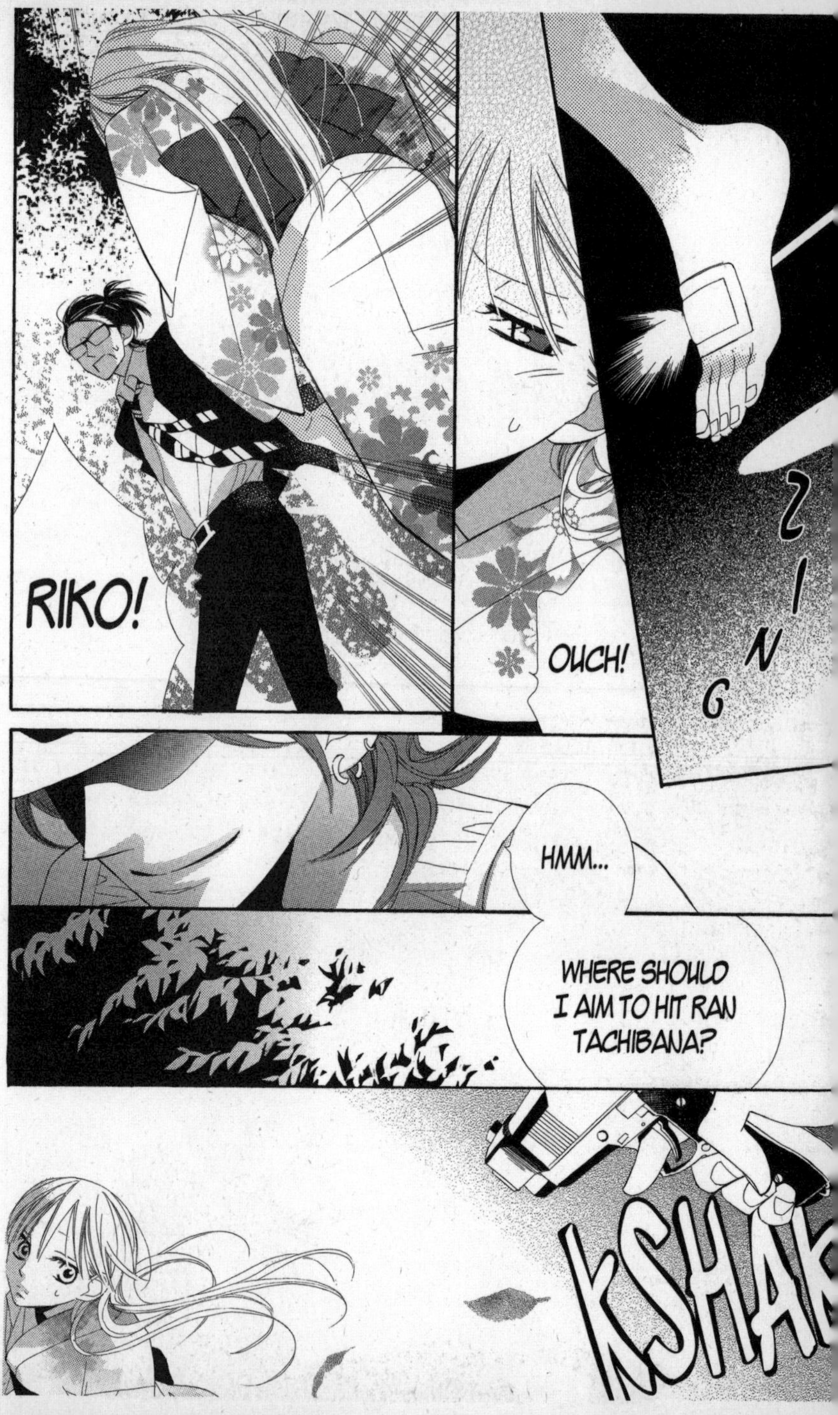
ZING
OUCH!
RIKO!
HMM...
WHERE SHOULD I AIM TO HIT RAN TACHIBANA?
KSHA

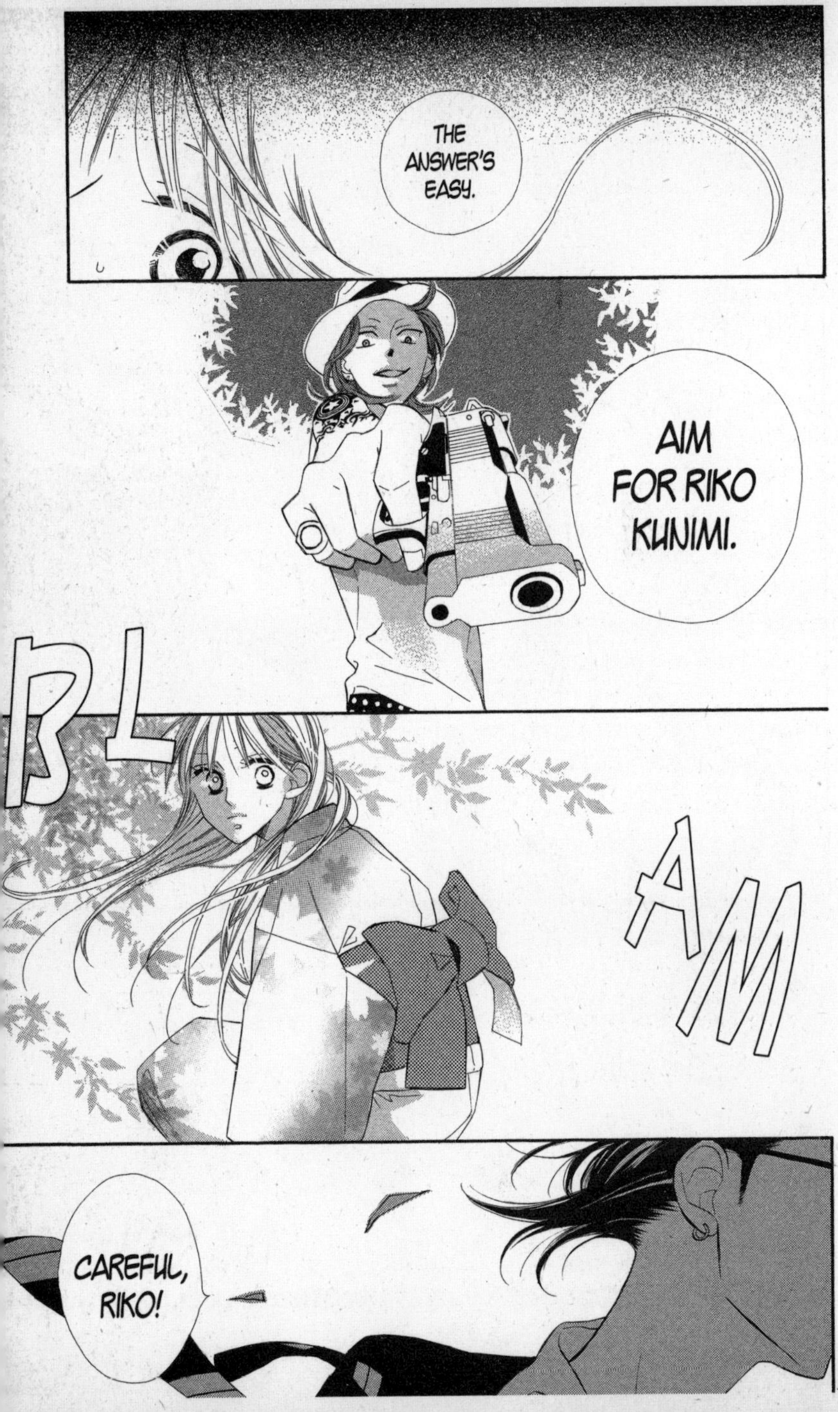
THE ANSWER'S EASY.
AIM FOR RIKO KUNIMI.
BLAM
CAREFUL, RIKO!

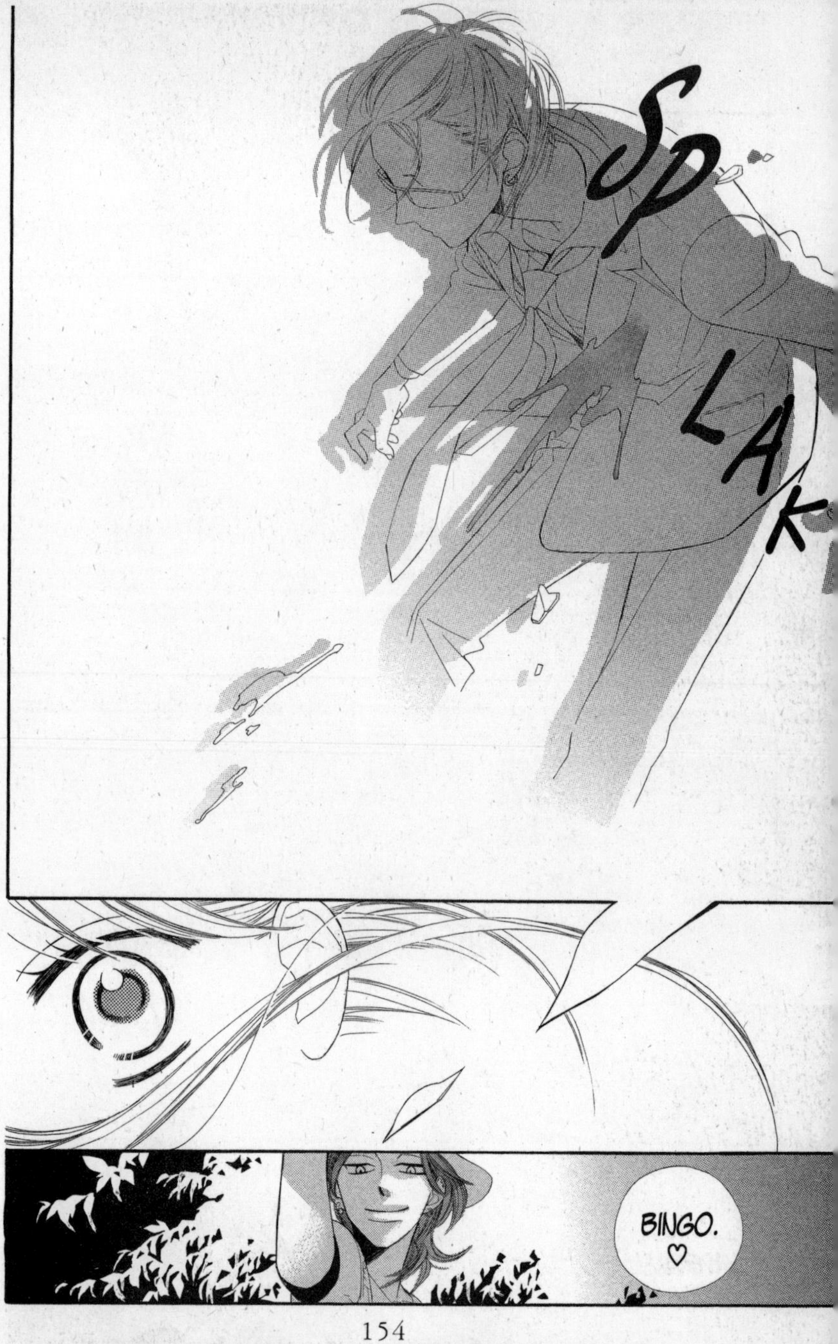
SPLAK
BINGO. ♡

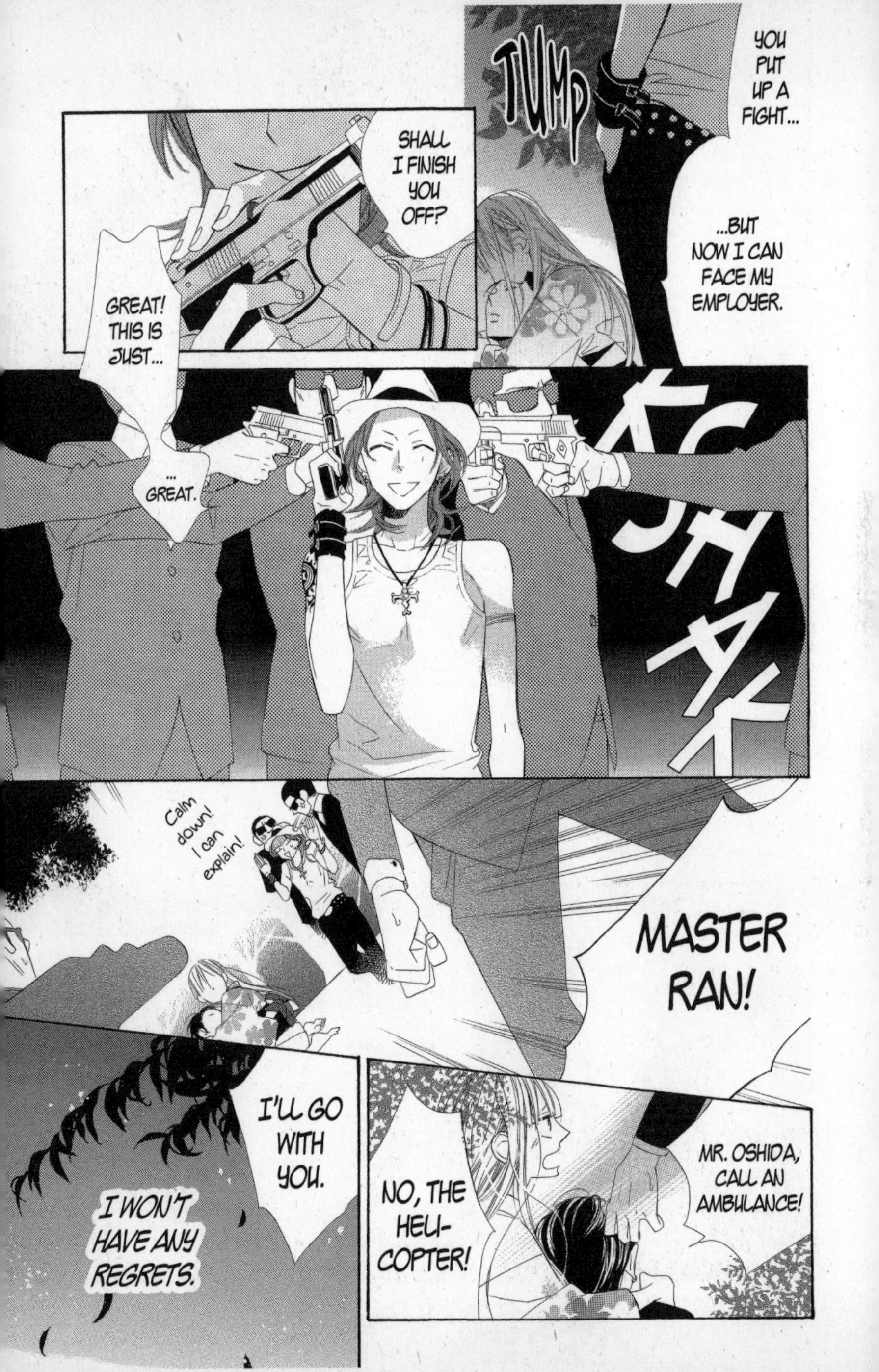
TUMP
YOU PUT UP A FIGHT...
...BUT NOW I CAN FACE MY EMPLOYER.
SHALL I FINISH YOU OFF?
GREAT! THIS IS JUST...
KASHAK
... GREAT.
Calm down! I can explain!
MASTER RAN!
MR. OSHIDA, CALL AN AMBULANCE!
NO, THE HELI-COPTER!
I'LL GO WITH YOU.
I WON'T HAVE ANY REGRETS.

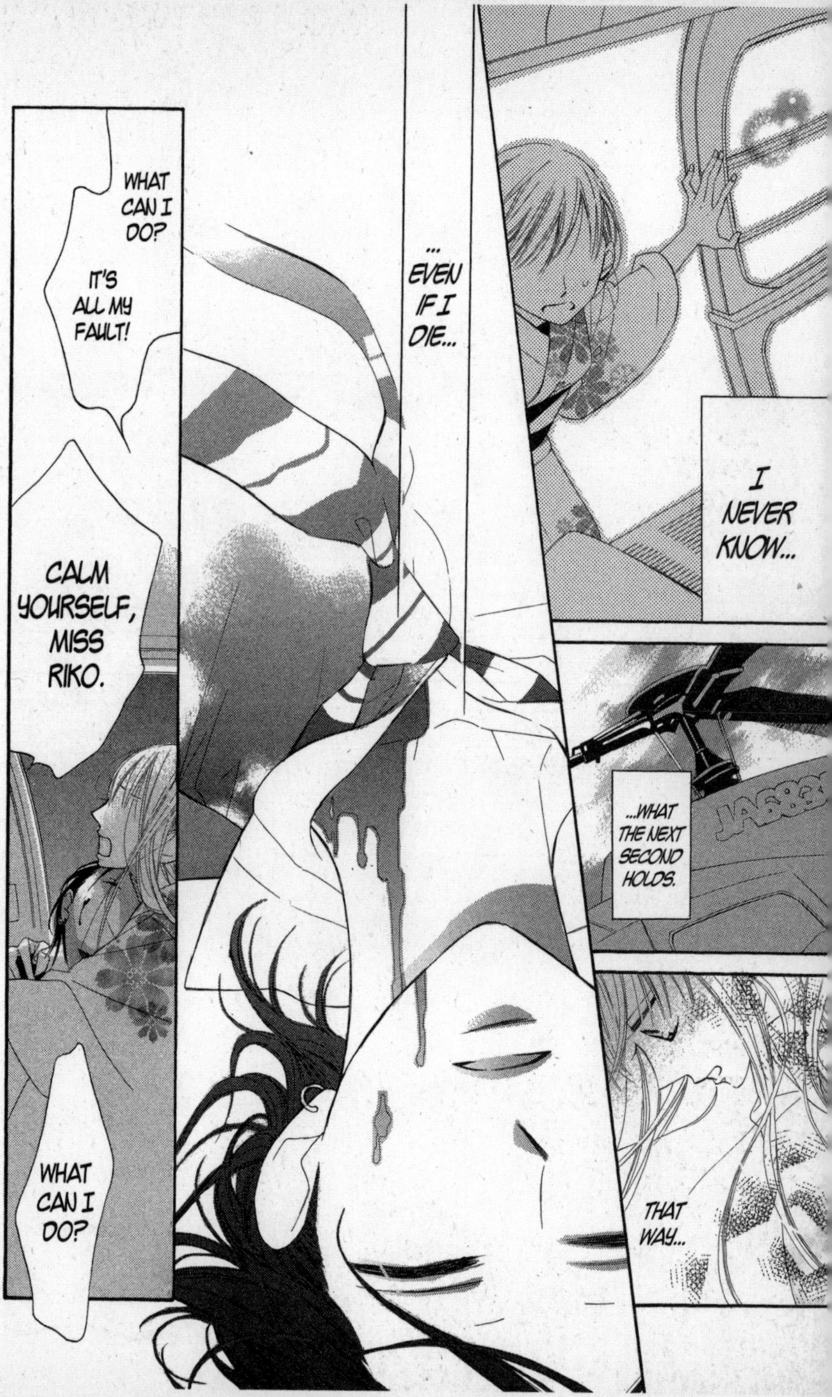
I NEVER KNOW...
...WHAT THE NEXT SECOND HOLDS.
THAT WAY...
...EVEN IF I DIE...
WHAT CAN I DO?
IT'S ALL MY FAULT!
CALM YOURSELF, MISS RIKO.
WHAT CAN I DO?

I COULDN'T BEAR TO LOSE HIM...

...TO DISAPPEAR.

I DON'T WANT THE ONE WHO STIRS EVERYTHING UP...

HM?

...

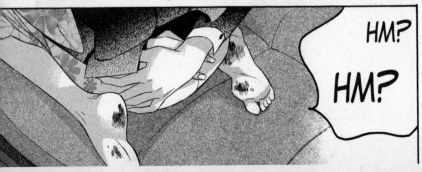

HM?

HM?

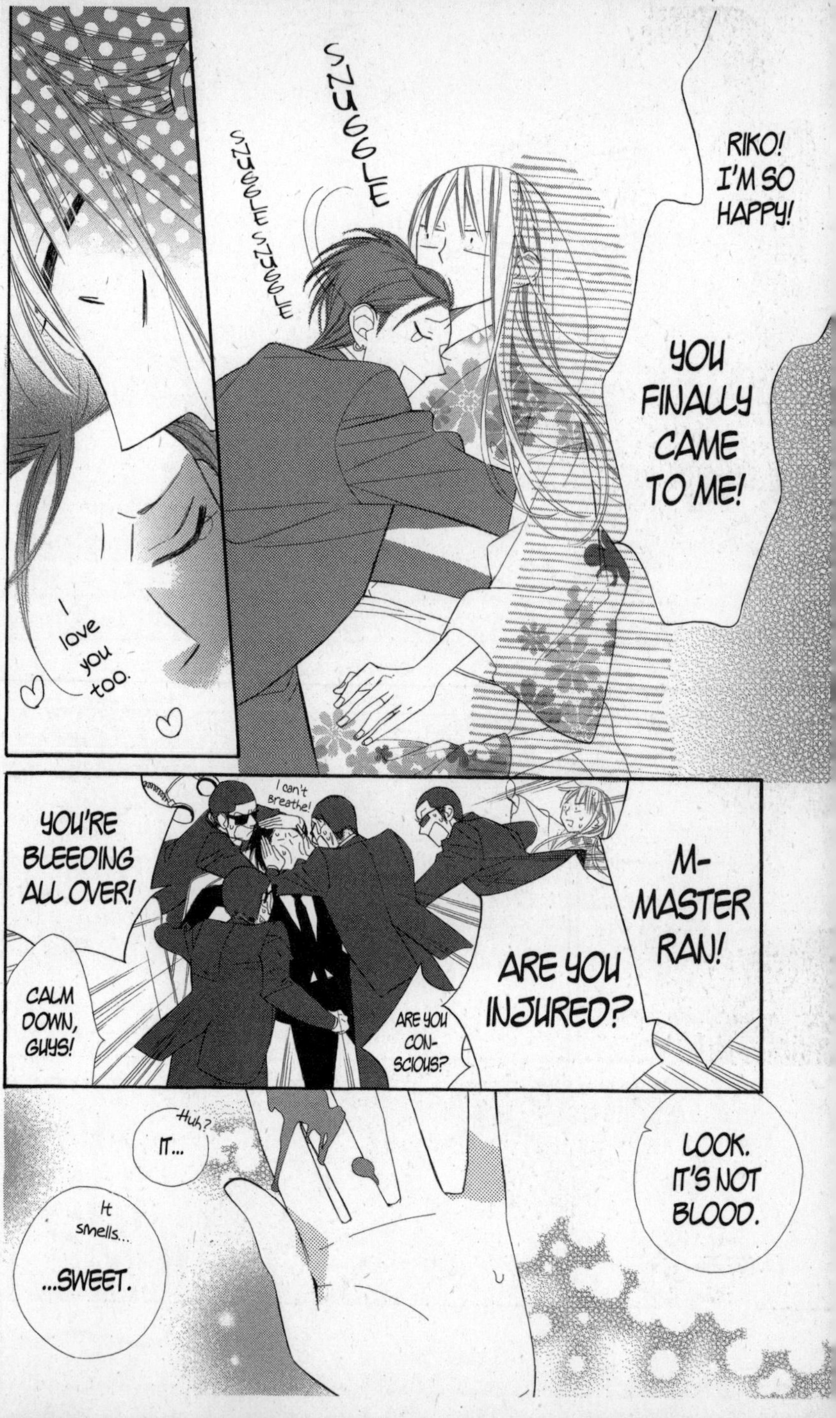
RIKO! I'M SO HAPPY!
YOU FINALLY CAME TO ME!
SNUGGLE
SNUGGLE SNUGGLE
I love you too.
M-MASTER RAN!
ARE YOU INJURED?
ARE YOU CON-SCIOUS?
I can't Breathe!
YOU'RE BLEEDING ALL OVER!
CALM DOWN, GUYS!
LOOK. IT'S NOT BLOOD.
Huh?
IT...
It smells...
...SWEET.

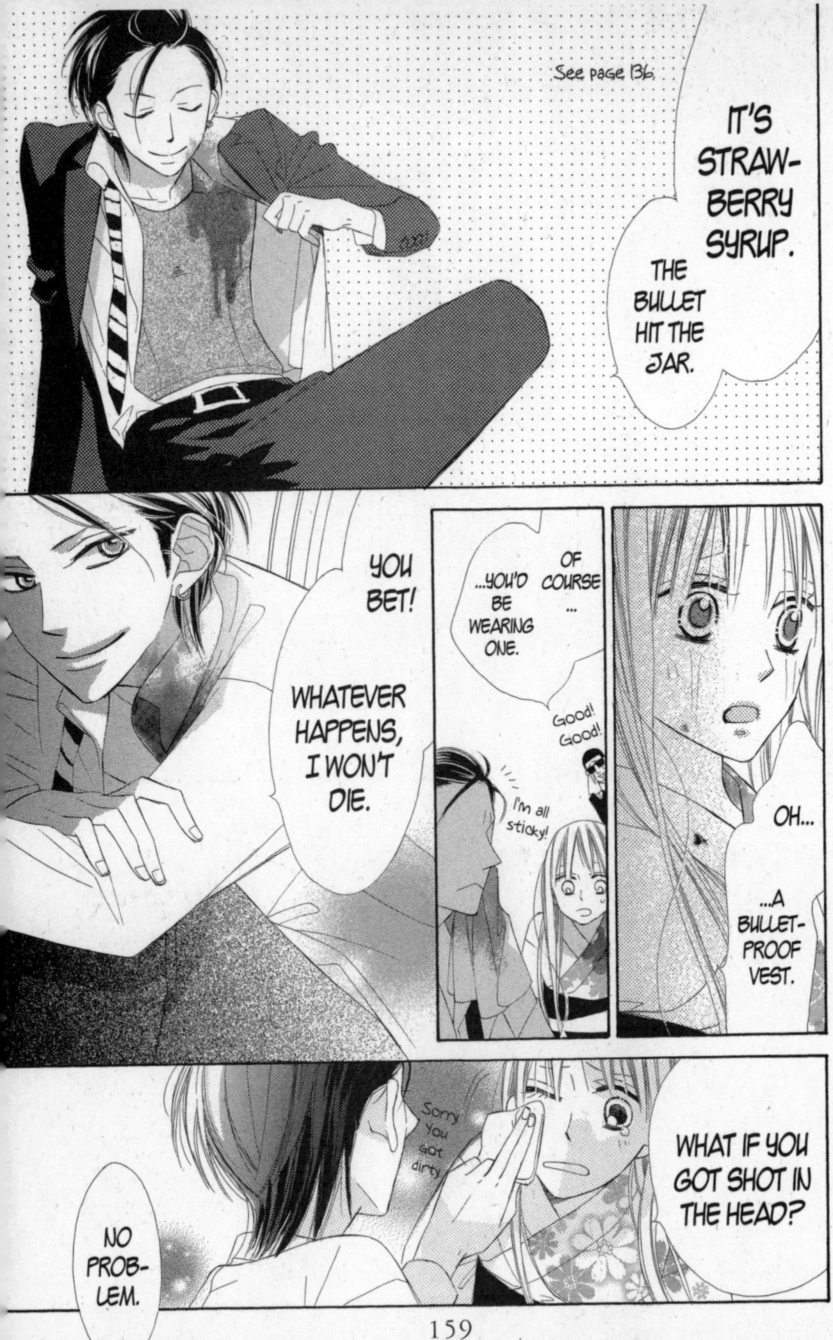
See page 136.
IT'S STRAWBERRY SYRUP.
THE BULLET HIT THE JAR.
OH...
...A BULLET-PROOF VEST.
OF COURSE...
...YOU'D BE WEARING ONE.
Good! Good!
I'm all sticky!
YOU BET!
WHATEVER HAPPENS, I WON'T DIE.
WHAT IF YOU GOT SHOT IN THE HEAD?
Sorry You got dirty
NO PROB-LEM.

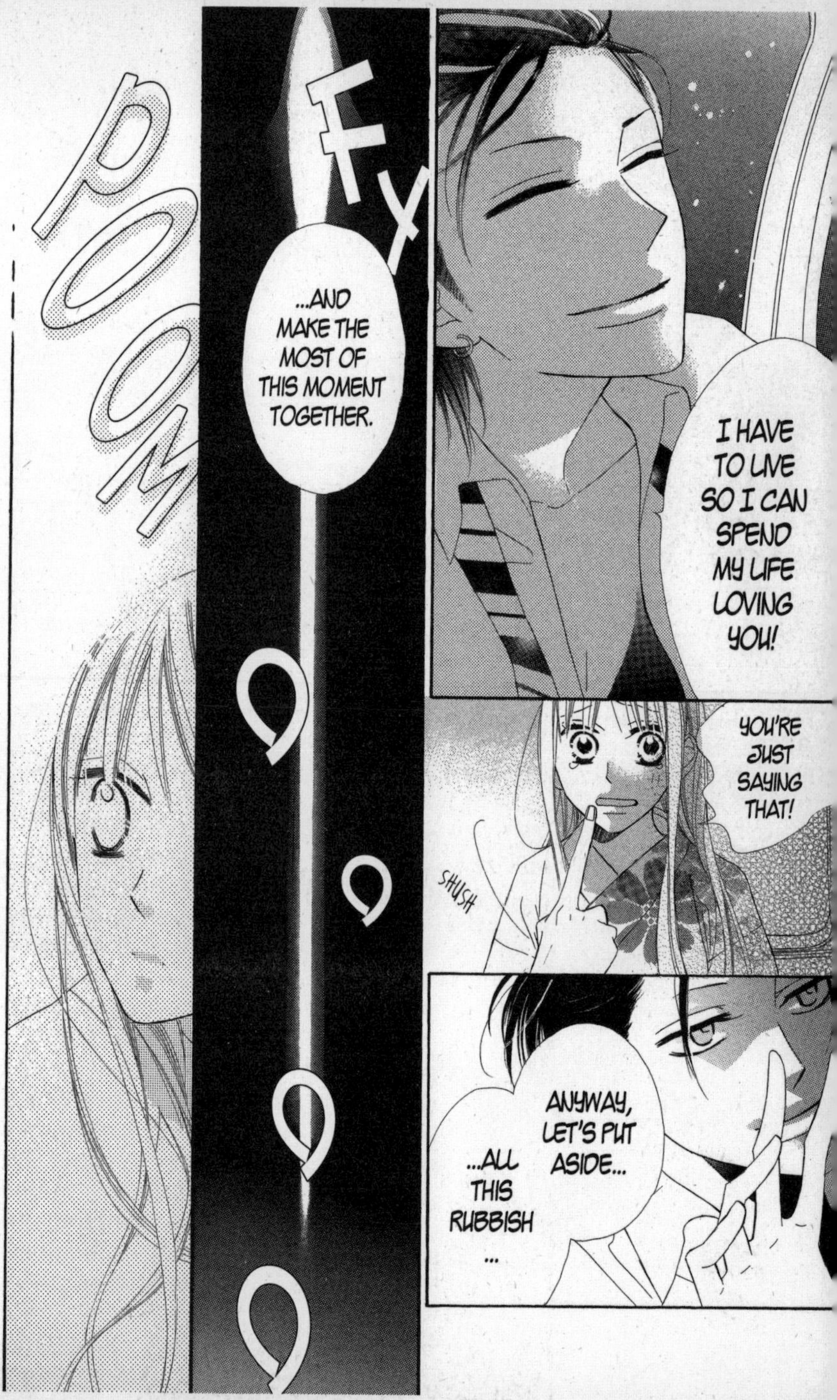
I HAVE TO LIVE SO I CAN SPEND MY LIFE LOVING YOU!
YOU'RE JUST SAYING THAT!
SHUSH
ANYWAY, LET'S PUT ASIDE...
...ALL THIS RUBBISH ...
...AND MAKE THE MOST OF THIS MOMENT TOGETHER.
POOM

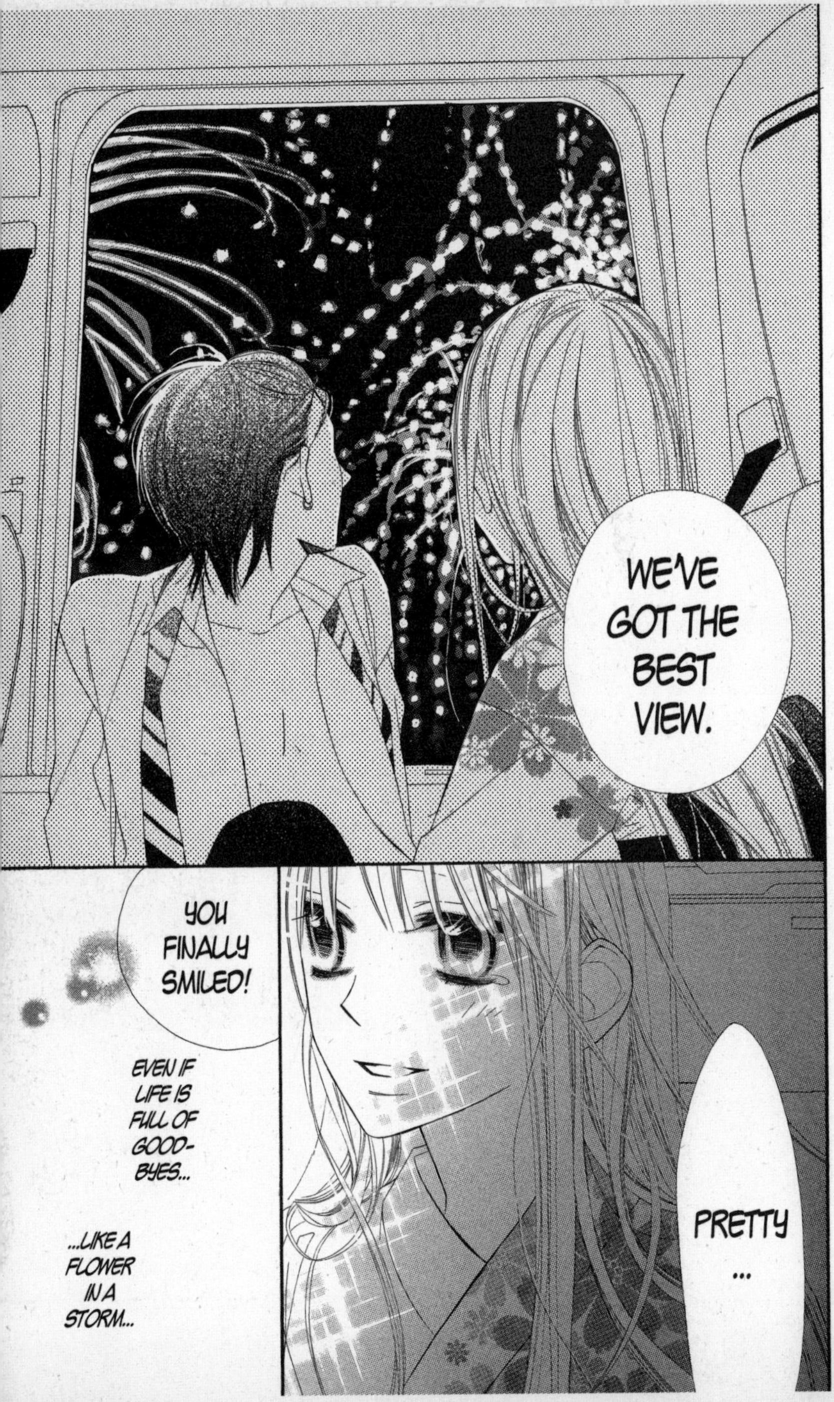
WE'VE GOT THE BEST VIEW.
PRETTY ...
YOU FINALLY SMILED!
EVEN IF LIFE IS FULL OF GOOD-BYES...
...LIKE A FLOWER IN A STORM...

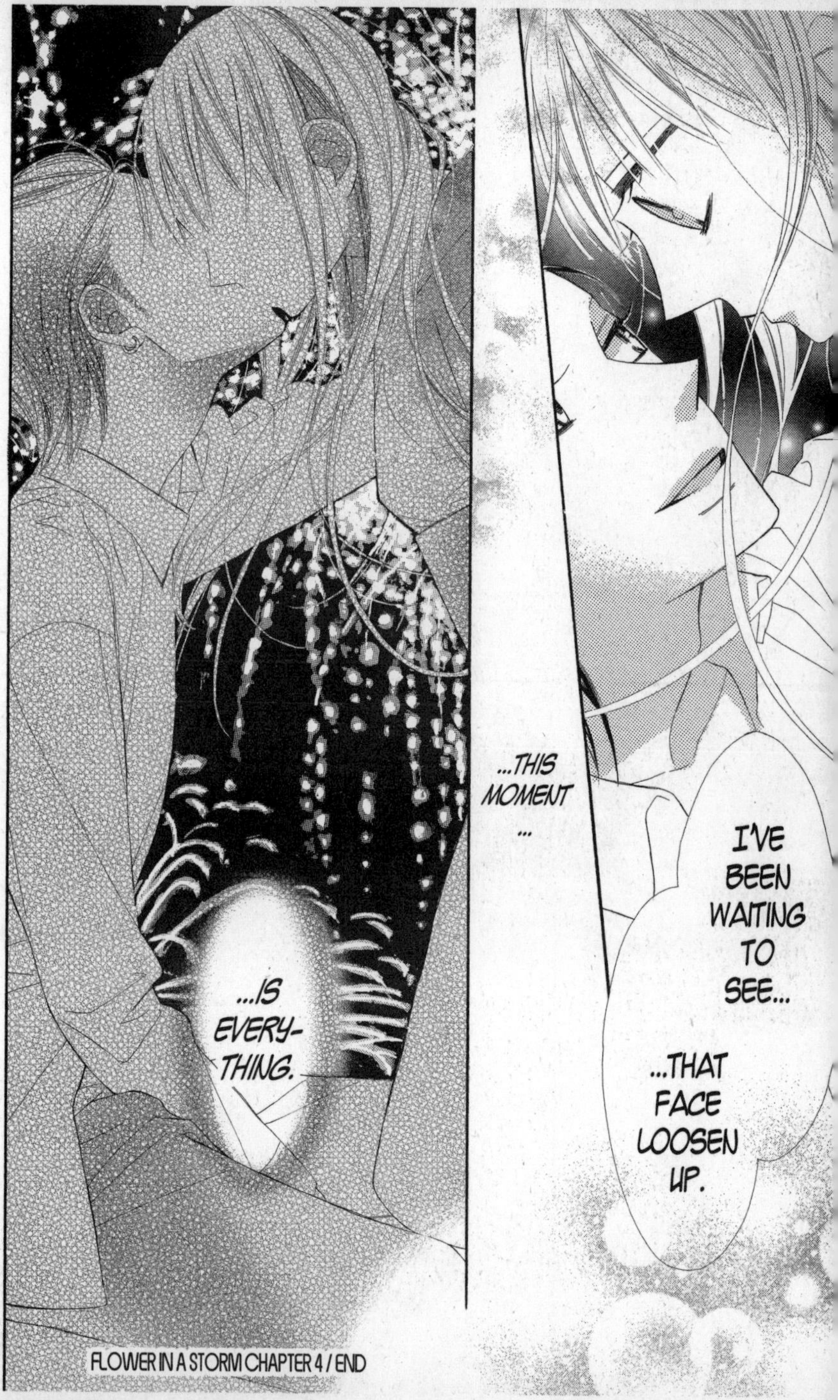
I'VE BEEN WAITING TO SEE...
...THAT FACE LOOSEN UP.
...THIS MOMENT ...
...IS EVERY-THING.

FLOWER IN A STORM CHAPTER 4 / END

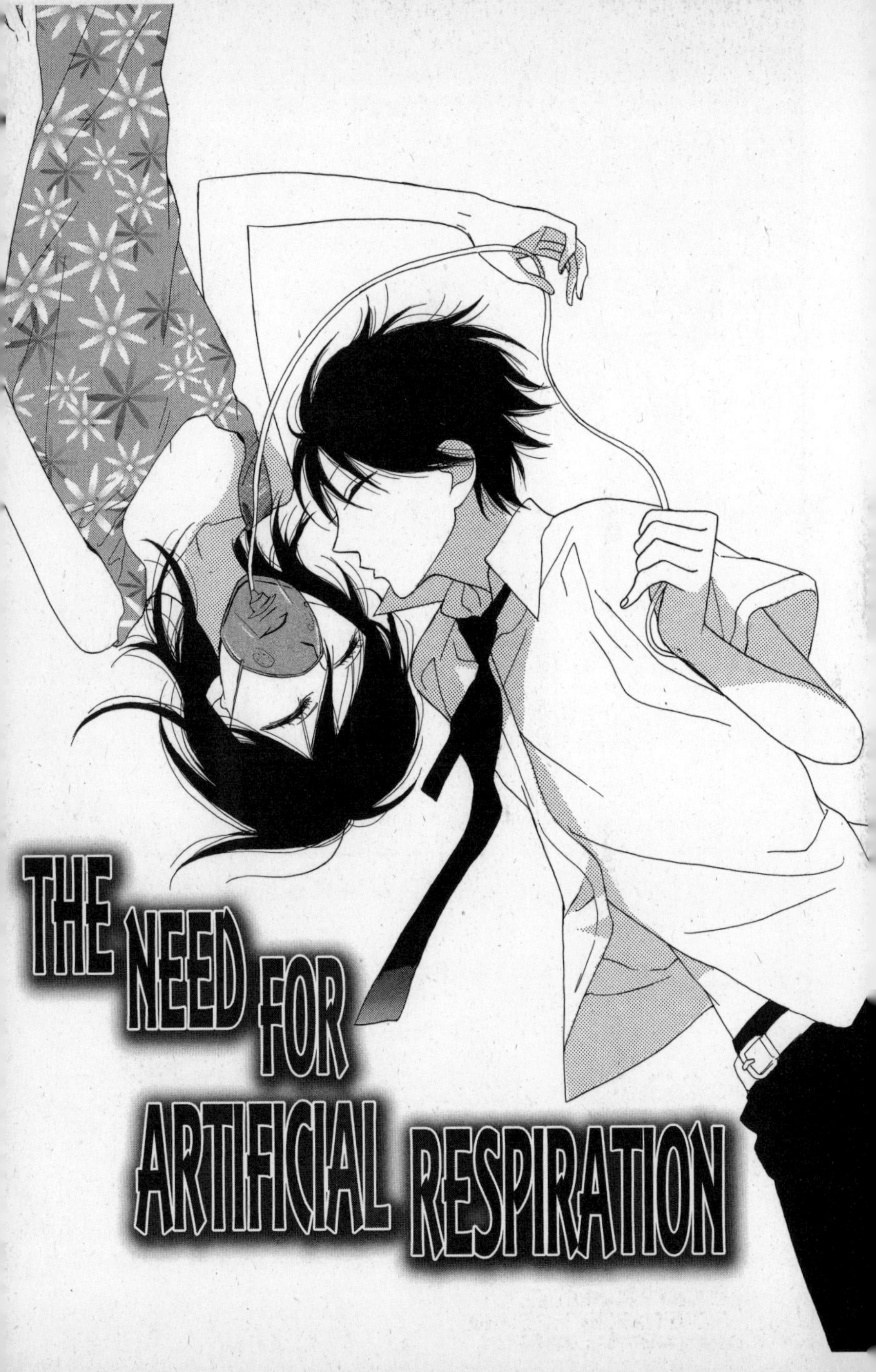
THE NEED FOR ARTIFICIAL RESPIRATION

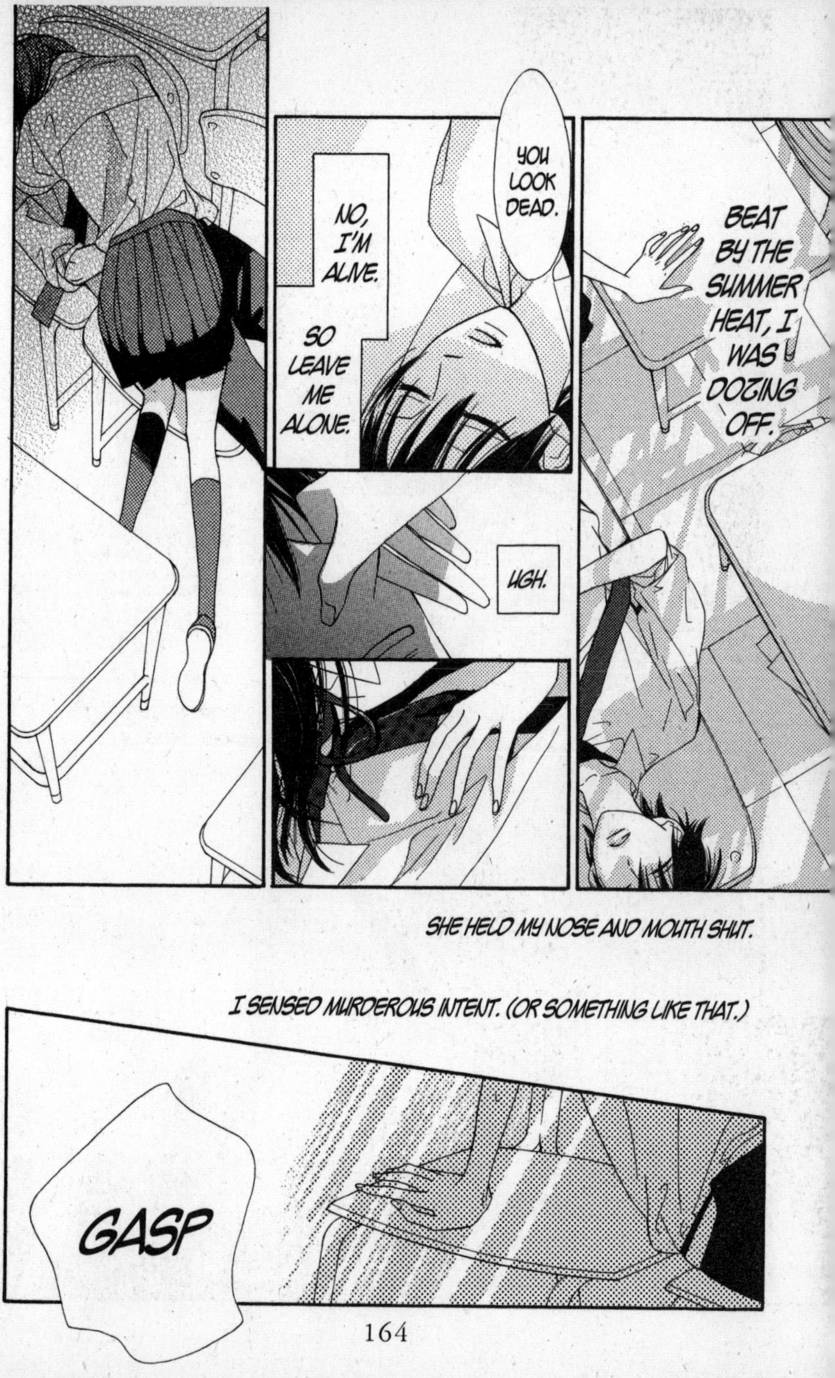
BEAT BY THE SUMMER HEAT, I WAS DOZING OFF.
YOU LOOK DEAD.
NO, I'M ALIVE.
SO LEAVE ME ALONE.
UGH.
SHE HELD MY NOSE AND MOUTH SHUT.
I SENSED MURDEROUS INTENT. (OR SOMETHING LIKE THAT.)
GASP

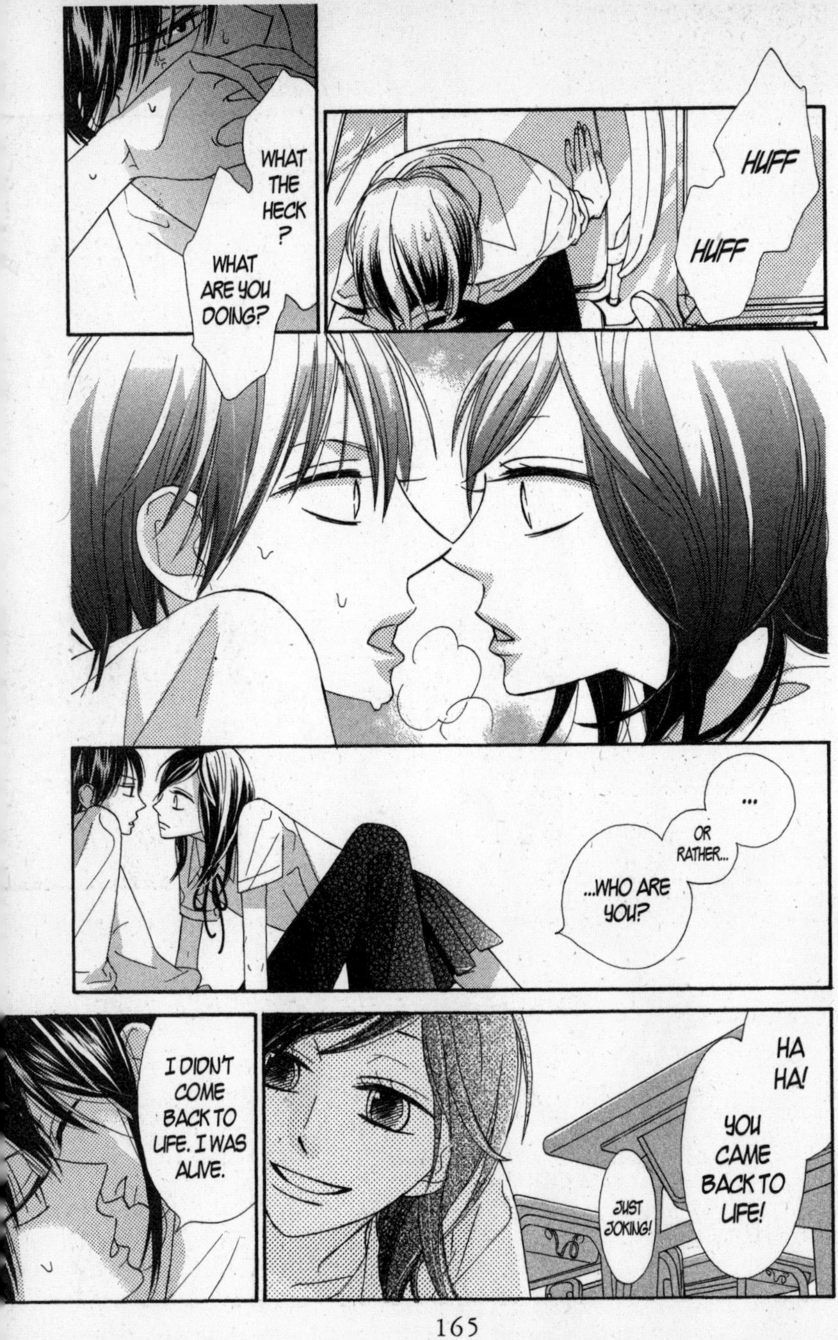
HUFF
HUFF
WHAT THE HECK?
WHAT ARE YOU DOING?
...
OR RATHER...
...WHO ARE YOU?
HA HA!
YOU CAME BACK TO LIFE!
JUST JOKING!
I DIDN'T COME BACK TO LIFE. I WAS ALIVE.

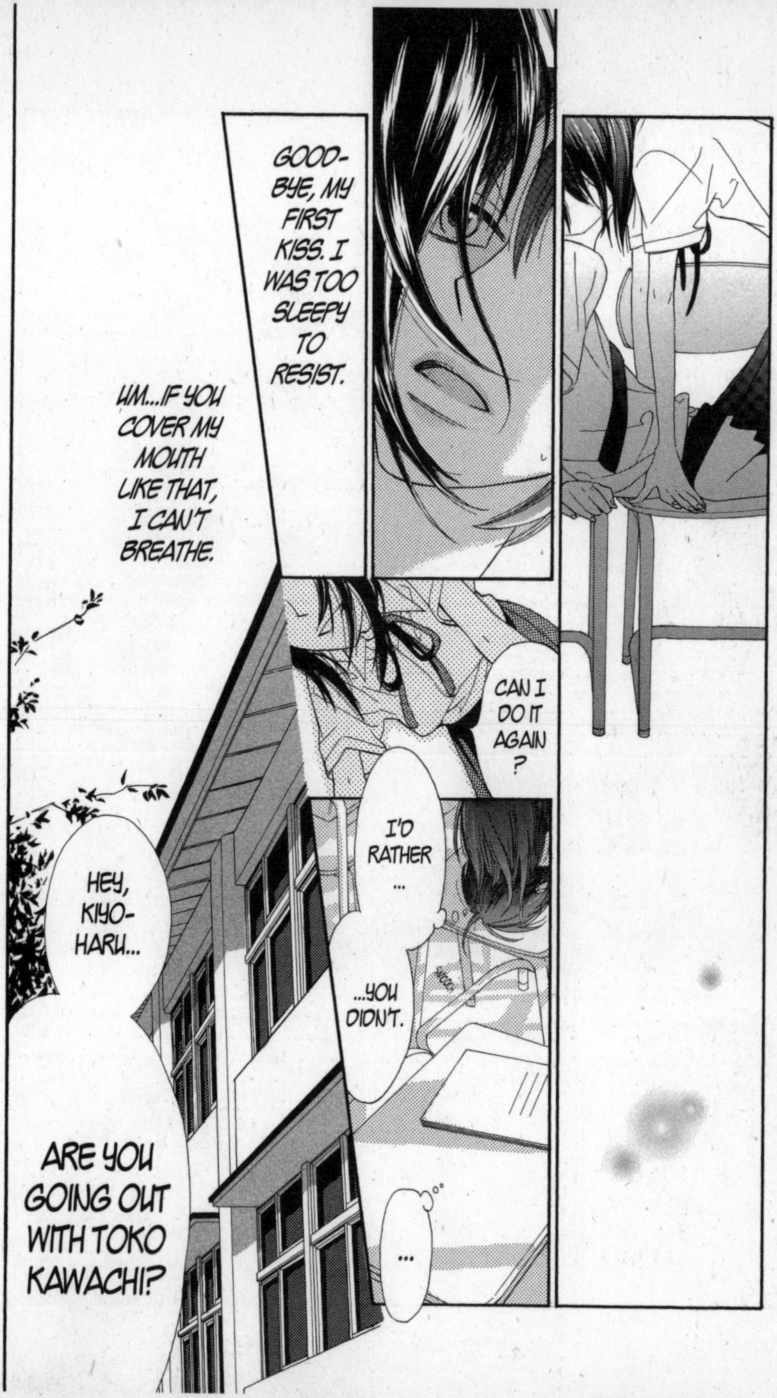
GOOD-BYE, MY FIRST KISS. I WAS TOO SLEEPY TO RESIST.
UM...IF YOU COVER MY MOUTH LIKE THAT, I CAN'T BREATHE.
CAN I DO IT AGAIN?
I'D RATHER...
...YOU DIDN'T.
...
HEY, KIYO-HARU...
ARE YOU GOING OUT WITH TOKO KAWACHI?

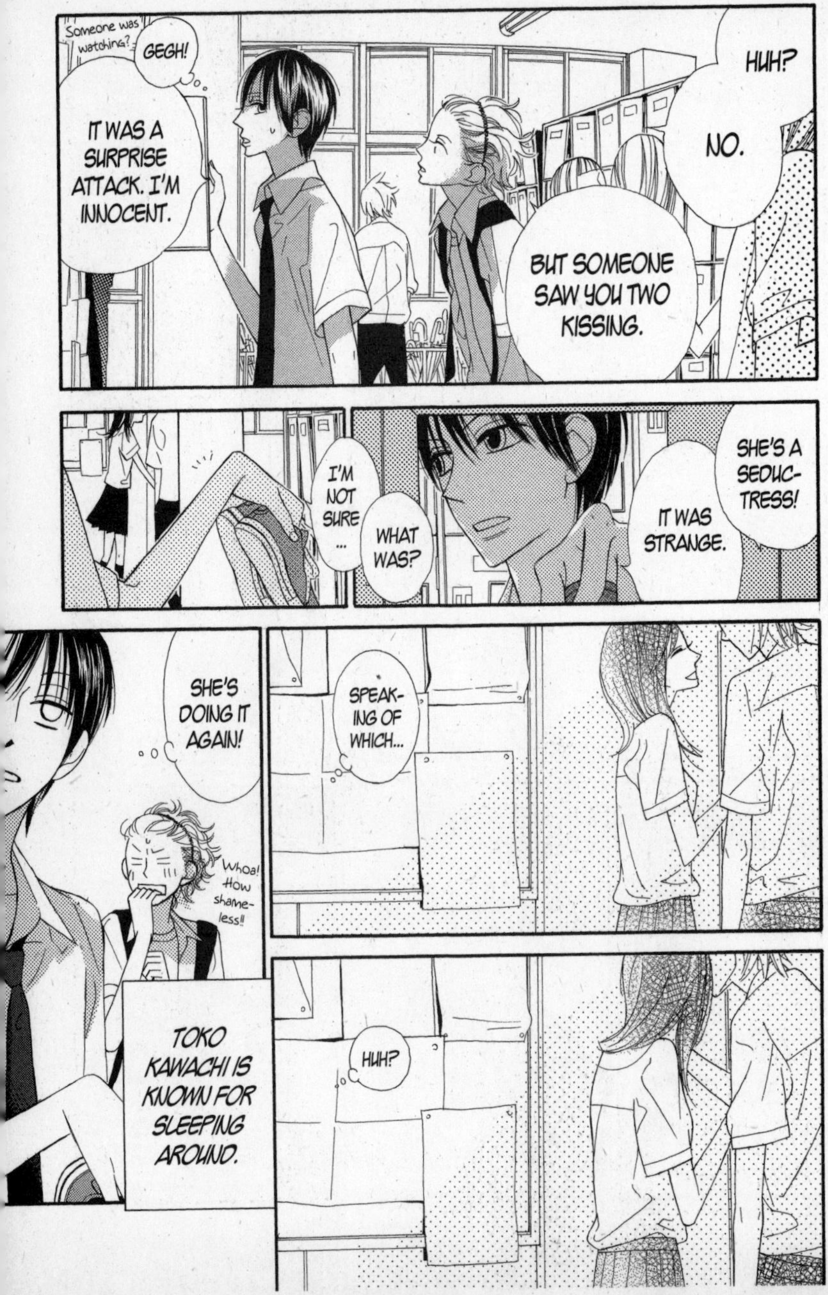
HUH?
NO.
BUT SOMEONE SAW YOU TWO KISSING.
Someone was watching?
GEGH!
IT WAS A SURPRISE ATTACK. I'M INNOCENT.
SHE'S A SEDUC-TRESS!
IT WAS STRANGE.
WHAT WAS?
I'M NOT SURE ...
SPEAK-ING OF WHICH...
HUH?
SHE'S DOING IT AGAIN!
Whoa! How shame-less!!
TOKO KAWACHI IS KNOWN FOR SLEEPING AROUND.

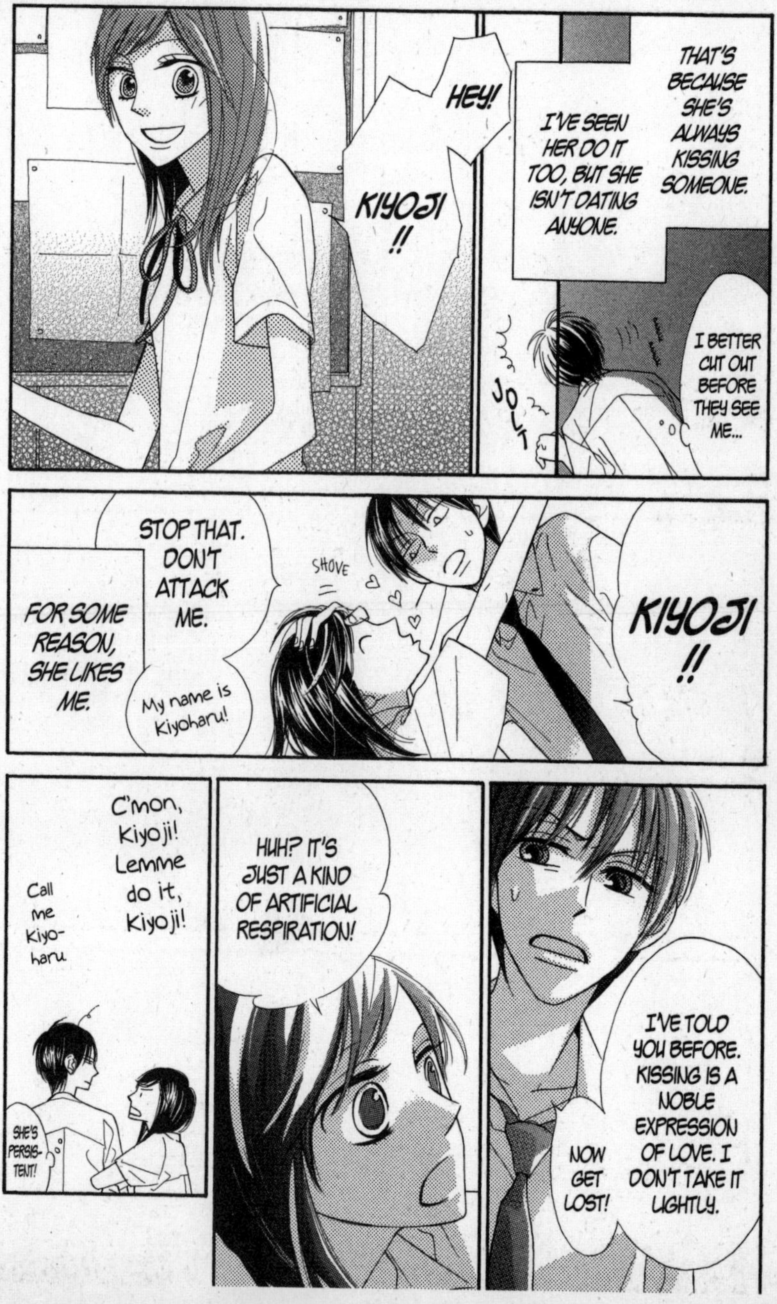
THAT'S BECAUSE SHE'S ALWAYS KISSING SOMEONE.
I'VE SEEN HER DO IT TOO, BUT SHE ISN'T DATING ANYONE.
I BETTER CUT OUT BEFORE THEY SEE ME...
JOLT
HEY!
KIYOJI!!
KIYOJI!!
STOP THAT. DON'T ATTACK ME.
SHOVE
My name is Kiyoharu!
FOR SOME REASON, SHE LIKES ME.
I'VE TOLD YOU BEFORE. KISSING IS A NOBLE EXPRESSION OF LOVE. I DON'T TAKE IT LIGHTLY.
NOW GET LOST!
HUH? IT'S JUST A KIND OF ARTIFICIAL RESPIRATION!
C'mon, Kiyoji! Lemme do it, Kiyoji!
Call me Kiyoharu.
SHE'S PERSISTENT!

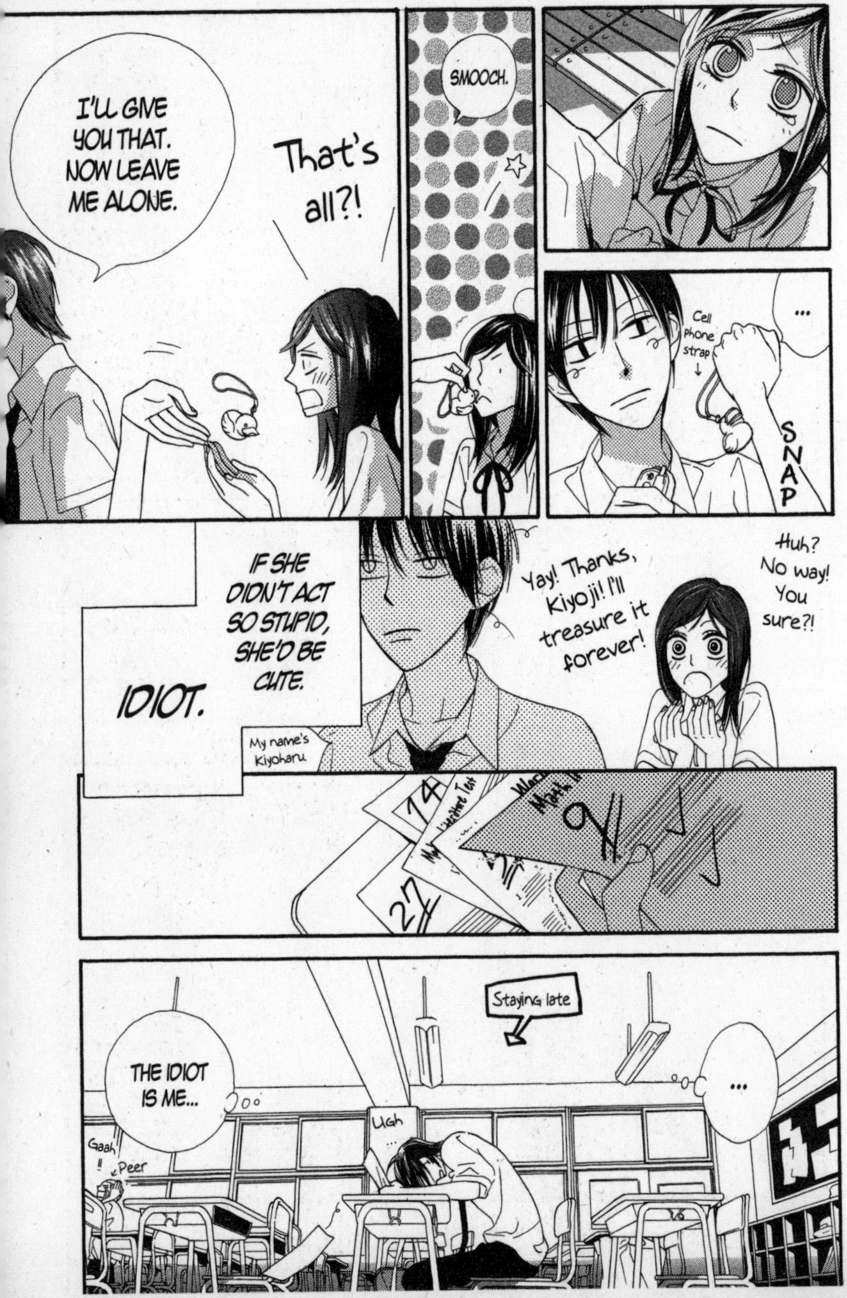
...
Cell phone strap ↓
SNAP
SMOOCH.
I'LL GIVE YOU THAT. NOW LEAVE ME ALONE.
That's all?!
Huh? No way! You sure?!
Yay! Thanks, Kiyoji! I'll treasure it forever!
My name's Kiyoharu.
IF SHE DIDN'T ACT SO STUPID, SHE'D BE CUTE.
IDIOT.
Staying late
...
THE IDIOT IS ME...
Ugh ...
Gaah !!
Peer

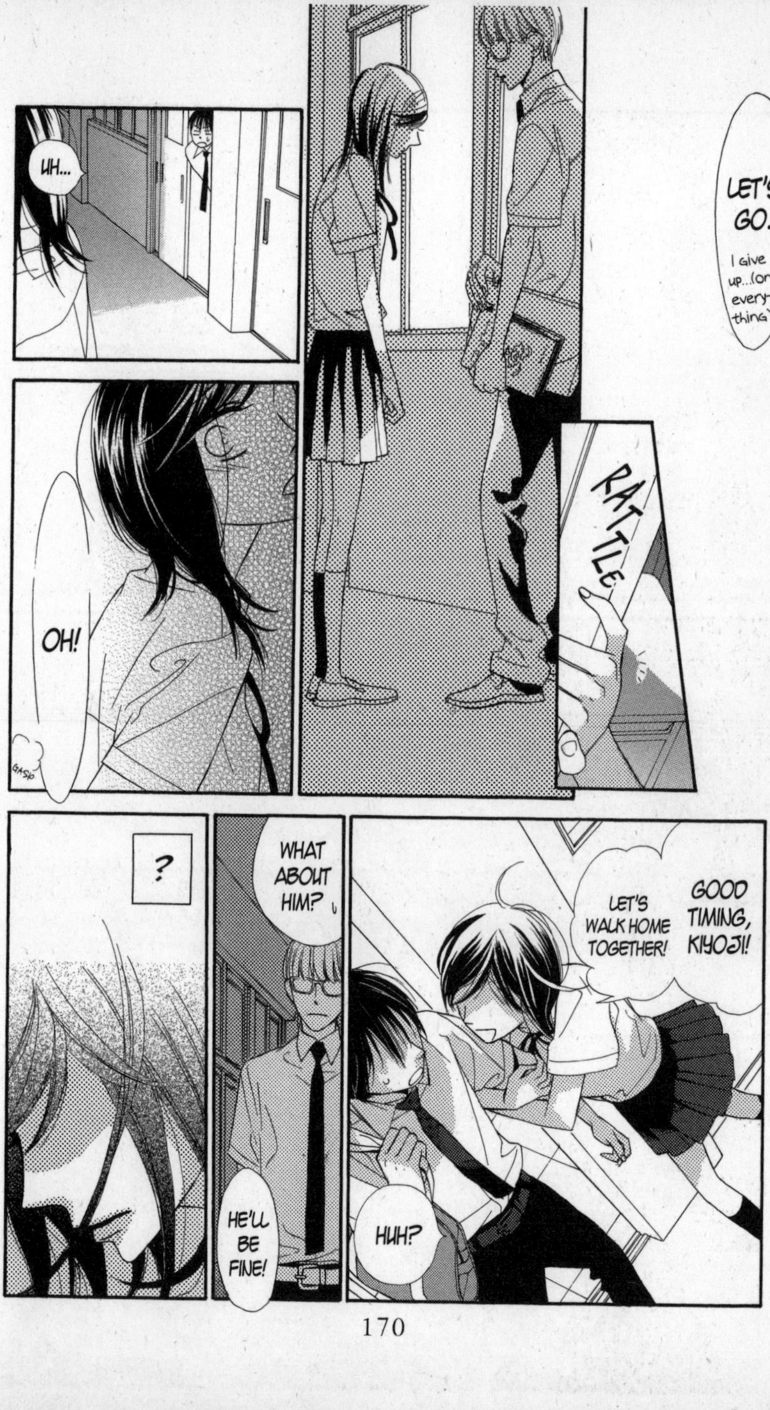
LET'S GO.
I give up...(on every-thing).
RATTLE
UH...
OH!
GASP
GOOD TIMING, KIYOJI!
LET'S WALK HOME TOGETHER!
HUH?
WHAT ABOUT HIM?
HE'LL BE FINE!
?

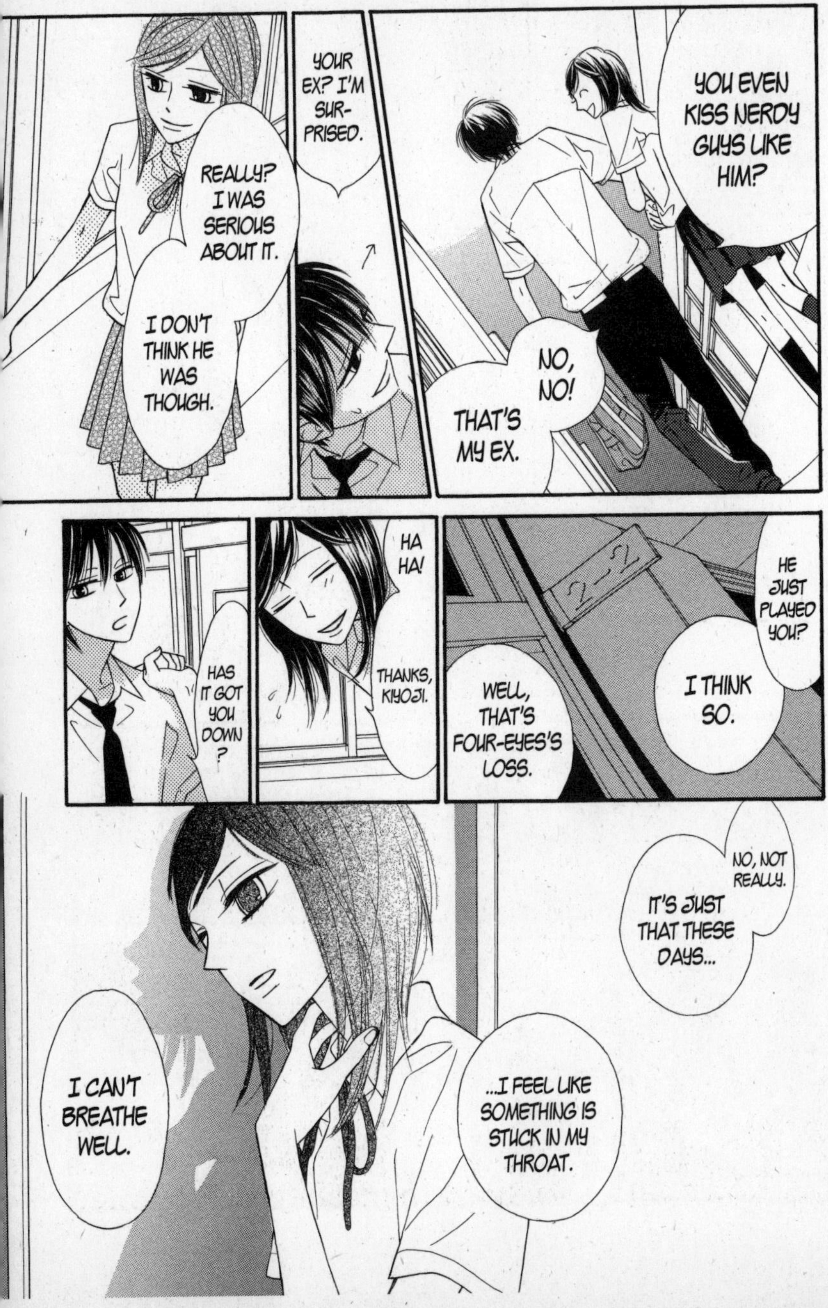
YOU EVEN KISS NERDY GUYS LIKE HIM?
NO, NO!
THAT'S MY EX.
YOUR EX? I'M SUR-PRISED.
REALLY? I WAS SERIOUS ABOUT IT.
I DON'T THINK HE WAS THOUGH.
HE JUST PLAYED YOU?
I THINK SO.
WELL, THAT'S FOUR-EYES'S LOSS.
HA HA!
THANKS, KIYOJI.
HAS IT GOT YOU DOWN?
NO, NOT REALLY.
IT'S JUST THAT THESE DAYS...
...I FEEL LIKE SOMETHING IS STUCK IN MY THROAT.
I CAN'T BREATHE WELL.

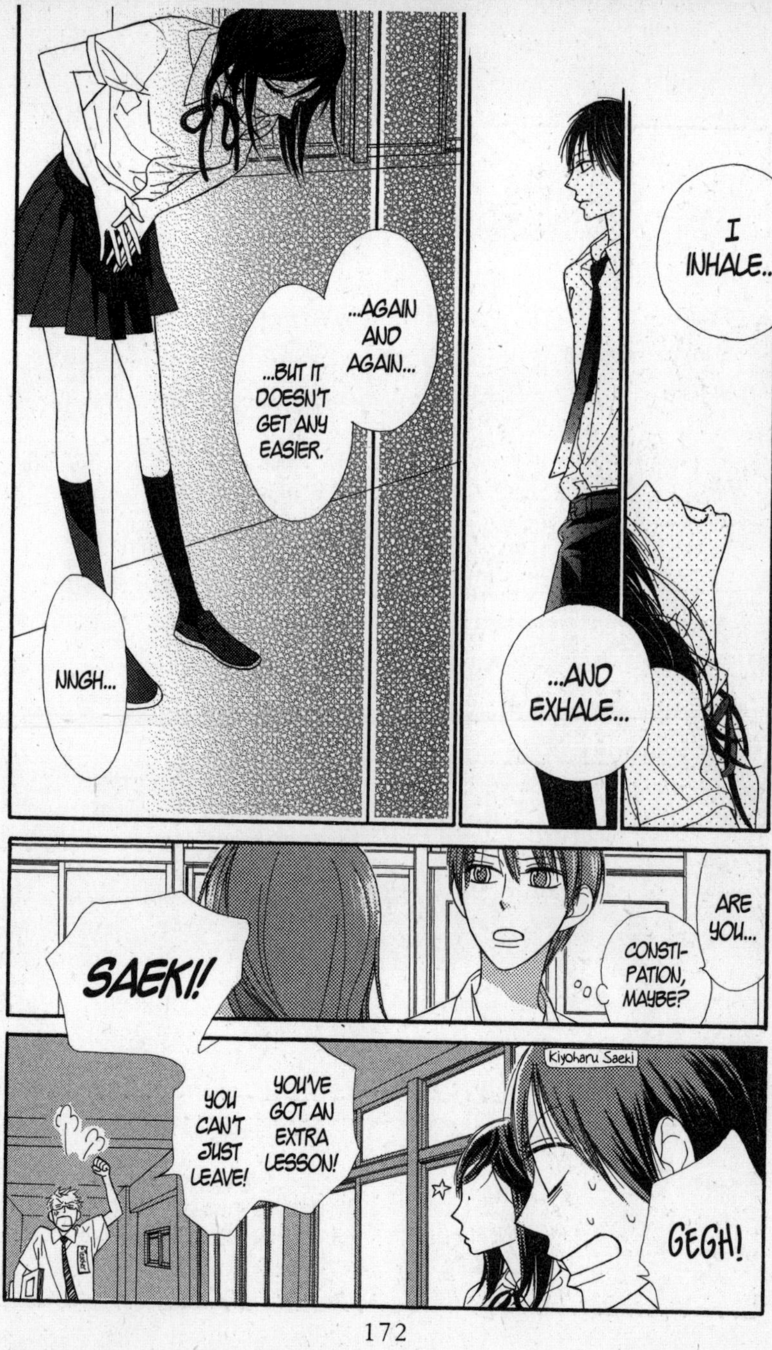
I INHALE...
...AND EXHALE...
...AGAIN AND AGAIN...
...BUT IT DOESN'T GET ANY EASIER.
NNGH...
ARE YOU...
CONSTI-PATION, MAYBE?
SAEKI!
Kiyoharu Saeki
GEGH!
YOU'VE GOT AN EXTRA LESSON!
YOU CAN'T JUST LEAVE!

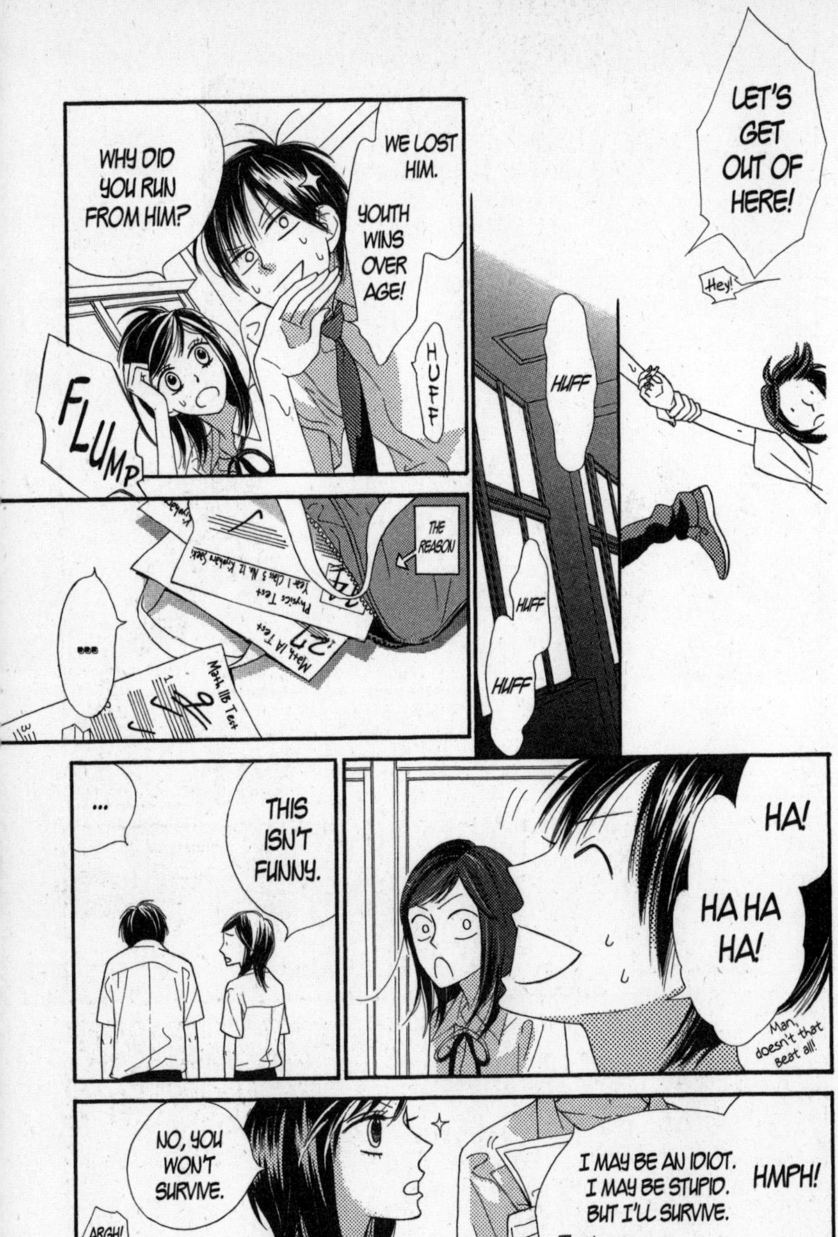

LET'S GET OUT OF HERE!
Hey!
HUFF
HUFF
HUFF
WE LOST HIM.
YOUTH WINS OVER AGE!
HUFF
WHY DID YOU RUN FROM HIM?
FLUMP
THE REASON
Physics Test
Math IA Test
Math IIB Test
...
HA!
HA HA HA!
Man, doesn't that beat all!
THIS ISN'T FUNNY.
...
HMPH!
I MAY BE AN IDIOT. I MAY BE STUPID. BUT I'LL SURVIVE.
That's the way Japan is.
NO, YOU WON'T SURVIVE.
ARGH!

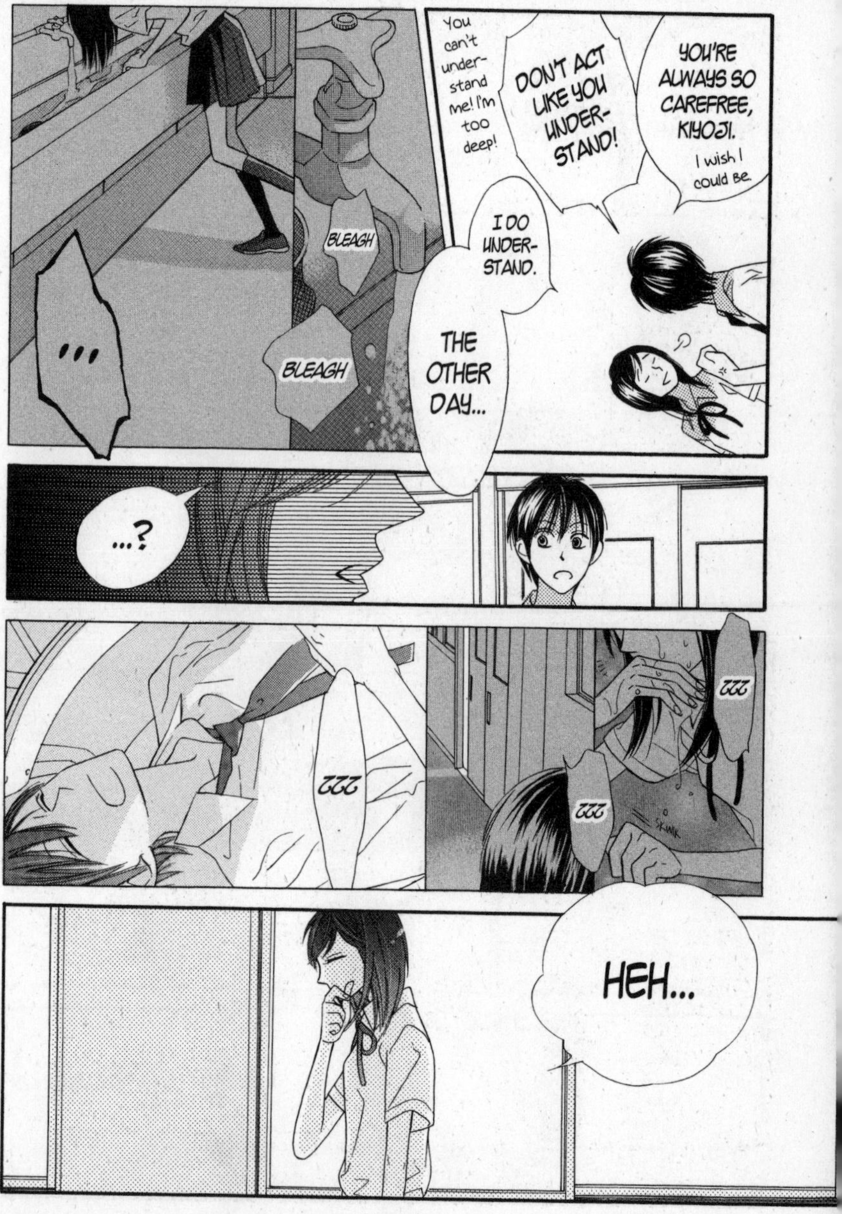
YOU'RE ALWAYS SO CAREFREE, KIYOJI.
I wish I could be.
DON'T ACT LIKE YOU UNDER-STAND!
You can't under-stand me! I'm too deep!
I DO UNDER-STAND.
THE OTHER DAY...
BLEAGH
BLEAGH
...
...?
ZZZ
ZZZ
SKWIK
ZZZ
HEH...

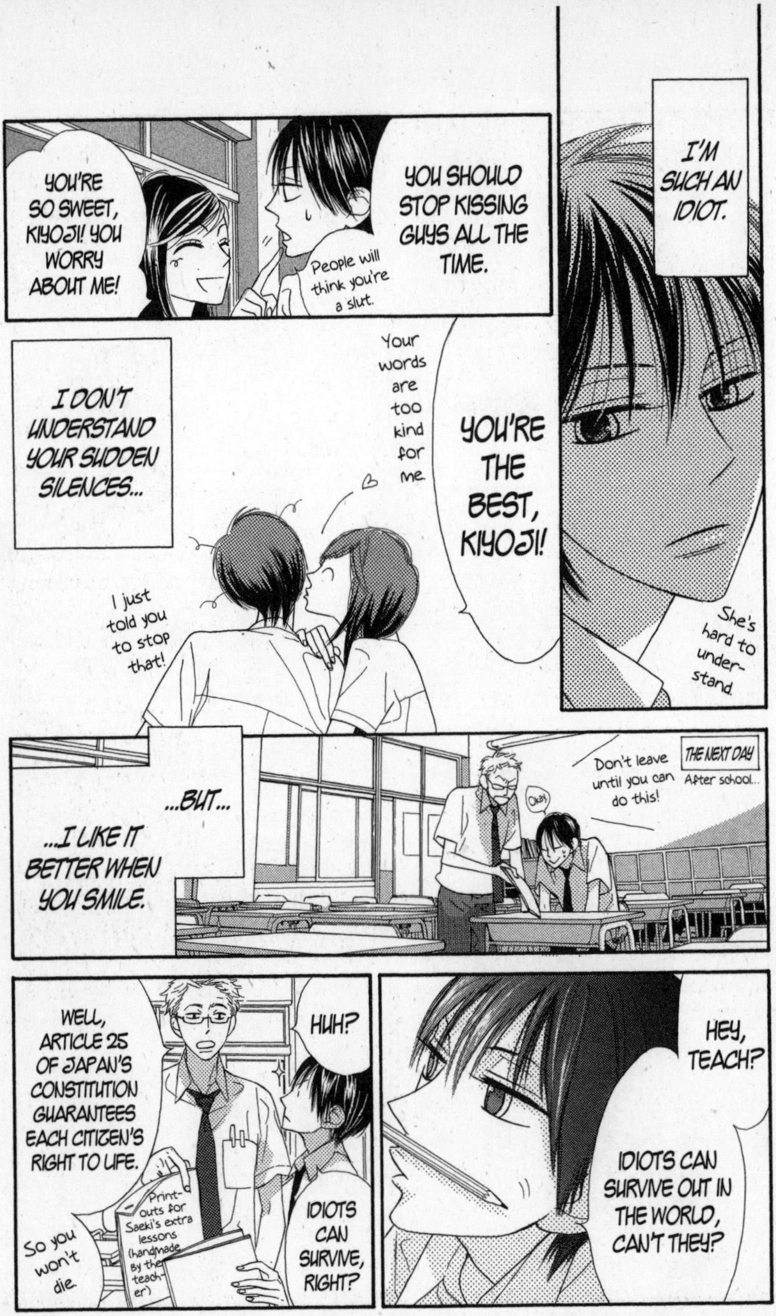
I'M SUCH AN IDIOT.
She's hard to understand.
YOU SHOULD STOP KISSING GUYS ALL THE TIME.
People will think you're a slut.
YOU'RE SO SWEET, KIYOJI! YOU WORRY ABOUT ME!
YOU'RE THE BEST, KIYOJI!
Your words are too kind for me.
I just told you to stop that!
I DON'T UNDERSTAND YOUR SUDDEN SILENCES...
THE NEXT DAY
After school...
Don't leave until you can do this!
Okay
...BUT...
...I LIKE IT BETTER WHEN YOU SMILE.
HEY, TEACH?
IDIOTS CAN SURVIVE OUT IN THE WORLD, CAN'T THEY?
HUH?
IDIOTS CAN SURVIVE, RIGHT?
WELL, ARTICLE 25 OF JAPAN'S CONSTITUTION GUARANTEES EACH CITIZEN'S RIGHT TO LIFE.
Print-outs for Saeki's extra lessons (handmade by the teacher)
So you won't die.

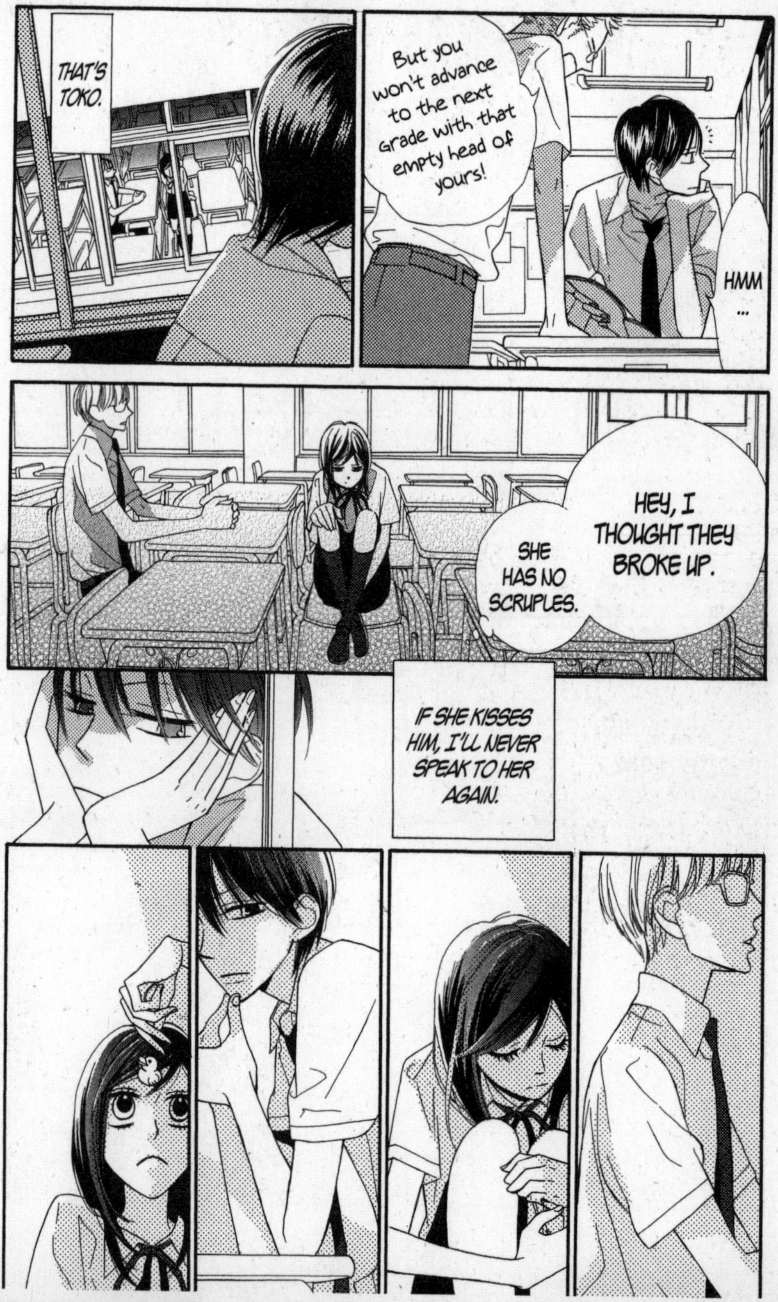
But you won't advance to the next grade with that empty head of yours!
HMM ...
THAT'S TOKO.
HEY, I THOUGHT THEY BROKE UP.
SHE HAS NO SCRUPLES.
IF SHE KISSES HIM, I'LL NEVER SPEAK TO HER AGAIN.

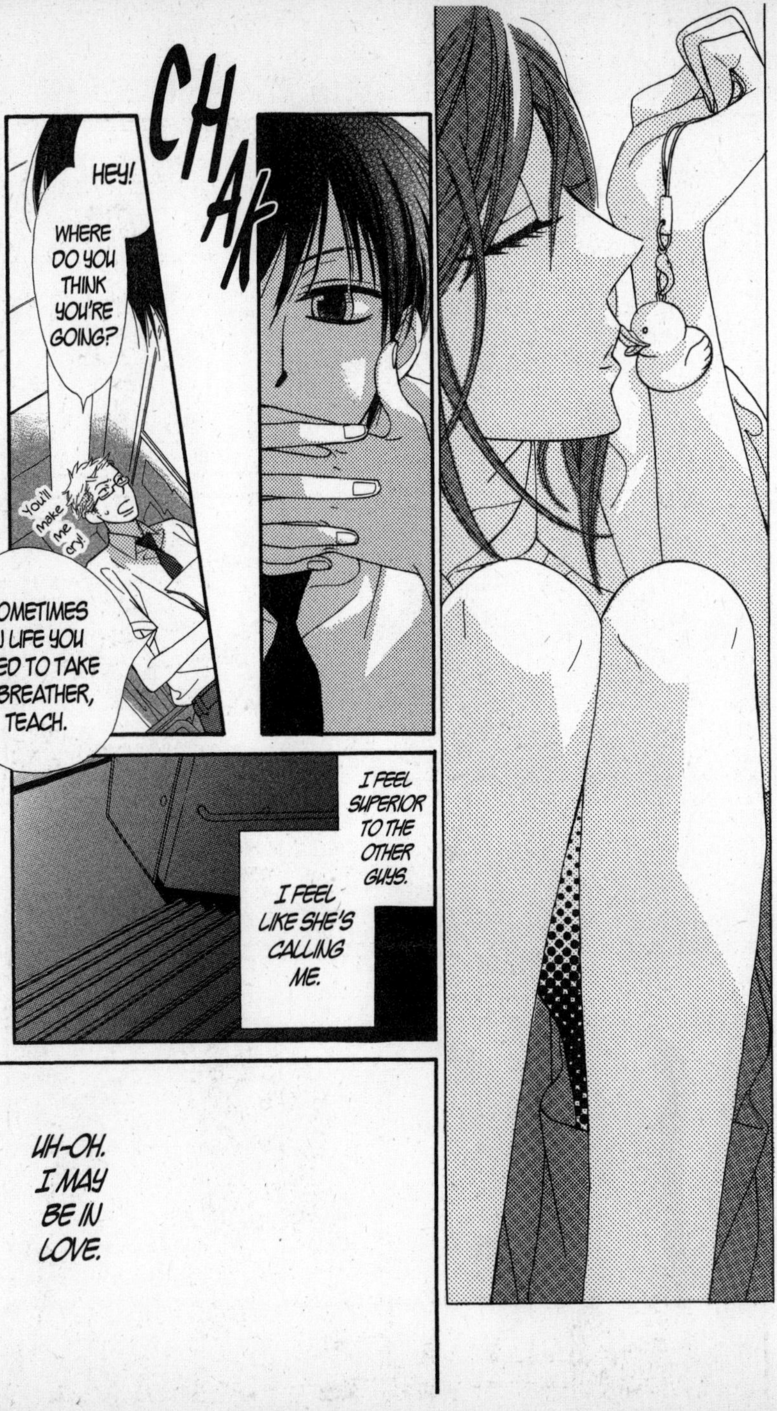
CHAK
HEY!
WHERE DO YOU THINK YOU'RE GOING?
You'll make me cry!
SOMETIMES IN LIFE YOU NEED TO TAKE A BREATHER, TEACH.
I FEEL SUPERIOR TO THE OTHER GUYS.
I FEEL LIKE SHE'S CALLING ME.
UH-OH. I MAY BE IN LOVE.

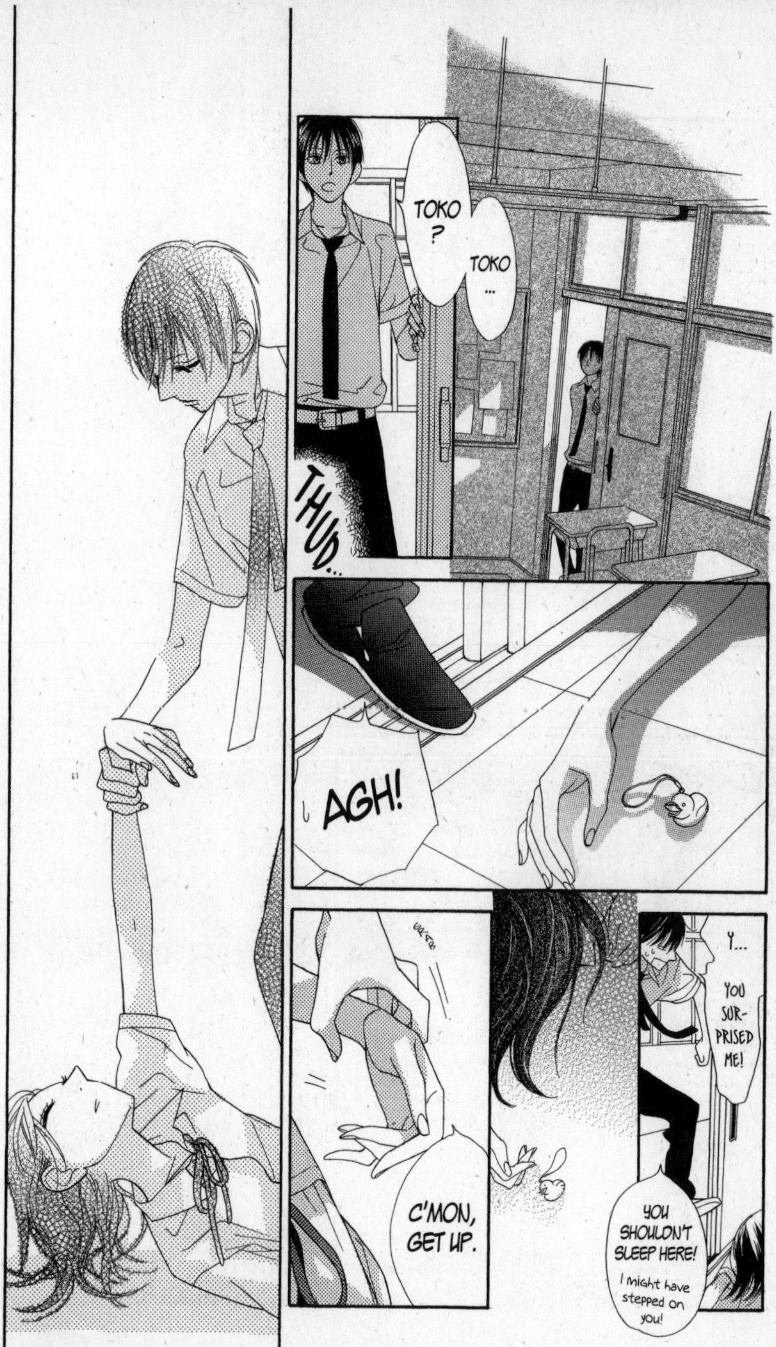
TOKO?
TOKO...
THUD...
AGH!
Y...
YOU SURPRISED ME!
YOU SHOULDN'T SLEEP HERE!
I might have stepped on you!
C'MON, GET UP.

...THESE DAYS...

...I CAN'T BREATHE WELL...

IDIOT. YOU FORGOT TO BREATHE.

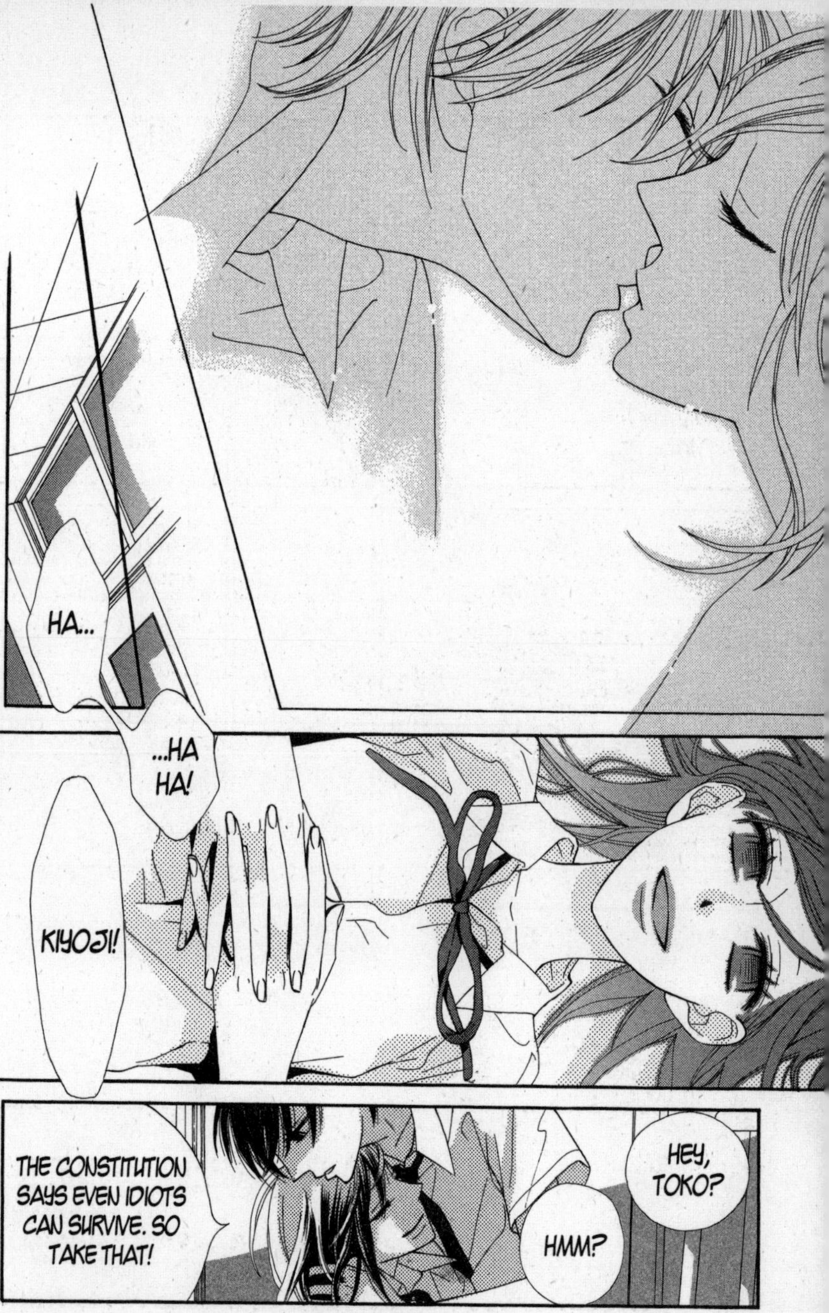
HA...
...HA HA!
KIYOJI!
HEY, TOKO?
HMM?
THE CONSTITUTION SAYS EVEN IDIOTS CAN SURVIVE. SO TAKE THAT!

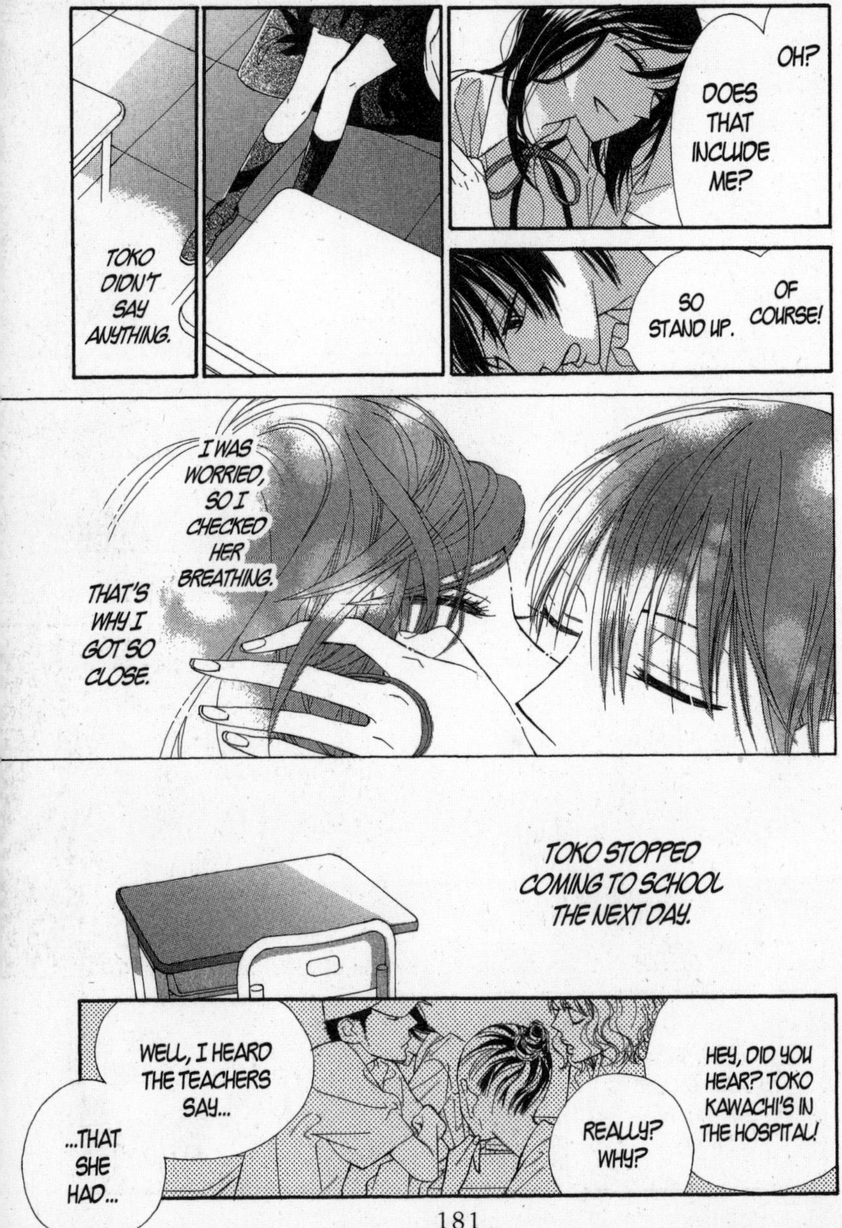

OH?
DOES THAT INCLUDE ME?
OF COURSE!
SO STAND UP.
TOKO DIDN'T SAY ANYTHING.
I WAS WORRIED, SO I CHECKED HER BREATHING.
THAT'S WHY I GOT SO CLOSE.
TOKO STOPPED COMING TO SCHOOL THE NEXT DAY.
HEY, DID YOU HEAR? TOKO KAWACHI'S IN THE HOSPITAL!
REALLY? WHY?
WELL, I HEARD THE TEACHERS SAY...
...THAT SHE HAD...

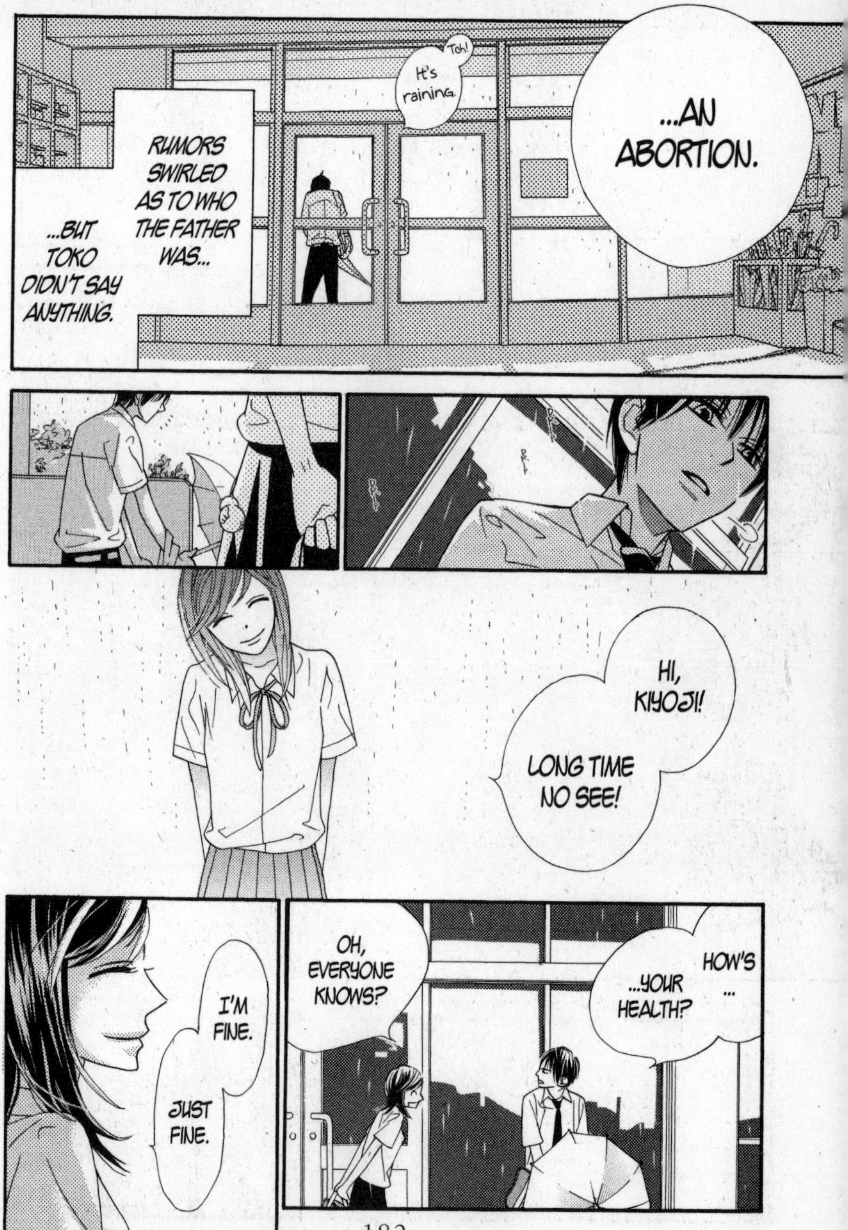
...AN ABORTION.
Toh!
It's raining.
RUMORS SWIRLED AS TO WHO THE FATHER WAS...
...BUT TOKO DIDN'T SAY ANYTHING.
HI, KIYOJI!
LONG TIME NO SEE!
HOW'S ...
...YOUR HEALTH?
OH, EVERYONE KNOWS?
I'M FINE.
JUST FINE.

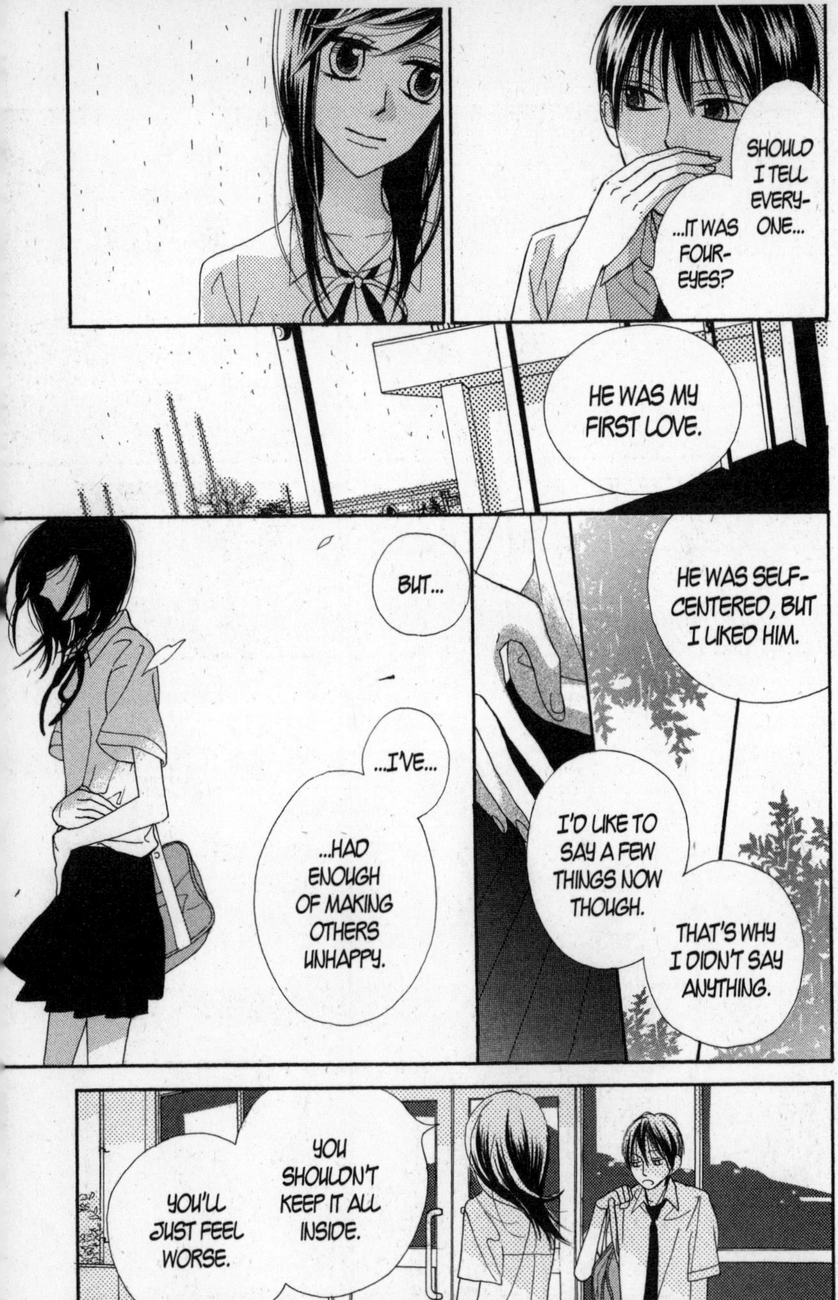
SHOULD I TELL EVERY-ONE...
...IT WAS FOUR-EYES?
HE WAS MY FIRST LOVE.
HE WAS SELF-CENTERED, BUT I LIKED HIM.
THAT'S WHY I DIDN'T SAY ANYTHING.
I'D LIKE TO SAY A FEW THINGS NOW THOUGH.
BUT...
...I'VE...
...HAD ENOUGH OF MAKING OTHERS UNHAPPY.
YOU SHOULDN'T KEEP IT ALL INSIDE.
YOU'LL JUST FEEL WORSE.

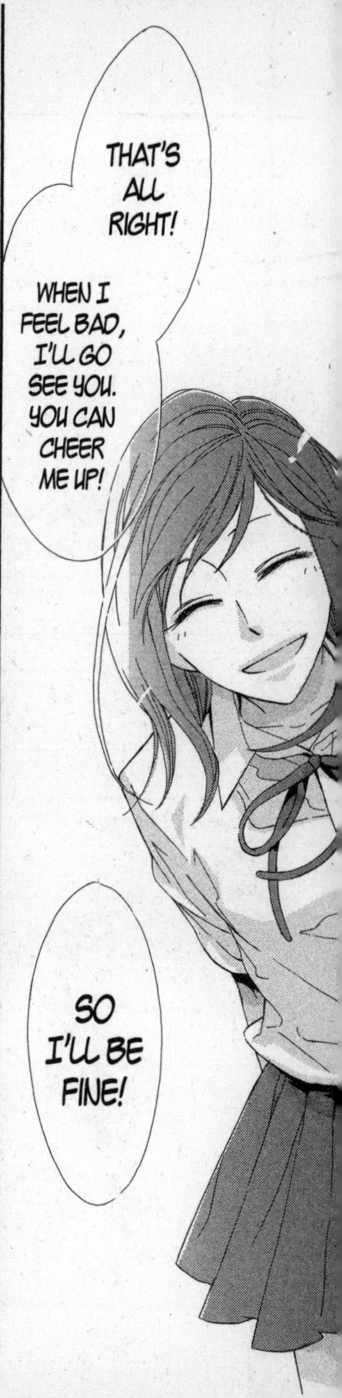
THAT'S ALL RIGHT!
WHEN I FEEL BAD, I'LL GO SEE YOU. YOU CAN CHEER ME UP!
SO I'LL BE FINE!

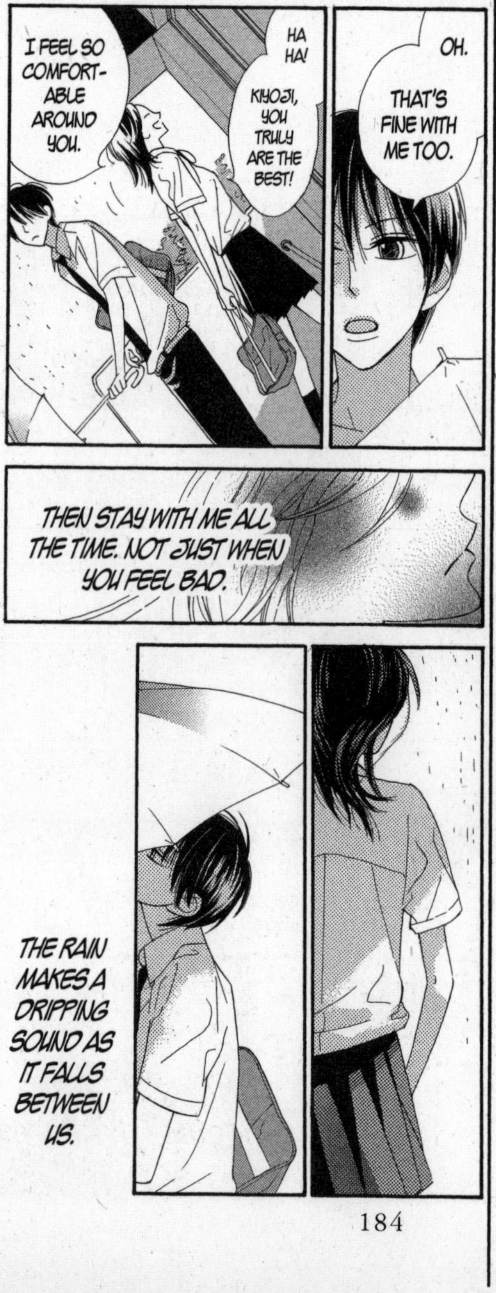
OH.
THAT'S FINE WITH ME TOO.
HA HA!
KIYOJI, YOU TRULY ARE THE BEST!
I FEEL SO COMFORT-ABLE AROUND YOU.
THEN STAY WITH ME ALL THE TIME. NOT JUST WHEN YOU FEEL BAD.
THE RAIN MAKES A DRIPPING SOUND AS IT FALLS BETWEEN US.

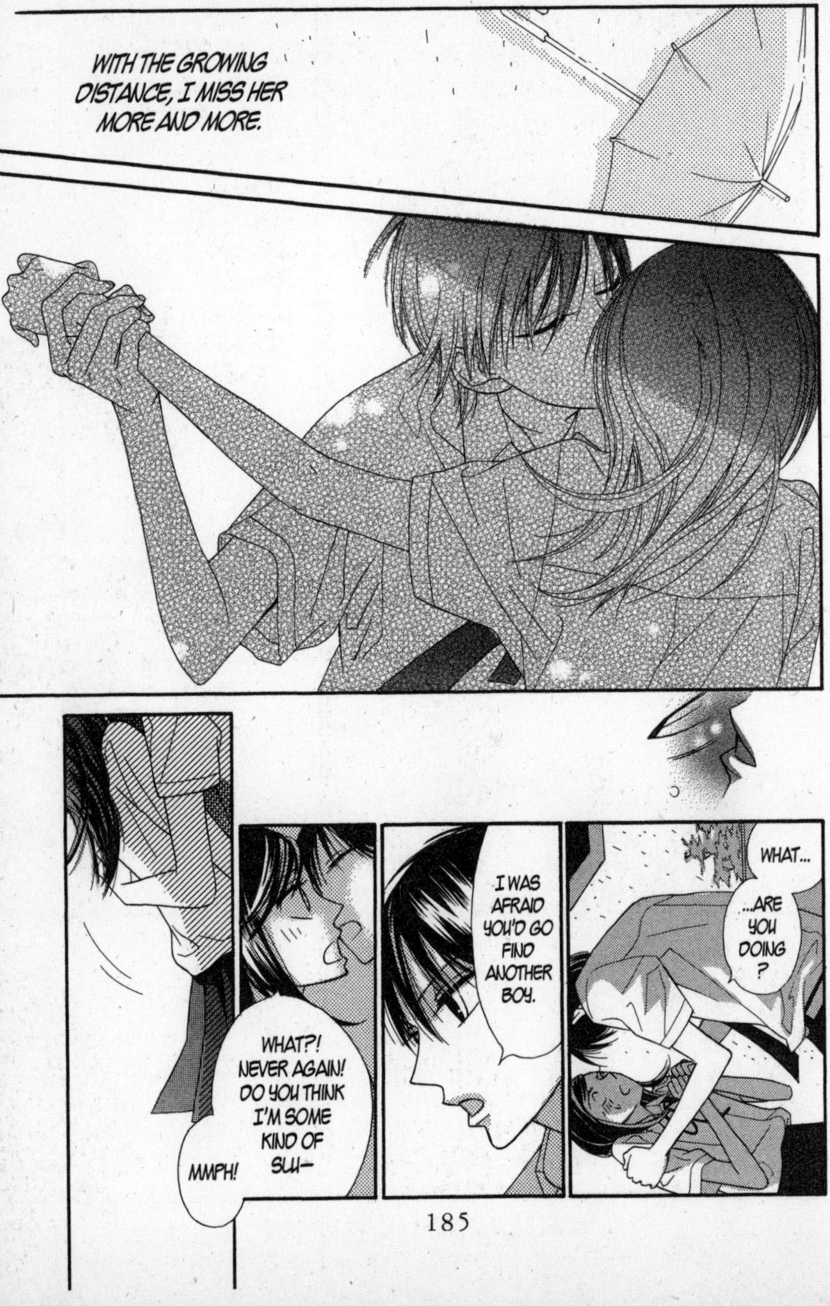
WITH THE GROWING DISTANCE, I MISS HER MORE AND MORE.
WHAT...
...ARE YOU DOING?
I WAS AFRAID YOU'D GO FIND ANOTHER BOY.
WHAT?! NEVER AGAIN! DO YOU THINK I'M SOME KIND OF SLU—
MMPH!

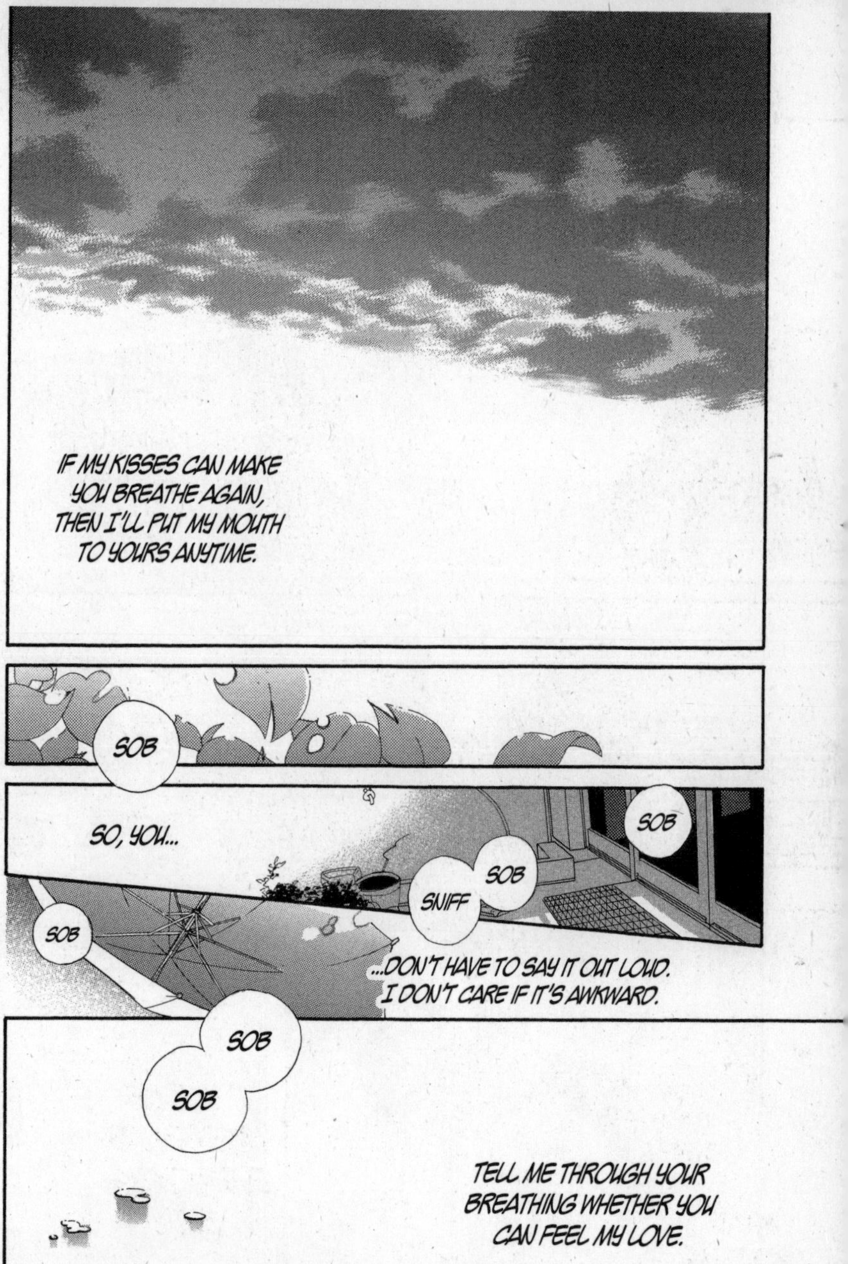
IF MY KISSES CAN MAKE YOU BREATHE AGAIN, THEN I'LL PUT MY MOUTH TO YOURS ANYTIME.
SOB
SOB
SOB
SNIFF
SO, YOU...
...DON'T HAVE TO SAY IT OUT LOUD. I DON'T CARE IF IT'S AWKWARD.
SOB
SOB
SOB
TELL ME THROUGH YOUR BREATHING WHETHER YOU CAN FEEL MY LOVE.

THE NEED FOR ARTIFICIAL RESPIRATION / END

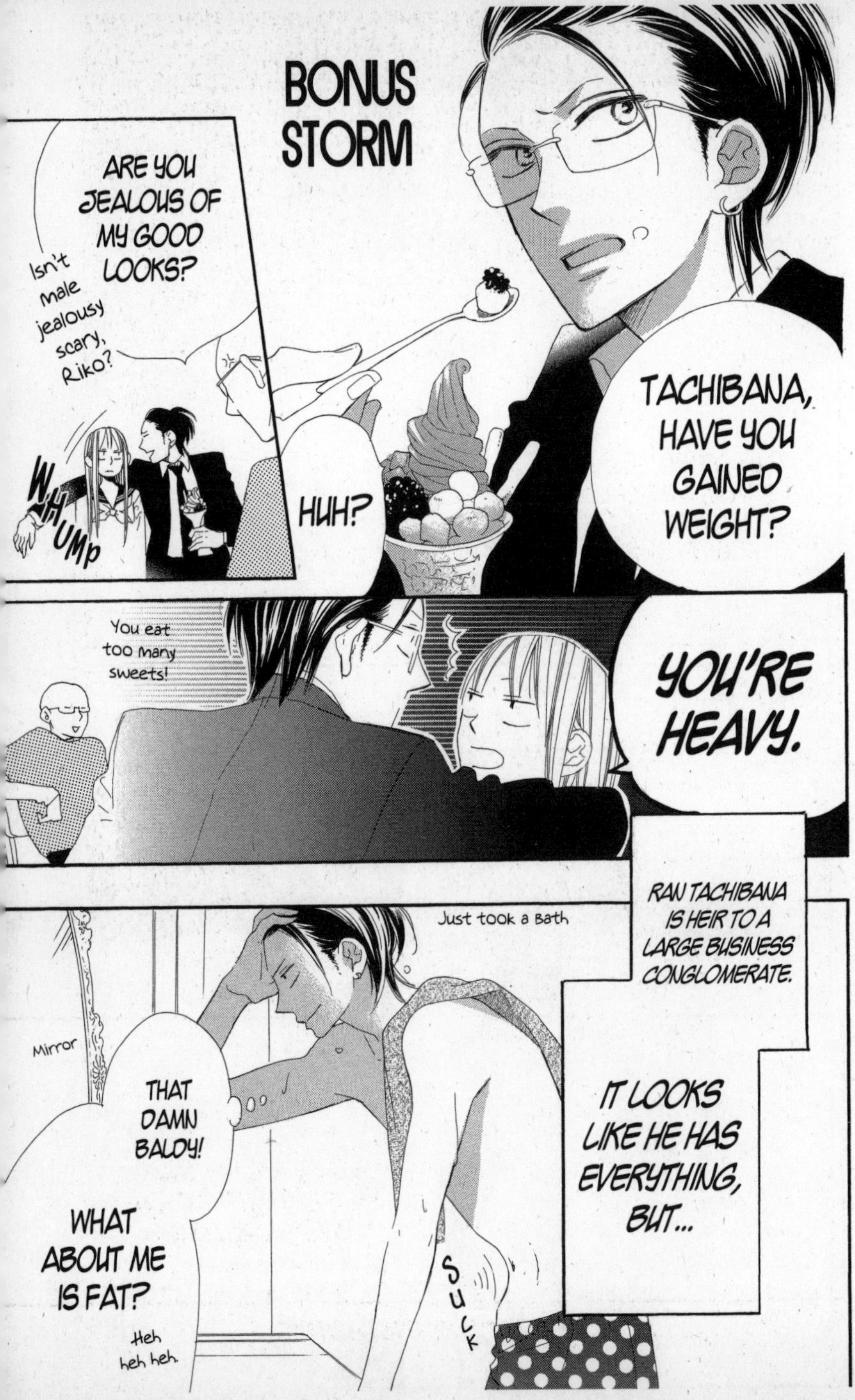
BONUS STORM
TACHIBANA, HAVE YOU GAINED WEIGHT?
HUH?
ARE YOU JEALOUS OF MY GOOD LOOKS?
Isn't male jealousy scary, Riko?
WHUMp
YOU'RE HEAVY.
You eat too many sweets!
RAN TACHIBANA IS HEIR TO A LARGE BUSINESS CONGLOMERATE.
IT LOOKS LIKE HE HAS EVERYTHING, BUT...
Just took a Bath
THAT DAMN BALDY!
Mirror
WHAT ABOUT ME IS FAT?
SUCK
Heh heh heh.

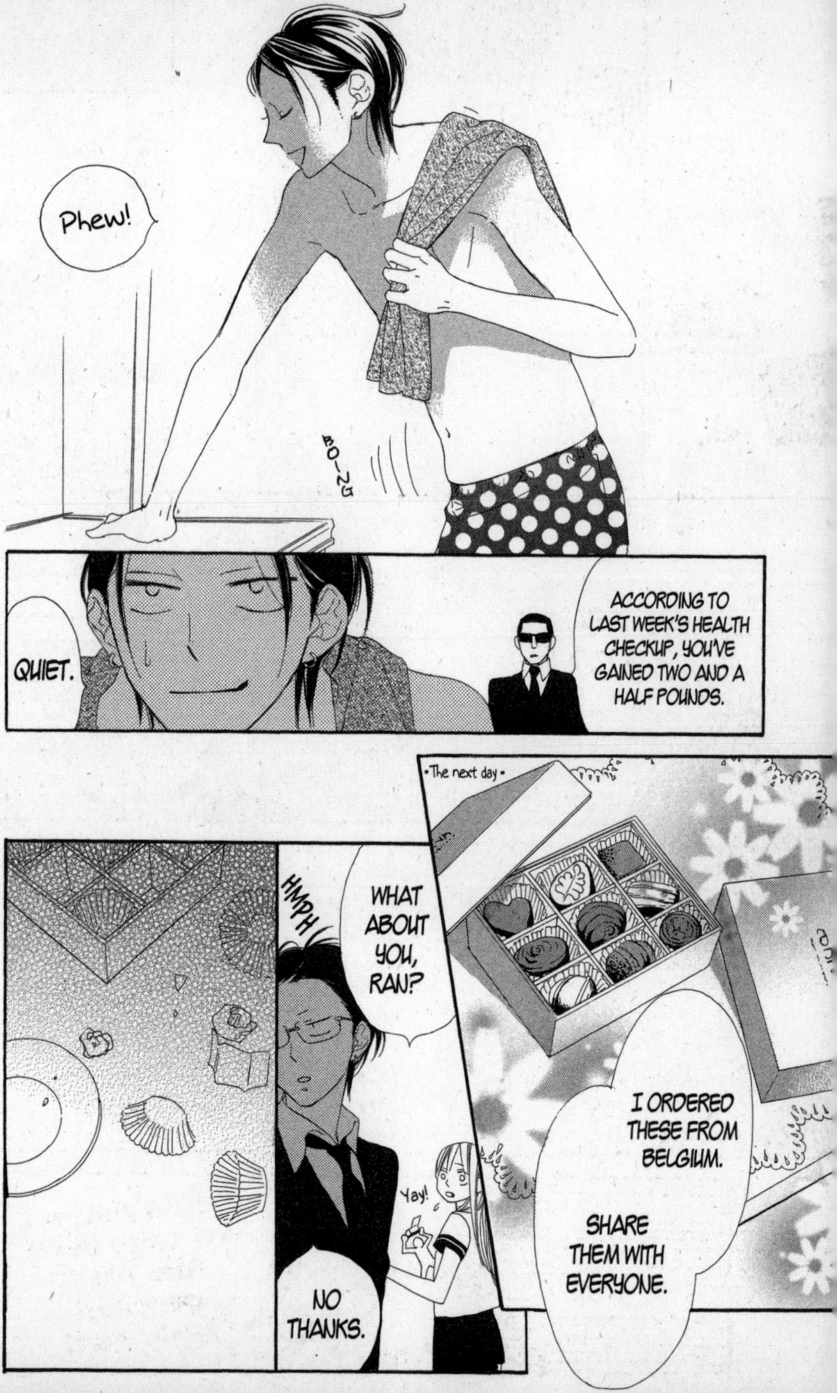
Phew!
BOING
ACCORDING TO LAST WEEK'S HEALTH CHECKUP, YOU'VE GAINED TWO AND A HALF POUNDS.
QUIET.
• The next day •
I ORDERED THESE FROM BELGIUM.
SHARE THEM WITH EVERYONE.
WHAT ABOUT YOU, RAN?
HMPH
Yay!
NO THANKS.

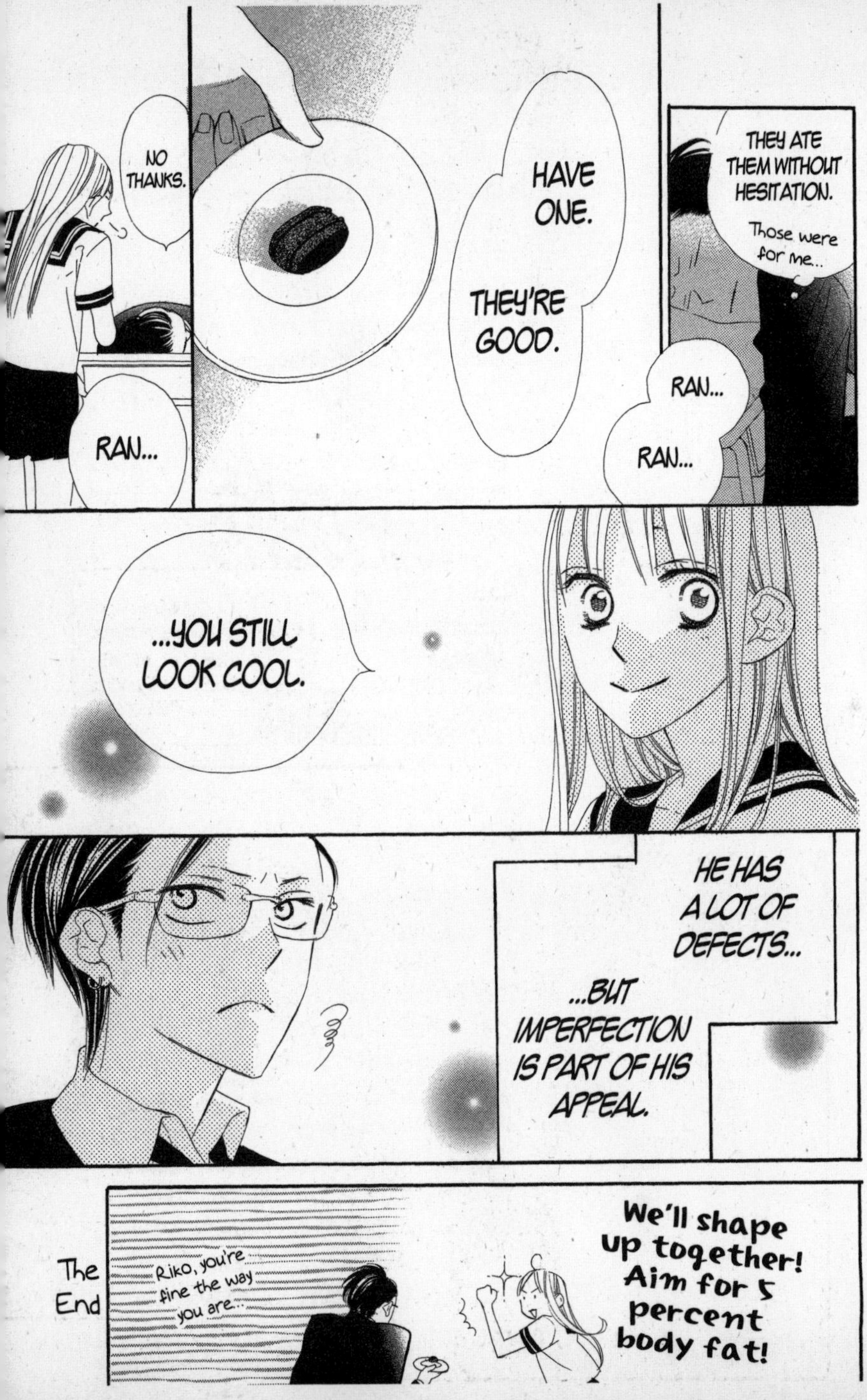
THEY ATE THEM WITHOUT HESITATION.
Those were for me...
RAN...
RAN...
HAVE ONE.
THEY'RE GOOD.
NO THANKS.
RAN...
...YOU STILL LOOK COOL.
HE HAS A LOT OF DEFECTS...
...BUT IMPERFECTION IS PART OF HIS APPEAL.
We'll shape up together! Aim for 5 percent body fat!
Riko, you're fine the way you are...
The End

Afterword

Hello! It's nice to meet you! I'm Shigeyoshi Takagi (a woman). Thank you so much for reading my very first graphic novel.

I began *Flower in a Storm* with the simple desire to write something that could be read quickly for a refreshing change of pace. I never thought it would make it into graphic novel format, so even now I can barely believe it. To tell the truth, the first chapter was so intense that plotting chapter 2 and later was quite difficult. How much of a natural high was I on when I wrote chapter 1?

This book also includes one of my prize-winning works. I spent a lot of time on the plot. It's one of my own favorites.

I hope you like these humble stories.

Lastly, I'd like to express my appreciation to my editor Sato; everyone in the editorial department; my parents; my twin sister; my friends; Shoko Asahina, who helped me out; everyone involved in the production of these works; and of course all of you who have read them. If it weren't for all of you, I would never have completed a single one of these stories. Thank you from the bottom of my heart.

I have six rose patterns in my house.

I'd love to hear your comments.

Shigeyoshi Takagi
c/o Flower in a Storm Editor
VIZ Media
P.O. Box 77010
San Francisco, CA
94107

BONUS STORM / END

ABOUT THE POEM

The poem that Ran quotes on page 142 is from Masuji Ibuse's Japanese translation of an old Chinese poem. It's worth noting that the kanji used for Ran's name means "storm."

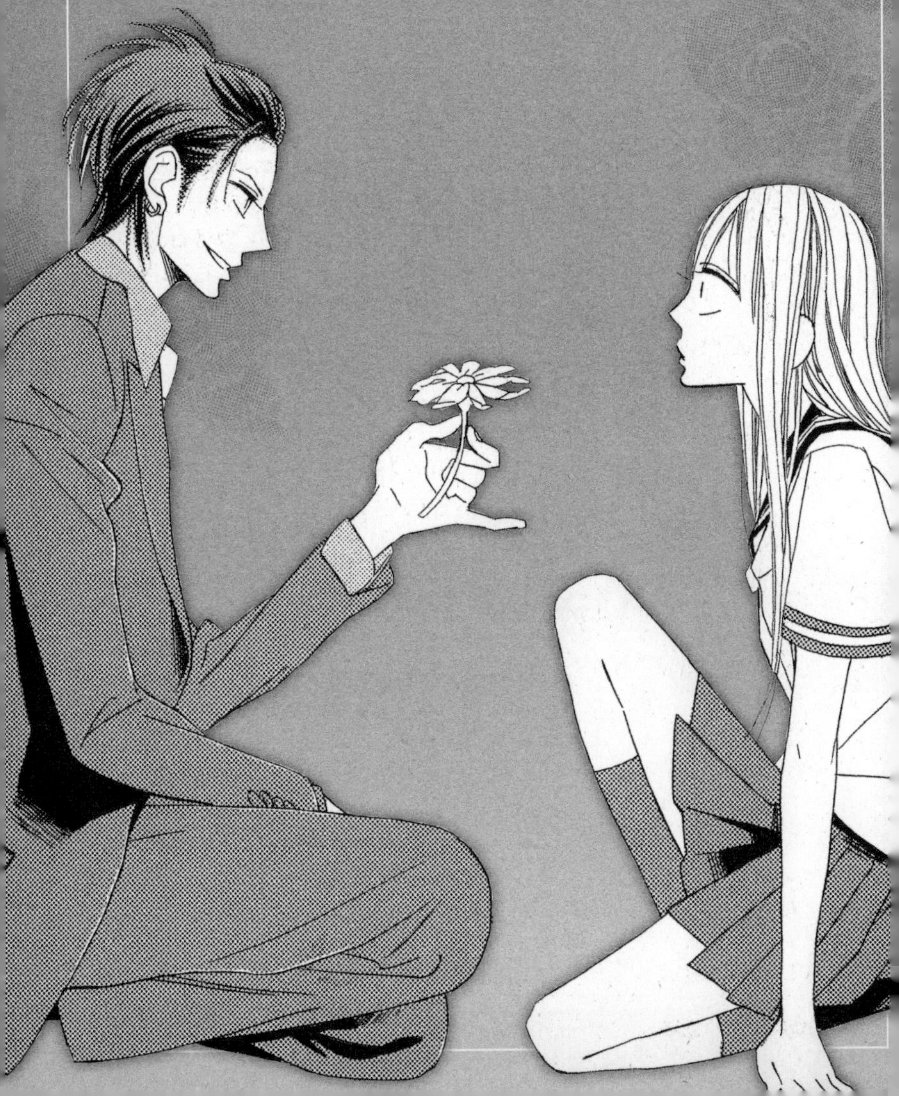

ABOUT THE AUTHOR

The author of *Flower in a Storm* uses the pen name Shigeyoshi Takagi. Her work has been published in the shojo manga anthologies *LaLa* and *LaLa DX* in Japan. *Flower in a Storm* is her first graphic novel.

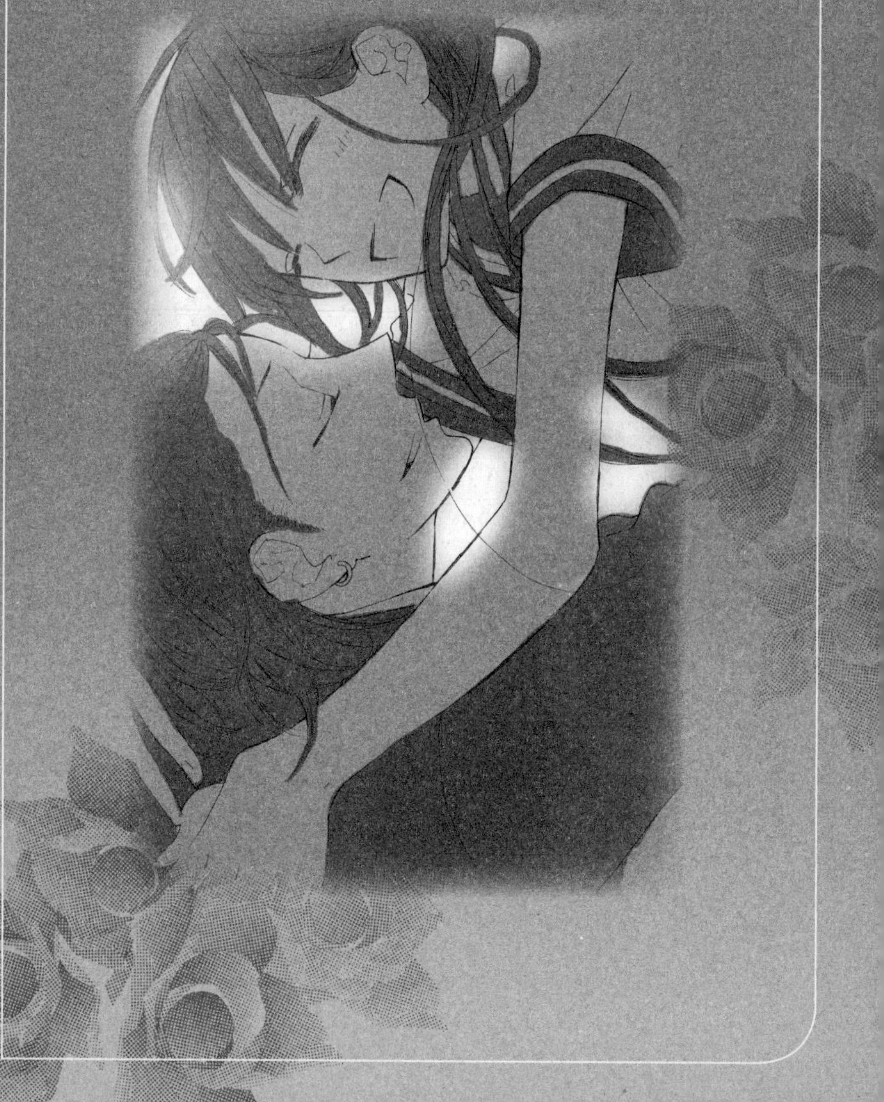

FLOWER IN A STORM

Volume 1

Shojo Beat Edition

Story and Art by Shigeyoshi Takagi

Translation HC Language Solutions, Inc.
Touch-up Art & Lettering Vanessa Satone
Design Frances O. Liddell
Editor Carrie Shepherd

VP, Production Alvin Lu
VP, Sales & Product Marketing Gonzalo Ferreyra
VP, Creative Linda Espinosa
Publisher Hyoe Narita

Hana ni Arashi by Shigeyoshi Takagi
© Shigeyoshi Takagi 2008
All rights reserved.
First published in Japan in 2008 by HAKUSENSHA, Inc., Tokyo.
English language translation rights arranged with HAKUSENSHA, Inc., Tokyo.

Printed in the U.S.A.

Published by VIZ Media, LLC
P.O. Box 77010
San Francisco, CA 94107

10 9 8 7 6 5 4 3 2 1
First printing, May 2010

Don't Hide What's Inside
OTOMEN
by AYA KANNO
Despite his tough jock exterior, Asuka Masamune harbors a secret love for sewing, shojo manga, and all things girly. But when he finds himself drawn to his domestically inept classmate Ryo, his carefully crafted persona is put to the test. Can Asuka ever show his true self to anyone, much less to the girl he's falling for?
Find out in the Otomen manga—buy yours today!
Shojo Beat Manga
OTOMEN
Aya Kanno
1
Shojo Beat
MANGA from the HEART
On sale at www.shojobeat.com
Also available at your local bookstore and comic store.
OTOMEN © Aya Kanno 2006/HAKUSENSHA, Inc.
RATED T FOR TEEN
ratings.viz.com
VIZ media
www.viz.com

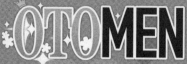

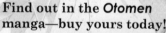

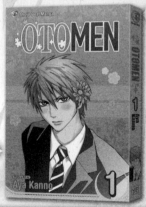

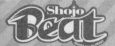

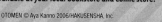

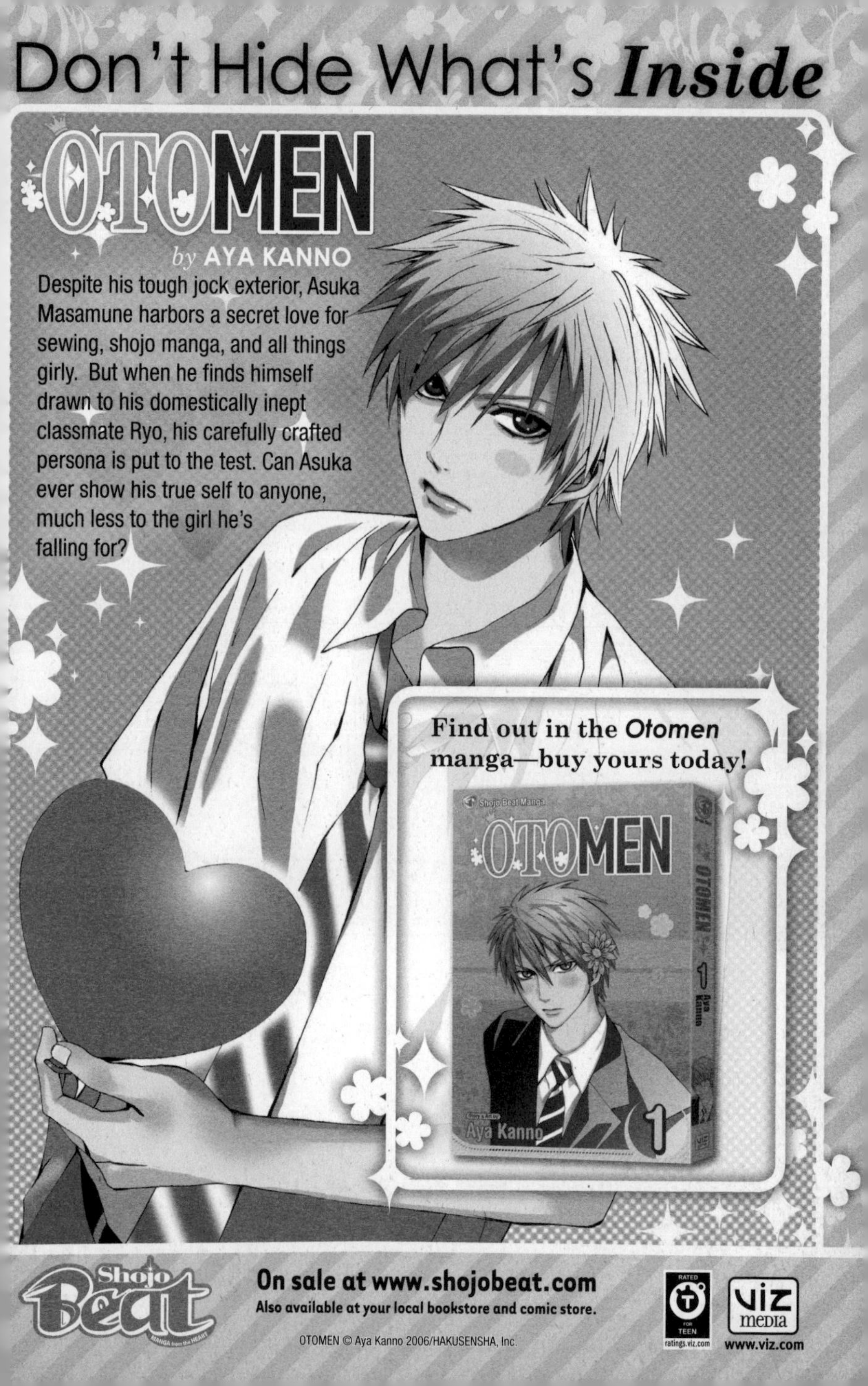

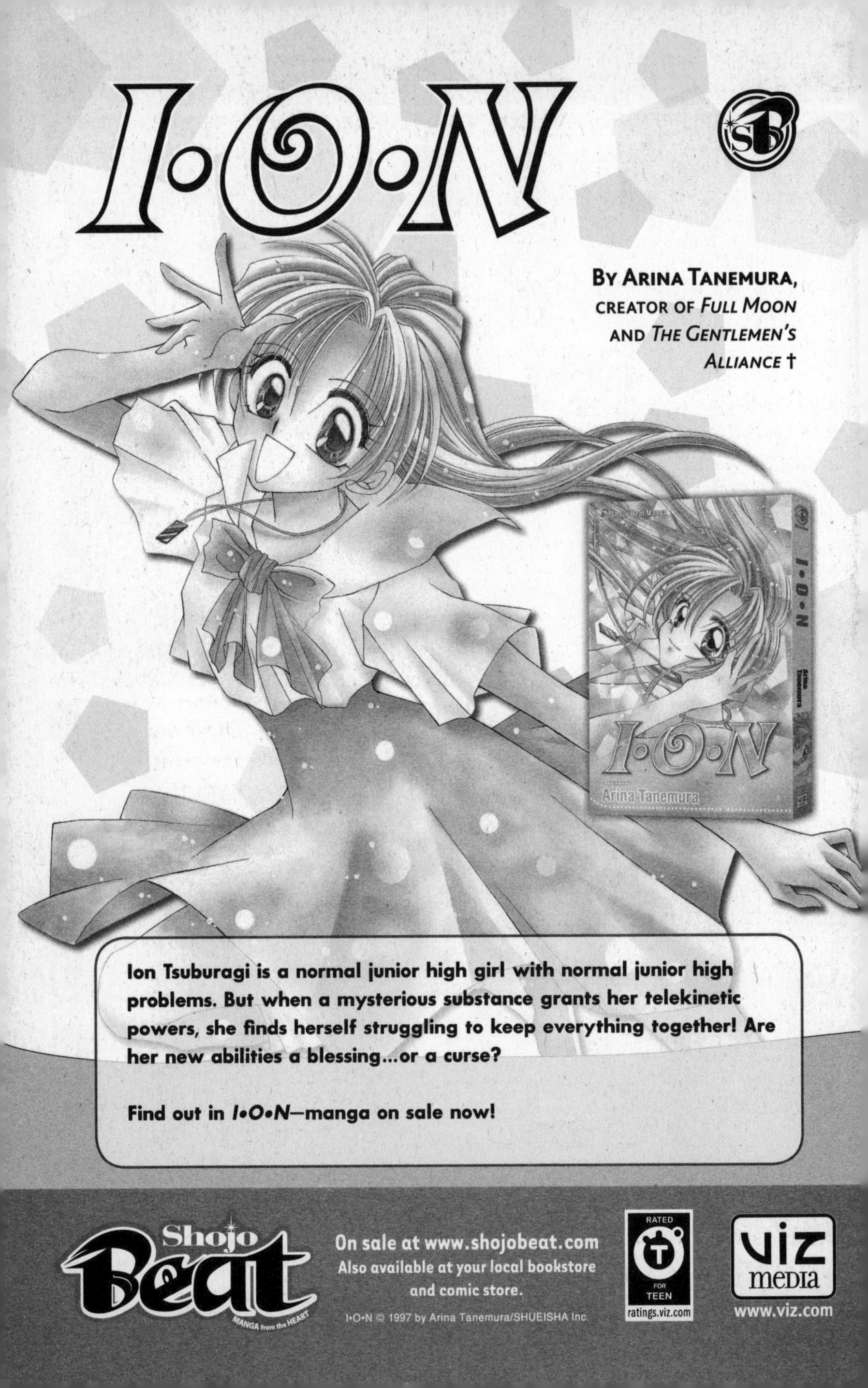
I•O•N
By Arina Tanemura, creator of Full Moon and The Gentlemen's Alliance †
Shojo Beat Manga
I•O•N
Arina Tanemura
Ion Tsuburagi is a normal junior high girl with normal junior high problems. But when a mysterious substance grants her telekinetic powers, she finds herself struggling to keep everything together! Are her new abilities a blessing...or a curse?
Find out in I•O•N—manga on sale now!
Shojo Beat
MANGA from the HEART
On sale at www.shojobeat.com
Also available at your local bookstore and comic store.
I•O•N © 1997 by Arina Tanemura/SHUEISHA Inc.
RATED
T
FOR TEEN
ratings.viz.com
viz media
www.viz.com

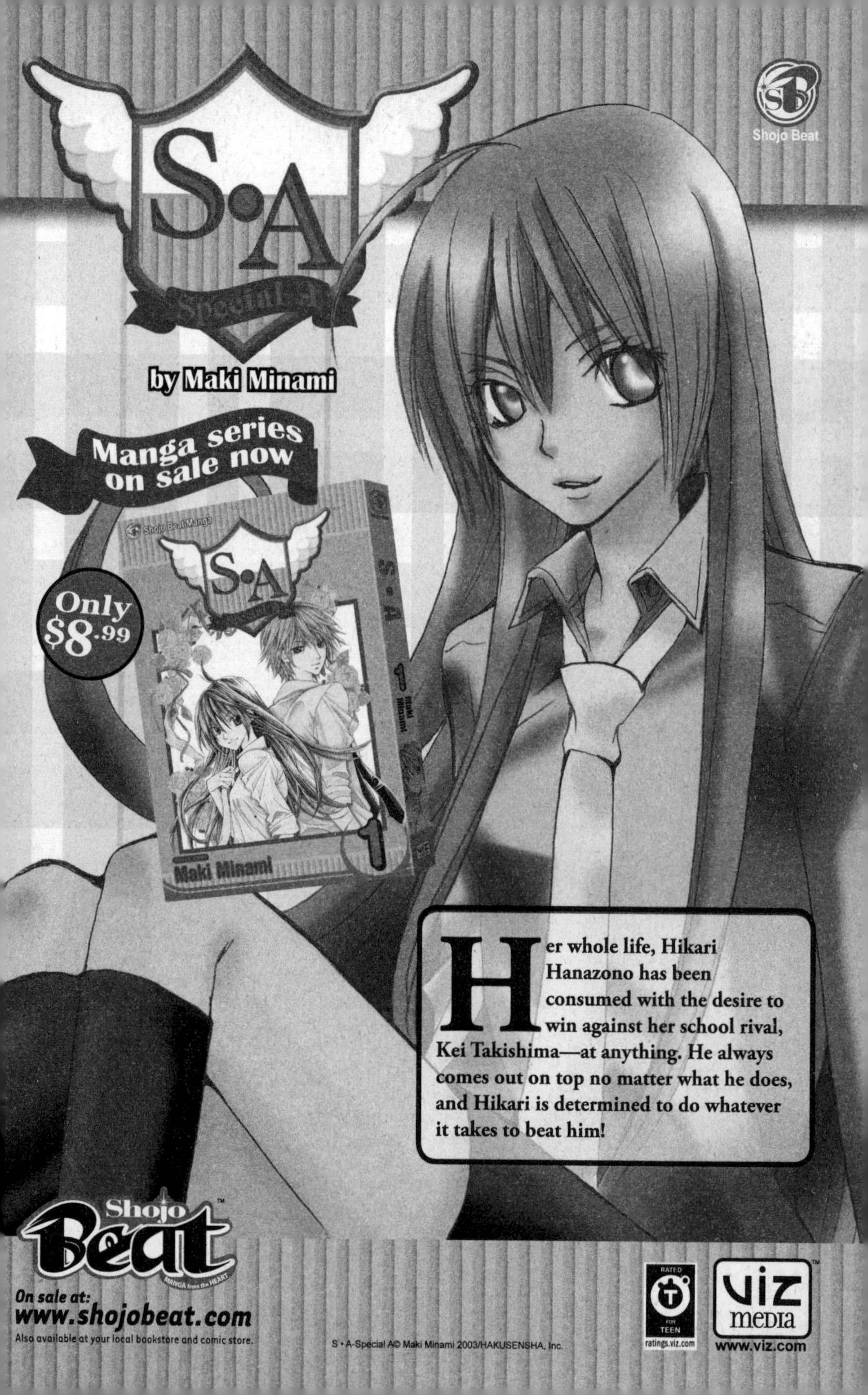
S•A
Special A
by Maki Minami
Shojo Beat
Manga series on sale now
Only $8.99
S•A
Maki Minami
Her whole life, Hikari Hanazono has been consumed with the desire to win against her school rival, Kei Takishima—at anything. He always comes out on top no matter what he does, and Hikari is determined to do whatever it takes to beat him!
Shojo Beat
MANGA from the HEART
On sale at:
www.shojobeat.com
Also available at your local bookstore and comic store.
S • A-Special A© Maki Minami 2003/HAKUSENSHA, Inc.
RATED T FOR TEEN
ratings.viz.com
VIZ MEDIA
www.viz.com

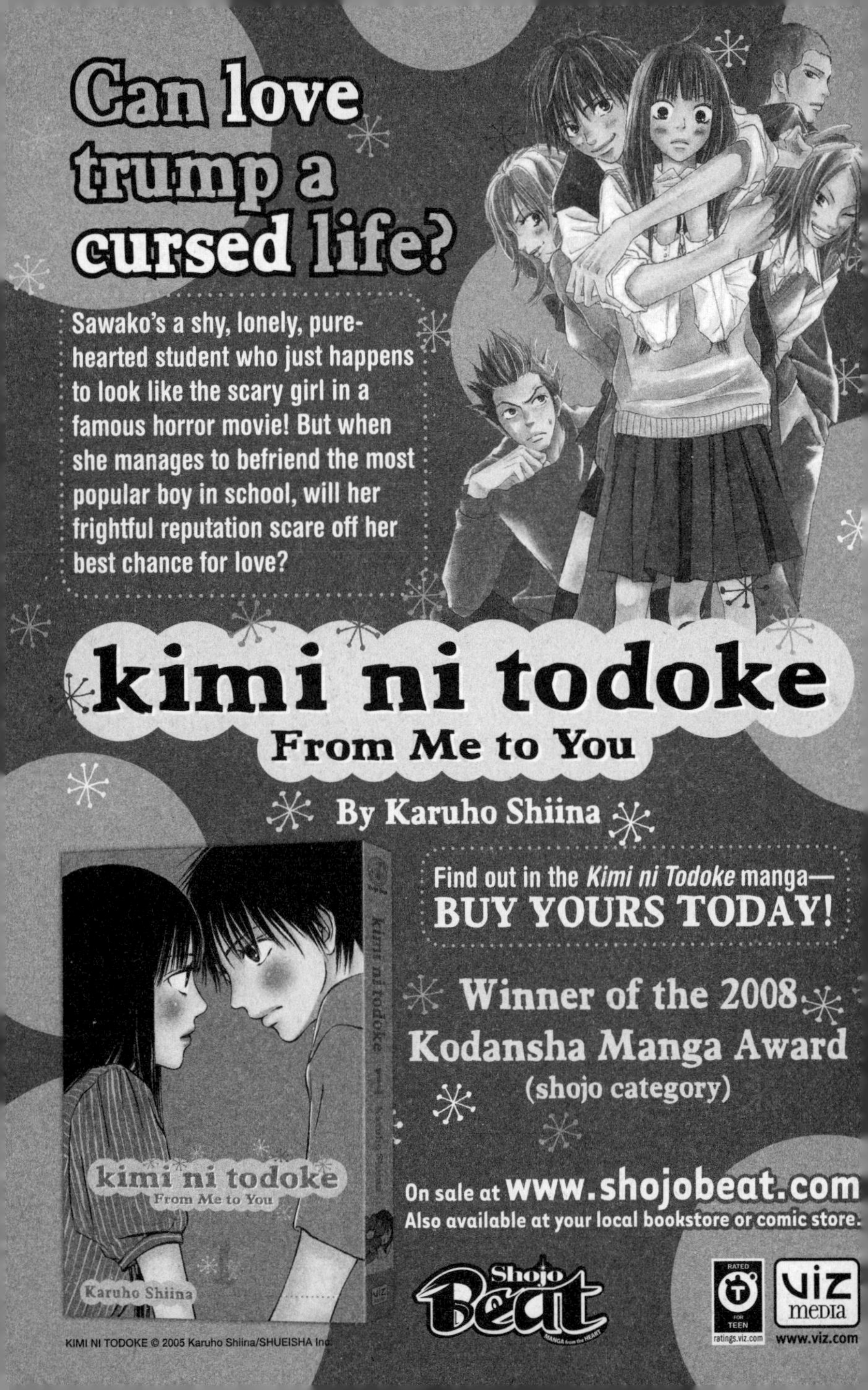
Can love trump a cursed life?
Sawako's a shy, lonely, pure-hearted student who just happens to look like the scary girl in a famous horror movie! But when she manages to befriend the most popular boy in school, will her frightful reputation scare off her best chance for love?
kimi ni todoke
From Me to You
By Karuho Shiina
kimi ni todoke
From Me to You
Karuho Shiina
Find out in the *Kimi ni Todoke* manga—
BUY YOURS TODAY!
Winner of the 2008 Kodansha Manga Award
(shojo category)
On sale at www.shojobeat.com
Also available at your local bookstore or comic store.
Shojo Beat
MANGA from the HEART
RATED T FOR TEEN
ratings.viz.com
VIZ media
www.viz.com
KIMI NI TODOKE © 2005 Karuho Shiina/SHUEISHA Inc.

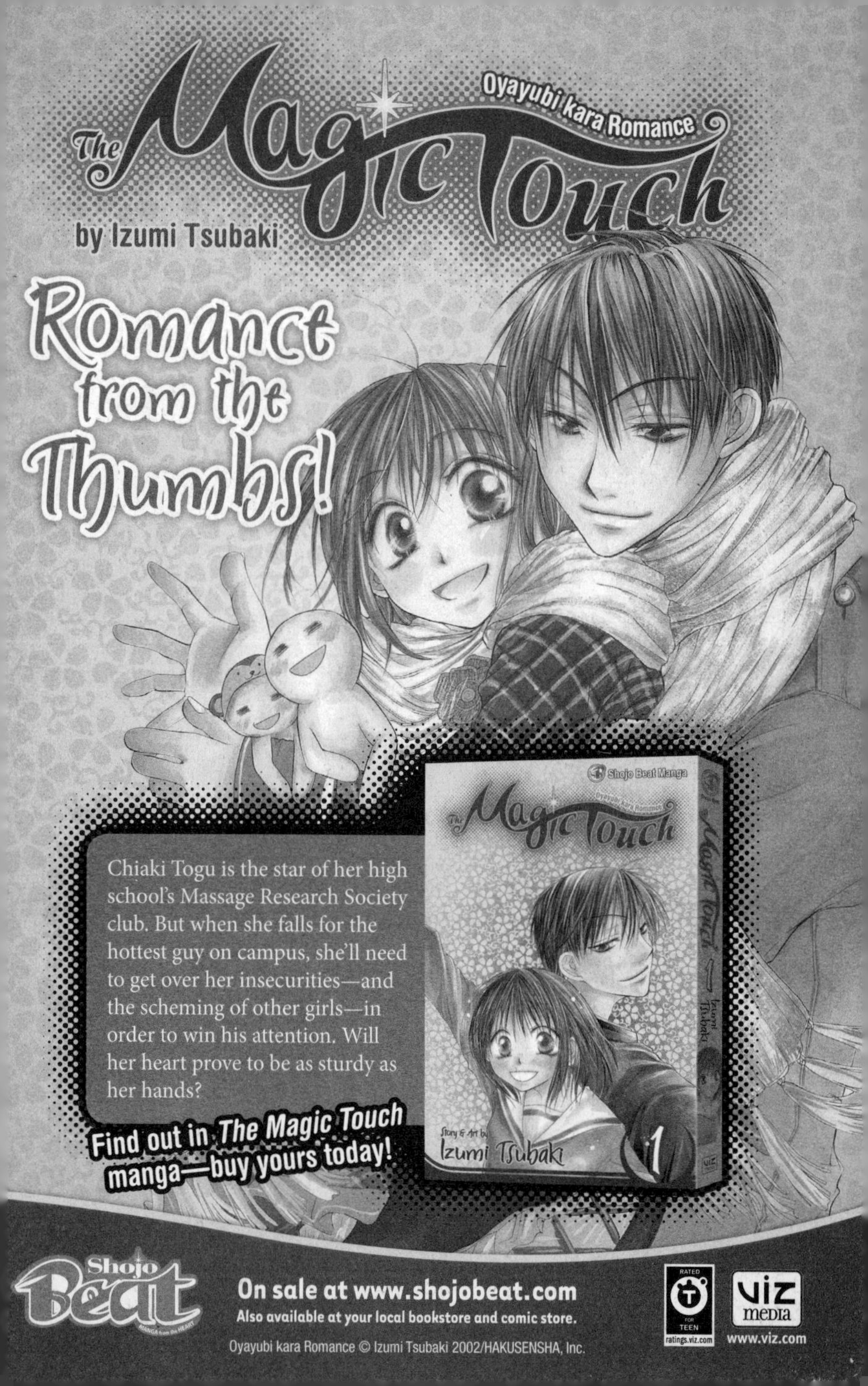
The Magic Touch
Oyayubi kara Romance
by Izumi Tsubaki
Romance from the Thumbs!
Shojo Beat Manga
Oyayubi kara Romance
The Magic Touch
Chiaki Togu is the star of her high school's Massage Research Society club. But when she falls for the hottest guy on campus, she'll need to get over her insecurities—and the scheming of other girls—in order to win his attention. Will her heart prove to be as sturdy as her hands?
Find out in The Magic Touch manga—buy yours today!
Story & Art by Izumi Tsubaki
1
Shojo Beat
On sale at www.shojobeat.com
Also available at your local bookstore and comic store.
RATED T FOR TEEN
ratings.viz.com
VIZ media
www.viz.com
Oyayubi kara Romance © Izumi Tsubaki 2002/HAKUSENSHA, Inc.

High School DEBUT

By Kazune Kawahara

When Haruna Nagashima was in junior high, softball and comics were her life. Now that she's in high school, she's ready to find a boyfriend. But will hard work (and the right coach) be enough?

Find out in the *High School Debut* manga series—available now!

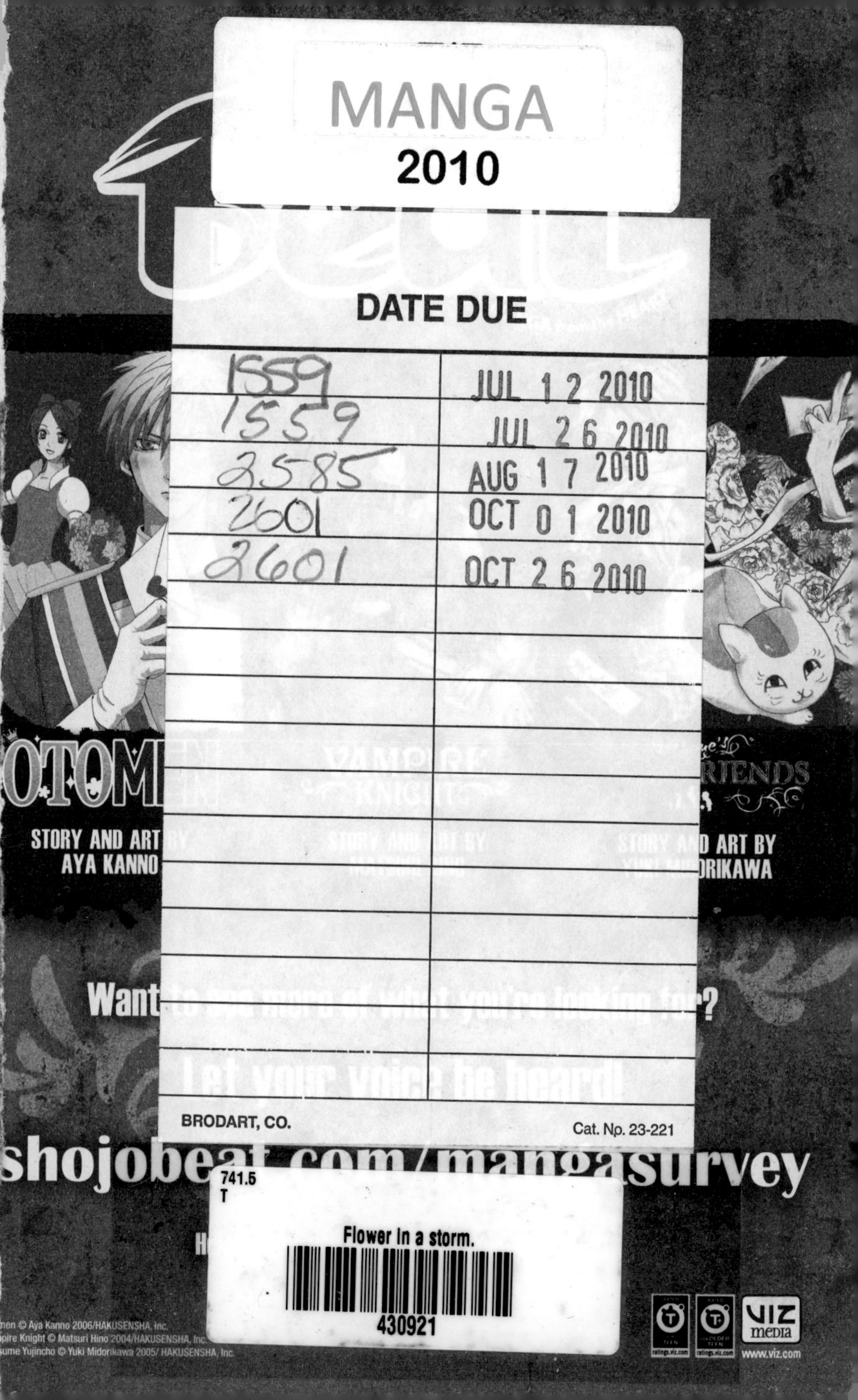
OTOMEN
STORY AND ART BY
AYA KANNO
VAMPIRE KNIGHT
STORY AND ART BY
RIENDS
STORY AND ART BY
RIKAWA
Want to see more of what you're looking for?
Let your voice be heard!
shojobeat.com/mangasurvey